THE RESU[illegible]ION

A CRITICAL EXAMINATION OF THE EASTER STORY

JONATHAN M.S. PEARCE

FOREWORD BY
DAVID FITZGERALD

The Resurrection: A Critical Examination of the Easter Story

Published by Onus Books

Cover design: Onus Books

Trade paperback ISBN: 978-0-9935102-8-1

OB 17/30

Praise for this book:

"Hitchens's Razor, not Bayes's Theorem, is the proper tool to use against the "absolute baselessness" of the resurrection belief (per David F. Strauss, as quoted in this book). There's no objective evidence for it. The testimonial evidence is abysmally poor. We should therefore dismiss this superstitious belief for what it is (per Hitchens). However, if you want to take such a belief seriously, read this thoroughly documented terminal case against the resurrection based on the latest research! This is the only book you'll need. Pearce is your expert guide on all the essential issues."

– John W. Loftus, author of *Unapologetic: Why Philosophy of Religion Must End*, and editor of *The Case against Miracles*.

"Jonathan MS Pearce puts the resurrection genie back in the bottle (and the body back in the grave). If you are digging for truth, this book is a goldmine!"

– Dan Barker, author of *Godless*

"This book is the definitive starting point for anyone intent on questioning or defending the resurrection of Jesus. Introductory and aimed at a broad audience, but thoroughly researched, all the key works are here cited and arguments addressed, and with sound reasoning. If this book cannot be answered, belief in the resurrection cannot be defended."

– Dr. Richard Carrier, author of *Jesus from Outer Space: What the Earliest Christians Really Believed about Christ*.

"This is a detailed, clear, and very readable survey of the evidence for the Resurrection, and it makes an overwhelming case for the conclusion that the Resurrection did not happen. It's an extraordinary fact that so many smart, educated people have managed to convince themselves that the historical case for the Resurrection is strong, when it is, patently, ludicrously weak."

– Dr. Stephen Law, author of *Humanism: A Very Short Introduction* and *Believing Bullshit: How Not to Get Sucked into an Intellectual Black Hole*

"An informative, enjoyable and even entertaining read. *The Resurrection* is clearly written and an especially helpful entry into philosophical questions surround the stories of Jesus' resurrection. Pearce's critiques of some of the unfortunately popular apologetic arguments are devastating and it is hoped his book will bury them for good."

– Dr. James G. Crossley, New Testament scholar and author of *Jesus and the Chaos of History: Redirecting the Life of the Historical Jesus*

"For too long, Christian evangelists have been able to get away with the outrageous claim that the resurrection of Jesus is one of the 'best-attested facts in history'. In this erudite and highly readable account, Jonathan MS Pearce demonstrates with devastating logic and clarity why this claim should be rejected."

– David Warden, Chairman of Dorset Humanists and Honorary Member of Humanists UK

"You'd think that a refutation of mythology wouldn't be necessary in the 21st century. But it is, and Pearce's corrective is both complete and approachable. Fascinating!"

– Bob Seidensticker, author at *Cross Examined,* Patheos Nonreligious

"No rational and honest scholar of religion or theologian who asserts that the resurrection of Jesus was an actual event would be able to do so without addressing the compelling counterarguments presented by Jonathan Pearce's The Resurrection. Drawing upon an array of sources and scholarly disciplines, Pearce offers a masterful analysis of the central miracle of Christianity, Jesus's purported return from death. He examines the events leading to the crucifixion, burial by Joseph of Arimathea, women visitors to the tomb, and the post-mortem appearances to demonstrate the irresolvable inconsistencies and contradictions in the gospels where these occurrences are described. All of this makes it difficult to refute the central argument presented in this book: that the entire narrative upon which the Christian faith is anchored is a fiction contrived by others long after the purported date of the crucifixion and related events."

– Dr. H. Sidky, Professor of Anthropology, Miami University, and author of *Religion, Supernaturalism, the Paranormal and Pseudoscience: An Anthropological Critique*

"Covering subjects as diverse as epistemology, archaeology, theology, metaphysics, and of course historical analysis, oceans of ink have been spilled to answer one question: is Jesus dead? Fortunately, in one place these various issues can be considered, sometimes just under the surface, but in the end getting to the bottom of the question. The final conclusions about what we can be confident about, what must remain uncertain, and what is just out-of-this-world, are well-addressed to help both a skeptic and a believer alike see why it just isn't likely that Jesus returned from the dead. The attempts to exhume him by this time stinketh, and Pearce shows why that is so."

– Dr. Aaron Adair, author of *The Star of Bethlehem: A Skeptical View*

About the author:

Jonathan M.S. Pearce is a teacher and author from south Hampshire, UK, who has dedicated many years to studying all manner of things philosophical and theological. A philosopher with a marked interest in religion, he became a founder member of the *Skeptic Ink Network* (SIN) before moving to write for *Patheos Nonreligious* (Pearce's blog is *A Tippling Philosopher*). As an original member of the Tippling Philosophers, from which his blog title comes (a friendly group of disparate believers and non-believers, and sort-of believers based in Hampshire), he is a big advocate of casual philosophy groups meeting over pints of good ale. He lives with his partner (and wonders how she puts up with him) and their twin boys (and struggles to put up with them...). Being diagnosed with primary progressive multiple sclerosis, he would like to personally thank God for that gift, though rely more reasonably on science to find a treatment (which he did do, with successful stem cell therapy that has kept him stable for several years – a resurrection of sorts, but certainly not a miracle).

Other books by Jonathan MS Pearce:

Free Will? An Investigation into Whether We Have Free Will Or Whether I Was Always Going to Write This Book

The Little Book of Unholy Questions

The Nativity: A Critical Examination

Beyond an Absence of Faith: Stories About the Loss of Faith and the Discovery of Self

13 Reasons to Doubt (ed.)

The Problem with "God": Classical Theism under the Spotlight

Did God Create the Universe from Nothing? Countering William Lane Craig's Kalam Cosmological Argument

Filling the Void: A Selection of Humanist and Atheist Poetry

Not Seeing God: Atheism in the 21st Century (ed.)

As Johnny Pearce:

Twins: A Survival Guide for Dads

Survival of the Fittest: Metamorphosis

The Curse of the Maya

A note about the book:

This book is a sister publication to my earlier *The Nativity: A Critical Examination* and I have dipped into it for an odd piece of text here and there in the early chapters when discussing the Gospel sources. A number of the points can be found in other writing, and on my blog (*A Tippling Philosopher* on the *Patheos Nonreligious* channel), though extended and elaborated for the purposes of this book.

There are many sections that require further reading. Some subjects receive a more cursory analysis since there are many involved arguments on either side of the religious aisle. I leave it up to readers to further any such research and come to their own conclusions. If nothing else, this book should stimulate the reader into researching more deeply into the topics at hand.

Each section of this text deserves a book in its own right and I hope I have done justice to summing up vast areas of historical and textual research as concisely and informatively as possible.

Where I have capitalised "Resurrection" and "Gospel" it is because it refers to *the* Resurrection of *the* Gospel (of, say, Luke). All other times, it is a case of lower cases because it is used more generally, like God and god. Jesus' is preferred to Jesus's, and a British spelling and style is used throughout, although skeptic with a 'k' is definitely preferred...

Acknowledgements:

So many people have helped polish this book to a shine. A great many thanks, as ever, to the various people who help on projects like these. Firstly, I have to say that Michael J. Alter is an officer and a gentleman who has really helped when asked, including in terms of proofing and editing. It was hard enough writing *these* pages; I shudder to think what 854 pages on the Resurrection would have done to my mental health, as he produced for his own book (the masterful *The Resurrection: A Critical Inquiry*)! He has put in what might be described by some as a supernatural effort; my deep appreciation to him. Richard Carrier has also been incredibly generous with his time and expertise, and certainly set me straight on a few issues in terms of evidence evaluation. What he doesn't know about the Resurrection narratives ain't worth knowing. Huge gratitude to him. These two fellow authors are due some serious cosmic credit.

David Austin, all the way Down Under, has also offered fantastic feedback and advice, again putting his obsession with the Resurrection to good use. Geoff Benson is such a wonderful chap, ably assisting with his tireless proofing. Speaking of proofing – welcome on board to Jörg Fehlmann, who has also done a tremendous shift in this regard. Thanks muchly to Bradley Bowen, who assisted with some early versions of the book. Ed Atkinson helped contribute some of the content for sections on Paul with contributions to my blog in a debate series with a Christian concerning the silence of Paul. Major kudos to him. Finally, a thumbs up, yet again, to David Fitzgerald, whose foreword and advice have added greatly to the text you are holding.

For doubters willing to nurture their seeds
to seedlings,
saplings,
trees
and ultimately forests.

But looking at it historically, as an outward event, the resurrection of Jesus has not the very slightest foundation. Rarely has an incredible fact been worse attested, or one so ill-attested been more incredible in itself.... Taken historically, i.e., comparing the immense effect of this belief with its absolute baselessness, the story of the resurrection of Jesus can only be called a world-wide deception.

– David Friedrich Strauss, *The Old Faith and the New* (1873)

Contents

Foreword

Sometime around the middle of the first century, writing to the tiny house church in the bustling ancient Greek seaport of Corinth, Paul poses to his flock an astonishing question:

> Now if Christ is proclaimed as raised from the dead, *how can some of you say there is no resurrection of the dead?* (1 Corinthians 15:12)

As jaw dropping as it is to imagine early Christians who are somehow dubious about life after death, Paul's opening reminder to them in chapter 15 is equally unthinkable. As I ask in my book *Nailed*:[1]

> Imagine you are Paul writing this letter. If the traditional picture of Paul were correct, you would have plentiful evidence to bring out here in support. You know Jesus' brothers. You know Jesus' disciples. It's not unthinkable that you know his mother. Jesus himself has appeared to you in a vision on the road to Damascus.
>
> So you should have access to the whole story from start to finish, including his miraculous birth, famous career, astounding miracles, bold new teachings, and all the amazing occurrences of his death, resurrection, return to his followers and his final ascension into Heaven. What would *you* say?

Any pastor (or even online amateur Christian apologist) can spend all day listing the convincing reasons why we should accept that Jesus' miraculous resurrection really happened.

So why can't Christianity's greatest apostle?

With all his allegedly available options – eyewitnesses, Jesus' relatives, Jesus' disciples, Jesus' miracles, even his own exciting conversion story – Paul offers next to nothing as evidence. First, what he claims to have "received": that Christ died for our sins – that is, according to the scriptures – and that he was raised on the third day – again, according to the scriptures... (1 Cor. 15:3-4).

He follows up these two scriptural-based assertions with no better proof or assurance than a suspicious list of a few "witnesses" – that is, those whom

---

[1] Fitzgerald (2010), p. 149.

Paul claims encountered the Risen Jesus the same way he did: speaking to them in visions, or from their study of the Hebrew scriptures.

According to Paul, Jesus "appeared" to the following, in this order: Cephas; then "the Twelve;" then more than five hundred brethren at once; then James; then "all the apostles;" and lastly, by Paul himself (1 Cor. 15:5-8). Apologists act as though Paul provides concrete corroborating evidence here of Jesus' post-resurrection appearances. But you only have to look at it to see that it doesn't tally with any of the Gospels – not that they agree with each other either, of course.

There are further problems, such as referring to the disciples as if they were two different groups. Why would Paul phrase this so oddly? Isn't Cephas (that is, Peter[1]) one of the Twelve?[2] So why wouldn't Paul just say Jesus was seen by his disciples and leave it at that?[3] And how could there have been five hundred brethren when Acts 1:15 says the total number of believers, men and women, was only "about one hundred twenty persons"?

Paul's tally of "witnesses" to his risen Lord raises more questions than it answers... and as we'll see later in this very book you're holding, his strange laundry list appears to be an older creedal formula he inherited from earlier Christian traditions. Following this he gets on a tedious hamster wheel, wheedling on for several verses[4] saying, in essence:

> Well, if that were so, then Christ isn't risen either, and if that's true, then you and I are just liars, and how sad would that be, because if the dead don't rise from the dead, then Christ can't be risen either, and that would make your faith empty and useless and if Christ isn't arisen then your sweet late Auntie Babs who loved Jesus would be gone forever and we would be the most pathetic losers if that were true. Which it isn't. Ahem.

As for the proof of this powerful and well-thought-out line of reasoning, Paul hits the doubters with—well, nothing. His scriptural quotes and list of his fellow "visionaries" is supposed to suffice. What actual evidence does he bring out to show that Christ rose from the dead, apart from telling us how bad it

---

[1] Though whether Cephas and Peter are really the same person has also been questioned.

[2] Though at this time Judas Iscariot was dead and his replacement Matthias not yet chosen (Acts 1:20-26), so it would have been the Eleven, not the Twelve.

[3] Actually, Paul never says that any of these people *were* Jesus' disciples – because Paul never says Jesus had any, or even uses the word "disciple," ever, in any context.

[4] Do give the verses a read (1 Cor. 15: 13-19) and see how little I'm exaggerating the feebleness of his case.

would be if he was just lying?[1] Not a word. So all this is the quality of proof and evidence we're talking about, *from Christianity's most famous promoter*. And we're only just getting started.

***

In 2012, Jonathan M.S. Pearce painstakingly took apart the myriad inconsistencies, incompatibilities and impossibilities lurking in the stories of Jesus' birth with his *The Nativity: A Critical Examination*. Now he returns to bookend the problematic story of Jesus with a new examination of the other end of the spectrum: his death and resurrection.

And just as he showed us with the Nativity story stories, how quickly the cornerstone of the Gospel turns out to be shifting sand... The usual suspects reappear: discrepancies, illogic, bad character development, plot holes, ahistorical details, anachronisms and other less-obvious mistakes of the evangelists. We get the sense, as Pearce notes repeatedly, that every single detail of the Gospels is contestable and problematic...

Pearce doesn't stop there. He also goes after the Gospels' bodyguards, the army of Christian soldiers surrounding and propping up the Gospels' shaky house of cards with logical fallacies and flawed arguments. It's a real treat to see him deflate the tiresome bluster spewing from such windbags as Wm. Lane Craig and all the others of his ilk who murk up the waters with their apologetic squid ink.

There's another facet of Pearce's approach that pleases. In the early 90's, when Christian filmgoers were still losing their minds over the blasphemy of a Jesus who has sex in *The Last Temptation of Christ*, virtually all of them missed a far more subversive film, *The Rapture* (1991). What made that later film so much more dangerous to Christianity is that it took their dogma – in this case, evangelical eschatological fantasies – and ran with them, showing how, even if their apocalyptic scenario actually was real in the first place, it would *still* be BS...

In the same way, Pearce tackles the Easter story not by simply dismissing its unbelievable miraculous and fantastical elements outright (which would certainly be fair enough) or by arguing (as I do) that none of this story ever really happened, but by taking them at face value and saying to believers, "Okay, let's say miracles *can* happen – *but did this one?*"

---

[1] Though I guess he *is* telling the truth, as Paul repeatedly and fervently assures us *he is not lying*: cf. Romans 9:1; 2 Cor. 1:23, 11:31; Galatians 1:20, etc.—why, even the forgers writing in his name swear to us they are not lying... (see 2 Thess. 3:17; 1 Timothy 2:7).

After hearing Pearce's exquisitely-reasoned case, any intellectually honest believer will have to agree – regardless of whether one believes divine resurrections can happen or not – that any claim to find historical reliability in the Easter story fails.

David Fitzgerald

Author of *Nailed: Ten Christian Myths That Show Jesus Never Existed at All*, *Jesus: Mything in Action* and *The Complete Heretic's Guide to Western Religion* series

Eureka, CA January 26th, 2021

Introduction

This book is designed to be a concise summary that looks critically at the Easter story, one of the most important theological and, ultimately, (supposedly) historical accounts and set of claims in the Bible for Christians now and since the time of Paul (and the birth of the belief system).

There are literally thousands of books and journals out there dealing with both skeptical analyses and Christian defences of the claims within the Christian Bible. My own offering is intended to be thorough but not exhaustive. Michael J. Alter, on the other hand, with his magnum opus *The Resurrection: A Critical Inquiry*, has been not only thorough, but nothing short of exhaustive. The book runs to a huge 854 pages, with over one hundred pages being dedicated to the bibliography and index alone. Speaking of which, he has since released *A Thematic Access-Oriented Bibliography of Jesus's Resurrection*, a 602-page reference text that identifies approximately 7,000 English sources, exclusively from books on the Resurrection, divided into twelve categories and thirty-four subcategories! My book is intended to be a rather brisker affair but with a no less robust, well-argued, and evidence-based conclusion:

That the Resurrection accounts are false (ahistorical) and the Gospels are not to be trusted.

Michael Alter's initial Resurrection book lists 120 differences and contradictions and 217 speculations involved in Paul's Epistles, the four Gospel accounts and Acts (see Appendix 1). That's an astoundingly high rate of issue per chapter and verse.

The way that I have organised this book is to start off by examining the ramifications of the conclusion to this text (to finding, in my and many others' opinion, that the Resurrection most probably didn't happen) – in other words, why this book is important. Next, I briefly set out the allegedly historical claims. I then look at the methodological approaches that I will be taking, discussing probabilities and how to assess them, including what kind of evidence and genre the Gospels are. After several chapters discussing these and connected topics and analogies, I start examining the Easter story claims, both from Paul and the Gospels. My analysis will reveal a well-known fact: there exist myriad problems associated with them. I also discuss the post-Resurrection appearances and what could explain these purported events. I finish with detailing (but not exhaustively) some far more probable naturalistic claims that I argue do a better job of explaining the data.

What I don't do is discuss the Ascension nor the events of Acts in any great detail, for the simple reason of time and length. It is my goal that this text is manageable, interesting and concise enough to promote readability. Similar to many authors, I had to draw a line somewhere and this was broadly with the Resurrection itself and appearances shortly thereafter.

What I am saying is that this book in your hands now, in paper or digitally, should not be the end of your investigations. It *can* be, as I believe my case is terminal; this book is enough to leave you in no doubt that the problems with the Resurrection are terminal and should undermine any rational belief in the theology and reality of the divine Christ.

That is not to say, of course, that there aren't attempted Christian apologetic rebuttals or answers to the issues that I raise here. But be warned: *an* answer is not *the* answer or necessarily *reasonable* or *probable*. There is a fallacy that has been named *possibiliter ergo probabiliter*, which is an approach I have seen countless times from Christian apologists: something is conceptually possible, so therefore it is probable. Or, "It's just about possible, so this is definitely what actually happened." Where I *do* supply Christian counter-arguments, it is because they are worthy of consideration. But I do not exhaust them because apologetics is an inexhaustible well of post hoc rationalisation.

It is worth mentioning that I am not a Jesus mythicist, which means that I do not believe that Jesus was a wholly constructed myth. However, my beliefs about Jesus are synonymous with mythicism: we know virtually nothing, not even a useful nugget (other than, perhaps, "he was an itinerant preacher from Nazareth" and "he was crucified") about Jesus; his story has been so mythologically overlaid onto what would have been an initial historical kernel; what we know about him now is as divorced from the original man as to effectively be myth. I am not a dyed-in-the-wool "historicist" such that I cannot be convinced towards mythicism. But I *am* convinced that what the Christian Bible tells us about Jesus is, to all intents and purposes, myth. Jesus most probably existed as an itinerant preacher originally from Nazareth and was probably executed in Jerusalem. However, that's all we can derive with any kind of certainty. Virtually everything else that the Christian Bible tells us is an ahistorical add-on. We may know what his *followers believed* but not what *actually happened.*

It is somewhat depressing that Lee Strobel, with his ninety-five tiny pages of text (*The Case for Easter*), will outsell both this book and Alter's combined, reaching a far greater audience. However, that's money and marketing for you.

And there's the rub. Christianity is a multi-billion-dollar industry and people have a lot to lose. In 2016, research found that religion generated $1.2 trillion to the US economy,[1] and you can bet your bottom dollar that atheism and agnosticism didn't contribute much of a proportion to that total! In

---

[1] Grim & Grim (2016).

addition, Americans give $74.5 billion to their congregations each year.[1] I could go on, but the point is that there is a lot of investment, *both psychological and financial*, in the "truth" of Christianity (qua the Resurrection). This means that people have a lot to lose by recognising the falsity of the Easter narrative. I will return to *motivated reasoning* later in this text.

These and other arguments aren't measured by many people on the merits of their intrinsic rational value. Oh, but I wish they were. Skeptics will herald these arguments as confirming their already-held position. Theists will dismiss them by either ignoring such conceptual problems wholesale or attaching more intrinsic value to their counter-arguments. This is known as *confirmation bias* and we all suffer from it. A few people in the middle might well be swayed. Good for them.

In one sense (and being frank here), I could not care less about the force of these arguments on receptive or non-receptive readers. You've bought the book, right? Well, I won't be quitting my day job on the back of these book sales, believe you me. However, I sincerely *do* care about truth and about my fellow members of society, of the world, having a more accurate appraisal of the universe around them. This is, for me, more about contributing to the repertoire of arguments towards finding a more accurate ultimate truth of the world, as far as that can be achieved. And, after all, I *enjoy* doing this. I am thoroughly convinced of the arguments and reasons for my position, philosophically starting from the very building blocks of reality – the ontology of abstract objects – and moving up to claims about history, as you will see here.

This isn't a project of *post hoc rationalisation*, of me scrabbling around for rational arguments *after* intuitively lumping for agnostic atheism. My position has been gradually arrived at over the course of twenty years or so, with constant refining and making sure that everything is coherent and consistent *from the ground up*. There are no missing bricks in any layers of my worldview wall. I don't have to justify anything spuriously in the world or universe around me. I stub my toe, I get primary progressive multiple sclerosis, I see cancer and malaria, I see tsunamis and earthquakes, wars and murders, and I don't have to square them with a loving god. The only thing that keeps me up at night is the age-old question, and this would apply to the notion of a god just as much, as to why there is something rather than nothing. Other than that, my worldview is utterly consistent and internally coherent, as far as I believe that I have thoroughly analysed it.

I am fine with changing my mind, too. Here are some things I have fundamentally changed my mind about over the years as a direct result of philosophising: the existence of God, free will, moral philosophy, politics, immigration, truth, knowledge, and so on. That's pretty much the scope of philosophy right there.

---

[1] Zauzmer (2016).

For me, the house of cards that is the Bible started collapsing when I began reading and writing about the Old Testament (that I will from hereon in call "the Hebrew Bible"). In my opinion (and that of many other skeptics), the Hebrew Bible is relatively easy pickings, being such a disparate set of writings from any number of varied sources with a host of different agendas and intentions. (Indeed, a project I am working on is a similar exposition to this, an analysis of the Exodus accounts.) Later, I came to analyse the life of Jesus more thoroughly and found the birth narratives to be incredibly problematic; hence my book on the Nativity (*The Nativity: A Critical Examination*). Naturally, the Easter story was next in line but it has taken me some years to pull previous writings together in a more coherent manner: this book.

I will discuss, in the first chapter, the ramifications of pulling the Easter rug out from under the feet of Christian theology and belief. After this, I look to establish some of the basic claims to ground an idea of what this book is looking to analyse. The Resurrection, as already set out in the first chapter, is central to Christianity, but what does it all mean? What is the rationale behind atonement? This is examined in Chapter 3, where I conclude that I need to continue writing since no theory of atonement makes requisite sense, and thus the whole project is doomed from the outset.

However, I do continue.

The next chapter concerns probability and an explanation of the idea that extraordinary claims require extraordinary evidence. This is important because it underwrites much of the rest of the book. This takes into sets out a Bayesian account my case, and the rest of the book maps this out. Up until this point, I have shown that the probability for a resurrection claim of this sort is very low and requires exceptionally good evidence to support it. After a short analysis of the Gospels as sources and exposing the fact that they do not constitute "exceptionally good evidence", the next few chapters investigate some ancillary extraordinary claims and the distinct lack of evidence for them, including silence form the earliest source, Paul.

In the spirit of a Bayesian analysis and looking at the data to support an extraordinary claim, the extensive "middle section" of the book examines the Pauline and Gospel claims, and some in Acts, concerning the trial, death and Resurrection of Jesus. Everything is dissected, from individual verses, events, prophecies, contradictions and "differences", to historical and cultural norms and evidence. All of which shows that the sources are combinations of being outright incorrect, incoherent, and historically and theologically problematic. This invalidates the conclusion that they warrant belief in the actual Resurrection of Jesus.

Following this, I present the conclusion that the events did not happen as claimed by either Christians then or Christians now. If this is the case, then what explains the existence of those early narratives? And so finally, I offer much more plausible theories as to what happened to Jesus at his death and shortly thereafter.

Suffice to say that, whilst none of the individual points within this book are groundbreakingly original, and even though the idea of a synthesis is in itself nothing new (though I do think such books often suffer from a lack of general philosophising, which I have furnished you with here), this book should be a useful weapon in the armoury of those seeking to critically assess Christianity, as well as being a vital instrument for those merely wanting to search for truth in a biblical melee of competing claims and counter-claims. The text will combine philosophy, history, archaeology, biblical exegesis and theology, all with a healthy dose of skepticism.

Who knows, for the occasional curious Christian, reading this text could be the spring shoot of doubt that sprouts forth from a seed that has found fertile ground, fortuitously bouncing off a rough-hewn pathway: new life ready to grow, blossom and bear fruit. It could be that fig tree that Jesus oddly got so angry about. Makes sense now.

1 – Why This Is Important: A Castle in the Air

The birth and death of Jesus are historical bookends to the life of Jesus, obviously, even if the theology continues in Acts and is evident in the Epistles of Paul, as problematic as these may or may not be (both historiographically and theologically). As historical bookends, they stand in stark contrast to the stories that take place between them, the life of the adult preacher who roams the land carrying out miracles. They are in contrast because there are at least, with the birth and death of Jesus, verifiable historical events that intersect with the Gospel claims. When it comes to the miracle claims and the interceding events of Jesus' life as mentioned in the four Gospels, these are historically vacuous.[1]

As part of the conclusion to my book *The Nativity: A Critical Examination*, I stated, after showing throughout the book that the Nativity claims were a-historical:[2]

> The ramifications for pulling the rug out from under the believers' feet is that we are left with no proper account of Jesus' life until, really, he starts his ministry. Furthermore, we have no real evidence for the claims that Jesus is the Messiah and is derived from Messianic and Davidic heritage. As a result, we have only the accounts of the miraculous events surrounding Jesus' ministry and death. However, the same problems afflict these accounts: they are uncorroborated by extra-biblical, non pro-Jesus attestation and rely on unknown authors writing in unknown places. What is particularly damaging, as I have already set out, is that if the birth narratives can be shown to be patently false, and the narratives involve sizeable accounts from two Gospel writers, then how can we know what other purported facts are true? If these infancy miracle claims are false, then what of the myriad of other miracle claims–the walking on the water, the water to wine, the resurrection? It is a serious indictment of these writers (especially since Luke is declared as being a reliable historian by so many apologists[3]).
>
> The undermining of these narratives does not disprove that Jesus was the Son of God, or that he had Davidic lineage, or whatever else these passages were trying to establish, per se. However, one has to

---

[1] I am not going to discuss extra-biblical mentions of Jesus, such as in Josephus, because they are largely problematic (as interpolations) and not wholly germane to the purpose of the book.
[2] Pearce (2012), p. 152-53.
[3] It is worth referring you to the work of Richard Carrier, *Not the Impossible Faith.* He does an excellent job of dispelling this ubiquitous assertion.

> recognise that some really damaging chinks are undoubtedly beaten into the apologetic armour of claims of Jesus' divinity....
>
> So while I have not proved anything entirely (in a Cartesian manner, what can be entirely 'proved' other than I exist?), I believe that I have provided a cumulative case which is overwhelmingly decisive in showing that the infancy narratives are almost certainly non-historical. As a result, it then follows that the rational belief in the divinity of Jesus, if based on such historical evidence in any way, then becomes equally damaged. Because these claims involve events which can be investigated in some way using existing sources outside of the Bible, we are in a more historically verifiable position to analyse these narratives. Other passages in the biographical accounts of Jesus' life are not afforded such verifiability, unfortunately. As such, the assertions of the rest of the Gospels are taken on their own merits rather than allowing historians to be able to see if they match up with extra-biblical evidence.

Projects such as mine do not seek to *prove* that Jesus did not rise from the dead because such an action is not possible. What they seek to do is show that it is *highly improbable indeed.* Consequently, anyone being *rational* should not believe that Jesus rose from the dead. Belief in the Resurrection, then, becomes more about faith than about a fair analysis of the source materials and a comprehensive historical investigation.

The great Catholic scholar, Fr. Raymond Brown, who did so much historical biblical exegesis for his seminal work *The Birth of the Messiah* (and let us not forget his monumental two-volume work *The Death of the Messiah*) spent a great deal of time and effort in eventually finding the historical foundations of the Nativity narratives to be seriously wanting, but that there was still theological "verisimilitude".[1] But on what foundations is the verisimilitude built if there is no history?

Thus, the accounts are inspired by trying to develop an "intelligibility" for the reader. These accounts would certainly be full of theological meaning and intelligibility, but then so do stories of pure fiction placed in historical settings. For Brown, it seems that, in terms of the Nativity, the Gospel of Matthew is all about integrating sources as both "interesting folklore" and "a salvific message that Matthew could develop harmoniously".[2] In other words, it arguably never happened as Matthew claimed it did. Jesus may offer salvation, but we cannot derive that truth from these narratives since they seem to contain little or no historical fact.

Brown observes:[3]

---

[1] For example, see Brown (1977), p. 188-90.

[2] Ibid., p. 229. See many other quotes, such as "Indeed, close analysis of the infancy narratives makes it unlikely that either account is completely historical." (p. 36).

[3] Ibid., (p. 37).

> Previous investigation with all its "hard-nosed" probing of historicity was necessary, even if it discovered that the probabilities were more often against historicity than for it. Necessary too was the quest for sources, even if it has led only to possibilities, and so was the quest for literary genre (the midrash discussion), even if attempts at classification have not been totally successful. Much of permanent value was discovered in all those quests, and it will be digested and preserved in the pages that follow. Nevertheless, the end result from some aspects of this past research has been almost an embarrassment about the value of the infancy narratives for educated Christians, as I pointed out in the Foreword.
>
> Now biblical scholarship seems to be moving into a more fruitful stage of research as it seeks to recover the value of the infancy stories as theology.

If you can't find historicity in the accounts, then there is always theology to fill the gap.

When we consider the Easter narratives, where we have a dying Messiah who is sacrificed for some reason (the atonement, which I will shortly discuss), if we find the historical claims of the death and resurrection to be wholly dubious, then what does this say about those reasons, about the atonement? What do the narratives say concerning current and theological beliefs about Jesus, about dying for sins and sacrifice if there was no dying for sins or sacrifice?

Let me exemplify. Imagine I tell you that, fifteen years ago, the alien Shwerb came down to Earth, and did X, Y and Z, and then was murdered by the intelligence agencies, and that these events had huge theological significance for Shwerbism. His death was somehow sacrificial and fed into theological ideas of sacrifice for others that permeates through Shwerbism.

But, on close analysis, it appears that X and Y and his death have no historical validity. This then leaves huge doubts for the, in this scenario, unverifiable claim of Z.

What does the falsification of the historicity of Shwerb say about Shwerbism and its theology? Well, the whole project should be doomed to the same mythology or even psychology textbook that every other religion should have been in the world (at least from the viewpoint of any given religionist, minus their own religion). Shwerbism, by all rights, should fall apart in such a scenario.

However, we all know the power of psychology and cognitive dissonance, in particular. Cognitive dissonance happens in a situation involving conflicting attitudes, beliefs or behaviours. A feeling is produced of mental discomfort (dissonance) leading to an alteration in one of the attitudes, beliefs or behaviours to reduce the discomfort and restore balance. It is what your brain does when presented with evidence against a core belief that you hold such that the belief and the evidence can somehow be harmonised.

To relate this example to another (actual real-world) example, let us turn to Joseph Smith and Mormonism. The historical claims of the golden tablets, a vanished and vanquished Indian civilization, revelations and visions, and other such wondrous things, are so historically dubious that the explicit theology pertinent to The Church of Jesus Christ of Latter-day Saints should be invalidated.

And yet, again, psychology, emotional and social blackmail, and cognitive dissonance reign supreme.

I don't want to be insulting by dismissing the Christian religion out of hand, which one might be inclined to do; I have committed an awful lot of writing on philosophy and biblical exegesis to debunking it in a rational and detailed manner; this book is a part of that project.

The simple fact of the matter is that the only times that the Gospel claims are historically verifiable, they are found to be wanting to the point that the unverifiable claims, using the power of induction,[1] must also be terminally cast into doubt. And this leaves the skeptic with nothing to convince them of the truth of the Christian religion and claims. Unfortunately for the believer, personal revelation is precisely that: personal. It is easy to explain away, as Christians will do with every single account of personal revelation from *every other* religion in the history of humanity.

Where the Nativity does have some limited theology dependent on it (such as setting out the Messianic heritage and properties of the new-born Jesus), the Easter accounts are *far more theologically important*, and so such a critical analysis of the Easter claims carries all the more weight in terms of ramifications.

But what do Christians themselves think about the ramifications of the Resurrection claims not being true? Let me turn to Christian apologist and theologian Don Stewart writing in his article "How Important Is the Resurrection to Christianity?":[2]

> According to Paul, if Christ has not been raised then the following five things would be true.
>
> 1. Christian preaching is empty and so is anyone's faith because the object of the faith, Christ, is not whom He said He was.
> 2. The apostles are liars for testifying to a resurrection that did not occur.
> 3. No forgiveness has been granted for anybody's sin.

---

[1] Using observations to justify some expectations or predictions about observations we have not yet made, so if a text is found to be false the first ten times, when we look at the eleventh time, we can be somewhat justified in thinking it may well be false again.

[2] Stewart (n.d.).

4. Those who have died believing in Christ have no hope.
5. If hope in Christ is limited to this life, Christians are to be pitied above all people.

There Is No Meaning For Humanity If Christ Is Not Risen

Without the resurrection, Christianity has no meaning for humanity - its founder would have been a liar and a failure, and its followers would have no hope. Thus the importance of the resurrection to Christian faith cannot be overestimated.

There are those who say that even without the resurrection, Christianity has significance. They hold that Christ's teachings provide ethical guidelines for humanity. The New Testament, however, testifies that this is not the case. Without the resurrection there is no meaningful Christianity.

I suppose one could ask, if you wanted to achieve those five Pauline objectives, whether the Resurrection is the best vehicle to employ. Since God is supposedly perfect, his decision to go through with this chain of events must be, in some way, a perfect choice.

Paul is referenced here, so let us see what he has to say:

Now if Christ is preached, that he has been raised from the dead, how do some among you say that there is no resurrection of the dead? But if there is no resurrection of the dead, not even Christ has been raised; and if Christ has not been raised, then our preaching is vain, your faith also is vain. Moreover we are even found to be false witnesses of God, because we witnessed against God that he raised Christ, whom he did not raise, if in fact the dead are not raised. For if the dead are not raised, not even Christ has been raised; and if Christ has not been raised, your faith is worthless; you are still in your sins. Then those also who have fallen asleep in Christ have perished. If we have hoped in Christ in this life only, we are of all people most to be pitied. (1 Corinthians 15:12-19)

The Catechism of the Catholic Church 652-58 states in no uncertain terms:

651 "If Christ has not been raised, then our preaching is in vain and your faith is in vain." The Resurrection above all constitutes the confirmation of all Christ's works and teachings. All truths, even those most inaccessible to human reason, find their justification if Christ by his Resurrection has given the definitive proof of his divine authority, which he had promised.

652 Christ's Resurrection is the fulfillment of the promises both of the Old Testament and of Jesus himself during his earthly life. The phrase "in accordance with the Scriptures" indicates that Christ's Resurrection fulfilled these predictions.

653 The truth of Jesus' divinity is confirmed by his Resurrection. He had said: "When you have lifted up the Son of man, then you will know that I am he." The Resurrection of the crucified one shows that he was truly "I AM", the Son of God and God himself. So St. Paul could declare to the Jews: "What God promised to the fathers, this he has fulfilled to us their children by raising Jesus; as also it is written in the second psalm, 'You are my Son, today I have begotten you.'" Christ's Resurrection is closely linked to the Incarnation of God's Son, and is its fulfillment in accordance with God's eternal plan.

654 The Paschal mystery has two aspects: by his death, Christ liberates us from sin; by his Resurrection, he opens for us the way to a new life. This new life is above all justification that reinstates us in God's grace, "so that as Christ was raised from the dead by the glory of the Father, we too might walk in newness of life." Justification consists in both victory over the death caused by sin and a new participation in grace. It brings about filial adoption so that men become Christ's brethren, as Jesus himself called his disciples after his Resurrection: "Go and tell my brethren." We are brethren not by nature, but by the gift of grace, because that adoptive filiation gains us a real share in the life of the only Son, which was fully revealed in his Resurrection.

655 Finally, Christ's Resurrection - and the risen Christ himself is the principle and source of our future resurrection: "Christ has been raised from the dead, the first fruits of those who have fallen asleep... For as in Adam all die, so also in Christ shall all be made alive." The risen Christ lives in the hearts of his faithful while they await that fulfillment. In Christ, Christians "have tasted...the powers of the age to come" and their lives are swept up by Christ into the heart of divine life, so that they may "live no longer for themselves but for him who for their sake died and was raised."

IN BRIEF

656 Faith in the Resurrection has as its object an event which is historically attested to by the disciples, who really encountered the Risen One. At the same time, this event is mysteriously transcendent insofar as it is the entry of Christ's humanity into the glory of God.

657 The empty tomb and the linen cloths lying there signify in themselves that by God's power Christ's body had escaped the bonds of death and corruption. They prepared the disciples to encounter the Risen Lord.

658 Christ, "the first-born from the dead" (*Col* 1:18), is the principle of our own resurrection, even now by the justification of our souls (cf. *Rom* 6:4), and one day by the new life he will impart to our bodies (cf.: *Rom* 8:11).

Or, as theologian and popular apologist William Lane Craig concludes:[1]

What justification can Christians offer, in contrast to Hindus, Jews, and Muslims, for thinking that the Christian God is real?

The answer of the New Testament is: the resurrection of Jesus.

I could furnish you with any number of quotes, here, from every corner of the denominational world of Christianity, but the end result would be the same: there is no doubt about the centrality that the death and Resurrection narrative has to the theology, and indeed the existence, of Christianity.[2] Therefore, if one can show that the historical claims of the Easter story are highly dubious, that the most probable hypothesis is that it did not take place, then there are serious threats to Christianity as a worldview. Christian preaching is empty, the apostles are liars, there is no divine forgiveness for sin, there is no hope for those dying in belief in Christ, and we should pity Christians. And Jesus was probably just a man. That's a pretty damning state of affairs. Christians *really need* the Resurrection to be true; they have a lot to lose.

Imagine, if you will, Christianity without the sacrificial death and Resurrection of Jesus Christ. What would we be left with? Would it be enough to move people to create and maintain a viable religion? We would have an itinerant miracle-working preacher who travelled around a Roman-occupied land now known as Israel. Such supposed messianic-type figures are ten-a-penny throughout history, so I posit that Christ without the cross and the Resurrection is not enough for Christianity.

I use the term "castle in the air" here not because Christianity is "daydream, an idle fancy, a near impossibility" (it is all those things) but because the idiom always makes one think of an edifice devoid of any foundation.

---

[1] Craig (n.d.).

[2] Unitarians and other nontrinitarians have a different position, that God is one single unity and not the triune version of orthodox belief; Jesus was merely a Saviour inspired by God, but not God. In some of these vastly different belief systems, you could find a version of Christianity that could work without the divine person of Jesus as God dying sacrificially and rising, but this would arguably not be "*Christ*ianity". Indeed, many Unitarians do not self-identify as Christian.

But to take the metaphor a step further, by showing the Christian edifice is without (historical) foundation, it means that with the slightest of skeptical winds, the whole structure comes toppling down.

Without the history (of the Nativity, of the Resurrection), there is no real theology, and without the theology, there is no substance to the remaining Christian worldview.

2 – What Do the Gospels Claim Happened?

After this discussion to analyse what happens if the Easter story is untrue, it is probably about time that we got on to what the death and Resurrection claims actually are. For ease of use, I will set these out in chronological order. Remember, many of these purported events happen (as we shall later see) only in one, two or three of the Gospels and/or Paul's letters, and/or contain contradictions about the claims made concerning the event.

- Jesus was God in human form. (This is a theological claim.)
- Jesus went to Jerusalem and he had a Last Supper with his disciples before going out to the Garden of Gethsemane and praying to himself.
- He was betrayed and arrested for the blasphemy of claiming to be divine.
- After being arrested, Jesus was condemned by religious leaders.
- Jesus went on trial before Pilate.
- He was sent to Herod and then returned to Pilate where he was sentenced to death.
- He was led away to Calvary.
- He was crucified.
- Whilst on the cross, the soldiers cast lots for Jesus' clothes.
- Whilst on the cross, he was mocked and insulted.
- Another criminal on the cross rebuked him.
- Jesus spoke to Mary and John from the cross.
- There was an earthquake, tombs were opened with dead saints parading around Jerusalem and the veil in the Temple was torn. There was darkness for three hours.
- Soldiers pierced his side.
- The death and suffering of Jesus contributed to a greater good and atoned, somehow, for all of humanity's sins; that God needed, for some reason, to have the books balanced (or some other similar theory that Christians themselves can't quite agree on). (This is a theological claim.)
- Jesus' body is taken and buried by a Sanhedrin member, Joseph of Arimathea.
- Pilate grants permission for guards to be placed at the tomb.

Three days later (depending on which Gospel you read), Jesus rose again with perhaps this chronology (contradictions aside):

- Some people (arguable as to who, exactly, and when) go to the tomb.
- No angels, or one, or two angels are there and the stone is rolled away.
- Jesus is resurrected; that is, as a fully-fledged human being, he comes back to life.
- He goes around appearing to many people in the local area as a resurrected human, and in Galilee (there are Gospel contradictions as to where), and over a forty-day period, including to more than five hundred people at one time.
- Jesus then ascends into heaven by rising into the clouds.
- Angels question why the disciples are staring into the sky.

Some of these points are somewhat theological and though I have produced a mainstream understanding of the events in these short bullet point list sentences, as we shall see, these understandings can and will be challenged in this book and often from within a Christian understanding. For example, I will later argue that Paul himself believed Jesus' resurrection to be a spiritual one and not a bodily one. For the sake of seeing these events in order, I have assumed a more orthodox appraisal of the events.

Although I haven't listed them here, there are many, many contradictions (or "differences", as apologists will maintain) concerning these apparent events between the four Gospel accounts in terms of the events, their order and the details thereof. The accounts are both terminally internally incompatible as well as being incompatible with external sources. One can reason why this came about (differing sources, agendas, times, places etc.) but there is no way of being able to resolve the accounts into a single coherent narrative, though I have tried.

What this means is that, in producing a seemingly coherent chronological narrative "list" such as above, we have to smash the Gospels together. This is how many Christians (and non-Christians alike) see the stories.

In *The Nativity: A Critical Examination*, I detail how the only two Gospels with details of the birth narratives (Matthew and Luke) diverge on details so fundamentally that explanations are absolutely necessitated. For example, despite how hard Christians try, you simply cannot marry (historically speaking) Luke's census with Matthew's Herod: the at least ten-year gap is insurmountable. This is a case of smashing the two Gospel accounts together in order to make one single narrative. It is why, in popular culture, you might go and see your child's Christmas Nativity play that has Joseph and Mary travelling to Bethlehem for a census and being visited by the three Magi, with the involvement of Herod. But critical analysis leads to the conclusion that the census cannot coexist in a single narrative form with Herod and the Magi.

With the Resurrection narratives, most Christians think that many of the contradictions still fit within an overall narrative flow, give or take to differing degrees, and so the contradictions are less foundational. For example, you could argue that, okay, there *are* contradictions but this might just be one of two Gospels being wrong, and the others being right but that this doesn't *really* affect the chronological narrative list and flow of events.

Of course, the Gospels or sources that could be right or wrong change from claim and contradiction to claim and contradiction (or "difference"). There is simply mass confusion, and who is to say where one Gospel may be admitted to be wrong that all those other claims remain as accurate? What does this say about the sources? What does this say about verifiability of the claims and believability of the readers?

As such, to the skeptic, these are still reflective of issues with sources, accuracy and reliability. In this way, an extended list of *all* of the events will need to be somewhat pared down as a result of problematic contradictions and/or omissions.

Internally, the Gospels disagree on a whole raft of different details that we will explore, but if you were so inclined, you could perhaps forgive many of them with some mental gerrymandering because you would have so much psychological capital invested in the overall truth of the story. Perhaps more critical to the Christian's claims of historical veracity are the external sources (burial practices and suchlike).

I will seek to challenge this approach of harmonising disparate accounts later (such as the four-newspaper article approach, or four witnesses to a car accident) in showing that some of the details are far more serious and represent much greater narrative issues. I will also take issue with claims that either all the Gospels or perhaps only one has: for example, Joseph of Arimathea and Matthew's guards at the tomb. It is not so much about coherence across the four accounts but that they are all wrong, or using techniques that are indicative of fictionalisation. All this will happen after an analysis of the Gospels, as a whole, as "reliable" sources for historical (and theological) claims.

But before this, we need to very briefly discuss the Holy Trinity of Jesus, God the Father and the Holy Spirit.

The Holy Trinity

It is important to mention the Trinity because the idea underwrites the whole concept of the commonplace understanding of the Resurrection. That Jesus was God in human form and part of the Holy Trinity is foundational to him resurrecting as a human incarnation of a divine being.

In other words, if you can't make sense of the Holy Trinity to the point that the whole idea becomes incoherent, and then you can't make sense of the atonement that we will next discuss, and you can't make sense of the Resurrection as an apparent event in history. The Holy Trinity suffers from being a theory that supposedly has three separate, distinguishable entities with their own different properties (The Father, the Son and the Holy Spirit) that are somehow the same but, by threat of heresy, meaning that they cannot be "parts" of a single entity, or wholly different "gods" (polytheism).

Yes, there are "unitarian" and "nontrinitarian" movements that dent the Holy Trinity, and there is theological debate as to how much the Bible actually supports such a theological position, either way. That said, *most* denominations adhere to some sense of the Holy Trinity, so let us, for the sake of argument, assume its truth.

Yet the Holy Trinity, as far as I am concerned, doesn't make sense; it *is* incoherent. I have written a fair amount on this topic elsewhere, and I cannot devote too much space to it here. You really have to start questioning things when the prevailing modern Christian approach to the theology of the Trinity is called *mysterianism*. This is the idea that we don't understand *how* the Trinity works (it's a mystery) but we've just got to have faith *that* it works. I believe that 2+2=7; I don't know *how* it works and I can't *show* you to convince you, I just have faith *that* it does. God moves in mysterious ways, end of discussion.

Professor of Philosophy Dale Tuggy sees five ways to understand such mysterianism:[1]

> [1]...a truth formerly unknown, and perhaps undiscoverable by unaided human reason, but which has now been revealed by God and is known to some... [2] something we don't completely understand... [3] some fact we can't explain, or can't fully or adequately explain... [4] an unintelligible doctrine, the meaning of which can't be grasped....[5] a truth which one should believe even though it seems, even after careful reflection, to be impossible and/or contradictory and thus false.

The subject of mysterianism is itself almost a book-length affair. Suffice to say:[2]

> Mysterianism is a meta-theory of the Trinity, that is, a theory about trinitarian theories, to the effect that an acceptable Trinity theory must, given our present epistemic limitations, to some degree lack understandable content. "Understandable content" here means propositions expressed by language which the hearer "grasps" or understands the meaning of, and which seem to her to be consistent.
>
> At its extreme, a mysterian may hold that no first-order theory of the Trinity is possible, so we must be content with delineating a consistent "grammar of discourse" about the Trinity, i.e., policies about what should and shouldn't be said about it. In this extreme form, mysterianism may be a sort of sophisticated position by itself–to the effect that

[1] Tuggy (2003), p. 175-76.
[2] Tuggy (2016).

> one repeats the creedal formulas and refuses on principle to explain how, if at all, one interprets them. More common is a moderate form, where mysterianism supplements a Trinity theory which has some understandable content, but which is vague or otherwise problematic.

The reason I belabour the point of highlighting mysterianism here is that, in the evident absence of a prevailing theory that coherently works and that is accepted by mainstream Christian thinkers, some form of mysterianism must hold for Christians to be able to hold *Christ*ian beliefs. And this Trinitarian belief, as I have said, underwrites understandings of Jesus that are necessary to make sense of the narrative of Jesus' bodily resurrection. That is, unless you just want to believe that Jesus is a special man, some non-divine Messiah favoured by God but not *actually* God. However, as already mentioned in the last chapter, this would invalidate such a believer as being called a "Christian" in the most popular sense.

The important point to understand is this: if the concept of the Holy Trinity is incoherent or broken, then it doesn't really matter what you think of a Trinitarian resurrection event. Again, one idea supervenes on another. Christians need to satisfy themselves rationally with the concept of the Holy Trinity before they can properly work through the rational analysis and subsequent belief in the Resurrection.

One could make the argument, considering we will soon be talking far more about probability, given this extra level of epistemic hoops the Christian has to jump through, that the chance of the Resurrection together with the Trinity being true is even less probable than having to consider the Resurrection alone.

Precedence

Resurrecting deities is not an uncommon motif in ancient religions. This is nothing new, and so the idea that some truth value can be extracted from the claims due to them being wild or original has no purchase. As Richard Carrier, with a PhD in Ancient History, points out:[1]

> Indeed, resurrection was wildly popular among the pagans. Of course, it was already a common Jewish staple, with past resurrections in its sacred stories and future resurrections in its imagined plan of salvation. But the claim that all pagans scoffed at the idea is simply false. The idea of a future resurrection for all the saved actually derives from pagan Zoroastrianism, then the Persian state religion, which had influenced many

[1] Carrier (2011), p. 59-60.

> popular cults in the Roman Empire (including Mithraism and religious Stoicism). Indeed, it's from them that the Jews got the idea in the first place, having picked it up when they were in captivity in Persia several centuries before Christianity began.
>
> But that wasn't the limit of it. Besides the many popular resurrected savior gods already mentioned, pagan tales of other resurrected heroes, gods, saints, and just-plain-lucky lads were incredibly common. One very popular example at the time: not only was "the savior" Asclepius a resurrected and deified son of god, but he was also the preeminent "resurrector of the dead," which was in fact a prominent reason pagans held him in such esteem. Since the ancient Christian apologist Justin could not deny this, he was forced to insist "the devil" must have introduced "Asclepius as the raiser of the dead" in order to undermine the Christian message in advance.
>
> Clearly, pagans would have no problem with one more dying-and-rising son of god and savior. That notion was actually conspicuously popular at the time, which is why Christians thought of it and why it was at all successful. Even the claim that Jews would never have bought the idea of a singular resurrection before the general resurrection of all Jews is false: such special resurrections already appeared in their own Bible and were readily believed to still be occurring.

The mention of Justin Martyr is pertinent, since the early church father declared to early Jews and Christians:[1]

> When we say that the Word, who is our teacher, Jesus Christ the firstborn of God, was produced without sexual union, and that he was crucified and died, and rose again, and ascended to heaven, we propound nothing new or different from what you believe regarding those whom you consider sons of God.

Given the context within which Christianity was set, and looking at it in a secular, anthropological manner, a dying and resurrecting god is something you could and arguably would expect.

The final point to make on this topic, desiring parsimony in these matters, is that it was only after the whole Easter story, only after Jesus' death, that his followers understood who Jesus supposedly was. This was a theology that looks now rather like a post hoc rationalisation given Jesus' death. He was supposed to be the Messiah, often expected to be a militaristic leader who would

[1] Justin Martyr, *Apology* 1.21.

command the chosen people and not someone who ended up being crucified at the first sign of opposition.

Cognitive dissonance kicks in and the disciples and early church followers had to rationalise such a potential let-down. The Messiah morphs into a sacrificial lamb and the Old Testament is ransacked for potential quotes (many taken out of context or based on a faulty translation) that might support this view. Hence the mental contortions one has to make to derive coherent prophecies from the Old Testament, often from non-prophetic sources. But more on this subject later.

Just to finish this chapter, it is worth noting that, either internally or externally, in terms of common sense or history, virtually every single claim (by this I mean almost every single verse) in the Gospels recounting the Easter story, as listed above, is contestable. There are *so* many problems with the Christian Bible claims, indeed, that I am actually having to cherry-pick a selection of them to focus on in this book. This is the sheer scale of the problem for the Christian defender.

3 – The Atonement: Why Bother?

If I was to be a little facetious here, I would question why an all-knowing, all-powerful, all-loving being would sacrifice himself to himself to sit on his own right hand[1] in heaven for eternity to pay himself for the sins of a being he designed and created. All things considered, this is not much of a sacrifice, one could argue, and one that makes little philosophical sense. Yes, I am admittedly being somewhat flippant and simplistic here, but you get the point.

It is always worth reminding readers that, in some way (mysterianism – the idea that though it is a mystery *how*, we just have to have *faith* that it works), the Holy Trinity apparently makes sense. That God the Father, the Son and the Holy Spirit are not the same but are, and are not different but are. Jesus sacrificing himself to pay for our sins, a payment to God the Father, is a wholly bizarre idea given that God the Son and God the Father are in some incalculable way *the same entity*: the Godhead (but not parts thereof as that is heresy).

The theological problems involved with the atonement are legion. Many of the problems start with the notion, as per classical theism, that God is indeed omniscient, omnipotent and omnibenevolent. The particular characteristic that causes most of the headaches for theists is divine foreknowledge.

It is worth noting here that not all Christian thinkers adhere to the line of thinking that God has full foreknowledge of all future events, including supposedly freely willed events. This is no surprise because the concept of divine foreknowledge is more than mildly problematic in terms of God's characteristics, making little sense of creation and the world, and even the Bible.

Indeed, the relatively new theology of *Open Theism* stipulates that God does not have full divine foreknowledge of future events because this plays merry havoc with the idea of his judgement and moral culpability. However, if God doesn't know future events, then it means that his creation is somewhat random. It is a bit like a computer game of *SimCity* or similar that he is playing in the hope that it will turn out well. This may, indeed, work with some notions of God but not with most orthodox others.

Of course, the idea that God is perfectly knowledgeable, as in omniscient, is that he has the full knowledge and understanding of all counterfactuals that have ever and will ever come to pass. A counterfactual is an "if statement". If Harriet is in causal circumstance C_1, she will do X. If she is in C_2, she will do Y.

---

[1] It might correctly be pointed out that this is symbolic and refers not to location but to favouritism. This is still incoherent, since if Jesus is identified as having a special place of honour to God the Father, we have all sorts of issues concerning the Holy Trinity and Atonement itself. Whichever way *Dextera Domini* is interpreted leads to problem.

If God genuinely knew every counterfactual, then this leaves no space, in my book, for any genuine libertarian free will (irrespective of the fact that the concept is broken anyway). That is because (as is shown in something called the grounding objection) there must be some reason and causality involved in why Harriet does X in C_1 and not ~X (not X). Harriet's causal circumstance has causality inherently wrapped up in it.[1]

Of course, if you have no free will, then a judgemental God and the notion of sinning is entirely nonsensical. Worse still, if God is perfect and has no lack, no needs, and if God knew everything in advance (and could even be able to experience scenarios – experiential knowledge – without having to create) then why would he create anything at all? Especially a creation that involved imperfection, pain and suffering... But let us park these thorny ideas and grant creation for the sake of the Christian and this argument. I have set out many more arguments along these lines in my book *The Problem with "God": Classical Theism under the Spotlight*.

Let us look at God's moral culpability and responsibility. If God designed the universe, the laws, humanity and *everything*, and *then* created the universe; and given that God could have chosen any other possible world out of infinite choices; and given that God could step in at any moment and change things; and given that God has complete foreknowledge of future events; how is God not in some way ultimately culpable for our sin?

For example, if I created a sentient lifeform in the laboratory – designed from scratch and created entirely myself – and I knew 100% (and I mean *infallibly*) that these things would break out of the lab and rampage through town causing harm (rape, murder, mugging) and *knew* this in advance, and then *still* decided to create these lifeforms and they went out and did their evil (qua morally bad) thing, would I not be in some way culpable? Yes, some of them might go out and paint pictures and do charity work, but the majority were pretty evil. Yes, they did it "of their own free will", whatever sense we may make of this. But I *knew* this in advance. I designed them in such a way. And I created them with this perfect foreknowledge of mine. Would the police, in evaluating the crime and suffering in the town, not see me as somewhat morally or causally culpable?

Let's put it another way. I am the CEO and chief designer of a massive car company. I design a car that I know 100% will have a certain number of faults and will cause pain and suffering through crashing as a result of those faults. Yes, some of the cars will be great, and provide good service to their end users. But many will crash and burn. Literally. And I create them *knowingly*. Would I not, as CEO and chief designer, be held accountable?

There are two issues here, seen when we consider a literal understanding of Adam and Eve, but extendable beyond that example:

---

[1] Dealing robustly with this topic would take a lengthy chapter, and of course theists have responses. I leave it to the reader to research this further.

(1) Adam and Eve, if they are representative of humanity, reflect a poorly designed humanity. If we are poorly designed and God knows it, then God is a poor designer and should be held morally or causally culpable for our Fall or failure.
(2) Adam and Eve are not representative of humanity, and we are being punished (vicariously through the Fall) for the actions of people who bear no proper connection to us, who are not reflective of who we are. Therefore, God is not fair.

Does God cause Adam and Eve's actions? Ultimately, if God designed and created a scenario over which he has ultimate power, and allows his creation to knowingly play out, then yes, in any meaningful sense of the concept, God caused Adam and Eve's actions.

Now let us extend this example from Adam and Eve to the whole of humanity. God has designed and created everything about this world, the entire garden into which he has planted us, *and* he has designed us – the seeds. He can control everything at every moment, in any way he sees fit. He can stop things, start things, change things, do anything. This situation is a mixture of will and omissive will. Omissive will is when an agent decides *not* to do something and the not doing something brings about a certain scenario. In other words, if God decides *not* to stop the tsunami from killing 230,000 people *but could have*, then this is functionally the same as God creating a tsunami *in order to* kill 230,000 people.

This is a really important concept to understand because the whole of Jesus' existence and sacrificial death hangs on this. Actually, it doesn't hang on this, it falls down and crumples into an incoherent mess as a result of this.

There are many theories of atonement. But what I'm trying to set out here is that it doesn't really matter what those theories are because none of them can make sense of the mess that is design, creation and Jesus. God sees fit to sacrifice his incarnated human self (to himself) as a result of some scenario involving humans *that he designed himself, created himself and knew, himself, would come to fruition from the beginning of time*.

I will lay out, very briefly, some of the prevailing theories of the atonement, but bear in mind that this is essentially an irrelevant task since none of it makes any sense in light of what I have just said.

First of all, it is rather pertinent to point out that there are many theories as to how the atonement works. This should tell you something. What this tells us is that there is confusion at the heart of *why Jesus existed at all* amongst the very cleverest of Christian thinkers. Let me just emphasise this point: the best Christian minds since the death of Christ can't agree on why Christ had to (live and then) die.

Furthermore, let me start my atonement list by saying that, as we can see with the approaches to understanding the Holy Trinity, a common tack to atonement is mysterianism (again, the position that, even though we don't understand *how* it works, the atonement *must* work). God works in mysterious ways. Or...we can't make sense of this; therefore, faith.

Please also take into account that entire books have been written on the subject of atonement, so I will only give these theories a cursory summarisation. And, of course, when you have so many different denominations (such as Calvinists, Lutherans and suchlike – there are some 42,000 denominations of Christianity worldwide), things get even more complicated. If you were so inclined, you could broadly split them into vicarious atonement (some kind of substitution), a defeat of Satan or victory for Christ, or participating, as humans, in the death and resurrection of Jesus, imitating him in some way.

Ransom from Satan

Supposing you believe that both God and Satan are literally real entities. Well, then, you'd be making no sense at all. Remember God's "omni-" characteristics: God can do anything (with logical permissibility, arguably). God could make Satan disappear, non-existent, at the click of his fingers. Any ontological argument for God, or claim that he is perfect (such as under *Perfect Being Theology*, for example) argues for God's supreme omni-abilities. To be the greatest being in conception, there can be no rival being as God could dispense with such a being on a whim.

This means that if Satan exists, he does so at the behest of God. Either God actively wants him to exist, or his disappearance would cause more grief than good, like some embodiment of the *Problem of Evil* (broadly the problem that suffering exists in the world given that God has the *ability* to do something about it, would *know* what to do about it, and would *want* to do something about it).

Thus, it appears that Satan, if he exists, is doing a job for God: providing a service, if you will. God, then, must accept corporate responsibility for him. In other words, anything that is laid at the feet of Satan, in terms of blame and moral responsibility, should actually be laid at the invisible feet of God. God allows (either by design, direct causation or act of omission) everything that Satan does.

So let's now consider this theory of the atonement. The ransom theory essentially states that Jesus liberated humanity from being enslaved to Satan (and by extension death) by giving his own life as a sort of ransom sacrifice to Satan. He swaps his life for the lives of imperfect humans. Adam and Eve, at the Fall, sold humanity to Satan, requiring God to pay the Devil a ransom to free us, though he tricked Satan into accepting Christ's death as this ransom.

This theory was popular with the early church and can take on slightly different forms, especially when considering the relationship of Satan to God, how the Fall works, and what rights that Satan has to our sinful souls. As St Augustine stated:[1]

> The Redeemer came and the deceiver was overcome. What did our Redeemer do to our Captor? In payment for us He set the trap, His Cross, with His blood for bait. He could indeed shed that blood; but he deserved not to drink it. By shedding the blood of One who was not his debtor, he was forced to release his debtors.

Some versions have God doing a deal with Satan, but this then falls victim to issues of God lacking some kind of omnipotence, as discussed previously. Essentially, as far as I can see, this is now quite an outdated view because the idea of a very real and tangible Satan is perhaps somewhat outdated itself in modern theological thinking. When, as stated, the concept of Satan is broken, then any atonement theories based on him suffer.

Recapitulation Theory

Early Greek bishop Irenaeus (130-202 CE), responsible for guiding the early church, first communicated this theory to sit alongside the ransom theory. In it, Christ rectifies Adam's earlier wrongs, helping humanity achieve eternal life and moral perfection. Jesus becomes, in a sense, the new Adam, balancing the wrongs of Adam (and Eve) during the Fall. But where the human Adam failed, Jesus succeeds.

Part of this is divinisation (or *theosis/theopoesis*), where divine grace transforms humans to a more godlike status or union. As Augustine of Hippo (354-430 CE) said, "To make human beings gods, He was made man who was God" (Sermon 192.1.1). In fact, a lot of the early church fathers had much to say on this transformative spirit of God and the process of divinisation.

As theologian William Barclay said, in capturing the essence of this belief:[2]

> Through man's disobedience the process of the evolution of the human race went wrong, and the course of its wrongness could neither be halted nor reversed by any human means. But in Jesus Christ the whole

[1] "Doctrine of Atonement", *Catholic Encyclopedia,* https://www.newadvent.org/cathen/02055a.htm (Retrieved 10/11/2020).
[2] Barclay (1961), p.100.

course of human evolution was perfectly carried out and realised in obedience to the purpose of God.

Of course, this theory relies on a coherency in the notion of Adam and Eve, fully designed and created by God, being ultimately responsible for failing and falling and thus requiring some kind of atonement to take place. As mentioned already, that foundation is terminally cracked.

Christus Victor

This theory was also a dominant theory in the historical church. Indeed, some ransom theories are called Christus Victor theories, but Gustaf Aulen's 1931 book *Christus Victor* studying atonement theories put a different spin on things. Christ dies in order to defeat the evil powers (of Satan, sin and death), freeing humanity from bondage to them. However, remember the philosophical problems with Satan.

Aulen saw this not so much as a ransom payment but as a liberation, so it is a move away from some sort of business transaction model that arguably somewhat diminishes God's power or moral superiority. This isn't about paying anyone off, but a classical understanding of defeating a foe.

As former minister and editor-in-chief of *Christianity Today* Mark Galli states:[1]

> The idea is this: Christ is victor. Christ in his death and resurrection overcame the hostile powers variously understood as the devil, sin, the law, and death. While the model assumes humanity's guilt for getting ourselves into this predicament - beginning with the original sin of Adam and Eve - the theory's anthropology (view of humanity) emphasizes not our guilt but our victimhood, at least the way it is often discussed today. The main human problem is that we are trapped and we need to be rescued.

Of course, astute readers will notice that God equally designed and created those hostile powers noted above, ultimately speaking.

This view is often used in tandem with other theories, though many argue (there being a debt owed to Satan) that this approach should not be carried out.

[1] Galli (2011).

Satisfaction Theory

Anselm of Canterbury (1033-1109 CE) was not enamoured of the previous theories (he didn't like there being a debt owed to Satan) and proposed an alternative one. Here, mankind has offended God and dishonoured him, and such offences require punishment. Humanity owed God; God did not owe Satan. But there is nothing we mere humans could do in terms of salvation for such crimes, and so Christ steps in to make the repayment, to satisfy God's needs – although "satisfaction" more properly means redeeming the affront to God with something of equal value.

We no longer need to satisfy our misdeeds with punishment thanks to the sacrifice of Jesus.

As theologian Stephen D. Morrison states:[1]

> Our debt, in this theory, is that of injustice. Our injustices have stolen from the justice of God and therefore must be paid back. Satisfaction theory then postulates that Jesus Christ pays back God in His death on the cross to God. This is the first Atonement theory to bring up the notion that God is acted upon by the Atonement (i.e. that Jesus satisfies God).

Although Christ *is* God, and a perfect God should have no needs. But I don't want to confuse matters.

This is the view favoured by the Catholic Church, with Thomas Aquinas and John Calvin developing it.

Penal Substitution

Protestant reformers, in the 16th century, did what they liked doing and reformed previous ideas – in this case, Anselm's satisfaction theory – into a more legalistic context. In terms of jurisprudence, crimes necessitate punishment, and no amount of "satisfaction" can get around this situation. Here, Christ substitutes himself for us and takes the actual punishment. We are saved from God's wrath by God in human form. Again, Morrison explains:[2]

> This theory of the Atonement contrasts with Anselm's Satisfaction Theory in that God is not satisfied with a debt of justice being paid by Jesus, but that God is satisfied with punishing Jesus in the place of mankind. The notion that the cross acts upon God, conditioning Him to

[1] Morrison (n.d.).
[2] Morrison (n.d.).

forgiveness, originates from Anslem's theory, but here in Penal Substitution the means are different. This theory of the Atonement is perhaps the most dominant today, especially among the Reformed, and the evangelical.

Instead of punishment being averted, punishment is absorbed.

Penal substitution is a theory of atonement favoured by conservative theologians, thinkers and Christians in general.

This penal substitution is conditional, however, and not afforded everyone, automatically; you need to have faith. And this *is* separate from deeds or actions (works). As with all theories, there are many Christians who do not adhere to this understanding of the atonement.

Moral Government Theory

This theory originally arose in opposition to a movement called Socinianism, an antitrinitarian movement that denied the pre-existence of Christ. The governmental view of atonement was that Christ suffered so that God could forgive us and in so doing, justice reigned. This is still a form of substitution, but Christ's punishment is not exactly equal to the one due to humanity. Jesus, in his sinlessness, was sacrificed as a form of *propitiation* whereby God is appeased. ("The word *propitiation* carries the basic idea of appeasement or satisfaction, specifically toward God. Propitiation is a two-part act that involves appeasing the wrath of an offended person and being reconciled to him."[1])

Some critics see this sort of appeasement in light of God's great wrath as somewhat "pagan" with defenders insisting that it is not, because it is God doing this act himself. As J.I. Packer observes:[2]

> In paganism, man propitiates his gods, and religion becomes a form of commercialism and, indeed, of bribery. In Christianity, however, God propitiates his wrath by his own action. He set forth Jesus Christ, says Paul, to be the propitiation of our sins.

The main difference here is that the payment is not exactly equal to that which was due, but acts more as an alternative.

---

[1] "What is propitiation?", *Got Questions*, https://www.gotquestions.org/propitiation.html (Retrieved 11/11/2020)

[2] Packer, J. I. (1993) [1973], p. 185.

Moral Transformation

We will now start seeing a slightly different paradigm in the next theories. Abelard (1079–1142) rejected the ransom and satisfaction theories to prefer one whose basis was in God's immutable, unchanging characteristics and existence. If a sinner accepted Jesus' sacrificial death as atonement, God's judgement upon them would change accordingly. Abelard wanted to concentrate not on a wrathful God who needed some kind of payment, but on a loving God. For him, Jesus died as the demonstration of God's love, which would in turn change the sinner's course to return them to God.

As theologian Brian Hebblethwaite states:[1]

> ...justification and sanctification-the two elements of atonement-are best understood in terms of God's free forgiveness and the effective transformation of sinners, the moral seriousness of the former being shown in the whole story of the Incarnation, including the passion and way of the cross, and the moral seriousness of the latter consisting in the fact that conformation to Christ is no easy, automatic transformation but a winning of our penitence and commitment by that incarnate love and an inspiration from within by the Spirit of that same Christ enabling us to become more Christlike in the Christian fellowship and eventually in the communion of saints. This may be regarded as objective a theory of atonement as we can hope for.

Though Hebblethwaite tries to make this theory objective here, this is a much more *subjective* theory that concentrates more on how God's actions and characteristics affect the believer and is favoured by those with more liberal theologies. The more conservative you are, the more you will (psychologically) favour a form of penal substitution. As ever, of course, both positions can be evidenced in the Bible. But, then again, the Bible has given birth to 42,000 different denominations, so you can pick and choose what you want from its pages. If you love slavery or hate it, love money or hate it, love authoritarian Yahweh or prefer liberal lovey-dovey Jesus, it's all there in those pages, if you are so inclined to find it.

Moral Example Theory

Similarly, this theory (as part of the aforementioned Socinianism), developed by Faustus Socinus (1539-1604 CE), sees Jesus as teaching us by example. Specifically, that Jesus' dedication to God and (self-)sacrifice is

---

[1] Hebblethwaite (2001), p. 82-83.

something to learn from. Such exemplary behaviour (*exemplar theories*) morally influences us to become better people, in the light and image of Jesus. We should live this way as set out by Jesus.

As Morrison opines of this theory:[1]

> Within this theory the death of Christ is understood as a catalyst to reform society, inspiring men and women to follow His example and live good moral lives of love. In this theory the Holy Spirit comes to help Christians produce this moral change....
>
> This theory focuses on not just the death of Jesus Christ, but on His entire life. This sees the saving work of Jesus not only in the event of the crucifixion, but also in all the words He has spoken, and the example He has set. In this theory the cross is merely a ramification of the moral life of Jesus. He is crucified as a martyr due to the radical nature of His moral example. In this way the Moral Influence theory emphasizes Jesus Christ as our teacher, our example, our founder and leader, and ultimately, as a result, our first martyr.

Scapegoat Theory

In this theory, Christ dies as a scapegoat for humanity, where Jesus is not so much a sacrifice as a victim. Referencing him again, theologian Stephen D. Morrison says of it:[2]

> There are many Philosophical concepts that come up within this model, but in a general sense we can say that Jesus Christ as the Scapegoat means the following. 1) Jesus is killed by a violent crowd. 2) The violent crowd kills Him believing that He is guilty. 3) Jesus is proven innocent, as the true Son of God. 4) The crowd is therefore deemed guilty.

But where most scapegoats are singled out as the cause for troubles and are killed or expelled (restoring the balance in some way), Jesus resurrects and one can see his innocence. In some again transformative manner, we can recognise the shortfalls of humanity in this process.

[1] Morrison (n.d.).
[2] Morrison (n.d.).

Other Theories

Other theories include the "embracement theory" where Jesus' divine kindness is in some sense embracing humanity in its murder of God on the cross, and the "shared atonement theory", where Jesus' death is shared by us all: as he died, we all died, and as he rose, we rose with him.

Concluding Remarks

As you can see, there are many competing theories to explain why Jesus, as a Messiah, would end up being crucified instead of leading the chosen people to some messianic victory in the more obvious short term. None of them is relevant if you take seriously the terminal issues with the classic notion of God, particularly if you believe he has divine foreknowledge. Furthermore, although not discussed in this chapter, the Hebrew Bible categorically refutes these ideas of atonement (e.g., see Hosea 14, Exodus 32, Numbers 35, Deuteronomy 24, etc.).

What we see here, and this is true whether you are an ardent believer or a skeptic, are early Christian thinkers trying desperately to make theological sense of the data in the centuries after the death of Christ to the point that theologians are still, to this day, producing refined or new theories. And, remember, many of these theories are believed to the exclusion of others, so that a modern adherent to a moral example theory must believe that all previous Christians who adhered to other "incorrect" theories didn't actually understand why Christ died – arguably why Christ even existed.

What this looks like to me is a rather surprising end, for his followers, of their leader dying and these people trying to work out why this happened, loaded with cognitive dissonance (more on this later). As such, they developed narratives that didn't always agree, and theologies that don't always agree. For example, Mark, Matthew and Luke appear to diverge from the theology of Paul. Specifically, Paul and John seem to have more in common, with a focus on seeing Jesus as fully divine right from the beginning of time. Having said this, it is worth pointing out an important difference: Paul adhering to a preexistence theory whereby it appears Jesus is seen as a first created being and an agent of God, and John proposing a dualitarianism. For John, Jesus and God are identical with the Holy Spirit yet to be incorporated into the Godhead.

Are these theologies merely post hoc rationalisations developed after both the disappointment and the theologically problematic death of the Messiah qua God? In my opinion, almost certainly yes! That very little agreement and, indeed, sense can be made of the death of Jesus and the Resurrection accounts, theologically, is pretty convincing evidence that the whole developed narrative has been constructed by his very human followers, cobbled together from the original sources.[1]

[1] For more information on the problems with atonement, see Ken Pulliam's excellent chapter "The Absurdity of the Atonement" in Loftus (2011), p. 181-94, p. 392-95.

4 – Probabilities and Extraordinary Claims: Dancing Skunks and Unicorns

Before we start looking at the actual issues with the Gospel accounts of the Easter narrative, we need to establish some ideas and approaches concerning what is probable and what is improbable in terms of assessing claims. We already know some of the claims and so bear these in mind as we consider our methodology.

Are we in a position to truly trust the sources of the Gospels (that I will shortly discuss), given the magnitude of their claims and the biases that they must obviously have? These claims purportedly prove (or strongly evidence) certain supposed events that the authors themselves did not witness.

"Prove" is a difficult word. As biblical scholar Bart Ehrman writes:[1]

> You will notice that I have worded the preceding sentences very carefully. I have not said that the *resurrection* is what made Jesus God. I have said that it was the *belief* in the resurrection that led some of his followers to *claim* he was God. This is because, as a historian, I do not think we can show - historically - that Jesus was in fact raised from the dead. To be clear, I'm not saying the opposite either - that historians can use the historical disciplines in order to demonstrate that Jesus was *not* raised from the dead. I argue that when it comes to miracles such as the resurrection, historical sciences simply are of no help in establishing exactly what happened.
>
> Religious faith and historical knowledge are two different ways of "knowing." When I was at Moody Bible Institute, we affirmed wholeheartedly the words of Handel's *Messiah* (taken from the book of Job in the Hebrew Bible): "I know that my Redeemer liveth." But we "knew" this not because of historical investigation, but because of our faith. Whether Jesus is still alive today, because of his resurrection, or indeed whether any such great miracles have happened in the past, cannot be "known" by means of historical study, but only on the basis of faith. This is not because historians are required to adopt "unbelieving presuppositions" or "secular assumptions hostile to religion." It is purely the result of the nature of historical enquiry itself - whether undertaken by the believers or unbelievers...

---

[1] Ehrman (2014), p. 132.

This brings me on to a certain maxim that was popularised by Carl Sagan. That maxim already existed in some form or other since the philosophising of David Hume, the Scottish Enlightenment philosopher. Sagan, the late popular scientist and science populariser claimed, “Extraordinary claims require extraordinary evidence.”[1] This is a self-evidently true maxim, even though many theists seek to deny its power. This is because they misunderstand its best application. This claim is a statement that is most aptly applied to secondary or tertiary evidence. Let me exemplify what I mean by way of five claims and how most people would assess them (as I used in my Nativity book):

Claim 1: *I have a dog.*
Nothing more than verbal testimony needed.

Claim 2: *I have a dog which is in the bath.*
As above, with one eyebrow raised.

Claim 3: *I have a dog in the bath wearing a dress.*
I would probably need a photo of this to believe you.

Claim 4: *I have a dress-wearing dog in the bath with a skunk wearing a SCUBA outfit.*
I would need some video evidence at the least.

Claim 5: *I have the above in the bath, but the bathwater is boiling and the animals are happy.*
I would need video and independent attestation that the video was not doctored agreeing that this is what appeared to be happening.

Claim 6: *All of the above, but the dog has a fire-breathing dragon on its shoulder and the skunk is dancing with a live unicorn.*
Well, I’ll be damned, I’ll need video, plus video of the video, plus independent attestation from multiple recognisably reliable sources, and assessment and evaluation by technological experts and biological experts, plus a psychological evaluation of the claimant, and so on.

Bayes’ Theorem

The point of this exercise is to show that when evaluating evidence that is not first-hand, we have different criteria for assessing its veracity depending on the type of claim. It is actually all about probability: claims that are highly improbable require a great deal of evidence, even if they are physically

---

[1] “Encyclopaedia Galactica”. Carl Sagan (writer/host). *Cosmos*. PBS. December 14, 1980. No. 12. 01:24 minutes in.

(naturalistically) possible claims. The claim that I climbed Mount Everest without using my right arm and with only one eye is something that is physically *possible* but ultimately very *unlikely*. As a result, people would naturally demand more evidence than me merely asserting this in a casual conversation. The more improbable my claim, the more incredible; the more incredible, the higher the demands for evidence. This reality is just intuitive. If we then make a claim that is about as unlikely as can possibly be, that a man-God dies and is resurrected (or performs any of his miracles), then these claims are of events that defy the laws of nature as we know them. This is, almost by definition, the most improbable set of claims. As a result, they should demand the highest level of evidence, especially when not witnessed first-hand.

The standard of evidence must meet the level of improbability in the claim. This can be mathematically set out and assessed using *Bayes' Theorem*. Essentially, and I will massively simplify here, this theorem involves the idea that one should believe the hypothesis, if one has to make such a decision at all, that is the most probable. This probability is made up from two different calculations: the *prior probability* and the *likelihood ratio*.

It can be written as follows:[1]

$$P(A \mid B) = \frac{P(B \mid A)P(A)}{P(B)}$$

Don't get too worried about the notations in the above equation as I will try to explain it in simple terms. And in simplest of terms, this looks like "the odds that a claim is true equal the prior odds it's true times the likelihood ratio". For the record, the above notations mean the following:

- P(A|B) – the probability of event A occurring, given event B has occurred
- P(B|A) – the probability of event B occurring, given event A has occurred
- P(A) – the probability of event A
- P(B) – the probability of event B

We can compare the relative likelihood of two theories for explaining an event, after analysing *background knowledge* and *evidence*. We will add to our background knowledge the *prior probability* or *prior odds* – the prior odds are the odds on any such claim being true before entertaining any evidence particular to the claim. The likelihood ratio is a ratio of two probabilities: firstly, how likely is all the evidence we do and don't have given the claim is true? Secondly,

[1] Michael Martin, in his chapter "The Resurrection as Initially Improbable" in *The Empty Tomb: Jesus Beyond the Grave* (Price & Lowder 2005) states it slightly differently and in a more complex form specifically for the Resurrection.

how likely all this same evidence if the claim is false? And if it's false, this means that something else happened than the original claim. The *posterior probability* is the final probability of the claim being true given all of the above.[1]

What is the prior probability of a god-figure being resurrected after dying, and of dead saints rising and parading around a city? Well, since no Christian, let alone skeptic believes any previous similar examples in those categories, then the probability of such a new claim being true, before evidence is evaluated, is exceptionally small indeed.

We do this kind of reasoning all of the time, including like when you are working out whether to cross the road. Given what you know about traffic, and the present observations at hand, it helps you conclude "it will be safe to cross the road, now, given the data". If there is rustling in a bush over there, I will conclude it is the wind as opposed to being a tiger. I take into account that tigers don't live in my country (background knowledge), it is windy and I don't see any orange, black and white. Now, if I had heard in the news of a locally escaped circus tiger and I saw some orange, black and white, then my conclusions would adapt to this new data and I might conclude that the hypothesis "this is a tiger" is the most probable explanation of the data.

To overcome this tiny prior probability at hand (of a god-figure being resurrected after dying, and of dead saints rising and parading around a city), one must have very high consequents. The evidence must be stunningly good. Think of the examples given above in claims 5 and 6. A dying and rising god and resurrection of many beings supposedly witnessed by many is mind-boggling as a claim. And the evidence needs to be exceptionally good to overcome this, to make the truth of this claim the most probable interpretation of the data. Christians are happy to dismiss *other* similar religious claims from rival religions and yet, it seems, their evidence threshold is lowered greatly to allow a supposedly rational acceptance and belief in *these* Resurrection claims.

Not only do we not have video evidence of the Resurrection claims, but we have no independent attestation. One would expect this given that supposedly five hundred plus people at one time (according to only one source) witnessed a risen god and yet there is absolute silence. Where one would expect to have evidence and voice, if we do not have it, then this absence of evidence *is* evidence of absence. Sometimes Christians claim that this does not follow, that there is usually the idea and claim that because you don't have some evidence for something happening it doesn't mean it didn't happen. But as you will see here, this is not always the case. I will return to this point in Chapter 8.

To look at one of the Easter claims, taking Matthew 27:51-53, we can put what I have explained into context:

> And behold, the veil of the temple was torn in two from top to bottom; and the earth shook and the rocks were split. The tombs were opened,

---

[1] See Carrier (2017b).

> and many bodies of the saints who had fallen asleep were raised; and coming out of the tombs after His resurrection they entered the holy city and appeared to many.

This is a truly miraculous and improbable claim. The passage claims that, at the death of Jesus, the saints rose out of their tombs (being a host of resurrected bodies) and paraded around Jerusalem. What is the evidence that we have in order to judge whether this claim is veracious or not? An anonymously written non-eyewitness account produced some decades after the event by a fervent follower and evangeliser that is unverifiable and some 2000 years old. It was not recounted in any sources we have upon which this Gospel might have been based, or in any other source.[1] It is strange that these publicly resurrected saints appeared to "many" in Jerusalem and yet we have no other accounts of this event, no corroboration from any other source – and this would have been the most amazing sight in any of the witnesses' lives. In this instance, we *should* apply the criteria that extraordinary claims require extraordinary evidence for the reasons mentioned. This is an event that patently demands such treatment, yet it has only very poor evidence to support it. As a result, this claim should be discarded as either false or highly dubious. At the very least, I would recommend agnosticism over its verisimilitude but, realistically, given the lack of evidential foundation, even agnosticism is seriously called into question.

More on this episode later.

As a Syllogism

Michael Martin expresses Bayes' Theorem as applied to the Resurrection as a logical syllogism as follows:[2]

1. A miracle claim is initially improbable relative to our background knowledge.
2. If a claim is initially improbable relative to our background knowledge and the evidence for it is not strong, then it should be disbelieved.
3. The Resurrection of Jesus is a miracle claim.
4. The evidence for the Resurrection is not strong.

---

5. Therefore, the Resurrection of Jesus should be disbelieved.

[1] Luke 23 includes the darkness and temple's veil tearing happening at a different time, but no earthquake and parading saints.

[2] Martin in Price & Lowder (2005), p. 46.

There really is nothing about syllogism with which I disagree. As he rightly alludes to, even the Catholic Church start out with the inductive conclusion that any new claim for a miracle at Lourdes is likely to be false. The Church then applies very charitable metrics for evidential value to conclude that only a minority of them are true. What this reality suggests, in looking at claims against supposed miracles, is that the initial probability of a miracle claim is still very low indeed, even if we are the very charitable Catholic Church.

As Stephen T. Davis, Christian philosopher and apologist (and miracles believer), concludes: "naturalistic explanations of phenomena ought to be preferred by rational people in the vast majority of cases".[1] Irrespective of whether you are a naturalist or supernaturalist (however you define those most slippery of terms), miracle claims have a very low probability of being true and require a high level of evidence to support them.

Preacher-turned-atheist Dan Barker recognised these problems concerning the Resurrection in his excellent chapter "Did Jesus Really Rise from the Dead?" in his book *Godless*:[2]

> When examining artifacts from the past, historians assume that nature worked back then as it does today; otherwise, anything goes. American patriot Thomas Paine, in *The Age of Reason*, asked: "Is it more probable that nature should go out of her course, or that a man should tell a lie? We have never seen, in our time, nature go out of her course; but we have good reason to believe that millions of lies have been told in the same time; it is, therefore, at least millions to one, that the reporter of the miracle tells a lie."...
>
> David Hume wrote: "No testimony is sufficient to establish a miracle unless that testimony be of such a kind that its falsehood would be more miraculous than the fact which it endeavours to establish."[3]

The circularity of Christianity and New Testament belief

As I have mentioned, the few times that New Testament claims intersect with history – namely, the Nativity accounts, and to a lesser degree, the Resurrection accounts – the claims fail, historically speaking. What epistemic right does the Christian then have for believing in Jesus, for being a Christian?

If you ask the Christian, "Why do you know that the Resurrection accounts are true?", they will likely reply, "Because I have faith (in Jesus)." Faith, in any meaningful sense, is belief absent evidence, and oftentimes merely hope.

---

[1] Davis (1993), p. 13.
[2] Barker (2008), p. 278-79.
[3] Hume (1902), p. 115-16.

The Christian Bible states clearly, "Now faith (πίστις) is the assurance of things hoped for, the conviction of things not seen. For by it, the people of old received their commendation" (Hebrews 11:1–2). This becomes apparent when we ask, "Why do you have faith in Jesus", and they likely reply, "Because of the Gospels and New Testament." But that is not evidential because it defers to the faith position.

The faith in Christianity comes predominantly from the New Testament, and faith that the New Testament is true comes from faith in Christianity qua Jesus. Here we have circular reasoning.

Perhaps the Christian can draw on personal revelatory experiences. However, an Amazonian tribesman will never have a revelatory vision or appearance or some kind of experience that will point to Christianity if he has never heard of or come across Christianity. Religious experiences of Christians concerning Christianity come about precisely because they already have knowledge of the Bible, of the New Testament. In other words, Christian religious experiences supervene on (depend upon) knowledge of the Bible. These experiences do not truly break the problem of circularity, but actually feed into that circle.

Even given critical historical analysis (such as this book) that points to the claims not having veracity, the Christian can still rely on mere faith. It is an epistemic circle that is not really sound, just relying on itself. Indeed, the process ends up looking like a presuppositional stance where the Christian might as well presuppose the truth of the New Testament to shore up faith in Jesus.

This is precisely why Christian apologists like William Lane Craig try so hard to get away from mere fideism (the doctrine that knowledge depends on faith or revelation) because they know this strategy is not convincing to a third party. Craig sets this out in his book (and resultant website) *Reasonable Faith*[1] to establish an evidential and rational basis for his belief, intending it to be ammunition to convert third parties (or, at the very least, for it to stop the haemorrhaging from the church).

Craig is absolutely intent on establishing the historicity of the Easter story and the Resurrection. I can understand this motive. He (and others, such as Gary Habermas with his *Minimal Facts* approach) does this because, as laid out in Chapter 1, he has everything to lose by not doing so.

If we relate this back to Bayes' Theorem, then we might look at the Background Knowledge part of the formula. This is where the naturalist atheist will diverge, before we even get started, from the supernaturalist theist.

The naturalist will *conclude* (i.e., not *presuppose*), based on pragmatism and inductive observation, that there is no recourse to supernaturalism:

- We can't assess eyewitness accounts (there are none).
- We have never experienced a god becoming a man.

---

[1] Craig (2008).

- We have never experienced any living organism dying and being resurrected.
- We have no evidence of a heaven.
- And so forth.

Therefore, in order for all of these Easter story claims to be true, we have to throw out everything we know about how the world works. Which is fine, if the evidence warrants this decision (it doesn't, by the way).

Now, the theist has different axioms but the problem is that they are circular.

The theist already believes in a world (background knowledge) where resurrections and general supernaturalism are possible (and perhaps even expected – though the question is where they derive this from). With this background knowledge, the probabilities of the resurrection claims are massively adjusted upwards. They already believe in a world where there is a god, God, and where this god has been in human form, Jesus.

But these are the very claims we are trying to evaluate. The existence of God as Jesus and resurrections are what we are analysing in the formula, so you can't presuppose the truth of the Resurrection by already having the Resurrection or resurrections in your background knowledge.

On the other hand, the theist will accuse the naturalist of already counting *out* such possibilities of resurrection. Craig Blomberg, in *Resurrection: Faith or Fact?*, in which he wrangles with the late skeptic Carl Stecher over the Easter story, does exactly this:[1]

> How then do we adjudicate among the remaining options? At this point the issue of preunderstanding, presuppositions, or worldviews looms large. If one is an antisupernaturalist (or, more simply, just a naturalist), then one excludes the possibility of an actual bodily resurrection at the outset. No amount of dialogue, discussion, or debate can change that. Dead men don't rise. Everyone today knows this. Therefore, however, we explain the rise of Christian faith, a literal physical resurrection is excluded *a priori*. We can debate the relative merits of the alternatives, but the historic Christian belief simply can't be the correct one.... Hume also claims that no one has sufficient reason for believing in something that has no analogy in their personal experience or an experience of anyone they know. Already in the eighteenth century, however, it was pointed out that by this logic, no person living in the tropics should ever believe in the ice.
>
> Today, the presupposition of antisupernaturalism is often phrased a little differently. Nothing may be admitted as genuinely existing, or as having occurred, unless it can be demonstrated empirically or logically.

---

[1] Stecher & Blomberg (2019), p. 234-35.

> But the truth of this presupposition is merely asserted; it is never demonstrated either empirically or logically! Indeed, by its very nature it cannot be true. So the argument is solipsistic, that is, it forms a viciously circular form of reasoning and therefore has no force. Only slightly different is the claim that unless something can be proven scientifically, there are no rational grounds for believing it. But again, this affirmation itself cannot be proven scientifically. We are reminded that science is not omnipotent and cannot be the final arbiter of reality.

However, this approach is not as sound as one might think since it would also support a belief in unicorns or anything that one can think and assert as being true; such a claim would obviously be nonsense and may even be an attempt to prove a negative. *Proving* that unicorns do not exist in the universe is to expect us to look under every rock and inspect every atomic conglomeration in the universe. Even then, we would be victim to claims of making mistakes and missing things.

We should not be able to just *assert* every divine claim (read in any ancient text) or any idea as being true without recourse to other arguments and evidence. This is a question not of proof but of probability.

The naturalist has inductive reasoning, observations over time and geography, that resurrections do not happen. A Christian usually applies this same reasoning to every other situation...outside of Christianity. However, the naturalist can also apply a *methodological* naturalism to underpin such *metaphysical* naturalism. By this, I mean that scientists always assume naturalism when doing any observational work since to posit that a ghost or God could have done something does not help any scientific experiment; these statements are untestable. This methodology has worked very well for science. Look where it has got us.

As such, the naturalist can use these tools and rationally expand methodology to conclude metaphysically, that, in all likelihood, supernaturalism is false. But one would really hope that this metaphysical conclusion isn't merely an assertion and it is at least based on inductive evidence and probability.

My favourite quote on this topic is as follows:[1]

> The cause of lightning was once thought to be God's wrath, but turned out to be the unintelligent outcome of mindless natural forces. We once thought an intelligent being must have arranged and maintained the amazingly ordered motions of the solar system, but now we know it's all the inevitable outcome of mindless natural forces. Disease was once thought to be the mischief of supernatural demons, but now we know that tiny, unintelligent organisms are the cause, which reproduce and infect us according to mindless natural forces. In case after case, without

[1] Carrier (2006b).

exception, the trend has been to find that purely natural causes underlie any phenomena. Not once has the cause of anything turned out to really be God's wrath or intelligent meddling, or demonic mischief, or anything supernatural at all. The collective weight of these observations is enormous: supernaturalism has been tested at least a million times and has always lost; naturalism has been tested at least a million times and has always won. A horse that runs a million races and never loses is about to run yet another race with a horse that has lost every single one of the million races it has run. Which horse should we bet on? The answer is obvious.

Skeptic author Jeffrey Jay Lowder explains further:[1]

If there is a single theme unifying the history of science, it is that naturalistic explanations work. The history of science contains numerous examples of naturalistic explanations replacing supernatural ones and no examples of supernatural explanations replacing naturalistic ones. Indeed, naturalistic explanations have been so successful that even most scientific theists concede that supernatural explanations are, in general, implausible, even on the assumption that theism is true. Such explanatory success is antecedently more likely on naturalism-which entails that all supernaturalistic explanations are false-than it is on theism. Thus the history of science is some evidence for naturalism and against theism.

The theist simply does not have this luxury because it all looks very circular:

(1) I believe in a world where resurrection is possible.
(2) Because I believe in a world in which Jesus was resurrected.
(3) Because I have analysed the accounts of Jesus' resurrection and found them to be a plausible account of the data.
(4) Because (1) I believe in a world where resurrection is possible.

And so the circle goes on, in perpetuity.

Read this again and truly take on board what I am saying here because this is absolutely fundamental to highlighting the foundational issues to the Christian worldview.

The skeptic or naturalist does not dismiss the claims of resurrection in the Easter story out of hand. To the contrary, they assess the evidence put

[1] Lowder (2012).

forward in light of what we know about the world and the standard of evidence of the Gospel accounts. Indeed, Stecher replies to Blomberg's arguments about presuppositions in this way:[1]

> I am certainly willing to consider the evidence for the resurrection, just as I call upon Craig to consider the evidence from natural explanations and the problems with the evidence for the resurrection as a fact of history. Both of us, certainly, have presuppositions, but the hope is for both of us to make the strongest possible cases for and against resurrection as history (given the limitations of the format and the voluminous arguments on both sides), then to clarify where and why we differ, and to discover, if possible, where we are in agreement. My position is not that Jesus' resurrection did not happen, but that the evidence is scant and deeply flawed, contradictory in almost every possible way, and therefore insufficient to establish Jesus' resurrection as a fact of history. Furthermore, I argue, there are many plausible natural explanations to explain why some of Jesus's disciples might have come to believe that Jesus had been raised from the dead.

And that is pretty much my approach and conclusion in this book.

In a sense, this book should present strong enough argument for a supernaturalist who believes in resurrection, for whatever reason, to assess the historical analysis of the Easter story claims and logically conclude: "Although I believe in resurrection being possible, I do not believe that the claims of the Easter story have historical veracity because they fail on grounds of probability irrespective of my supernaturalist beliefs."

Hope springs eternal. Though, of course, the supernaturalist would then be invalidated in any adherence to Christianity on account of having no evidential foundation to their belief.

Another point to add is that faking histories at the time was so common as to be seen as something of a crisis of the time. Such behaviour was...

> ...attested in the very source Craig [Blomberg] himself cites: Lucian of Samosata's *How to Write History* (similarly, in Plutarch's *On the Malice of Herodotus*). And modern historians note many episodes contained even in otherwise proper histories of the day, are fictions (as documented by Michael Grant in *Greek and Roman Historians: Information and Misinformation* - just for a start, but examples are endless, and extend all the way from Tacitus to Josephus). So we cannot rescue the

[1] Stecher & Blomberg (2019), p. 155-56.

> fabulous and unverified tales of encountering a risen Jesus in the Gospels as fact by appealing to the claim "no one did that back then."[1]

Given this observation, then our probabilities should likely be lowered that the Gospel claims are a true representation of what happened in history (and we are going to look further at Gospel issues in the next chapter), especially when we also have numerous examples of pagan divine figures dying and rising (Bacchus, Romulus, Osiris, Zalmoxis) and we (Christians and non-Christians together) don't believe *them*.

As Dan Barker astutely points out:[2]

> "Why have you ruled out the supernatural?" is a question believers sometimes ask. I answer that I have not ruled it out: I have simply given it the low probability it deserves along with the other possibilities. I might equally ask them, "Why have you ruled out the natural?"

Unfortunately, I think we have a scenario whereby biblical scholars spend inordinate amounts of time in their protective bubbles discussing the minutiae of form and source criticism, theology and symbolism, that they don't see the wood for the trees. The whole notion of a resurrected Jesus becomes so normalised and plausible when immersed in the topic so deeply. They need to step out of their own reality to assess the data from as objective a position as they can.

In doing so, however, they must be prepared (and I say this knowing that, at the time of writing, biblical scholar Gary Habermas is some 5,000 pages into his magnum opus on the subject) to realise that all of the theology and symbology, textual analysis and subsequent meaning, come tumbling down like a house of cards.

When you remove the keystone, the bridge collapses.

---

[1] Carrier in Stecher & Blomberg (2019) p. 211.
[2] Barker (2008), p. 281.

5 – The Gospels: An Overview

> Indeed, it may seem blindingly obvious that people invent stories and the sifting of fact from fiction or fiction from fact has been one of the most notable features in the history of critical biblical scholarship. What this really boils down to is very basic, namely that the historical probability of a story must be taken on a case by case basis. But it is important to point out such creative storytelling traditions because when [Christian apologist N.T.] Wright discusses those arguments rejecting the historicity of the resurrection stories they are the complex, highly speculative and sometimes unnecessary tradition-histories of, for example, Lüdemann, and are rightly dismissed. All we need to posit is a general practice of rewriting history which makes heroes greater and justifies beliefs in the present in order to account for divergent resurrection traditions. It is not the case, of course, that Wright is unaware of storytelling tradition. For example, when discussing a dispute between the Roman Emperor and Gamaliel II's daughter (b. Sanh. 90b-91a), he can say it is 'no doubt fictitious' [Wright (2003), p. 196]. Most would agree. But this degree of suspicion is never applied to the story of the resurrection, an empty tomb, and all the strange accompanying stories, stories that for many people are much more unlikely than a rabbi's daughter meeting an emperor. If we are to take stories on a case by case basis, why is it that pagan and Jewish texts can be deemed fictitious but Christian stories, including the obviously secondary Mt. 27.52-53, are not? If we are going to take Christianity seriously in its Jewish and pagan contexts then we must expect the Gospel writers to make up stories just as Jews and pagans did. Historically speaking it is extremely unlikely that the Christians behind the Gospel traditions were immune to this standard practice.[1]

This seemed a particularly pertinent quote to start this chapter with; James Crossley, skeptical New Testament scholar, takes aim at Bishop and theologian N.T. Wright's attempts to ground the Resurrection narrative in history, and the double standards employed.

There are, generally speaking, three aspects to the debunking of the Resurrection:

(1) The Gospels are not reliable sources of information; they are poor quality evidence.

---

[1] Crossley (2005), p. 181.

(2) The claims of the Resurrection are incredible claims that require very good quality evidence.

(3) If the Christian claims of the Resurrection are not true, then what, if anything, actually took place, and what hypothesis can better explain the data?

Let us look at the first aspect in this chapter, point (1).

The Gospels are not reliable. This much is true in at least a number of places (not least the Resurrection). Yet, in the places where they *could* be reliable, we have no way of verifying or knowing that they are (for example, the wedding at Cana – how can we verify those claims?).

Firstly, I have documented in my book *The Nativity: A Critical Examination*, as I have mentioned, the plethora of contradictions, differences, omissions and issues with just two of the Gospels, bizarrely the only two to mention the birth of Jesus.

Many lay-Christians are unaware that the Gospels are, for example, not written by eyewitnesses to Jesus' ministry. They are not eyewitness testimony. Indeed, the problems with the provenance of the Gospels are legion.

We don't know for sure, but can only guess:

- who wrote the Gospels,
- when they were written,
- where they were written,
- who the sources were,
- who the audiences were,
- in what genre they were penned.

What we *do* know is that they (1) were written by people who already believed in Jesus as Messiah, (2) were not eyewitnesses, (3) were trying to evangelise and thus had open agendas and (4) were not writing objective history, (5) were writing 40-100 years after the death of the person they were writing about, and (6) had no recognisable historical methodology that we can actually see in other contemporaneous historians.

It's not looking good.

We might ask:

Why is it more probable that your god exists than man made him up?

Let's return to the previous chapter: we have an exceptionally high prior probability that your god is false given that we both believe that every other god claimed to be true (before and after Jesus) is false. Thus, on prior probability, Jesus as man-God is *highly* unlikely to exist. How does the Christian overcome this dilemma? They have to provide high *posterior probability* by providing exceptionally good evidence. But the evidence is poor. Really poor (though they don't like to admit this and it is why William Lane Craig realises that he has to spend so much time in asserting the reliability of the Gospel Resurrection accounts).

Let's take the four Gospels, written by unknown people at unknown dates in unknown places with *ex post facto* agendas to evangelise, at least forty years after the person they are writing about and whom they have never met has died. As Bart Ehrman opines:[1]

> [H]istorians presuppose that some evidence is better than other evidence. Eyewitness reports are, as a rule, superior to hearsay from years, decades, or centuries later. Extensive corroboration among multiple sources that show no evidence of collaborating with one another is far better than either collaboration or noncorroboration. A source, who provides disinterested off-the-cuff comments about a person or event is better than a source, who makes interested claims about a person or event in order to score an ideologically driven point. What historians want, in short, are lots of witnesses, close to the time of the events, who are not biased towards their subject matter and who corroborate one another's points without showing signs of collaboration. Would that we had such sources for all significant historical events!

There is an idea perpetuated by many apologists, and often with reference to sociologist Rodney Stark, that the speed of growth of Christianity (possibly related to the quality of the sources, they claim) is prima facie evidence of the truth of Christianity. No such mythological or largely untrue claims wrapped up in a worldview would produce such startling success, so they say. Stark reasoned that the Christian religion grew at the rate of 40% every decade. The problem for such a claim as to "success meaning truth" is that the Mormon Church grew at precisely this rate (a little more, indeed) in the 19th century (and there are similar claims for other movements, such as the Moonies). And yet no one other than Mormons think that they have exclusive claims to truth, and no non-Mormon Christian believes the truth of Mormonism on the basis of its speed of growth.

Let's now look very briefly at the mainstream accepted views of the four Gospels. I will discuss Paul in a later chapter separately; however, one must be aware that Paul is our earliest source for Jesus and knowledge of his supposed resurrection. There is actually very little we know about the Resurrection from Paul, which leads skeptics to think that the vast amount of narrative was invented after Paul wrote, starting with Mark.

---

[1] Ehrman (2014), p.146.

Before we start, it is probably a good time to read the words of Celsus (a Greek philosopher and opponent of Christianity who, sadly, only survives in the critiques of his work in *Contra Celsum* by Origen, written in 248 CE):[1]

> It is clear to me that the writings of the Christians are a lie, and [their] fables have not been well constructed to conceal this monstrous fiction. [Their] interpreters, as if they had just come out of a tavern, are onto the inconsistencies and pen in hand, alter the original writings three, four, and several more times over in order to be able to deny the contradictions in the face of criticism.

Damning words, and an early belief and accusation pretty much contemporaneously levelled at the Christian writers; an opinion that still holds credibility today.

An Introduction, and Mark

As with everything biblical, there is a spectrum of approaches to the interpretation of the texts: who wrote them and when they were written, as well as what type of texts they are (genre), for what reasons they were committed to "paper" and whether they represent historical fact or religious symbolism. Quite often in biblical exegesis (the study and interpretation of biblical texts), scholars are prone to starting with a conclusion and then massaging or searching for evidence that supports their conclusion (post hoc rationalisation), as opposed to surveying all the evidence, piecing it together and seeing in what direction it takes them. One should build a conclusion from the brickwork of evidence rather than vice-versa.

The general consensus amongst scholars is that non-eyewitnesses wrote the Gospels, meaning that the people who are giving us arguably the only detailed sources of information about Jesus never actually met him. To make matters worse, the Gospel of Mark (if one assumes Markan priority, which means that Mark was written first) was generally thought to have been written about forty plus years after the death of Jesus (around 70 CE), probably in Syria.[2] As such, all of the other Gospels were written later, and most probably in other countries, using the lingua franca, Greek, and not the native tongue of Jesus, Aramaic, and were arguably based to differing degrees on Mark.

Alongside these points, it is generally thought that Mark, together with an unknown source (called Q by modern scholars), provided the source material for the Gospels of Luke and Matthew, although there is some debating of

---

[1] Celsus (1987), p. 64. See also the Ante-Nicene Fathers translation at *New Advent*, Chapter 27, Book II, https://www.newadvent.org/fathers/04162.htm (Retrieved 08/03/2021).

[2] Theissen & Merz (1998) p. 24-27.

this opinion by recent scholars such as Mark Goodacre. The implications of there being no Q are interesting since, if this is correct, it seems that the parts that do overlap (Q) are essentially instances where Luke has copied Matthew (who reworked Mark). Thus the Gospels are *even less independent*. As David Fitzgerald expounded in *Nailed: Ten Christian Myths That Show Jesus Never Existed At All:*[1]

> The three share a truly astonishing number of near-identical passages, arranged in much the same order and in many cases using the exact same wording. Luke reproduces 50% of Mark's text, and Matthew a whopping 90%. Of the 661 verses in Mark's Gospel, Luke's Gospel uses about 360 and Matthew's Gospel uses about 607. The parallels are so widespread and apparent that the majority opinion among Biblical authorities has been in agreement ever since; namely that Matthew and Luke based their material upon Mark's. If the Farrer or Goodacre Hypotheses are correct (and I believe Goodacre's modified Farrer hypothesis is), Luke also copied from Matthew (while others speculate both used a hypothetical second source, "Q").

I will return to this issue later in the chapter.

The names "Matthew, Mark, Luke and John" were names later ascribed to the writings by early church fathers. However, modern scholars rarely believe that the names have any real relevance to the authors of the works.

It is essentially unclear what or who the sources for Mark were, but it is assumed that they included a mixture of certainly oral and possibly written pieces of sayings of Jesus, the passion narrative (Easter Story), some miracle stories and so on.[2]

What interests me is how there are so many examples of speech in the Bible, particularly the New Testament, and often passages of speech to which there were almost certainly no witnesses (Jesus talking to Pilate) available to the Gospel writers. In addition, Matthew 4 and Luke 4 both have private conversations recorded between Jesus and the devil. All these speeches seem to have been remarkably well-preserved considering the people listening (if there were any, and often there weren't) would most likely have been illiterate or certainly did not have notebooks or Dictaphones handy. This raises the question as to the authenticity of the direct speech reported in the Gospels (and elsewhere in the Bible), and whether these speeches were historically factual.

So the situation we have is that that unknown people in essentially unknown places wrote these accounts of Jesus, and at a time we can only make good guesses to. None of the Gospels detail their sources – something you would expect from good historians. Some earlier and contemporaneous

---

[1] Fitzgerald (2010), p. 67.

[2] Ibid.

historians to the Gospel writers such as Josephus (and ones close to the time, such as Thucydides, Polybius and Arrian) included some of their sources, and some of the lesser historians such as Suetonius did so too. These vital references to sources are missing in the cases of all the Gospel accounts. This essentially means that the verifiability of the events that are claimed to have happened is nigh on impossible.

Another issue with the Gospels, in general, is the fact that they are not attested by extra-biblical sources. This means that no other source outside of the Bible, and contemporary with the events or with the Gospel accounts, reports and corroborates the events claimed within the Gospels. Theists make much out of what is mentioned in extra-biblical sources such as Josephus, Tacitus,[1] Suetonius, etc. However, all that these sources can validate (when they are not shown to be interpolations or edited additions, or forgeries) is that Christians, who followed Christ, existed. Not really the greatest of conclusions. An intellectually honest assessment is that these sources do not offer dependable conclusions.

Archaeology doesn't particularly support the accounts of a historical Jesus or any of his apostles.[2] There are some events and places referred to that are of course verified, but that amounts to the analogy of the places and events of Victorian London being mentioned in Sherlock Holmes by Conan Doyle being real. Obviously, it in no way follows that Sherlock Holmes was a real historical figure.

A further problem is that people wrote these accounts with a vested interest in seeing the life and teachings of Jesus evangelised to those in the world around them. One might question the reliability, for example, of a biography of David Koresh or Sathya Sai Baba (and the many miracles his followers have claimed of him) if it were written by their most fervent of followers. People who believe after the time of some such events that they were miraculous will create accounts of those events that might not reflect their true nature, ex post facto. In this way, the Gospel writers, without knowing Jesus, come to believe that he was resurrected and carried out miracles (without witnessing them) and *then* go on to write his biography with those beliefs already firmly embedded. They are presupposing the truth of what they are writing about to help prove to others that truth, again creating a sort of circularity. Are we in a position to truly trust these sources, given the magnitude of their claims and the biases that they must obviously have? These claims purportedly prove (or strongly evidence) certain supposed events that the authors themselves did not witness.

---

[1] See Carrier (2009), and more recently Carrier (2014b), p. 332-49. I will not be spending any time discussing Josephus and Tacitus in this book, as interesting as the subject is – I have done so on my blog (Pearce [2020a, 2020b], for example – also see Zindler [1998]) – but there is general scholarly consensus that the most "Christian" parts of Josephus are interpolated (added later by Christian writers), as well as there being similar issues with Tacitus, including robust claims of forgery.

[2] Cline (2009), p. 103.

Mark, and this is extremely important for the purposes of this book, did not originally include the Resurrection narrative – where the resurrected Jesus appears to many – after Mark 16: 1-8.[1] The ending after these verses was interpolated later, first arising in the second century CE. What does this say about the truth of the Resurrection claims if the earliest source with any detail of the post-Resurrection appearance events is shown to be added by a later author?

Luke

The Gospel of Luke was written perhaps around 80-90 CE (although some conservative scholars favour an earlier date), or perhaps later, possibly by a Gentile companion of Paul. Many scholars who think that the letters of Paul contradict the Gospel of Luke, however, contest this view. Consequently, the author may not have known Paul. Some scholars claim that Luke is an anonymous or unknown author. Either way, it is generally accepted that Luke also wrote Acts. The early church fathers believed that the Gospel was written by Luke (a travelling physician), hence the name of the Gospel being attributed to him. As Gerd Theissen and Annette Merz in their seminal classic *The Historical Jesus* say, this view is only "occasionally put forward these days".[2] There are, though, many contrasting opinions from every side of every fence, and huge works have been dedicated to what I am summing up in a paragraph or two.

By Luke's (and I will name the author so as to avoid confusion, cognisant of the point that this was probably not his name) own admission, he was trying to create some sort of a history. As the preface to Luke (1:1-3) sets out:

> Inasmuch as many have undertaken to compile an account of the things accomplished among us, just as they were handed down to us by those who from the beginning were eyewitnesses and servants of the word, it seemed fitting for me as well, having investigated everything carefully from the beginning, to write it out for you in consecutive order, most excellent Theophilus; so that you may know the exact truth about the things you have been taught.

This introduction admits the author to being a non-eyewitness and sets out his stall. Many Christian theologians and scholars claim that Luke is an excellent historian. However, as I mentioned earlier, Luke does not use a wide range of historiographical techniques that one would hope for from a good historian. Luke does, though, mention places and events with some degree of accuracy. However, once again, I refer you to the Sherlock Holmes analogy. We

[1] See Carrier (2014c), p. 231-312 ("Mark 16:9-20 as Forgery or Fabrication").

[2] Theissen & Merz (1998), p. 24.

know that even the very best ancient historians made mistakes and reported falsities. As Richard Carrier (holding a PhD in ancient history) writes in *Not the Impossible Faith*:[1]

> It is a universal principle accepted throughout the professional community that no ancient work is infallible. Even the most respected and trusted of historians–Thucydides, Polybius, Arrian–are believed to have reported some false information, especially when it came to private matters witnessed by only a few, and when material was important to an author's personal or dogmatic biases and presuppositions. And the further any ancient author is from these men in explicit methodology, by that much less are they trusted.

This is unquestionably important because it shows that, even with the best will in the world, Luke's Gospel will have at least a good sum of mistakes or false information. Some might say that this is easy to determine when the accounts disagree directly with the letters of Paul himself. And yet, it becomes very difficult to know otherwise, with any certainty, what is definitely true and what might be false when there is nothing to compare accounts to, when there is no contradicting information. As Carrier continues:[2]

> But on top of that we know he lied. For instance, his account of Paul's mission and the division it created in the Church contradicts Paul's own account (in his letter to the Galatians) in almost every single detail, and in a way we can discern was deliberate. And if Luke lied about that, he could be lying about anything else. Moreover, Luke cannot be classed with the best historians of his day because he never engages discussions of sources and methods, whereas they did–and that is a major reason why modern historians hold such men as Thucydides and Polybius and Arrian in high esteem: they often discuss where they got their information, how they got their information, and what they did with it. It is their open and candid awareness of the problems posed by writing a critical history that marks them as especially competent. Even lesser historians (like Xenophon, Plutarch, or Suetonius) occasionally mention or discuss their sources, or acknowledge the existence of conflicting accounts, and yet Luke doesn't even do that.

So that leaves us thinking that Luke, though he is probably more reliable than the other Gospel writers, is not a pillar of rectitude by any stretch of the imagination.

---

[1] Carrier (2009), p. 162.
[2] Carrier (2009), p. 163.

In addition, Luke probably used the Gospel of Mark and Q, as mentioned, as sources. If they are inaccurate, Luke is inaccurate. His theology looks to designate "Jesus the Saviour anointed with the Spirit of God, who accepts the weak and outcast in the name of God and proclaims salvation to them."[1] As seen, the idea of Q could be wide of the mark, leading to the probability that Luke copied from Matthew. However, it potentially gets worse for Luke since there are some well-founded theories that posit that Luke plagiarised Jewish historian Josephus in much of his writing in Luke-Acts. Academics such as Josephan scholar Steve Mason and Richard Carrier favour such a conclusion. As Carrier notes in "Luke and Josephus":[2]

> This thesis, if correct, entails two things. First, it undermines the historicity of certain details in the Christ story unique to Luke, such as his account of the Nativity, since these have been drawn from Josephus, who does not mention them in connection with Jesus, and thus it is more than possible that they never were linked with Jesus until Luke decided they were. This does not prove, but provides support for the view that Luke is creating history, not recording it. Second, it settles the *terminus post quem* of the date Luke-Acts was written: for in order to draw material from *The Jewish War*, Luke could not have written before 79 A.D., and could well have written much later since the rate of publication in antiquity was exceedingly limited and slow, requiring hand copies made by personal slaves (though at first oral recitations would be more common than written copies); and in order to draw material from the *Jewish Antiquities*, as he appears to have done, Luke could not have written before 94 A.D., and again could have written much later for the same reason.

This view fits better with the claims that the story has been "handed down to us" (1:2). It is also pertinent to note that Luke claims that "many" others have set out to write Gospels (1:1) but that this, with an air of special pleading, is the real deal!

Matthew

As with the other Gospels, there are differing views as to the date, sources and composition of the Gospel of Matthew. One has to be careful because presuppositions over either the truth or the falsity of biblical narratives lead scholars to favour early or late dating (or compositional conclusions) accordingly. This is why I have favoured the work of Theissen and Merz who give an

---

[1] Theissen & Merz (1998), p.32.

[2] Carrier (2000).

overview of most of the relevant research, hopefully getting as close to an objective conclusion as possible.

Matthew's Gospel was written by an anonymous author sometime towards the end of the 1st century CE, probably in Syria.[1] Again, like Luke (and with those caveats), it seems to be based on Mark and Q. Matthew contains almost the whole of the Gospel of Mark in one form or another; the birth narrative, though, being a clear addition. Richard Carrier in "Why Do We Still Believe in Q?" argues that Matthew *is* Q:[2]

> In fact all the evidence for Q is 100% consistent with Q being a redaction (a later edition) of Mark.... And that means Q sounds pretty much exactly like Matthew. In fact, it's almost certainly Matthew.

The author was probably a highly educated Jew. This is because he corrects some fairly basic mistakes that Mark made about Judaism that any Jew would not have made. These include such things as misquoting the Ten Commandments, as well as attributing God's words to Moses, and having Jews buy things on the Sabbath[3] (something that was forbidden). He also showed an intimate knowledge of Jewish law.

It is thought that Matthew references the destruction of the Temple in Jerusalem that happened in 70 CE, so it must have been composed later than that date.

Matthew's theology is one that reflects Jesus' dignity, showing his life to fulfil the Law and Prophets, and presents him as a teacher who "unfolds the will of God".[4] It is generally accepted that he was writing for a Jewish audience.[5] Matthew seems to use the miracles of Jesus in a different way to his source, Mark, showing the more divine nature of Jesus. However, we still have no ascension account in Matthew.

John and the Synoptic Problem

John is right out.

Okay, so Monty Python and their Holy Hand Grenades of Antioch aside, John is an outlier in the Gospel tradition. What explains the differences and similarities between the first three Gospels? This has become known as the Synoptic Problem, as the first three Gospels are called the Synoptic Gospels, or

---

[1] It refers (19:1) to Judea being *beyond* Jordan, thus implying the writer is not in Judea, as well as giving other hints.

[2] Carrier (2017).

[3] Mark 15:46 says that *that same evening* Joseph of Arimathea "bought a linen cloth." Matthew, however, drops the idea of a Jew buying something on the Sabbath.

[4] Theissen & Merz (1998), p.31.

[5] As according to many scholars, such as Delbert Burkett (Burkett [2002]).

Synoptics (meaning "seen together"). Add to this the huge gulf in difference between John and the other Gospels, and the problem is greater. Something like 90% of the material in John cannot be found in the other Gospels.

John was written (and many Christian scholars disagree about John's date) from about 90 CE–110 CE, at least a full generation (arguably) after the other Gospels. There are some things he shares with Mark and Luke, in terms of vocabulary and some of the events. However, there are key differences, key absences, from the other Gospels when reading John.

There has been debate that the Gospel of John sprang out of a Johannine community, though this is being challenged more and more. A Christian community was manifesting itself more obviously and Jerusalem had fallen some time previously. Consequently, this might well have affected John's views, intentions, and writing.

This work is well written in Greek and shows a sophisticated theology, and this latter point marks it out as significantly different to the other Gospels. The Synoptic Gospels have a much tighter relationship with each other than they do with John, in vocabulary, order, quotations and narration. This might well be because of interdependence as well as shared dependence on another source or sources (such as the famed "Q" source).

For example, with Mark being written first, there is the idea that Matthew and Luke, with their own agendas and access to other sources (including each other, particularly Luke of Matthew) embellish upon Mark. All the Gospels suffer from the same problem that Jesus spoke in Aramaic and they are written in Koine Greek.

There are many theories concerning the sources for Luke and Matthew, including the following:

- The Two-Source Theory has Mark and Q both being the sources for Matthew and Luke.
- The Farrer Theory has Mark influencing Matthew and both influencing Luke.
- The Three-Source Theory adds Q into the mix for also influencing Matthew and then Luke.
- The Wilke Theory has Mark influencing Luke and both influencing Matthew.

And so on. When you add Proto-Gospels, Marcion and other unknown sources into the mix, things can get complicated.

The key difference that John has to the others is how Jesus is seen. In Mark, he was the authoritative, miracle-working Son of God (where this is a turn of phrase to denote importance, not the actual, biological son of God). For Matthew, Jesus is portrayed as the fulfilment of the Old Testament Law and prophecies, something that I make very clear in my book on the Nativity. Matthew expresses Jesus not simply as the Messiah prophesied in the Hebrew Bible

(Matthew 1:21), but also as the new Moses (chapters 5–7 and the Nativity), the new Abraham (1:1-2), and the descendant of David's royal line (1:1-6). Luke, and again I discuss this in my other book, is at pains to appeal to Gentiles, connecting Jesus to outcasts, women, the poor, the sick and suchlike. The Synoptics have their agendas wrapped up largely with the intended audience demographics.

John, on the other hand, takes his *high Christology* very seriously; it is what drives his more spiritual Gospel. It's about theology, not audience. There are no demon exorcisms but there is teaching on eternal life. John looks to try to solve the issues that people were wrangling with, proposing the idea (or building the foundation for it) that Jesus was both fully man and fully God. You can argue that the Synoptics didn't really actually see Jesus as God, more as a great man or a Messiah. John, though, puts his Christology centre stage.

John has Jesus as the divine Word, as the *Logos* (John 1:1).

This approach can also explain some differences in the Easter story that we can see between the Synoptics and John, as we shall examine later (such as when the Last Supper was eaten). The differences between John and the Synoptics regarding the Resurrection narrative are incredibly numerous and also very theologically important. It may well be that John admits this, too, as he declares in John 20:

> **Why This Gospel Was Written**
>
> 30 Therefore many other signs Jesus also performed in the presence of the disciples, which are not written in this book; 31 but these have been written so that you may believe that Jesus is the Christ, the Son of God; and that believing you may have life in His name.

That's quite an admission as to his agenda and an indication of the driving force behind his differences (discrepancies qua contradictions qua embellishments qua legendary mythological theological overlay). We might ask whether the narrative invokes theology (a Christian approach) or whether theology drove the narrative to be written in the way it was (the skeptic's approach, broadly speaking).

It might be pertinent to refer back to James Crossley here:[1]

> The resurrection traditions themselves would suggest this [creative storytelling]. As we have seen, it is certainly not impossible that Mark has invented his empty tomb story to explain what happened after Jesus was buried. After that, as we might expect from Jewish rewriting of history, anything can follow which can easily be seen as secondary with no grounding in what actually happened shortly after Jesus was buried.

[1] Crossley (2005), p.181-82.

> Surely some degree of suspicion is required when, after Mark's statement that the women told no one, we find Peter suddenly present at the empty tomb (Lk. 24.11 -12; Jn 20.6-8) and the disciples suddenly being told what happened by the women (Mt: 28,8-9), just as we should be suspicious of a rabbi's daughter in the presence of an emperor. Surely some degree of suspicion should be aimed at the historical accuracy of grounding the Gentile mission, something of great importance for the early Church, in the words of the bodily raised Jesus on a mountain (Mt. 28.16-20). Surely some degree of suspicion should be aimed at Luke, particularly in the context of the theology of Luke-Acts, virtually eliminating the possibility of Galilean appearances by having the two dazzling men replace the Markan promise of Jesus' return to Galilee with what he said in Galilee (Lk. 24.6-7; cf. Mk 16.7) and having all resurrection appearances and the ascension all in the Jerusalem area (Lk. 24). Surely some degree of suspicion should be aimed at Thomas's confession of high Johannine Christology (Jn 20, 28). If Thomas really had said something as staggering as this it is highly unlikely that we would have to wait until John's Gospel to hear of it. Matthew, Luke and John are surely more than just adapting primitive tradition for contemporary needs: these are monumental embellishments of the Markan tradition which ground some of the most important Christian beliefs in the resurrection.'' This all makes good sense in the tradition of Jewish storytelling and creative rewriting of history.

Legendary embellishment is certainly something that I claim took place. I refer again to Dan Barker in his chapter about the Resurrection in *Godless*, who dates the Christian Bible sources, including noncanonical texts, and observes:[1]

> I made a list of things I consider "extraordinary" (natural and supernatural) in the stories between the crucifixion and ascension of Jesus. These include: earthquakes, angel(s), rolling stone, dead bodies crawling from Jerusalem graves..., Jesus appearing out of thin air (now you see him) and disappearing (now you don't), the "fish story" miracle, Peter's noncanonical "extravaganza" exit from the tomb..., a giant Jesus head in the cloud, a talking cross and a bodily ascension into heaven.
>
> Perhaps others would choose a slightly different list, but I'm certain it would include most of the certain events. I do not consider events that are surprising to be extraordinary.... Then I counted the number of extraordinary events that appear in each resurrection account. In the order in which the accounts were written, Paul has zero, Mark has one,

[1] Barker (2008), p. 291-92.

> Matthew has four, Luke has five, Peter has six and John has at least six. (John wrote, "And many other signs truly did Jesus in the presence of his disciples which are not written in this book." 20:30) Putting these on a time graph produces a curve that goes up as the years pass. The later resurrection reports contain more extraordinary events than the earlier ones, so it is clear that the story, at least in the telling, has evolved and expanded over time.

Barker goes on to detail this with reference to messengers at the tomb and bodily appearances, before concluding:[1]

> The mistake many modern Christians make is to view 30 C.E. backward through the distorted lens of 80-100 C.E., more than a half century later. They forcibly superimpose the extraordinary tales of the late Gospels anachronistically upon the plainer views of the first Christians, pretending naively that all Christians believed exactly the same thing across the entire first century.

Progressive Embellishment

When we read the Gospels chronologically, there is a progressive embellishment, and this is something to which we will return later in the book. Here is one example for now:[2]

Mark: Several women who were "looking on afar off" at Jesus on the cross, later "beheld where he was laid". There was no detail as to their proximity to the tomb.

Matthew: The women "there beholding afar off", later "sitting against the sepulchre" (against the grave) as a vigil (and thus concerned).

Luke: "And all his acquaintance, and the women that followed him from Galilee, stood afar off, beholding these things" (23:49), later "beheld the sepulchre" and "how the body was laid", returning to their homes to prepare "spices and ointments" to anoint this body and prepare it for Sabbath (showing discipleship and piousness).

John: He details how Jesus' mother and the disciple "whom he loved" were at the cross, and Jesus had a conversation with them, and orders said disciple to take care of his mother, amongst other details.

These examples and others are commonplace and lead to some good deal of suspicion. Why is there a consistent embellishment in an additional manner

[1] Barker (2008), p. 292.
[2] Alter (2015), p. 27-28.

correlating with chronology? Why does it rarely seem to go in the other direction? Why would the earlier Gospels not seek to include the details of the later ones (consistently, too)?

Taking all this into account (and bear in mind that each of these tiny sections on the individual Gospels requires book-length expositions), what can we take away from this? And before I list some take-away points, it is worth noting that there were other gospels that never made it into the canon partly because four was a good, round number but mainly because these others were just *too* extraordinary in their claims, as if there is some invisible line of acceptability under which the four canonical gospels sat. Earthquakes and dead saints parading, a god-man Messiah being resurrected and rising into the sky was somehow acceptable, but the claims in the non-canonical gospels (say, Thomas) were just *too* unbelievable?

Back to what we can derive from reading the four Gospels:

- They were all non-eyewitness accounts, written anywhere between forty and seventy years or so after the events.
- They used no recognisable historiographical methodology as even some contemporaneous historians were doing (because they are not historians or not presenting history, arguably).
- They recounted private conversations (including a private meeting between Jesus and Pontius Pilate) – how could they do this?
- They were not written in the language of the protagonists.
- We are unsure of their sources, though we are fairly certain they relied to some degree on each other.
- We are unsure exactly where and when they were written though we can hypothesise some pretty good guesses.
- They were written ex post facto, by which I mean they were presenting quasi-histories after coming to believe in the conclusions to their theses. That is, already believing Jesus was the Messiah *and then* writing an account looking to show how Jesus was the Messiah.
- They are all laden with agendas (they were *evangelising*, for a start), both in the sense referred to above but also regarding the audiences they were appealing to.
- In this sense, they were biased towards their agenda, affecting the reliability with which they were presenting their "facts" if indeed they were intending to be primarily factual.
- The claims made therein were both unverified and unverifiable.

Let us return to the idea that extraordinary claims require extraordinary evidence. The above points invalidate the four Gospels from being labelled reliable sources, and they are certainly not, by any stretch of the imagination, *extraordinarily good* evidence.

We are starting now to understand why believing in the historical veracity of the Easter story is a thoroughly problematic enterprise.

The Four Newspaper Accounts Apologetic

Theologian N.T. Wright and others have espoused the view that the four Gospels are like four different newspaper accounts of an event or four witnesses to a car crash. These are common apologetic tactics for attempting to harmonise the very numerous and oftentimes serious discrepancies and contradictions. We could concentrate on all the issues we now have with eyewitness testimony:[1]

> Psychologist Elizabeth Loftus has been particularly concerned with how subsequent information can affect an eyewitness's account of an event.
>
> Her main focus has been on the influence of (mis)leading information in terms of both visual imagery and wording of questions in relation to eyewitness testimony.
>
> Loftus' findings seem to indicate that memory for an event that has been witnessed is highly flexible. If someone is exposed to new information during the interval between witnessing the event and recalling it, this new information may have marked effects on what they recall. The original memory can be modified, changed or supplemented.
>
> The fact the eyewitness testimony can be unreliable and influenced by leading questions is illustrated by the classic psychology study by Loftus and Palmer (1974) *Reconstruction of Automobile Destruction...*

But we don't need to get into the details of this because the Gospels don't even constitute eyewitness testimony – they are at least a level or so below this – maybe third- or fourth-hand evidence if we're lucky.

Furthermore, there are situations whereby there can only have been one or two actual eyewitnesses to an event reported (e.g., the guards at the tomb in Matthew). However, and even if one assumes that the eyewitnesses survived the forty or more years until the Gospels were written (given low life expectancies), there are differences and discrepancies in the accounts that should not be there given that the original source must have been the same person or few people. We have the empty tomb narratives whereby different people were claimed to have been present, one reporting one angel, and another reporting two and a third reporting none (more on this later). If modern newspapers were reporting such an amazing event in which all witnesses saw, say, two angels, you can guarantee that all the papers would agree on that one main fact given the nature

[1] McLeod (2014).

of the extraordinary claim. And if they didn't, explanations would be robustly sought.

Let us consider eyewitnesses briefly. Christian author (and ex-homicide detective) J. Warner Wallace opines:[1]

> In evaluating alleged "contradictions" of this nature, I think it's important to remember a few overarching principles related to eyewitness testimony (I describe many of these principles in my first book, *Cold-Case Christianity*). Even though I accept and affirm the inerrancy of Scripture, inerrancy is not required of reliable eyewitnesses. In fact, I've never had a completely inerrant eyewitness in all my years as a homicide detective. In addition, I've never had a case where two witnesses have ever agreed completely on the details of the crime. Eyewitness reliability isn't dependent upon perfection, but is instead established on the basis of a four part template I've described repeatedly…

What a bizarre position: to admit that eyewitnesses are not reliable, not inerrant, but to affirm the inerrancy of Scripture that happens to be based on eyewitness testimony! I just can't understand adhering to this *obvious* contradiction. How can Scripture, based at some level at some point (perhaps several levels removed) on eyewitness testimony, be inerrant, but eyewitnesses be not inerrant (*always* to some degree)? Either this is a totally incoherent position or the Gospel writers magically transformed inaccurate claims into accurate ones. In which case, the eyewitness testimony is in some large sense worthless as some powerful methodological tool because it is consistently reformulated by magic.

I will finish this section with a quote from anthropologist of religion, Homuyan Sidky, writing about the Resurrection narratives:[2]

> The inconsistencies and mutual contradictions in these texts make their historicity highly suspect. Here we have to refer back to Hume (1902 [1748]: 112–13) who advises extreme caution in any matter of fact "when the witnesses contradict each other; when they are few, or of a doubtful character; when they have an interest in what they affirm." We have no eyewitnesses in this case, and our only sources are the individuals who wrote the gospels working with second- and third-hand information, meaning anecdotes in circulation for years, passed on from person to person and between communities before they were written down. They had no personal knowledge of the facts, lived decades apart from the events and far away from the locations they discussed, and did not even speak the same language as the alleged witnesses. Also, the authors of

[1] J. Warner Wallace (2015).

[2] Sidky (2019), p.459-60.

> these texts not only contradict each other on significant points but were exceedingly credulous and as evangelists had plenty of interest in the tales they narrated. Religionists may vouch that such factors do not affect the quality of the evidence. However, as Gorham (1908: 76) queried long ago, "If testimony is not weakened by internal contradictions, credulity on the part of the witness, and the absence of corroboration, by what is it weakened?"

Verifiability

Richard Carrier (as well as many others[1]), in his book *Not the Impossible Faith* broadly criticising the notion that Luke, in particular, was an accurate historian of sorts, wrote very relevant chapters to this section ("Was Christianity Vulnerable to Disproof?" and "Would the Facts Be Checked?"). There is too much to summarise in a short paragraph or two, but the claims are hugely important. It's not so much that people *didn't want* to fact-check (though this is the idea I will contest), it's that they *couldn't* (which I hope to also set out). These chapters set out what we would intuitively know and claim anyway – that contemporary cultures and people were not skeptical in the way we are today. Goodness me, people until recently attributed supernatural causes to natural events such as eclipses and thunderstorms. It's easy, therefore, to realise why it was so hard for them to be able to exercise any level of skepticism. People did not have the requisite knowledge or methods to skeptically challenge claims.

Referring to Christian authors Bruce Malina and Jerome Neyrey,[2] rather than assuming that everyone knew everything, he argues that "secrets were of paramount priority in groupthink cultures, far more so than even today, and that outsiders often would not even be told in-group truths, much less personal truths."[3]

The standard of evidence that people presented (to defend or put forward a claim) was very different to the standards we see and use today. For instance, modern Christians...

> ...assume ancient Christians acted like modern Jehovah's Witnesses and just went knocking on random doors to coldsell the faith. That is not what they did. Instead, they mostly *relied* on groupthink to sell the faith. By first appealing to a group they were already a part of, they were not

---

[1] For example, see New Testament scholars Robert M. Grant (Grant 1963, p. 145), A.J.M. Wedderburn (Wedderburn 2004, p. 217), Philip F. Esler (Esler 1989, p. 97), Richard Pervo (Pervo 2006, p. 161-66, 2008, p. 1-16), amongst others.

[2] Carrier uses apologist JP Holding reference to Bruce Malina & Jerome Neyrey's *Portraits of Paul: An Archaeology of Ancient Personality* and turns the tables on Holding, using the source to refute Holding's position of verifiable accuracy.

[3] Carrier (2009), p. 330.

> seen as strangers, but comrades (in respect to whatever relation was being exploited at the time, whether family, race, trade, etc.). Then, once they were accepted into that group locally, that group could then introduce them to their neighbors. So again the Christians were not perceived as complete strangers, but as friends recommended by friends. Though Christians did not always rely on this tactic, it was their most common and important strategy, and it greatly reduced the burden on them to prove their merit and thus win trust.

It seems that, as according to Acts 2:1-42, the earliest recording we have of the Resurrection being preached publicly is at Pentecost where about three thousand people convert instantly. No other research or fact checking takes place – we have instant conversion based on claims of visions and supposed validation in Scripture. Peter or early Christian authorities are not consulted whatsoever. All it took was a powerful speech, and Acts tells us so. Carrier continues:[1]

> Seriously. Look at what was actually *said* to the public or the authorities. In Acts 2:14-40 we have Peter's first, and longest, public presentation of the case. Yet his argument consists entirely of irrelevant appeals to the disciples' private, unverifiable claim to have "seen" Jesus in some unspecified sense, to an obscure exegesis of the Psalms, and to various other "miracles" that actually have no bearing on whether Jesus actually rose from the dead. That's it. According to Peter's exegesis of scripture, a descendent of David *had* to rise from the dead (Acts 2:24-31 & 2:34-36), and Jesus must have been that descendent simply because "we" saw him, though (conveniently) "you" only get to see us speaking in tongues (Acts 2:32-33). He tacks on as a final flourish a typical *ad baculum* fallacy that they'd all better believe or they're doomed (Acts 2:38-40). That's a feeble argument. Yet (supposedly) it wins thousands of instant converts.

About two thousand more were converted on listening to Peter's speech as recorded in Acts 3:1-4:4. Immediately! No fact checking whatsoever.

Philip evangelises to the Samaritans in Acts 8:4-14. More instant conversions with no fact checking. All the inhabitants of Lydda and Sharron (Acts 9:33-35), the many believing Peter's healing of Tabitha (Acts 9:36-42), the household of Cornelius (Acts 10), the Roman Governor Sergius Paulus (Acts 13:6-12), the merchant Lydia (Acts 16:14-15), the jailer and his household (Acts 16:22-34), a great multitude of Jews and pagans in northern Greece (Acts 17:1-

[1] Ibid, p. 343-44.

4). So on (Acts 8:25) and so forth (Acts 8:27-39 and Acts 9:1-19). And there were more examples.

The point here is that there is no record of anyone checking assertions made of Jesus' resurrection in Acts. People just instantly converted, or converted with minimal persuasion.

Rather amusingly, certainly from the position of the skeptic, is what happens in reverse situations. When the facts are challenged at the debates in Athens and at the various trials, in Acts, *no one is converted* save a "few" in Athens!

Converts were won without evidence. *This* is what Acts inferentially or by assertion claims. In other words, using evidence from Acts itself, converts did not fact-check and were happy converting so the inference is that they didn't *want* to check the purported facts.

The idea that the empty tomb miracles *would have been* checked is denied by internal biblical evidence. And *exactly the same* can be said for the early church fathers: there is no evidence that they or anyone else seriously tried to fact-check the claims they were presented with, believing them wholesale.[1]

But, even if they *had* wanted to, could they have verified the claims of the Resurrection accounts?

Firstly, the scientific method and double-blind tests had not been properly developed by this point in history. Consequently, the methods of verification were somewhat limited and probably constrained somehow to merely asking the people involved (on both sides).

It is certainly the case that we can no longer verify the Resurrection claims. Nonetheless, we do now have some tools at our disposal as you will shortly see (burial practices, internal and external coherence of the texts and so on). However, contemporary potential converts had, in principle at least, access to eyewitnesses.

The Christian notion that the facts could have been verified "requires that most people in antiquity – particularly actual converts to Christianity in its first hundred years – were *also* excellent and studious historians, which is even *more* improbable."[2]

What we need to understand is that most of the early converts to Christianity did not live in the area where the events took place. People living in the Jewish diaspora in places like Greece (remember that the Gospels were written in Greek) would have been completely hampered by geography in any desire to fact-check. People at the time couldn't check newspapers, couldn't go to public libraries, couldn't use a telephone or the internet, and struggled even to travel to neighbouring towns (there were no cars or even bicycles and certainly no airplanes). The methods of fact-checking were not established, let alone did they have the sheer practical ability.

---

[1] See Carrier (2009), p. 352-64 for analysis of early church father fact-checking, or lack thereof.
[2] Ibid., p. 163.

Even contemporaneous "historians" at the time had very different ideas about what was plausible and what was implausible and had a habit of making things up. And these were the most accurate written historical sources of the era!

> Thucydides and all his successors felt at liberty to invent entire speeches, based on limited data in conjunction with assumptions about what *they themselves* thought was "probable" (and that would depend on their religious, ideological, personal, and philosophical commitments). This would never be tolerated today, and with very good reason....
>
> F.W. Wallbank, an expert on speeches recorded by ancient historians, concludes that the most reliable speech preserver in antiquity is Polybius, and yet Wallbank notes that even he "shows perhaps less critical judgment than we are entitled to expect" and "there is no evidence that Polybius' protest" against other historians taking greater liberties "had much effect in changing the current attitude towards writing history" in subsequent centuries.... Thucydides famously described his own method thus: "my practice has been to make the speakers say what *in my opinion* was demanded of them by the various occasions–or what *in my opinion* they *had* to say on the various occasions–of course adhering as closely *as possible* to the general sense of what was really said," insofar as he knew (he preceded this remark by mentioning the general nature of his sources).[1]

And Thucydides was one of the strictest of ancient historians! This shows what I previously stated, that we must treat any speech in such documents as incredibly dubious and most probably inaccurate.

Let me list the challenges to fact-checking, even if people had the background knowledge and desire to do so:

- Travel was too expensive, very time-consuming and oftentimes dangerous, whether on land or at sea.
- Mail, in any conventional sense, was practically impossible, certainly from strangers.
- Library access was incredibly limited and of little use to the potential Christian convert, and most likely inaccessible.
- Given the near practical impossibility of foreign or distant travel from outside of Palestine or even from far-off places within, this leaves us with localised fact-checking. The skills of interrogating were not known let alone implemented, especially given the in-group secretive

[1] Ibid., p. 166.

> world of the nascent Christian cult or sect. Such people would have really wanted to fact-check and then been in a position to be able to do this at a personal and social level.

Therefore, I would conclude that the readers or hearers of the Gospels *would not have wanted* to fact-check, and often not because *they didn't* fact-check, but because they *couldn't* fact-check. What this means is that the Gospels were both unverified *and* unverifiable.

Simply put, we do not know who the eyewitnesses were; we cannot (and nor could anyone contemporaneously, realistically) verify them; and eyewitnesses are never completely inerrant, anyway (as according to the previous quote from J. Warner Wallace). All of which, added to the previous arguments about provenance, leads us to conclude that we should treat the Gospel accounts with a massive amount of healthy skepticism.

6 – 75% of New Testament Scholars…

"75% of New Testament scholars believe in the Empty Tomb" is a claim, often without the percentage or with a differing percentage, made by popular apologist and theologian William Lane Craig – and others who follow in his lines of arguments – based on a claim made by Gary Habermas (in debate and in other various sources). It is used to set up the Resurrection account as likely to be true.

In "Resurrection Research from 1975 to the Present: What are Critical Scholars Saying?" by Habermas, he writes:

> Since 1975, more than 1400 scholarly publications on the death, burial, and resurrection of Jesus have appeared. Over the last five years, I have tracked these texts, which were written in German, French, and English. Well over 100 subtopics are addressed in the literature, almost all of which I have examined in detail. Each source appeared from the last quarter of the Twentieth Century to the present, with more being written in the 1990s than in other decades. This contemporary milieu exhibits a number of well-established trends, while others are just becoming recognizable. The interdisciplinary flavor is noteworthy, as well. Most of the critical scholars are theologians or New Testament scholars, while a number of philosophers and historians, among other fields, are also included….
>
> A second research area concerns those scholars who address the subject of the empty tomb. It has been said that the majority of contemporary researchers accept the historicity of this event. But is there any way to be more specific? From the study mentioned above, I have compiled 23 arguments for the empty tomb and 14 considerations against it, as cited by recent critical scholars. Generally, the listings are what might be expected, dividing along theological "party lines." To be sure, such a large number of arguments, both pro and con, includes very specific differentiation, including some overlap.
>
> Of these scholars, approximately 75% favor one or more of these arguments for the empty tomb, while approximately 25% think that one or more arguments oppose it. Thus, while far from being unanimously held by critical scholars, it may surprise some that those who embrace the empty tomb as a historical fact still comprise a fairly strong majority.

Let's look at "Contemporary Scholarship and the Resurrection of Jesus" by William Lane Craig to see a similar sort of claim:[1]

> For these and other reasons, most scholars are united in the judgment that the burial story is fundamentally historical. But if that is the case, then, as I have explained, the inference that the tomb was found empty is not very far at hand....
>
> One could go on, but perhaps enough has been said to indicate why the judgment of scholarship has reversed itself on the historicity of the empty tomb. According to Jakob Kremer, *"By far most exegetes hold firmly to the reliability of the biblical statements concerning the empty tomb"* and he furnishes a list, to which his own name may be added, of twenty-eight prominent scholars in support. I can think of at least sixteen more names that he failed to mention. Thus, it is today widely recognized that the empty tomb of Jesus is a simple historical fact. As D.H. van Daalen has pointed out, *"It is extremely difficult to object to the empty tomb on historical grounds; those who deny it do so on the basis of theological or philosophical assumptions."* But assumptions may simply have to be changed in light of historical facts.

I use these extensive quotes because this argument is so common in debates concerning the historicity of the Resurrection and it needs dealing with. There are several things to say here, and we will need to start with what might seem obvious to the skeptical reader: who are these scholars? Is there a selection bias?

The short answer to the last question is "Yes".

Let me make a couple of points. Firstly, almost 100% of Islamic scholars believe in the truth of the Qu'ran but this does not say anything at all about the intrinsic truth-value of the book. Historically, most New Testament scholars are Christian and enter the field of study in order to ratify their own beliefs. Of course, they will find this cornerstone of the Resurrection narrative true.

That most people asked were Christians should be obvious, but it is worse when many are studying at Christian universities where they have to make doctrinal statements. Relating this back to Habermas's claims, it is ensuring that those asked *had* to believe in the empty tomb! As we will see soon, Mike Licona lost his job because he wouldn't subscribe to the literal interpretation of Matthew 27![2] We could say that, even with such a huge selection bias, *only* 75% believed the minimal facts thesis of the empty tomb and this shows that fully 1 in 4 still do not think it viable. That is no small proportion of people who are

[1] Craig (1985b).

[2] More on this, and references, to come.

predominantly Christian! The fraction, perhaps coincidentally (perhaps not), roughly reflects the proportion of the US population who is non-Christian.

When I first became interested in these sorts of arguments, I took it upon myself to email every single university in the UK that offered such courses and ask for data on the beliefs of the faculty and the undergraduates. Although I didn't get a huge response from my unsolicited request, the data I did receive was almost unanimous – virtually every single undergraduate and teacher was Christian. So, if most undergraduates and those who study the New Testament are Bible-believing Christians, again, I am in all honesty surprised that the data is as low as 75%!

Let me indulge a further complete deconstruction of Habermas's work (read the whole article for a more complete analysis):[1]

> As an overview, note that Habermas's methodology falls far short of the basics of performing meta-analysis in the social sciences and would not, for example, pass peer review in a secular academic journal....
>
> But I don't want to limit my criticism of this model to form; it's not just that Habermas is summarizing where he should be regressing. Fundamentally, the problem is that a meta-analysis is only as good as the underlying data being aggregated. Most "biblical scholars" are, by definition, believing Christians: why would you spend your entire adult professional life researching something if you think it's ultimately worthless?
>
> The underlying problem is one of selection bias: if an intelligent and informed person thinks the Bible is probably *true* and therefore significant, he or she is more likely to pursue a career in biblical study and then publish his or her findings (confirming that the Bible is true). If, however, an identically-qualified person thinks the Bible is probably *false* and therefore not significant, he or she is dramatically less likely to trundle off to seminary regardless, and is exponentially less likely to publish his or her findings confirming that the Bible is false....
>
> In other words: Habermas's argument is a strategy for ignoring Biblical critics outside the mainstream, by padding the universe from which his meta-analysis is drawn with Christians. At its core, Habermas can tell us *what Christians believe*, but not what actually happened....
>
> In other words: a meta-analysis doesn't give you facts; it gives you a summary of the data compiled by the sources comprising your universe. Similarly, Habermas's meta-analysis/literature review doesn't tell us

[1] 'Why The "Minimal Facts" Model is Unpersuasive', *Evaluating Christianity*, https://evaluatingchristianity.wordpress.com/2009/03/05/why-the-minimal-facts-model-is-unpersuasive/ (Retrieved 08/03/2021).

> what actually *happened* – it tells us what his sources (almost all of whom are Christians) mostly *believe* to have happened.
>
> Worse, Habermas also concedes that for the linchpin "fact" in his argument – the empty tomb of Jesus – the level of agreement among his sources is not 95% but only 70%. Think about that for a moment. What Habermas is really saying is that, among Christians who have dedicated their lives to studying the Bible, ***nearly one in three denies the empty tomb***!
>
> Isn't that staggering?? I mean, if three out of every ten biologists denied the common descent of all living animals from a last universal common ancestor, then the creationists would really be on to something. Imagine if three out of every ten cosmologists thought it was possible that the universe was 6,000 years old instead of fourteen billion, or if three out of every ten astronomers thought that the Moon landing was faked, or... you get the idea.
>
> In other words: Habermas's case is, on close inspection, a powerful argument *against* the historicity of the resurrection of Jesus Christ, and a good reason for even Christians to take seriously the work of skeptics, such as Robert Price and Jeffrey Jay Lowder's *The Empty Tomb*.

Richard Carrier in "Innumeracy: A Fault to Fix" also provides an excellent critique of Habermas's arguments relating to the minimal facts, and the associated statistical problems.[1] The fact that hardly any agnostics or skeptics are included as scholarly sources for the survey is dubious to say the least. Indeed, in his chapter in *Resurrection: Faith or Fact?* he states:[2]

> But also, the only data ever collected (but still never published) by Gary Habermas on how many experts believe there was an empty tomb, though purported to show three quarters do, actually show *less than half do* - when we remember to exclude *non*experts, and to *not* exclude empty tomb *agnostics*. So that an empty tomb was discovered is probably *not* the majority opinion of experts, which is why Gary Habermas has dropped the empty tomb from his ever-shrinking "minimal facts" apologetic.

To recap: that almost 100% of Islamic scholars believe the Qu'ran does not mean that the Qu'ran is more likely to be true, it just means you have a huge

[1] Carrier (2013).
[2] Stecher & Blomberg (2019), p.199.

issue with selection bias. The selection bias for this Christian claim is thus highly problematic.

Or, in other words, this claim is utterly worthless.

When William Lane Craig has used this claim, it has not been known whether he was basing it off of Gary Habermas or Jakob Kremer[1] (a biblical scholar) or both.

The issues with Habermas's claim are obvious from the points above. If the claim is based on Jakob Kremer, then this was a bald assertion with no backing at all, and Kremer himself was apparently agnostic about the empty tomb anyway. Craig's use of Kremer has been critically analysed.[2] In an interview with Kremer, it is apparent that his own position is a little more nuanced:[3]

> Mulder: If somebody would ask you, let's say, you do an interview on the radio and somebody asks you the question: Prof Kremer, did Jesus rise with a body, and does it mean that the grave is empty? What would your answer be?
>
> Kremer: Ahh, maybe possible that the grave was deserted, but it is no proof, no proof....
>
> Mulder: So the empty grave is not that important?
>
> Kremer: No, no, it's got nothing to do. [sic]
>
> Mulder: OK.
>
> Kremer: Probably it is an expression of the church, but we know nothing.

Not that this is hugely important, but it was interesting that Craig, in debate with Richard Carrier, and when Carrier spent a long time critiquing Habermas on this point, switched and claimed he was using Kremer as a source, and of course Carrier had not prepared for this sidestep (considering Craig was almost certainly using Habermas: a sort of bait and switch tactic).[4] However, to

---

[1] Kremer (1977), p. 29-50.

[2] "(Infidel Guy radio) Richard Carrier, William Lane Craig, Jacob Kremer, and the Empty Tomb", *Infidel Guy Radio*, http://war-on-error.xanga.com/2009/05/01/infidel-guy-radio-richard-carrier-william-lane-craig-jacob-kremer-and-the-empty-tomb/ Transcripts from external interviews with Kremer can be found here, including a broken link to F. Mulder's thesis (pg. 180): "...it is significant that he [Jacob Kremer], generally known for his staunch defense of the empty tomb, revised his position on the empty tomb and resurrection of late. This is significant as Craig and Habermas continue to use Kremer to support their belief in the empty tomb."

[3] Kremer, J. (2006), Interview with Mulder, F. Evangelische Fakultät, Vienna, 5 July 2006, as detailed in the previous footnote link.

[4] "Did Jesus Rise from the Dead? Richard Carrier debates William Lane Craig", found variously online (e.g., https://www.youtube.com/watch?v=rCFuhlnsF9c).

use either source is problematic, especially as Kremer never even appears to cite a statistic: this is at best a subjective opinion lacking citation or reference to empirical evidence.

I have included this chapter also because of how often the "Minimal Facts" argument is used and buttressed by this supposedly statistical evidence. As Gary Habermas states of his "Minimal Facts" approach:[1]

> The half-dozen facts we usually use are these: 1) that Jesus *died by crucifixion*; 2) that very soon afterwards, his followers had *real experiences* that they thought were actual appearances of the risen Jesus; 3) that their lives were *transformed* as a result, even to the point of being willing to die specifically for their faith in the resurrection message; 4) that these things were *taught very early*, soon after the crucifixion; 5) that *James*, Jesus' unbelieving brother, became a Christian due to his own experience that he thought was the resurrected Christ; and 6) that the Christian persecutor *Paul* (formerly Saul of Tarsus) also became a believer after a similar experience.
>
> One "secret" not readily known is that these skeptical scholars are quite willing to cite New Testament texts in order to buttress the historical nature of these six events. While not believing that these passages are inspired or even generally reliable, they still employ the individual texts that meet their standards of evidence. It is largely from these passages, plus occasionally from extra-New Testament writings, that they find plenty of data to accept these half-dozen events.
>
> If you are interested in the historical back-up for these six facts admitted by virtually all scholars, as well as how these six can show that Jesus' resurrection really happened, you can buy a downloadable audio recording of my *2017 NCCA talk on the Evidence for the Minimal Facts* on the SES Store.

There are some seriously asserted claims here, and the historical claims of the minimal "facts" are what this book is looking so closely at, and facts they are not.

Just for the record, it is well worth pointing out that Habermas started out his Minimal Facts project with twelve supposed facts. This shrank to six, as listed above. Noteworthy in its absence here, crucially, is the empty tomb. As highlighted earlier, even Habermas now concedes the divergence in beliefs concerning this claim.

---

[1] Habermas (n.d.).

7 – Why Not Believe the Claims Concerning David Koresh and Sathya Sai Baba?

Let me now analogise.

I *really* get David Koresh, the Messiah who led his initial followers to an ultimately terminal 1993 conclusion. I dig him. I come to believe *now* (actually, in another 20 years plus, to be accurate), whilst in another country, that David Koresh was the living Messiah. But, it is worth remembering, I have no telephone or internet, car or public transport, to research this great being. Now, after being converted, coming to already claim that this man is the Messiah, I *then* write a "history" or account of him and his Messiahship. Remember, I have never met him, and there is no way of you knowing (and it is unlikely, given my geography) whether I have met any of his disciples. I call myself an evangelist, one whose job it is to convince other people, using persuasive techniques, of the Messiahship of Koresh.

Would you think this, my writing that you read long after my death, to be a reliable account of David Koresh, that I am a reliable source? Should *my* account be trusted?

No. Not at all. You would be mad to think my account should be trusted (prima facie), or certainly very irrational.

Taking just one little portion of the accounts, Matthew 27 (again, it should be fresh in your mind), we can take a further look. Dead and resurrected saints appear, parading around Jerusalem for many to see. Except no one else in the world apart from Matthew, writing in the context stated above, makes note of this purported event happening. No Jew ever mentions what would have been, for them, one of the greatest things ever seen.

Or take the idea that the Nativity accounts (a point I bring up in my Nativity book) stake claims on the "facts" of Jesus' birth. They are pretty much the only claims or events able to be cross-referenced in the New Testament, bar a couple that we will discuss later. Matthew and Luke fail on every claim. They are empirically wrong. So, given the basis that the first claims in two of the Gospels are empirically false, and these are the only ones that are properly verifiable (claims concerning censuses, dates, Herod and so on), on what basis do we have the justification to believe the rest of the Gospel claims that are not verifiable? The Wedding at Cana: who was there? How do we know? These are miracle claims that happen in conveniently unverifiable, nebulous contexts. And yet people are happy to drop the Nativity when they get into such difficulty and more readily believe *these other* nebulous (miracle) claims?

Of the Gospel accounts, we should be thoroughly skeptical.

As far as the Resurrection goes, there are many contradictions. As atheist Bob Seidensticker writes:[1]

> How many days did Jesus teach after his resurrection? Most Christians know that "He appeared to them over a period of forty days" (Acts 1:3). But the supposed author of that book wrote elsewhere that he ascended into heaven the same day as the resurrection (Luke 24:51).
>
> When Jesus died, did an earthquake open the graves of many people, who walked around Jerusalem and were seen by many? Only Matthew reports this remarkable event. It's hard to imagine any reliable version of the story omitting this zombie apocalypse.
>
> The different accounts of the resurrection are full of contradictions like this. They can't even agree on whether Jesus was crucified on the day before Passover (John) or the day after (the other gospels).

- What were the last words of Jesus? Three gospels give three different versions.
- Who buried Jesus? Matthew says that it was Joseph of Arimathea. No, apparently it was the Jews and their rulers, all strangers to Jesus (Acts).
- How many women came to the tomb Easter morning? Was it one, as told in John? Two (Matthew)? Three (Mark)? Or more (Luke)?
- Did an angel cause a great earthquake that rolled back the stone in front of the tomb? Yes, according to Matthew. The other gospels are silent on this extraordinary detail.
- Who did the women see at the tomb? One person (Matthew and Mark) or two (Luke and John)?
- Was the tomb already open when they got there? Matthew says no; the other three say yes.
- Did the women tell the disciples? Matthew and Luke make clear that they did so immediately. But Mark says, "Trembling and bewildered, the women went out and fled from the tomb. They said nothing to anyone, because they were afraid." And that's where the book ends, which makes it a mystery how Mark thinks that the resurrection story ever got out.
- Did Mary Magdalene cry at the tomb? That makes sense–the tomb was empty and Jesus's body was gone. At least, that's the story

[1]Seidensticker (2013).

according to John. But wait a minute–in Matthew's account, the women were "filled with joy."

- Did Mary Magdalene recognize Jesus? Of course! She'd known him for years. At least, Matthew says that she did. But John and Luke make clear that she didn't.

- Could Jesus's followers touch him? John says no; the other gospels say yes.

- Where did Jesus tell the disciples to meet him? In Galilee (Matthew and Mark) or Jerusalem (Luke and Acts [and John])?

- Who saw Jesus resurrected? Paul says that a group of over 500 people saw him (1 Cor. 15:6). Sounds like crucial evidence, but why don't any of the gospels record it?

- Should the gospel be preached to everyone? In Matthew 28:19, Jesus says to "teach all nations." But hold on–in the same book he says, "Do not go among the Gentiles or enter any town of the Samaritans" (Matt. 10:5). Which is it?

And there are lots more.

The question then becomes, are these contradictions (or "differences"), and are the claims themselves better explained by an ultimate truth in them, or by an alternative theory? We know from the Nativity accounts that when the claims of the Gospels are verifiable and able to be cross-referenced with external sources, they fail dismally. Therefore, on what basis are further claims (that themselves might be internally inconsistent like the Resurrection claims) believable when one cannot cross-reference them or verify them whatsoever? These are literally *incredible* claims, so the evidence must be pretty damned good to make them believable. How do we know what was privately being said by Pilate? Who recorded all of these speeches "on the fly"? Who are the sources that we can check? Why is there not one single external reference or witness to any of Jesus' amazing miracles? (We will talk about arguments from silence in coming chapters.)

Sathya Sai Baba in India has far more miracles claimed of him, attested to with more technology and by a far greater number of people, than Jesus. Sai Baba has more followers than Jesus did at a comparable time. And yet Christians do not believe him to be a miracle-worker!

Sathya Sai Baba is still one of India's most famous Swamis and has been one of the most enigmatic and remarkable religious figures in recent times. Millions of people, in these contemporary times, have followed him and accepted his claim of being a modern-day Avatar – a God Man. He has been far more successful than Jesus ever was in a comparable timeframe. Hundreds of miracles concerning both him and his followers (on account of following him) have been attested to with far more credibility and evidence than those claimed of Jesus. If Christian followers think that the Bible provides good evidence of Jesus' miracle-working, then they really should consider following Sathya Sai Baba. They really *should* believe the claims of Sathya Sai Baba in order to be evidentially consistent.

Except Christians don't. The rationale is simple: because they cherry-pick their reasons and evidence and employ double standards.

No, the evidence is shoddy, utterly filled with unknowns and contradictions and a lack of verifiability. Sathya Sai Baba and Jesus both. As Dan Barker states in *Godless:*[1]

> Protestants and Catholics seem to have no problem in applying healthy skepticism to the miracles of Islam or to the "historical" visit between Joseph Smith and the angel Moroni. Why should Christians treat their own outrageous claims any differently? Why should someone who was not there be any more eager to believe than Doubting Thomas, who lived during that time, or the other disciples who said that the women's news from the tomb "seemed to them as idle tales, and they believed them not?" (Luke 24:11)

Whilst we are talking about believing things without epistemic warrant, it is probably a good time to mention Noah's Flood.

The Case of Noah's Flood

I wrote an article once bemoaning how normal people can believe ridiculous things – in this case, Noah's Flood. I produced a whole host of arguments explaining how the story is in every way impossible.[2] The point is that people often don't question received stories told as fact from their childhood. They use the critical faculties they eventually pick up on other religions later in their lives, but they do not apply them equally to their own embedded, culturally inherited stories. These myths, whether Noah, the ten plagues, the Genesis Creation, the Tower of Babel or Matthew 27 and the Resurrection as a whole, bypass the

---

[1] Barker (2008), p. 279.

[2] For example: it being based on the pre-existing Epic of Gilgamesh; there not being enough water molecules in the world for the claims; water destroying everything would destroy previous biblical written claims; eight people looking after the world's biggest zoo; no wooden vessel could do that job; all of the world's animals from polar bears to pubic lice, sloths and lions – how do you get them there, feed them and clean them out?; the population of the world could not rebound from eight in the timeframe; the weight of the water would have had disastrous effects on the Earth's crust; no evidence for it; presently 100,000-year-old reefs exist that would have died; all sea fish would have died from rainwater influx; so on and so forth. You get the picture. See Pearce (2016).

vetting process by point of fact of being embedded before the process was learnt. It is like a computer with viruses that eventually gets a virus scanner. But the virus scanner can only pick up new viruses that come onto the system, rather than already existing ones. Those pre-existing viruses last the life of the computer. Unless it has a motherboard breakdown, goes to the shop, and gets refitted with new, decent software and hardware. In short, it has a mid-life crisis.

The second option is also prevalent. Many Christians do learn to be critical and do apply that vetting process to their embedded learning. However, cognitive dissonance means that the disharmony of having an embedded story and associated worldview with also having evidence against both of these triggers procedures in the mind that seek to harmonise these conflicting beliefs.

What happens, of course, as we all know, is that the stronger, more desired belief wins out. Not on account of the strength of the evidence, mind you, but on account of the *desire* for it to be true. The theist ends up discounting the evidence out of hand, or creating wildly ad hoc reasons as to how the evidence can fit in with so-called biblical "facts". I have been involved in such discussions with theists who offer the most incredible harmonisations and reasons as to how the flood myth could be true. All they do is destroy their epistemological credibility whilst producing some of the most amusing mental contortions known to intelligent man.

Obviously, there are difficult questions for the theist who actually discounts such myths (as symbolic or similar). It is a potentially slippery slope as to discerning what is myth, what is allegory and what actually happened in the Bible.

This childhood indoctrination (since that is what it is), a theist might respond, is merely a genetic fallacy. By knowing *how* something comes about, it does not necessarily discount its truth-value. No, not necessarily. But it does illustrate double standards, and it does illustrate how the case for the historicity of such accounts is built on very shaky cognitive foundations.

The Resurrection is one such cultural myth. Christians get wrapped up in the narrative, in each and every detail of the Easter story. It is ritualised, it is culturally embedded, it is acted out in society, on film, in schools, in church. "How can it not be true?" they might ask. But don't let the fact that something is culturally embedded impair your judgement. The Resurrection, like Noah's Flood, is full of unlikely claims, theological agenda and historically problematic supposed events.

8 – Earthquakes, Saints and an Absence of Evidence

Let us again return to Matthew 27: 51-53:

> And behold, the veil of the temple was torn in two from top to bottom; and the earth shook and the rocks were split. The tombs were opened, and many bodies of the saints who had fallen asleep were raised; and coming out of the tombs after His resurrection they entered the holy city and appeared to many.

The first thing we need to mention here is that the earthquake and parading saints only feature in the Gospel of Matthew (the three-hour darkness and veil tearing happen in Luke 23 at a different time, before Jesus dies). This should raise some serious concerns. Let it be stated that the fact that no other Gospel thought to mention this incredible set of details helps to cast serious doubt on Matthew's claims.

There is no other corroboration of this massive claim inside or outside of the Christian Bible.

Let that reality sink in.

(1) We have a book written by an unknown person (2) at an unknown time and place, (3) not being an eyewitness, (4) claiming, amongst other things, that the tombs of Jewish saints were opened and the dead bodies paraded around the capital appearing to many people. At the time, we can estimate that the population of Jerusalem would have been 55,000. But that number would have swelled to about 180,000 at this time of religious festivity.

And no one else reports this miraculous event. Anywhere.

This incident alone would qualify, ceteris paribus, as one of the most amazing claims in history given it is broadly seen as true by Christians, a large proportion of the world's population. From the Greek myths to the Epic of Gilgamesh, from South American divine mythology to the Qu'ran, we do not believe the truth claims of such worldviews. But we are expected, and many do, to believe this one unverified claim about something utterly unparalleled in world history? Furthermore, no Jewish person in Jerusalem deems it appropriate to record this event, or to pass it down to their descendants? It only appears as evidence this once, and this miraculous event is expected to be believed?

Swiss theologian and biblical exegete Ulrich Luz concludes:[1]

[1] Luz (2005), p. 587.

> There is no historical report; it is a polemical legend told by Christians for Christians or, more precisely, a fiction largely created by Matthew for his readers.

One problem with assessing the historicity of the Gospels is knowing which passages are reporting historical fact and which are written as symbolic passages: allegories to put forward a particular theme. It seems perfectly obvious to me that these claims of Matthew express a theological significance in the death of Jesus, whilst not being themselves historically accurate. Many theologians, conservative and liberal alike, agree because it is hard not to given the scope of the claims. R.T. France, a conservative New Testament scholar, states, "The symbolism is fairly clear, but we do not have the resource to determine the status of the story as sober history."[1] Theologian Hugh Anderson (who served as Professor of the New Testament at Edinburgh University for over twenty years) agrees: "What we have here is surely not a historical note, but a theological reminiscence."[2]

In 2011, renowned New Testament scholar Mike Licona was forced to resign from his teaching post and position as research professor of New Testament at Southern Evangelical Seminary and was ousted as apologetics coordinator for the North America Mission Board. This resignation was because, in one of his books relevant to our project here, *The Resurrection of Jesus: A New Historiographical Approach*, he examined the above passage in Matthew 27. In researching this passage, Licona came up with a theory that annoyed the biblical literalist camp. He recognises the problem that there is no other evidence to support this extraordinary biblical claim. As Licona has said:[3]

> Based on my reading of the Greco-Roman, Jewish, and biblical literature, I proposed that the raised saints are best interpreted as Matthew's use of an apocalyptic symbol communicating that the Son of God had just died.

In the original analysis Licona was here referring to (i.e., in his book), he stated:[4]

> [I]t seems to me that an understanding of the language in Matthew 27:52-53 as "special effects" with eschatological Jewish texts and thought in mind is most plausible. There is further support for this interpretation. If the tombs opened and the saints being raised upon Jesus' death was not strange enough, Matthew adds that they did not come

[1] France (1994), p. 1943.
[2] Anderson (1965), p. 45.
[3] Ross Jnr. (2011).
[4] Licona (2010), p. 552-53.

> out of their tombs until after Jesus' resurrection. What were they doing between Friday afternoon and early Sunday morning? Were they standing in the now open doorways of their tombs and waiting?
>
> ... It seems best to regard this difficult text in Matthew as a poetic device added to communicate that the Son of God had died and that the impending judgment awaited Israel.

Because he was bucking a conservative trend of not reading the passage literally, *he had to go* as his colleagues and peers were more literal in their understanding of the text. This just shows that one scholar can read an account as being symbolic whilst another concludes antithetically. But there is often motivated reasoning in believing more conservatively and literally.

Matthew's account is contradicted by Acts 26:23 that says that Christ should be the first to rise from the dead. This is clearly not the case since this parading mass of saints got there first.[1] The whole notion that Christ is the first of the general resurrection (that Jews believe in) is put to bed by this Matthean claim.

To make matters worse, the Matthew 27 account is actually less well attested than a particular Hindu miracle (just a random one that I have found):[2]

> An incident concerning Raghavendra Swami and Sir Thomas Munro has been recorded in the Madras Districts Gazetteer. In 1801, while serving as the Collector of Bellary, Sir Thomas Munro, who later served as the Governor of Madras is believed to have come across an apparition of Raghavendra Swami who had died almost two centuries back.

Yet none of us, Christian, atheist, non-Hindu, believe this supernatural claim.

Extraordinary claims require extraordinary evidence. Remember Chapter 4 – this is of utmost importance now.

We are evaluating the extraordinary claim that resurrected hordes of saints paraded through a municipal city. This raising of the saints, coming out of their graves, and walking through the Holy City went unrecorded or unreferenced by everyone until some half a century or so later, and only then by an evangeliser with a theological agenda.

Thus, since this is unverified and not independently attested, even on historical grounds, this is poor evidence to support a resurrection. It is also a wildly supernatural claim that, as far as we know, has never happened and

[1] There is some debate concerning the translation, as to whether the saints resurrected after Jesus' death or after his resurrection.

[2] From "miracle" on the reference website *Sensagent*, http://dictionary.sensagent.com/miracle/en-en/ (retrieved 18/11/2020)

cannot happen naturally, except in the claims of the Christian Bible. However, the Christian would, I imagine, deny all other supernatural claims from religions outside of the Bible. It must be inquired: on what grounds can Christians deny the supernatural claims of other religions? I would posit that it would actually be on special-pleaded *naturalistic* grounds, thus employing double standards, though I could be wrong. In other words, miracles in other religions are denied on account of being naturalistically implausible as a gut reaction (together with all other religions being false), but this benchmark is not assigned to miracle claims from within the Christian's own religion.

If I told you tomorrow these two things:

(1) I ate two apples yesterday.

(2) I swam the English Channel with my hands and feet tied, yesterday, in two hours.

You would believe (1) on my simple testimony alone. You would not believe (2) on my simple testimony alone.

Therefore, extraordinary claims do indeed need extraordinary evidence, as I have at some length set out already. We would need to apply a Bayesian analysis to the claims of Matthew, here, and we would find that the hypothesis that Matthew's claims are true, over and above the claims that he is making it up or mistaken, is improbable. Importantly, they are less probable than the rival, naturalistic hypothesis; and this should be so from a Christian perspective, too, if they are being honest with their evaluation.

But let us bring up the oft-heard claim that "the absence of evidence is *not* an evidence of absence".

This is something that you hear very often from theists in their defence of certain claims from within the Bible: the maxim "absence of evidence is not evidence of absence", or, "the fact that there is no evidence that it *didn't* happen doesn't mean that it didn't happen. It still *could have* happened." Just because I do not have evidence that you went to the shops today does not mean that you didn't go to the shops today. Sounds fair, right?

Remember that we are dealing in probabilities, so it is always difficult to say that something didn't indubitably happen; what we prefer to say is that, *in all likelihood,* it most *probably* didn't happen. Given the Bayesian approach to these claims, though, we know that the prior probability of such claims as in Matthew 27 are vanishingly small. In order to overcome those vanishingly small probabilities, we need to have extraordinarily good evidence.

We have Matthew's paragraph above. And that is all!

We lack any other evidence *for* the hypothesis that Matthew's claims are correct. We have an absence of evidence.

Mathematician John D. Cook casts his learned eye over this maxim and opines:[1]

> Here's a little saying that irritates me:
>
> Absence of evidence is not evidence of absence.
>
> It's the kind of thing a Sherlock Holmes-like character might say in a detective novel. The idea is that we can't be sure something doesn't exist just because we haven't seen it yet.
>
> What bothers me is that the statement misuses the word "evidence." The statement would be correct if we substituted "proof" for "evidence." We can't conclude with absolute certainty that something doesn't exist just because we haven't yet proved that it does. But evidence is not the same as proof.
>
> Why do we believe that dodo birds are extinct? Because no one has seen one in three centuries. That is, there is an absence of evidence that they exist. That is tantamount to evidence that they do not exist. It's logically possible that a dodo bird is alive and well somewhere, but there is overwhelming evidence to suggest this is not the case.
>
> Evidence can lead to the wrong conclusion. Why did scientists believe that the coelacanth was extinct? Because no one had seen one except in fossils. The species was believed to have gone extinct 65 million years ago. But in 1938 a fisherman caught one. Absence of evidence is not proof of absence.
>
> Though it is not proof, absence of evidence is unusually strong evidence due to subtle statistical result. Compare the following two scenarios.
>
> **Scenario 1:** You've sequenced the DNA of a large number of prostate tumors and found that not one had a particular genetic mutation. How confident can you be that prostate tumors never have this mutation?
>
> **Scenario 2:** You've found that 40% of prostate tumors in your sample have a particular mutation. How confident can you be that 40% of all prostate tumors have this mutation?
>
> It turns out you can have more confidence in the first scenario than the second. If you've tested N subjects and not found the mutation, the length of your confidence interval around zero is proportional to N. But if you've tested N subjects and found the mutation in 40% of subjects, the length of your confidence interval around 0.40 is proportional to √ N. So, for example, if N = 10,000 then the former interval has length on the order of 1/10,000 while the latter interval has length on the order of

[1] Cook (2011).

> 1/100. This is known as the rule of three. You can find both a frequentist and a Bayesian justification of the rule here.
>
> Absence of evidence is unusually strong evidence that something is at least rare, though it's not proof. Sometimes you catch a coelacanth.

The differentiation between what is logically possible and what is plausible or probable is pertinent here, and that's not to talk about logical possibilities given laws of nature and supernaturalism vs. naturalism.

The point is that we would absolutely, almost one hundred percent *expect* there to be corroborating evidence. The fact that there is none definitely adds to the probability of Matthew's account being false. We shouldn't just believe any old claim on the basis that an absence of evidence is supposedly not an evidence of absence, otherwise we would end up believing anything. Where we should expect evidence in support of a claim and find none, we find that this does indeed provide evidence against that claim.

This should lead the skeptic (well, everybody, really) to conclude that the prior probability, the evidence, the likelihood ratio *and therefore* the posterior probability are very low indeed. This is a very improbable and implausible scenario that one is barely epistemologically justified in believing. Either, then, the original claims or the data are wrong, or there is a better explanation for the data, or a mixture of both.

Why would Matthew do this? It's impossible to tell this with any kind of certainty. But any explanation that we could give, within reason, will lead to a more probable account of the data than believing Matthew's claim. That he might be outright fabricating the data for some kind of gain is far more probable. That he genuinely believed this purported event but heard it from an unreliable source that was ultimately false is more probable. There is no doubt in my mind that Matthew would definitely *want* these claims to be true, just as any modern Christian does. Wishful thinking does not an argument make, though.

Mike Licona provides a very reasonable theological and thematic reason as to why Matthew included this passage.

Again, if we fully expect evidence of an extraordinarily improbable claim to exist but find none, then this leads us to have further doubt in the truth of that claim.

9 – The Silence of Paul

We have just discussed the absence of evidence conundrum and I would like to continue this train of thought by bringing into play the curious case of the apostle Paul. Here is a good deal of the "detail" that Paul, in all of his writing, gives on the death and the Resurrection of Jesus:

> 3 For I delivered to you as of first importance what I also received, that
> Christ died for our sins according to the Scriptures, 4 and that He was buried, and that He was raised on the third day according to the
> Scriptures, 5 and that He appeared to Cephas, then to the twelve. 6 After
> that He appeared to more than five hundred brethren at one time, most
> of whom remain until now, but some have fallen asleep; 7 then He appeared to James, then to all the apostles; 8 and last of all, as to one
> untimely born, He appeared to me also. (1 Corinthians 15)

This excerpt is important and shows that Paul's main source was a personal revelation – not the most trustworthy of attestations. He doesn't mention evidence, refer to an empty tomb, talk of the testimony of Doubting Thomas, and didn't even talk to any supposed eyewitnesses for the first three years of his evangelical belief.[1] Nebulous scriptures and personal, subjective revelation is all that he presents as evidence. That's it.

Who is Paul, for the uninitiated? Some say he is the creator of Christianity in a very meaningful sense. Paul, according to Acts, was a Jew who originally persecuted Christians before having an appearance experience of Jesus on the road from Jerusalem to Damascus. As a result, he "converted" to become an early Christian. He was also the earliest source that we have for Jesus.

Acts spends about half of its time dealing with Paul's life, and fourteen of the remaining books of the Christian Bible have traditionally been attributed to Paul, though most are not authentically written by him (written some twenty years plus after the death of Jesus). Indeed, only seven epistles are deemed to actually be Pauline. Paul was involved in starting early church communities and developing theology for the movement.

There is often a tension between those who effectively think that Paul "invented" Christianity and those who believe that Jesus himself had more of a say, together with some early followers. James Tabor, in his book *Paul and Jesus*, sees this very much in terms of the former scenario:[2]

---

[1] See Galatians 1:11-18. Also, Carrier (2010), p. 301, for discussion of this.

[2] Tabor (2012), p. xv-xvi.

> [T]he Christian faith, confessed by millions each week in church services all over the world, originates from the experiences and ideas on one man - Saul of Taurus, better known as the apostle Paul- *not* from Jesus himself, or from Peter, John, or James, or any of the original apostles that Jesus chose in his lifetime. And further, I maintain there was a version of "Christianity before Paul" affirmed by both Jesus and his original followers, with tenets and affirmations quite opposite to these of Paul. This is the lost and forgotten Christianity of James the brother of Jesus, leader of the movement following Jesus' death, and the Christianity of Peter and all the apostles. In other words, the message of Paul, which created Christianity was we know it, and the message of the historical Jesus and his earliest followers, were not the same. In fact, they were sharply opposed to one another with little in common beyond the name Jesus itself.

Whether you see Paul as fundamental to Christianity or merely very significant is perhaps besides the point. The point being that Paul is the earliest known written source concerning Jesus and is *at least very important* to Christianity.

Paul's Silence

A striking aspect of the New Testament is the way the letters attributed to the apostle Paul have so little material in them about the historical figure of Jesus and his teaching. Paul's letters contain teachings largely from his own thinking or derived from the Hebrew Bible. Paul speaks of "Christ" a lot but this is usually concerning more abstract theology, especially on what Jesus' crucifixion implies.

It is not merely that there is little material regarding Jesus' teachings and deeds in Paul's epistles, it is that when Paul uses quotes and references very frequently, he does so of the Hebrew Bible (over 180 times), of creeds/hymns (about seven) and even Roman poets (two) – this has been laid out by many scholars, including E.P. Sanders and Margaret Davies in *Studying the Synoptic Gospels*.[1] So, we should *expect* a large volume of quotes from Jesus' teachings and deeds as well. But they are not there; the evidence from Jesus is exceptionally meagre with just one actual quote and a few references (more on this below). When Paul wants to make a point, he rarely draws on the body of information that he and his readers supposedly must surely have had on the life of Jesus; yet, he nearly always goes elsewhere.

[1] Sanders & Davies (1989), p. 323.

A good case in point is Paul's letter to the Romans 12 where he says:

> 17 Never repay evil for evil to anyone. [t]Respect what is right in the sight of
> all people. 18 If possible, so far as it depends on you, be at peace with all
> people. 19 Never take your own revenge… 21 Do not be overcome by evil,
> but overcome evil with good.

This is just the kind of thing Jesus taught on, with memorable quotes from the later Gospels like "if anyone forces you to go one mile, go with them two miles", "turn to them the other cheek", "blessed are the peacemakers" and "love your enemies and pray for those who persecute you". If Paul and his audience were familiar with this material from the Sermon on the Mount and Jesus' teachings carried authority, he would surely have used it. Paul could also have mentioned Jesus' exemplary behaviour at his arrest, flogging, trial and crucifixion.

Instead, Paul uses two quotes from the Hebrew Bible (Deuteronomy 32:35 "It is mine to avenge; I will repay" and Proverbs 25:21,22 "If your enemy is hungry, feed him..."). They do the job of backing up Paul's points, though I guess you will have to assess whether it is better than Jesus' material. I think not! It is hard to imagine a *Christ*ian preacher today teaching on not taking revenge by quoting these passages rather than Jesus himself!

An obvious conclusion to draw from this silence is that Paul was either ignorant of the life of Jesus and his teachings, or that these matters did not interest him (or they never occurred). The further option that Paul knew of Jesus' teachings, but his audiences did not, seems implausible, as Paul would want to remind them of Jesus' words. That Paul's audience knew Jesus' life and teachings is usually given as a reason as to why Paul gives so little information: they didn't need it. But that argument doesn't hold water. Because Paul is continuously reminding them of things they already know – doctrines, creeds, practices, beliefs, scriptures, even his own past statements. So why is content from or about Jesus the only thing he never reminds them of?

The circumstances under which arguing from silence is valid is where the evidence that we should *expect* to see is missing, as previously discussed. For example, if we visit an apartment and find no food in the refrigerator or cupboards, no books or magazines strewn about, no toothbrush or soap in the bathroom, no clothes, no rubbish in bins, and so on, then it is valid to conclude that the apartment is unoccupied. What we would *expect* to see in an occupied apartment is missing. And that is like the case here; the way Paul (and the authors of James and Peter) use the Hebrew Bible and other authorities so much leads us to expect similar widespread use of the traditions about Jesus should they both be held in common with their readers and considered authoritative. The lack of such material is therefore very telling. If we find just a chocolate bar wrapper in the bin in the apartment and one book placed neatly by the slightly disturbed bed, we don't have enough evidence to conclude that the apartment is occupied; instead, we assume that there is another explanation. That is the case here.

I would say that if we have the hypothesis "Paul and his readers knew the deeds and teachings of Jesus (pre-Easter) and considered them authoritative", then the near silence on them is extremely unlikely, and thus undermines the hypothesis.

Why did Paul seem to have little interest in or apparently slim knowledge of Jesus almost entirely in this narrow "Christ died for sins" way and not more widely as a teacher and figure, with his source appearing to be "according to Scripture" (*kata grapha*)? Remember this is in the context of Paul's love for quoting and alluding to authoritative sources in his letters, about two hundred in all. If Jesus was believed to be the Son of God, or God incarnated as man on Earth as "part" of the Godhead itself, this silence is astounding. Moreover, Paul's direct claim that he got his gospel about Jesus direct from revelation from heaven,[1] rather than the teachings of Jesus passed on to the church, only makes this worse.

Had the Resurrection account based on followers discovering an empty tomb been a pre-existing oral or written tradition, in all likelihood, the apostle Paul would have mentioned it; not in all of his letters, since many were about local church issues. However, he surely would have in 1 Corinthians 15 at least, I would posit. We learn very little from Paul about the historical Jesus, but 1 Corinthians is slightly different. After all, Paul reminds the Corinthians of their general acceptance of Jesus' resurrection, that he was buried and raised. And yet there is no mention of an empty tomb, or of its discoverers. Paul goes to length in persuading the reader of how important the reality of the Resurrection of Jesus was. Surely, then, to help persuade, as the Gospel writers do, then mentioning the "facts" about this event would have been vital![2] As British theologian Geoffrey Lampe states:[3]

> If Jesus' resurrection is denied, he says, the bottom drops out of the Christian gospel. And the evidence that he raises consists in the appearances to himself and to others. Had he known that the tomb was found empty it seems inconceivable that he should not have adduced this here as a telling piece of objective evidence.

Similarly, skeptic Kris Komarnitsky affirms in *Doubting Jesus' Resurrection*:[4]

---

[1] Galatians 1:12, 2:2; 1 Corinthians 2:10, 11:23; 2 Corinthians 12:1.

[2] See the later chapter on whether Paul believed the resurrection was spiritual or bodily.

[3] Purcell (1996), p.43.

[4] Komarnitsky (2009), p.12.

> Given Paul's ability to defend ideas, and given his effort above to defend Jesus' resurrection, it is hard to understand why Paul did not mention a discovered empty tomb if he knew about it. It would have been a great bolstering point for Jesus' resurrection and in turn for the general resurrection, which Paul argues for right after arguing for Jesus' resurrection (1 Cor 15:20-57), including giving a seed/plant analogy that attempts to describe how a dead body is raised (1 Cor 15:35-54). The discovered empty tomb is the only piece of major evidence missing from Paul's argument for Jesus' resurrection.

Thus we appear to have good reason to hypothesise a later development of this perhaps legendary overlay. Absence of evidence, when expected and as previously mentioned, *is* evidence of absence.

Concerning 1 Corinthians 15:3-8, it is hard to know when it was written, but a good guess is around 55 CE or later, being approximately twenty-five years after the death of Jesus. Given a lexical analysis, it is a fair conclusion to say that Paul "received" such statements from others before him, as Bart Ehrman superbly sets out: [1]

> In other words, this is what New Testament scholars call a *pre-Pauline tradition* - one that was in circulation before Paul wrote it and even before he gave it to the Corinthians when he first persuaded them to become followers of Jesus. So this is a very ancient tradition about Jesus. Does it go back even to before the time when Paul himself joined the movement around the year 33 CE, some three years after Jesus had died? If so, it would be very ancient indeed!
>
> ... Scholars have devised a number of ways to detect these preliterary traditions. For one thing, they tend to be tightly constructed, with terse statements that contain words not otherwise attested by the author in question - in this case Paul - and to use grammatical formulations that are otherwise foreign to the author. This is what we find here in this passage. For example, the phrase "in accordance with the scriptures" is found nowhere else in Paul's writings; nor is the verb "he appeared"; nor is any reference to "the Twelve."
>
> The passage almost certainly contains a pre-Pauline confession, or creed, of some kind... In its original form, then, the creed would have read like this:
>
> 1a Christ died
>
> 2a For our sins

[1] Ehrman (2014), p. 138-39.

3a In accordance with the scriptures

4a And he was buried.

1b Christ was raised

2b On the third day

3b in accordance with the Scriptures

4b And he appeared to Cephas

I have not included much of Ehrman's (and others') analysis here for reasons of time and space. However, I think this is a fascinating place to start when considering the very foundations of the Resurrection narratives. Paul goes on to expand the end by adding some other witnesses, including Jesus "appearing" to him some two or three years after Jesus died.

There are two theological points to be made here: one that Jesus died for our sins and the second that it happened in accordance with the Scriptures on the third day. The third day is not necessarily relevant in and of itself, but it points towards the Scriptures of the Hebrew Bible. Scholars are split as to whether the day three raising refers to...

Hosea 6:2 "After two days, he will revive us; on the third day he will raise us up that we may live before him."

or

Jonah 2, whereby Jonah is consumed by a great fish and stays in his belly for three days and three nights before being released.

Either way, there is scriptural significance here. We know that the Gospel writers (in particular Matthew, playing to his Jewish audience) took great care to link Jesus to, or predict him using the Hebrew Bible.

Another essential nugget to take away from this very short set of creedal statements is the reference to Cephas. We are not told anything about who buried Jesus and certainly hear nothing of Joseph of Arimathea (Paul makes no mention of him anywhere in his writings); we are merely given reference to Cephas.

The 1 Corinthians 15:3-8 quote from the beginning of this chapter is very revealing because it appears that Paul is giving a definitive and exhaustive list of those people to whom Jesus appeared. Nowhere is mentioned the women at the tomb or tomb guards or even the empty tomb itself. The women were clearly the first people to see Jesus alive in the Gospels and yet, for someone who loves to quote others, and for someone keen to list evidence, *there is no mention of these women*. He doesn't mention them anywhere in his writings.

Kris Komarnitsky recognises this issue as lying at the heart of the matter, as we saw from his earlier quote. This Pauline silence is an issue that is all too often glossed over or simply ignored by apologists. G.W.H. Lampe, theologian and priest, admitted:[1]

> If Paul and the tradition which he cites lay no emphasis on the empty tomb the question arises whether Paul nevertheless may have known of it. Many New Testament scholars hold that he did.... Certainly it would be quite unsafe in the ordinary way, to infer that he did not from the fact that he does not actually allude to it. But in this case I think that the argument from silence has unusual force. For the situation in which Paul wrote I Corinthians 15 was that some of the Corinthians were denying that there is a resurrection of the dead (I Cor: 15: 12). In answer to them Paul marshals every possible argument, and in particular, he adduces the known fact that Jesus was raised from the dead as the foundation for belief in the future resurrection of Christian people.

And remember this from his previous quote:

> Had he known that the tomb was found empty it seems inconceivable that he should not have adduced this here as a telling piece of objective evidence.

In conclusion, Paul's silence about Jesus is highly controversial, or at least should be for the Christian. What this means is that (and I claim this has very high probability indeed) at the time of our earliest source, some twenty-five years after Jesus died, the empty tomb narrative didn't exist, and this leads on to the high probability that it was a later narrative construction of the Gospel authors or their own sources.

Or, as time progressed, the Resurrection narratives became progressively embellished with legendary and mythological overlay. This then leaves us with the mere Pauline assertion that Jesus resurrected and, as we shall see later, Paul perhaps saw this as a spiritual resurrection and not a bodily one, and his visionary experience of Jesus appearing was most probably hallucinatory and/or subjectively religiously experiential rather than objectively physical.

But you will have to wait for that chapter. First, let's look at the Gospel claims of the details of Jesus' death and ensuing resurrection.

---

[1] Lampe (1966).

10 – The Events Leading up to the Crucifixion

For the purposes of this chapter and to keep the length of the book to a manageable level, I am going to be as succinct as I possibly can with listing the events and critically analysing the Gospel claims in light of the vast number of problems that arise. However, this chapter will necessarily be the longest in this book.

I will start with the Last Supper. However, that is not to say that there aren't more problems with the Gospel claims of Jesus prior to this supposed event and after entering Jerusalem (there are).

The Last Supper

There is debate as to whether the Last Supper is actually a Passover[1] meal as is generally accepted. Mark, and subsequently Matthew and Luke, seem to indicate that it was a Passover meal. In direct contrast, John, as we have seen before, differs and many academics have argued that there is a significant variance here, and that, in fact, the meal is *not* a Passover meal. John's meal occurred at a different date, the fourteenth of Nisan. Moreover, when Judas Iscariot leaves with a moneybag, the other disciples think he is taking money to purchase food for the festival meal. This action implies that they had not already had that meal (see John 13:29). John does not mention the Passover lamb as the other Gospels do (presumably because Jesus *was* the Passover lamb). John 18:28 reads:

> **28** Then they led Jesus from Caiaphas into the Praetorium, and it was early; and they themselves did not enter into the Praetorium so that they would not be defiled, but might eat the Passover.

We later have John referring to the tradition of releasing a prisoner at Passover, and if they had already had their Passover meal, then this period was over. John 19:30-31 again confirms that Jesus died prior to the Passover. It is absolutely clear, then, that John is reporting the Last Supper as not happening at Passover, and therefore not being a Passover meal.

Why is the accuracy of the claims of this purported historical event important? Well, it shows that there are obvious contradictions between the Gospels and that the traditions in these communities were different, arguably

[1] The Jewish holiday or festival to mark the passing over of the children of Egypt by the angels during the ten plagues of Egypt. It includes the Passover sacrifice – the paschal lamb.

quite different. It certainly points to confusion as to the sources for the Synoptics as opposed to John.

Where it gets a little more interesting is that Paul appears to agree with John. As you will see later, and together with the idea that he apparently had no idea of the empty tomb narrative, it seems that Paul differs hugely from Mark, Matthew and Luke.

Paul doesn't mention the Last Supper meal as being the actual Passover meal at all. Instead, he refers to Jesus as "our Passover" in 1 Corinthians 5:7, similar to John. Likewise, in 1 Corinthians 11:23, Paul seems not to have been aware of a Passover observance, again mentioning nothing of the Passover such as the meal happening on Passover or similar. He refers to the evening as "the night in which the lord was betrayed", though this maybe apologetic spin and better translated as "handed over" (as it does in other contexts for him).[1] In 1 Corinthians 11:23, Paul uses the Greek word for "bread" and not the word for "unleavened bread" that would be the case for an actual Passover meal.

Even Bishop N.T. Wright, who has written exhaustively on the Resurrection, recognises an obvious issue here. He tries to harmonise the passages with "it seems to me virtually certain that the meal in question was *some kind* of Passover meal".[2] I think he is stretching plausibility here and there is definitely a contradiction, and certainly a disconnect between the earlier Paul and the three earliest Gospels.

Where would John have gotten the idea that Jesus was buried on a different day? It is most likely, in my opinion, that he would have taken this from Paul himself, who declares Jesus as our Passover lamb. I believe that Paul, and later John being familiar with Paul, wanted to get rid of the Passover feast from within Christianity. In this way, Jesus replaces the Passover feast and meal by becoming the new form of Passover.[3] Paul is moving the Jewish observances into a new schema. This hyper-literal manifestation of the Passover lamb is seemingly not picked up at all by Mark and the other Synoptics.

John's Gospel (starting, as it does, with John the Baptist) is the only one that sees Jesus as "the Lamb of God who takes away the sins of the world". His gospel is the only one that sees Jesus as dying on the same day as a Passover lamb (the day of preparation); indeed, he dies at the exact same hour, the same place (Jerusalem) and at the hands of the same people (the Jewish leaders) as Passover lambs.[4] The whole narrative has immense theological significance.

---

[1] This means there is arguably no betrayal narrative in Paul's writing, either.

[2] Wright (999), p. 84.

[3] See Hebrews 8:13. Mark, and by extension Matthew and Luke, sees Jesus in the breaking of bread – in the context of transubstantiation – as a sort of metaphorical Passover lamb, but not in John's hyper-literal sense.

[4] Alter (2015), p. 76-77.

Furthermore, John's Gospel is the only one where the Roman soldiers pierced Jesus' side rather than break his legs on the cross. It is forbidden in Exodus 12:46 to break the bones of the paschal lamb.

Michael Alter points out another issue:[1]

> In Mark 14:2, the chief priests and scribes express a desire to apprehend Jesus and dispose of him two days *before* the Passover meal. However, in verse 12, the Passover meal has *already* arrived. These two conflicting chronologies are seemingly left unreconciled.

Furthermore, Jesus leaves the house (importantly for a Passover meal, where his family is absent – another Passover issue) after the meal to go into the garden, which is against Passover tradition (Exodus 12:22) where one must stay in the house until morning.

Theissen and Merz, in their seminal *The Historical Jesus: A Comprehensive Guide,* add a number of other issues surrounding the claim that leave the reader in little doubt that this was indeed a Passover meal.[2]

There is certainly something amiss here. It looks very much like John has a far greater theological agenda than the other Gospels. This is interesting because either the Gospels of Mark, Matthew and Luke have got their theology wrong and the details of Jesus' final chronology (claiming it was a Passover meal and the details relevant to this when it wasn't), or John is making things up in order to paint a theological picture of Jesus that simply was not evidenced in the facts of Jesus' last days. You simply can't have it both ways. There is core Christian theology wrong with at least some of the Gospels here, one way or another. Is this history "scripturalised", as some apologists like to think, or theology "historicised", as I see it (where "historicised" implies "making history up").

In my opinion, John sounds theologically more sensible (though no less post hoc rationalised) and this throws huge doubt and confusion over the claims of the Synoptics. If these claims are problematic or wrong, what does it say about all of the others, and ones that aren't so obviously verifiable or contradictory? Might these still be incorrect? There is little way to tell if the claims that they make are both unverified and unverifiable, especially this late in the day. Our quest for truth is far from over, though: we shall see how many further problematic claims there are.

---

[1] Alter (2015), p.74

[2] Theissen & Merz (1999), p. 425-27.

Capture and Trial

The Synoptics claim that a "great multitude" of people were present for the capture of Jesus: chief priests, scribes, elders, and captains of the Temple. As Michael Alter contends:[1]

> Initially, the priests had just completed their busiest day in the year, the fourteenth day of Nisan, presiding over and organising the slaughter of thousands of lambs in the Temple, to say nothing of the obligation to attend their own paschal meal. That very evening, the evening of the Passover meal, they were to leave their families in the dead of night to assist in the arrest of Jesus.
>
> Second, the synoptic Gospels report that the Sanhedrin held two trials immediately after the arrest of Jesus. It is not plausible that the Sanhedrin would have convened twice, once in the night and once in the morning on the fifteenth of Nisan. Now that the evening had started...and the Passover Seder had commenced, the chief priests and the elders were supposedly going to leave their families in the dead of night to participate in not one, but two trials. Further, those present at the trial were not just the chief priests and elders, the scribes and members of the Temple guard were also present. Mark 14:55 went so far as to state that this trial occurred in the presence of "all the council," the entire Sanhedrin: "And the chief priests and all the council sought for witness against Jesus to put him to death; and found none." It is totally implausible to believe that between sixty and up to one hundred people would have left their Passover meal, leaving their families and guests in order to participate in two separate trials.

The whole trial of Jesus was itself illegal. In addition to these claims above, we can argue that there are further impossibilities: (1) Trials could not take place in the evening, (2) nor on the Sabbath or other Jewish feast days, (3) nor could they be brought in a private home, (4) one could not convict a man without witnesses, (5) nor without any charge (as per Luke), (6) one could not execute a man without a death sentence (since the Sanhedrin did not condemn him to death) and (7) death sentences could not be pronounced until at least a day after the interrogation, to name but a few of the illegal trial issues.

If the arrest was after the Passover meal, the fifteenth day of Nisan, then the people arresting would not be carrying weapons on a feast day, and Peter was also illegally carrying a weapon; it would be a serious problem that Simon the Cyrene was coming out of the country or fields (from whence he was taken to help Jesus carry the cross), implying he was working (and on this day, one

[1] Alter (2015) p. 89-90.

could not enter or leave Jerusalem); and the high priest tore his clothes during the questioning, again problematic. The high priest acting as prosecutor in the trial is problematic – because there *are no Prosecutors in Jewish trials...* In fact, virtually every facet of the trial account violates Jewish laws and customs.[1] David Fitzgerald says, in his book *Nailed: Ten Christian Myths That Show Jesus Never Existed At All*, referring to the work of Jewish legal authority Haim Cohn (Attorney-General of Israel and later Justice of the Israeli Supreme Court), who scrutinized in fine detail the different Biblical accounts of Jesus' trial:[2]

> The trial is incompatible with multiple well-established provisions of ancient Jewish law; in fact the violations of Jewish law in Jesus' trial dog-pile on each other so fast it's hard to keep up. All of them are virtually inconceivable, and of course highly improper: neglecting Passover, meeting by night, holding trial in a private home, conducting a trial in secret, the High Priest acting as interrogator himself and even striking the defendant with his hand, the failure of the witnesses to agree, mocking and beating the prisoner, and many more, any of which should have resulted in a mistrial. Even worse, they appear to have deliberately misrepresented certain aspects of the trial to paint the Jewish religious leaders as stereotypical villains. There are other less obvious implausibilities as well. Luke has the beloved rabbi Gamaliel make a cameo appearance to save Peter at his trial in Acts, so he should have been present and prominent at Jesus' trial, too. But there is no mention of this in any account, Biblical or Jewish.[3] Of course, if he had been there, it would have been utterly out of character for him to take part in such a gross miscarriage of justice (which the Gospels say was unanimous). And if such an outrageous trial really had broken all these rules in a rush to condemn a man the whole city had joyfully acclaimed just days before (John 12:13, Matt. 21:8-10), then how is it none of the historians and writers of the day ever mentioned it, especially when they give detailed accounts about so many much less interesting would-be messiahs and scandals in Jerusalem from the same period?
>
> The Gospels are also completely wrong about first century Jewish religious politics. The Pharisees and the High Priest were never in cahoots with one another. Nothing could be further from the truth - they were bitter political enemies. In reality, most everyone in Judea hated the High Priest, who was both a Sadducee (the Pharisee's political opponents), and a puppet appointee working for the hated Romans. The Pharisees regarded the Temple priesthood as mere ceremonial

[1] Fitzgerald (2010), p. 92-100.
[2] Ibid., p. 92-93.
[3] Cohn (2000), p. 132.

> functionaries doing the nation's spiritual grunt work, keeping the sacrifices going and maintaining the Temple.[1] Even in the best of times the Pharisees seemed to regard most high priests as little more than trained monkeys, saying "a learned bastard takes precedence over an ignorant High Priest."[2]

These issues might individually seem to some people minor issues, but together, they form a raft of problems for this narrative.

John's chronology is somewhat different, but no less challenging. For John, the trial would be held on the fourteenth of Nisan. The high priests and all the other members of the religious organisations would have been carrying out the arrest and attending the trial on the same day that they should have been "presiding over the preparation of thousands of Passover lambs".[3]

Executions were not permitted on holy days, and nor were trials, and trials could not be split over two days. Capital cases required two days, and so in John trying to correct the error of the Synoptics, by having the trial the day before Passover, we have further invalidation of the chronology. It seems that none of the Gospels can have it right.

Matthew 26:57 says that on the night Jesus was arrested, the priests and scribes were gathered together prior to Jesus being brought to the high priest. In direct contrast, Mark 14:53 says they were gathered on the night of Jesus' arrest *after* Jesus was brought to the high priest. Luke 22:66 says they assembled the *day after* Jesus was arrested whilst John mentions only the high priest, and no one else plays a role. Such multitudinous discrepancies, and we are only just getting started!

Luke states (23:7-11) that Pilate sent Jesus to Herod Antipas (tetrarch and ruler of Galilee and Perea), who questioned Jesus for some time before returning him. However, *the other Gospels do not mention this event at all.* Moreover, jurisdiction for a crime is determined by where it took place, not where the criminal came from, presenting even more problems with this narrative.[4] This whole scene makes no legal sense.

---

[1] Maccoby (1987), p. 26-27.
[2] Maccoby (1987), p. 23.
[3] Alter (2015), p. 91.
[4] In private correspondence (07/03/2021), Richard Carrier pointed out that "the author of this material [i.e., Luke] seems to incorrectly imagine Palestinian politics operating like the Greek Achaean League where one held citizenship in a *polis* and various *poleis* had treaty agreements regarding the prosecution of each other's citizens, e.g., the way he treats Paul's ability to cite Roman citizenship to change the jurisdiction; no such system existed between Palestinian cities, much less vague 'regions'…"

As far as the dates for these events are concerned, but also in looking again at the legality of the trial in terms of Jewish customs, Richard Carrier argues that there are just too many impossibilities and incongruities:[1]

> So none of this really works. But the more devastating point is that none of these dates *is even possibly true*. Under Jewish and (governed by a local treaty) Roman law at the time, executions could not be performed on holy days. Trials for capital crimes by the Sanhedrin (as all the Gospels depict) had to be conducted over the course of two days and could not be conducted on or even interrupted by a Sabbath or holy day–nor ever conducted at night. The Gospel trial narratives violate every single one of these rules. Their authors thus did not even know (or didn't care) how Jewish law in early Roman Judea worked, and can't have been recording anything that actually happened. In historical reality had Jesus been arrested during or immediately before Passover he would have been held over in jail until Sunday morning, and could only have been convicted on a Monday evening at the earliest. Days *after* any Passover could have occurred. (On all this, with primary sources, see my chapter on the "Burial of Jesus" in *The Empty Tomb*; with Mishnah, *Sanhedrin* 4.1j-k and 5.5a).
>
> The idea of having Jesus killed on a Passover Friday was entirely a mythical-theological contrivance.... Mark constructed his myth to reify the teachings of Paul, and Paul tells us Jesus was known in Christian doctrine as both the Passover Lamb (1 Cor. 5:7) and the "firstfruits" of the general resurrection (1 Cor. 15:20-23) and as having risen from the dead "on the third day" after his death (1 Cor. 15:3-4). The Torah commands that the Day of Firstfruits take place the day after the first Sabbath following the Passover (Lev. 23:5-11). In other words, on a Sunday. Thus Mark has Jesus rise from the dead on Sunday, the "firstftuits" of the resurrected, symbolically on the very Day of Firstfruits itself, and thus dying on Passover day, and rising the third day after (ancient Jews reckoned inclusively, so Passover is day 1, the Sabbath day 2, and the Day of Firstfruits day 3)
>
> There were several other reasons Mark had to choose Sunday as the day of resurrection: Sunday was also traditionally the first day of creation (since God rested on the seventh day of creation, making that the Sabbath, hence Saturday; so creation began on a Sunday, the first day of the week: Gen. 1:5 and 2:2), and Jesus was also imagined as inaugurating a new creation (e.g. 2 Cor. 5:17), and thus logically *had* to rise on a Sunday. Mark also found this confirmed in the Psalms: scholars have long noted that he saw the crucifixion in Psalm 22, and then the sojourn

[1] Carrier (2021).

> among the dead in Psalm 23 (a rest, corresponding to a Sabbath), and then the resurrection in Psalm 24, which in the Septuagint text is ordered to be sung "on the first day of the week," meaning–again–Sunday. That line is essentially directly quoted by Mark in 16:2, using the same distinctive idiom in the Greek. So we know this is what he was doing. When we combine all that with Paul's Passover and Firstfruits and third-day doctrines, it becomes clear that Mark *had* to pick this arrangement of days and dates. Matthew and Luke simply copied him. And John made only a slight mythical adjustment to it.

I really don't think Christians understand the scope of problems associated with their claims and the data that they provide to back up their claims.

What is pertinent about the Gospels is how much they try to pin the blame for Jesus' death not on the Romans, but on the Jews. Pilate famously offers to release one prisoner and the *Jews* call for Barabbas (where Mark has him up for insurrection and murder, but John contradicts and has him for robbery). The problem here is not so much the contradiction but the claim that Pilate *would do this at all.* The only recourse to such a decision would concern postponing the execution until after a holy festival, and Pilate was hardly known for his mercy.

The only reasons one can realistically suppose for this mercy is to, firstly, further absolve Pilate and the Romans of blame and to give a very explicit opportunity for the Jews to deny Jesus mercy and to be openly responsible for his crucifixion. Secondly, the event could well be an allegory for Yom Kippur, the Jewish Holy Day of Atonement, an important symbolic point for the Gospel writers.[1] We shall see in a later section that the real reason Pilate's releasing someone is included in the narrative is to represent Jesus or Barabbas as the Yom Kippur scapegoat – theology, but not history.

Pilate supposedly gives in to an unruly mob. This action is so unlike everything we know about the brutal ruler, who would much more likely send in the troops (as is evidenced by recounts of Pilate's actions by Josephus[2]). We know that he was *so* brutal that he was eventually pulled back to Rome,[3] so this public display of mercy is utterly incongruous with known history.

No matter which source you want to believe, the credibility is stretched to breaking point, both in terms of contradictions and general plausibility.

The other side of the trial coin is that the mistakes in Jewish law not only evince the distance between Judaism and the Gospel writers (who end up embellishing their accounts by "making things up"), but they also defend the

---

[1] See, for example, discussion of this in "Jesus as Goat of the Day of Atonement in Recent Synoptic Gospels Research" by Hans Moscicke (Moscicke 2018).

[2] E.g., Josephus, *Antiquities of the Jews,* XVIII, Ch. 3:1-2.

[3] Ibid., XVIII, Ch. 4:1-2.

hypothesis that writers were completely creating this part of the narrative from scratch. When analysing the details of the trial, with so many errors of procedure, I am led to also hypothesise that the whole episode is entirely fictitious, and inserted in the narrative to put the blame on the Jews. In other words, Jesus claiming to be "King of the Jews" was seditious, and the Romans wouldn't think twice about executing a possible revolutionary who threatened their rule. It is reasonable to conclude that the Romans just arrested Jesus on sedition and simply had him summarily executed, as a "trouble-maker". Perhaps the Jews weren't actually involved in any of this, with their part in the story retrojectively added due to the animus generated between the nascent sect and the established religion in the intervening period between Jesus' death and the compilation of the Gospels.

Either way, the arrest and trial is thoroughly problematic for the belief in the historical accuracy of narrative proposed in the Gospels.

The Day of Crucifixion

We have already dabbled a little into this subject. The first and most important thing to say is that, if Jesus really was captured and executed, it certainly didn't happen just before (and on) the Sabbath or a holy day (they would have held him over in jail to specifically avoid that inconvenience if it really happened at such a time). Moreover, it almost certainly would not have taken place during the Passover week. These are theological contrivances that actually play merry havoc with historical plausibility. We can discount the accuracy of the Gospel claims already, it seems.

Indeed, as we will see in later section, the Sanhedrin (or Romans, depending on what your theory might be) will have wanted maximal suffering for the worst of crimes; this would have meant executing the victim as far away from the Sabbath or holy day as possible (i.e., towards the beginning of the week) so they can be left to suffer before death for as long as possible.

Different theories abound as to what day of the week (Wednesday, Thursday or Friday) that Jesus was crucified due to the lack of clarity between the Gospels. John has Jesus being crucified after midday on the day before Passover (John 18:28; 19:14-16) whilst Mark has it mid-morning the day after the Passover meal (Mark 14:12; 15:25).

The time of day, as you can see, is also different. Specifically, Mark being the third hour (9 am, the third hour after the 6 am sunrise), Matthew having him crucified sometime after the sixth hour, or noon, (Matthew 27:45), with John agreeing to the sixth hour (as above). Some apologists claim John must be using a Roman civil day, and thus harmonise him with Mark in this way. Raymond Brown, a Catholic exegete, shows such attempts short shrift:[1]

> In the commentary we have seen that such harmonizations are implausible and unnecessary, so that the calculation from 6 A.M. should be accepted throughout, even if that leaves the accounts in conflict. It is not demonstrable that any evangelist had a personal, chronologically accurate knowledge of what happened. Most likely they found a time indication like "the sixth hour" (mentioned by all) in the tradition and attached it to different moments in the passion ***according to their respective dramatic and theological interest.*** [my emphasis]

This is one of those diamond quotes that open up a whole can of worms for Christian apologists, and from within their own ranks. This is an *explicit admission that the Gospel authors were manipulating data to fit their own theological and dramatic agendas.* Facts and truth play second fiddle to politics and theology.

American biblical scholar Jack Finegan, writing in the *Handbook of Biblical Chronology*, agrees, after laying out a series of issues with any attempted harmonisation:[2]

> The foregoing attempts at reconciliation between the Synoptics and the Fourth Gospel are relatively unconvincing.

Before concluding:[3]

> Therefore, Mark 15:25, and John 19:14 are "plainly irreconcilable" and Mark 15:35 can be thought to be an "interpolation."

There are vast amounts of scholarship and argumentation surrounding the issue of on what day and at what time Jesus was crucified. The fact that each Gospel makes their own different, solid stipulations as to when the crucifixion took place gives rise to further doubt based on such repeated discordance. Who were the sources and why would they cause such divergence on a continued basis? It's almost as if the details are constantly of little value to the Gospel authors.

Finally, it is worth noting that Mark, Matthew and John have Jesus being scourged and handed over to soldiers. They place a scarlet robe and a crown of

---

[1] Brown (1994, 2), p. 1352-53.
[2] Finegan (1998), p. 357.
[3] Ibid, p. 359.

thorns on Jesus (see later references to Yom Kippur here). Luke does not mention a crown of thorns *at all*, and has the robe *placed on him by none other than Herod*, whom Jesus visited, much earlier. Coincidentally, this event was *not recounted in any of the other Gospels*.

Carrying the Cross

In Mark, Matthew and Luke, Roman soldiers compel another man to carry the cross on behalf of Jesus, namely Simon the Cyrene, who appeared to be randomly accosted for the job. It is not clear that carrying a cross was even a done thing (as we will discuss, it is highly unlikely to have been a cross anyway) and would appear to be nigh on impossible.[1] No reason is stated as to why Simon was asked to do this task. John, again in contradiction, has Jesus explicitly carrying his own cross. Modern scholars (against the imagery depicted in art) concede by assertion of inference that this must have just been the crossbar (*patibulum*) that Jesus and/or Simon carried, and that Simon must have started and Jesus took over. This subject will also be discussed in the later section on execution.

A typical Christian apologetic with all sorts of modal irregularities looks something like this:[2]

> Jesus **carried the cross-beam**. Notice, it said "As they were going out." **Most likely**, Jesus was so exhausted from being nearly beaten to death that it became apparent that he would literally not be able to carry it to the crucifixion. It would be very embarrassing to the Roman soldiers if Jesus died before reaching the execution place. He had to be crucified. **For this reason**, when Jesus collapsed, **they chose** an innocent bystander, Simon the Cyrene, to carry it for him. **I will admit** that this is to some extent the **Roman Catholic version of events. I do not know for sure that** Simon of Cyrene was forced to carry it the rest of the way because Jesus had collapsed, but it is a **reasonable conjecture. What is for sure is that** the eye-witnesses reported that Jesus carried his cross (John 19:17), and that **Simon was forced to carry it part of the way** (Matthew 27:32 and Luke 23:26). [My emphases.]

This is a wonderful example of terrible heuristics and methodology, liberally smashing together modal ***most likely***s with ***what is for sure***s, and suchlike. *What is for sure* is pretty much *nothing* here or anywhere else in the Gospels.

---

[1] There is no evidence this happened outside of Rome; see van Wingerden (2020).
[2] Oakes (2006).

Another anomaly: Jesus only addresses his followers verbally on this journey in Luke (23:27-32).

It is also interesting to see that an oral, legendary embellishment has arisen as a result of consistent harmonisation attempts. In order for both people to have carried the cross, we have apologists claiming that Jesus collapsed from exhaustion or having a "hypovolemic shock" as a result of the flogging. Indeed, we are now at the point where Christians often generally believe he collapsed three times. It was at this point that Simon took over the carrying of the cross, so they assert without evidence. It has even been baked into a Catholic devotion, the Stations of the Cross: the three "stops" devoted to his "falls". Of course, this is not evidenced anywhere in the Gospels and is a mere apologetic assertion, showing how easy it is for "facts" or beliefs about an event to appear over time and get written into ritual.

The popular apologist website *Got Questions*, in answering the question "Why did blood and water come out of Jesus' side when He was pierced?", declares:[1]

> Those who were flogged would often go into hypovolemic shock, a term that refers to low blood volume. In other words, the person would have lost so much blood he would go into shock. The results of this would be:
>
> 1) The heart would race to pump blood that was not there.
>
> 2) The victim would collapse or faint due to low blood pressure.
>
> 3) The kidneys would shut down to preserve body fluids.
>
> 4) The person would experience extreme thirst as the body desired to replenish lost fluids.
>
> **There is evidence from Scripture** that Jesus experienced hypovolemic shock as a result of being flogged. As Jesus carried His own cross to Golgotha (John 19:17), **He collapsed**, and a man named Simon was forced to either carry the cross or help Jesus carry the cross the rest of the way to the hill (Matthew 27:32-33; Mark 15:21-22; Luke 23:26). **This collapse indicates Jesus had low blood pressure. Another indicator** that Jesus suffered from hypovolemic shock was that **He declared He was thirsty** as He hung on the cross (John 19:28), indicating His body's desire to replenish fluids. [My emphases.]

---

[1] "Why did blood and water come out of Jesus' side when He was pierced?", (n.d.), *Got Questions*, https://www.gotquestions.org/blood-water-Jesus.html (Retrieved 22/10/2020).

I include this quote because it shows the low bar that Christian apologists and apologetics websites often stoop down to. There is no direct evidence at all of Jesus collapsing; it is merely a bare assertion based in the somewhat dubious inference that, because there is a contradiction in who carried the cross, there must have been two people, and the best way to make sense of this problem is to have Jesus collapsing. This *could* have happened but to make the assertions so strongly and suggest the claims above as "evidence" is methodologically problematic.

We will return to this point later when discussing the blood and water streaming from Jesus' pierced body.

The Thieves on the Cross

Matthew very clearly has both robbers (robbers, criminals or men, depending on which Gospel you read) mocking Jesus. In direct contrast, Luke has one mocking him and the other rebuking the first.

Whilst Mark, Luke and John recount that Jesus' crucifixion took place between two thieves, Matthew provides no details of where the three were crucified in relation to each other. Furthermore, Mark and John failed to report any speech between the other condemned criminals and Jesus. However, Luke reports that the second rebukes the first of the robbers for mocking Jesus, made a confession of their crimes and that both the thieves were being rightly punished, and then claims that Jesus was innocent and asked that he be remembered by Jesus as they enter the kingdom. Jesus replies (Luke 23:43): "'Truly I say to you, today you shall be with Me in Paradise.'"

Again, we are faced with the same problem as to why certain Gospels omit such seemingly important details.

There is another contradiction involved here, comparing what Luke and John claim. John says *three days later*:

> Jesus said to her, "Stop clinging to Me, for I have not yet ascended to the Father; but go to My brethren and say to them, 'I ascend to My Father and your Father, and My God and your God.'"

So, does Jesus ascend on the day he dies on the cross as Luke claims or does Jesus ascend three days later?

There are some wonderful attempted harmonisations to this apparent contradiction, such as trying to differentiate "todays", claiming an Earthly "today" being a specific day, but when Luke mentions it, it is a heavenly "today", where heaven is outside of time. It is incredible the lengths that Christian apologists go to try to harmonise such disparate accounts.

Luke is supposedly a very good historian. At least, according to Christian apologists. Luke used Mark and Matthew's accounts as sources, apparently investigating everything carefully (as according to his own prologue). Matthew very clearly claims that both thieves mocked Jesus, and yet Luke only has one. Indeed, the following verses in Luke are not attested to in any other gospel:

> **39** One of the criminals who were hanged *there* was hurling abuse at Him, saying, "Are You not the Christ? Save Yourself and us!" **40** But the other answered, and rebuking him said, "Do you not even fear God, since you are under the same sentence of condemnation? **41** And we indeed are suffering justly, for we are receiving what we deserve for our deeds; but this man has done nothing wrong." **42** And he was saying, "Jesus, remember me when You come in Your kingdom!" **43** And He said to him, "Truly I say to you, today you shall be with Me in Paradise."

Where has Luke received this information given that it is contradictory to what the other Gospels state?

And again, we come back to a recurrent problem that exists actually throughout the entirety of the Christian Bible: how do the biblical authors know what was said in private conversations? I don't want to belabour the point, but any accounts that are purported to be history, or at least historical, that include speech are *prima facie* worthy of serious skepticism (as mentioned, who heard and recorded this speech and how?). One also has to ask how this thief appears to know how Jesus is innocent. Jesus was arrested at night and immediately taken for interrogation by the chief priests, elders and scribes, before being brought in front of Pilate for trial. How is this thief able to access any of this information?[1] How would Luke and all of the Gospel authors have access to all of the conversations involved in the final week of Jesus' life?

This is not written history, I wager, but fiction.

Jesus' Followers – the Women

There is much to be said about the discrepancies between the Gospels with regard to the women (as with every single verse and claim, it seems). I discuss issues concerning the women who visit the empty tomb in later chapters, so, for this section, we will only concern ourselves with those people present at the crucifixion.

Mark and Matthew (going back to the time of Jesus' arrest) are clear that there are no disciples at the crucifixion, that all of Jesus' disciples forsook him at the cross, but Luke (23) confuses matters by saying:

---

[1] Alter (2015), p. 121.

> 48 And all the crowds who came together for this spectacle, when they observed what had happened, began to return, beating their breasts. 49 And all His acquaintances and the women who accompanied Him from Galilee were standing at a distance, seeing these things.

Who are "all His acquaintances"? If Luke were, as is widely accepted, largely dependent on Mark and Matthew, then why would he change their narratives to have a different account?

Mark has *several* and Matthew has *many* women at a distance from the cross. Luke 23:49 could be seen to also support or contradict this description by nebulously including "*all his acquaintances*" being present. John, again the outlier, takes it one step further and claims that at least one disciple was there, the one "whom he loved". Tradition denotes this person as John himself but who could be, as has been proposed, one or none of the following: Lazarus, Mary Magdalene, James (Jesus' brother) or an unknown priest or follower. Luke could be seen to be "harmonisable", at a stretch, with Mark and Matthew, but John is in plain contradiction. Additionally, John includes Mary, Jesus' mother, present with several other women. John contradicts either all of the other authors or all minus Luke. Luke could be seen to agree with Matthew and Mark or disagree with everyone, essentially saying everyone was there. It's a mess.

It would be quite the issue if Luke *truly* meant that *everyone* was literally there at the cross. This casts doubt as to who either his sources were or those of Mark and Matthew.

What another mass of confusion.

Jesus Is Mocked

John does not mention any mocking (by people other than those on the cross). We are at a point now where discrepancies are wholly unsurprising. Matthew has the most embellished accounts when it comes to Jesus being mocked by those who passed by and by the chief priests themselves. He even adds in some elders for good measure.

The interesting point here is that, especially if (as some adherents to the early church tradition believe) John was present at the cross, why did John omit these noteworthy occurrences?

If we take into account the chronology that John used for a crucifixion, then the paschal lamb would be in the process of being slaughtered by the chief priests. Consequently, their non-presence would explain why they were not there to mock Jesus. This plays into the notion that, for John, Jesus *is* the paschal lamb. For the Synoptic Gospel authors, this crucifixion event took place on the day *after* the busiest day of the year (the day of preparation), and so the elders and priests were freely available to do so. However, this just re-highlights a previous contradiction.

Blood and Water, Wine and Myrrh

According to Mark (15:23) and Matthew (27:34), Jesus was given a drink of wine before and then after crucifixion but in Luke and John this happens only after crucifixion. "Vinegar" is a type of cheap and sour wine and could be confused with "wine" as a contradiction but it is not. However, Mark has the wine mixed with myrrh and Matthew has the "vinegar"[1] mixed with gall; gall and myrrh *are* a contradiction (not just a difference) – not one that will sink the Bible, mind, but a discrepancy nonetheless. Myrrh is a nice-tasting ingredient whilst gall is exceptionally sour; however, both have pain-relieving qualities. The issue here is why the Roman soldiers would be giving Jesus pain-relieving drinks. It makes no sense considering they had just beaten, scourged and mocked him. A minor contradiction within an action that is incoherent at best.

Dividing up Clothes and Casting Lots

I will deal with this topic separately due to the incident being a case of bizarrely fulfilling a Hebrew Bible prophecy. It is, however, worth noting a contradiction in when the soldiers part Jesus' clothes. In Mark and Matthew, it is *before* the criminals are crucified, in Luke and John, *afterwards*. Why such consistent divergence?

Matthew 27

The chronology of the claims that I will discuss here is perhaps confused given the events I have already discussed and those I will soon discuss, but I will keep Matthew's supernatural events together in this section. I have spoken at length about this part of the story (see Chapter 8) and the incredulous nature of the claims surrounding the darkness, the earthquake, the parading of dead saints around Jerusalem and the rending of the Temple veil. The earthquake and resurrected saints only appear in Matthew, and are not attested to in any

[1] See in a later section how this could be a reference to the metaphorical representation of the Jewish celebration of Yom Kippur.

other source in the world outside of the Christian Bible. The same lack of external corroboration goes for the rending of the veil and the supernatural darkness (where Mark and Luke make claims about the veil tearing *and* a three-hour darkness, both at differing times to Matthew's claim). Either worldwide or localised darkness, seismic shifts, a city full of ghosts or even zombies witnessed by many, and a religious totem being damaged in the most sacred space for the Jews, going completely undocumented by every other human being on Earth, is somewhat ridiculous, to say the least.

Again, Mark, Luke and John see these quite remarkable events of earthquake and zombie apparitions as not worthy of inclusion in their own accounts. Is that action by these writers probable? What does this say about the overall probability of either Matthew or the other Gospels being representative of the truth?

I will, however, add some very pertinent points to my previous discussion. Darkness at death is a common motif throughout religions and history.[1] Whether it be Julius Caesar, Krishna in Hinduism, Romulus, Aesculapius, Hercules, Alexander the Great, Atreus of Mycenae, darkness is so often a symbol associated with the death of important people. We also see many such precedents being set in the Hebrew Bible. As I set out in my book *The Nativity: A Critical Examination*, Jesus had to be bigger and better than contemporary historical and religious figures, both externally and internally to the Jewish context. Whatever Caesar did, Jesus could at least do. Moses? Jesus was the new upgrade.

Matthew is very keen on relating his account of Jesus back to the Hebrew Bible in order to appeal to his Jewish audience. The three-hour darkness of Matthew could well be significant in terms of the three-day darkness in Egypt's last plague. As we saw with the Nativity accounts, Matthew is portraying Jesus as the new Moses, coming out of Egypt, to fulfil prophecy. Such a parallel is surely not accidental. Matthew was also the only Gospel author to use an astral sign, the Star of Bethlehem, to signify Jesus' birth. Just as the star is completely lacking in evidence in contemporary literature, so too is this bookend of an astral sign of darkness lacking any evidence. Both mechanisms appear to be literary and theological vehicles.[2] Michael J. Alter concludes:[3]

> If the darkness was, in fact, a miracle, the silence from history is equally miraculous. Would it not be common sense to expect the Greeks, Romans, the Chinese, or others to have noticed and reported such darkness occurring at the time of the month when a solar eclipse was

[1] Alter (2015), p. 133-34

[2] For an in-depth discussion on this, see Alter (2015), p. 135-40 ("SPECULATION #24 Astronomical and Physical Explanations for the Darkness").

[3] Ibid, p. 139.

impossible? There is no historical evidence that this astronomical event occurred!

As far as the tearing of the Temple's veil is concerned, it is worth considering how much of a major deal this was for contemporary Jews. The curtain was about 83 feet high and 24 feet wide and one handbreadth thick and made from four different thread types, making it a hugely substantial piece of material. It held huge importance and the fact that its tearing is not corroborated in any source in the world other than Mark and Luke, as I have amply mentioned, makes the claim (in my opinion) completely unbelievable. I can't put it any other way. I am entirely confident that this never took place. All Jews in Judea would have known about this tearing.

There are a number of non-biblical accounts of phenomena concerning the curtain, such as Titus, a Roman general, entering the Holy of Holies, slashing the curtain supposedly causing blood to miraculously spurt out.[1] In this case, we rightfully do not believe this of Titus. No one does.

Luke's account of the tearing of the veil happens before Jesus dies as opposed to afterwards, as in Matthew. Luke 23 says, "because the sun was obscured; and the veil of the temple was torn in two". This massive holy material appears to have been torn in two and there is no Jewish record of this event occurring. The fact that, in one book alone,[2] there are over thirty-five interpretations of the tearing of the veil means that this is not a very clear revelation in any case, and leaves the reader wondering why on earth God would make this happen!

When Matthew says...

> **54** Now the centurion, and those who were with him keeping guard over Jesus, when they saw the earthquake and the things that were happening, became very frightened and said, "Truly this was the Son of God!"

...we have a problem because the guards would not have been able to see those things whilst guarding the cross, such as the veil in the Temple tearing (standing west of the Temple as they would have been).

As far as the earthquake is concerned, considering that, as Matthew claims explicitly, the rocks were rent or split; this would have been a pretty significant earthquake. We know that Luke does not mention this event and we also know that he claims to have investigated his sources carefully (Luke 1:3). Does this mean that he investigated Matthew to find that such a claim was

---

[1] See Gittin 56b, *The William Davidson Talmud*, https://www.sefaria.org/Gittin.57a?lang=bi (Retrieved 28/01/2021).

[2] Geddert (1989), p.141-43.

erroneous? That the claim of the saints rising from the dead was equally erroneous?

What Jesus Said

All of the Gospels disagree on what Jesus said and when he said it (both the sayings throughout his time on the cross and what he said at death). Some theories even propose that the sayings were increased to seven because this was a symbolic number for Jews and Christians, where six was deemed as negative, leading to a Lukan interpolation of an additional saying.[1] Whatever it was he was supposed to have said, the classic apologist's line, similar to the four newspaper accounts thesis, is as follows:[2]

> 'What were the last words of Yahshua before he died?'... This does not show a contradiction any more than two witnesses to an accident at an intersection will come up with two different descriptions of that accident, depending on where they stood. Neither witness would be incorrect, as they describe the event from a different perspective. Luke was not a witness to the event, and so is dependent on those who were there. John was a witness. What they are both relating, however, is that at the end Yahshua gave himself up to death.

This is, of course, a very convenient way of looking at things (and I am ignoring the assertion that John was a witness here). The contradictions and omissions are so varied and so numerous that one has to think about how much of the writing was driven by agenda, how much depended upon the reliability of their sources, and how much was legendary embellishment upon previous Gospels. We already know about the numerous issues concerning the provenance of the Gospels as mentioned throughout this book. This isn't history, these aren't historical texts! These are non-eyewitness, agenda-driven, ex-post-facto-evangelising texts written decades after the events with which they are-concerned.

Luke is the only Gospel to have Jesus forgiving his tormentors.

Mark and Matthew have Jesus crying out at the end but not knowing what Jesus said.

Luke is the only Gospel to have Jesus cry out to God (as nonsensical as this might seem).

John is the only Gospel that has his followers by the cross and then Jesus talking to a disciple and his mother.

---

[1] Whitlark and Parsons (2006), p. 201.

[2] Smith, Chowdhry, Jepson & Schaeffer (n.d.).

John is also the only Gospel to have Jesus asking for a drink. The other Gospels have witnesses from afar, where hearing Jesus ask for a drink becomes somewhat problematic.

This following one may seem like a minor point but Jesus supposedly cried out loud as per the Synoptics just before he died. Physiologically, this would have been impossible. A dying man on a cross simply wouldn't have had the energy or capability to cry out just before he died. It depends how seriously you take "fully man" or whether you can just accept some supernatural element here where anything is possible.

Roman soldiers didn't permit bystanders at executions and so hearing what Jesus said and reporting it to the Gospel authors somehow (over time) seems somewhat fanciful.[1]

Concerning bystanders, theologian and bishop E.J. Tinsley observed:[2]

> The Romans did not permit bystanders at the actual place of execution. John's account is influenced by his symbolic aim. The mother (old Israel) is handed over with care of the "beloved disciple" (who represents the new Israel of the Christian Church.)

In clearly presenting a problem for Christians, this position is contested by some. But, here, German priest and New Testament scholar Rudolf Schnakenburg agrees by recognising John as being more interested in symbolism than historical accuracy:[3]

> They are standing "by the cross." Apparently near Jesus. Whether this is historically probable, since the guard would scarcely allow spectators to approach so close does not worry the evangelist; he is concerned with the deeper meaning of the scene.

So on and so forth. Problem after contradiction after discrepancy.

The sayings seem to be, in general, vehicles for theological ends for each Gospel writer. Yet again, theology not history.

The Roman Soldier, Broken legs, and Piercing Sides

Although we have a moment where, in Mark, Pilate asks for a soldier to go and confirm Jesus' death and the soldier does so (without any more detail),

---

[1] See Alter's discussion, (Alter 2015), p. 170-72.
[2] Tinsley (1965), p. 294, cf Alter (2015), p. 170.
[3] Schnakenburg (1982), p. 277, cf Alter (2015), p. 172.

the Synoptics have no mention of the breaking of legs or the piercing of sides. This only happens in John's Gospel.[1] Yet again, we have this same discrepancy (embellishment) and yet again we are looking at John adding theological overlays.

In this case, John is fulfilling prophecy and seeing Jesus as the lamb of God. For details of this, see the next chapter, as it deserves more time, space and analysis.

Judas

Judas betrayed Jesus and is definitely a figure of blame and disgrace in the story. However, what happened with Judas is thoroughly contradictory. Matthew 27:3-5 has Judas repenting, casting his money down at the temple, leaving and going to hang himself.[2]

On the other hand, Acts (with many people thinking Acts was written by the same author as the Gospel of Luke) does not have him repent and has him buying a field (some contest this, claiming it better translated as a farm or similar) with the "price of his wickedness" and him falling "headlong" where he "burst open in the middle, and all his intestines gushed out". All in Jerusalem presumably knew this incident ("And it became known to all the residents of Jerusalem"). There was no repentance, no throwing his money on the floor of the temple. There is no element of Judas choosing his own end here as he dies by an act of God – this represents a huge shift in theology and philosophy. And, yet again, we have a claim of this, as according to Acts, being an event to fulfil scriptural prophecy (Acts 1:16):

> "Brethren, the Scripture had to be fulfilled, which the Holy Spirit foretold by the mouth of David concerning Judas, who became a guide to those who arrested Jesus."

Acts 1 then states:

> 19 And it became known to all who were living in Jerusalem; so that in their own language that field was called Hakeldama, that is, Field of Blood.

The most likely explanation of this narrative addition is name aetiology (where one story is later created to attribute an origin to a name already in use).

---

[1] Well, more on this in more detail later in the chapter on prophecy.
[2] Alter (2015) extensively analyses the Judas episodes. For those seeking a detailed analysis, see p. 442-531.

This Greek name, taken from two Aramaic words meaning "field of blood", is better explained this way:[1]

> It seems to me that that was the traditional name of the area of the field of the potter in the Kidron valley because it was fertilized by the mixture of water and blood from the Temple sacrifices.

There are huge differences. Matthew and Luke/Acts diverge considerably (and even Luke from Acts).

As ever, we find attempted harmonisations from typical apologists, such that both were suicides, with perhaps the branch breaking in Acts or something similar. These are pretty desperate:

- Judas fell headfirst (his head would more likely be injured than his guts).
- If he was hanged, he would fall feet first.
- Exploding guts is more likely metaphorical.
- It's pure conjecture.

I am not going to talk about what the metaphor could be, and what this all could mean. Suffice to say that, if it was metaphor, it didn't happen. In which case, the author is making up events to fit a theological (metaphorical) reading and meaning. There are such clear contradictions that harmonising them is a step too far outside the realms of warranted rationality, for me.

Theology not history.

Now that we have a sense of the range of problems and contradictions (or, of course, "differences") concerning the events leading up to Jesus' death and just afterwards, let us now investigate some of these (at times bizarre) claims to see why they might be there. It is time to consider what the Gospel authors thought was prophecy.

---

[1] Yadin (1985), p. 134.

11 – Prophecies: Scrabbling back in Time to "Prove" the Present

This chapter will deal with a subject that doesn't actually turn up as often as it should when discussing the Resurrection narratives in skeptical contexts. We are quick to focus on the contradictions and the big supernatural claims and can forget to question why, precisely, some of the other details end up being there at all.

Right out of the gate, let me say this: if Jesus really had prophesied his death and resurrection, there would have been an awful lot of people at the tomb waiting for him and no one would have been surprised at his death or his resurrection. But there was no one waiting for him (some women were coming to anoint his body but nobody was *waiting*), and everyone was surprised to the point that hardly anyone initially believed it.

Therefore, Jesus did not prophesy his own death and resurrection. They were post hoc rationalisations by followers seeking validation. All you are left with is some puzzle that only the cleverest followers could work out long after the fact, long after Jesus was dead. But does that work to actually convert people, at the coalface, in modern society?

N.T. Wright, theologian and bishop, in his magnum opus *The Resurrection of the Son of God*, declared:[1]

> We are forced to postulate something which will account for the fact that a group of first-century Jews, who had cherished messianic hopes and centred them on Jesus of Nazareth, claimed after his death that he really was the Messiah despite the crushing evidence to the contrary.

His death was certainly evidence to the contrary, given Messianic expectations, and so many followers sought to find evidence of his death as being Messianic by looking back into the Hebrew Bible. As New Testament scholar James Crossley, a more skeptical scholar countering Wright, agrees and observes:[2]

> Wright has a point: the followers of these would-be Messiahs might well have been deluded to claim them Messiah after such spectacular defeat. But an exercise in historical imagination should not allow us to forget the historical peculiarities of a given situation. First, we should

[1] Wright (2003), p. 562.
[2] Crossley (2005), p. 172.

note that Simon bar Giora and bar Kochbah were military figures expecting military victories. Of course their deaths would be deemed as a failure. This was not the case for the historical Jesus.

Let us now discuss some philosophy before we go on to discuss biblical exegesis and theology.

The Philosophical Problems with Prophecies

In order for God to need to send Jesus down from heaven for our salvation, we needed to be pretty sinful. So, at the time of, say, Psalm 22 or Daniel (who supposedly prophesied Jesus) some 600 years before Jesus came, we had prophecies dictating that Jesus was to come and rebuild Israel and destroy the wicked, amongst other things. Leaving aside arguments over Daniel's historicity (and the timing of the writings of the Psalms), and claims that it was written in the second century BCE, it seems there was a six hundred-year time-span from the prophecy to the moment of Jesus' arrival. What this scripture implies is that, in those six hundred years, there was nothing that not just one person but the whole of humanity could do to avoid needing Jesus to come and atone for our sins. This means that all of humanity was without the possibility, without the actual ability, to be able to act in any way to divert the necessity for Jesus to atone for our sins; we were going to be evil, and that's that. We know this because it was predicted to be so, and God's predictions are infallible.

Even given Christian apologists' defences and mental contortions (see the idea that God could have something called "Middle Knowledge"), we have a scenario where we humans were still "freely" choosing to be sinful and an onus on God that he chose this world to actualise. This meant that God would *have to* send Jesus to atone for our sins. He chose the world that, even with six hundred years' forewarning, humanity would or could do nothing to avert a sinful and punishable outcome.

The difficult issue for Christians is that if one believes that this is the best possible world that God could create, then his design is a poor, since even with such foreknowledge, we would be unable to divert imminent sinfulness and resultant atonement. If we, with God's best choosing, still could not act differently, given God's foreknowledge that we wouldn't, then God simply didn't do a good enough job at designing us. If we are the apex of God's creation, as the Bible leads us to believe, then God is responsible for our design when we find ourselves unable to act in any other way than sinful enough to deserve atonement. It seems odd that, as the apex of creation, we are so poor as to constantly incur the wrath of God but that he chose this world to create, knowing full-well we would act like this! How can God be angry if he knows what is coming? If he has divine foreknowledge? If he designed, chose and created us this way?[1]

One imagines that in another possible world that God could have chosen to create, there could be a humanity that did not necessitate Jesus coming down to pay the debt for our bad behaviour and evil ways. In *that* world, humans would be better behaved, though (one would assume) would arguably have less free will. If we did have the same amount of free will and could avert the sacrifice of Jesus, then why did God not create *that* particular world for us?

In the world in which we live, Jesus supposedly knew and indicated the main perpetrator of his betrayal – Judas Iscariot – and it seems that there was nothing that Judas could do to avert his own desperate and condemned future (Luke 22:3). There was no way he would sit at the Last Supper and say, "You know what, Jesus, I'm really going to surprise you, with my ability to choose freely, and not leave the table now and report you. Instead, I quite fancy some more bread and a glug of wine. Incidentally, I am considering supporting you to the death now, in case any nasty traitors decide to report you. You've really made an impression on me, and I've had a change of heart." Unfortunately, it seems his path was chosen many years before. If he *could* have chosen otherwise, then why didn't he? I would state that Judas would have to be someone just a little bit different to have chosen differently but let's not get drawn into a full-blown free will debate.[2]

Moreover, it is vital to note that six hundred years of foreknowledge is no small undertaking. Knowing what will take place in six hundred years' time does not entail simply adding the odd thing here and there to the potion of life. Not a bit. To do that, with the massive enormity of variables that exist in the universe, you have to lay in place something *of such intricacy that it is nothing other than completely deterministic*. The classic mantra of chaos theory is that of the butterfly effect: if a butterfly flaps its wings in Brazil, it could set off a tornado in Texas. The theory entails the small variation in a system having a large effect on the variables of that system in the long term.

Given that the causal connection between events in a system can mean that the variation in initial conditions can have truly profound effects, in order to know that Jesus is to come down in about six hundred years and atone, in order to know that humans will not be able to act in any other way but evil enough to necessitate Jesus' arrival, God has to know and manage *the whole world on a micro-scale to a staggering degree*. And I mean *really manage*. Which Christians and Jews believe, according to the Hebrew Bible, as God manages the world an awful lot.

---

[1] There are many different concepts about God within Christianity, and also differences between Christianity and Judaism.

[2] These claims and debates would look different in the contest of Judaism, as opposed to Christianity.

The Hebrew Bible is filled to brimming with accounts of the times that God has intervened, interfered and got generally involved with events on Earth. This idea that God has simply chosen the world with its freely willing humans happily doing as God has actualised is somewhat negated by the fact that God spent some three thousand years or so intervening, and making sure cities got burnt here; armies got massacred there; entire tribes and nations were killed there, right down to their women, children and animals; a man was struck down there for picking up sticks on a Sabbath; or, over there, making sure that forty-two children got mauled by two bears for calling Elisha "bald".

So, for Jesus to be prophesied, God has to ensure that he has the right parents, who have to be, for prophetic reasons and reasons of Jewish authority, in the male lineage of David. This is no small organisational feat – the family line must be kept alive throughout the years. In fact, the order is taller than you might think since it is often not a case of ensuring things *do* happen, but ensuring that things *don't* happen. Mary, for example, cannot be bitten by that poisonous snake when she was twelve, must not have injured her uterus when the plough skewed into her abdomen at fourteen, must not have slipped off the wall she was walking along a week later, must not have starved due to a poverty-stricken lifestyle, must not have been miscarried, must not have contracted an early form of cancer, must not have... the list is tremendous.

And that is just for Mary, in her short life. One has to map out the entire history of the world to ensure the rest. It has to be ensured that Jesus doesn't die in some way before his time of preaching and atonement. The entire ancestral line of his parents must be preserved (well, he actually only has one parent – quite where his genetic makeup on his father's side came from, we'll never know). The Egyptians must have been in a scenario to integrate with Hebrew slaves, the surrounding empires must not have obliterated the Israelites in a major conquest, a volcanic eruption must not have wiped out the Middle East, a meteorite must not hit Earth, man must have evolved in a certain way from the original life-form. So on, and so on, to the point that, in order to ensure that Jesus would come down in the fashion predicted, some six hundred years or so later, God has to micro-manage the entire universe, and this smacks, just a little, of determinism. For something to happen with any kind of certainty later down the causal chain, God, pretty much literally, has to make the butterfly flap its wings (or not, as the case may be).

Even if God was to choose some random carrier for his child on an ad hoc basis (such that he surveyed all mothers in the Middle East and lumped for one but that it could still fulfil prophecy without *having to be Mary*), there needed to be a Middle East that looked contextually like it did in terms of the Hebrew Bible. In addition, there still needed to be receptive mothers and a father that wouldn't think she was having an affair; there still needed to be world history and the evolution of man; so on and so forth again. Such an apologetic wouldn't get the Christian off the hook. Prophecy is a real headache for a host of reasons.

There is no other way that a consistently intervening God (and these are the explicit biblically recorded interventions, not the multitudinous unknown ones that must have happened) can be explained, other than for achieving certain ends, for managing his world and universe, otherwise he would simply not have bothered intervening.

All too often, people view prophecy and foreknowledge with a relatively benign outlook, without thinking about the implications involved. The example of prophesying Jesus arriving to atone for the sins of mankind concerns itself, predominantly, with foreknowledge, but intertwined with this is the difficult idea of theological determinism. It is one thing to argue that Jesus fulfils prophecy in his birth, life and death; it is another thing entirely to show prophecy as a coherent divine mechanism. Both should be criticised. In other words, I am just about to talk skeptically about the details of the supposed instances of prophecy in the Easter story narrative, but I would argue that prophecy is wholly problematic (terminally so) before we even get to the following issues. Problems built on a foundation of incoherence.

Scourges, Piercings, Broken Bones and Other Car Crashes

If you are familiar with the Mel Gibson film *The Passion of Christ*, you will know that many people believe Jesus was scourged in a pretty horrific manner. Whether it happened to quite that extent is unknown. What do the Gospels say about what happened to him before he had to carry his own cross to his eventual crucifixion?

This is another rather bizarre story.

But it's not so bizarre if you understand why it might be incorporated into the Gospel sources.

Psalm 22 does a good job of "predicting" the casting of lots for Jesus' clothing; or, more accurately, the Gospel authors do a good job of mining the Hebrew Bible for small nuggets of "prophecy" that they could fit into the Jesus narrative to give it the seal of approval. Every detail of Jesus' death, it seems, is painstakingly extracted from the Hebrew Bible. Could it really have been contrived in such a way? Why would God have wanted himself to die in a particular way with seemingly random details just to cohere with apparently cherry-picked verses of, but not whole, Hebrew Bible psalms or chapters?

Could God have really ensured such a replication of history without constraining people's free will? Simply put, no.

Matthew 27 has this following account:

> 27 Then the soldiers of the governor took Jesus into the Praetorium and gathered the whole Roman cohort around Him. 28 They stripped Him and put a scarlet robe on Him. 29 And after twisting together a crown of

> thorns, they put it on His head, and a reed in His right hand; and they
> knelt down before Him and mocked Him, saying, "Hail, King of the
> Jews!" 30 They spat on Him, and took the reed and *began* to beat Him
> on the head. 31 After they had mocked Him, they took the *scarlet* robe
> off Him and put His *own* garments back on Him, and led Him away to
> crucify Him.
>
> 32 As they were coming out, they found a man of Cyrene named Simon, whom they pressed into service to bear His cross.
>
> 33 And when they came to a place called Golgotha, which means Place
> of a Skull, 34 they gave Him wine to drink mixed with gall; and after tasting it, He was unwilling to drink.
>
> 35 And when they had crucified Him, they divided up His garments among themselves by casting lots.

We have a record of the Roman soldiers casting lots for Jesus' clothes. Casting lots for or dividing up Jesus' clothes when he has been beaten in such a way is a pointless or gruesome exercise and it is another example of the Gospel writers not thinking things through very well in a hurry to make the Jesus narrative appear to be a midrashic exposé of the Hebrew Bible. (Midrash is the Jewish/rabbinical interpretative method of finding new meaning in a story, often using similarity of content and analogy.)

Casting lots for Jesus' clothes, as mentioned, makes little sense, until you become aware of Psalm 22:

> 15 My strength is dried up like a potsherd,
>
> And my tongue cleaves to my jaws;
>
> And You lay me in the dust of death.
>
> 16 For dogs have surrounded me;
>
> A band of evildoers has encompassed me;
>
> They pierced my hands and my feet.
>
> 17 I can count all my bones.
>
> They look, they stare at me;
>
> 18 They divide my garments among them,
>
> And for my clothing they cast lots.

This is a perfect confluence of claims! Not only do we have a prophecy of casting lots and dividing garments, but we also have people looking on and staring, and being surrounded by evildoers (criminals on the other crosses) and Jesus' feet and hands being pierced. But his bones not being broken (John 19:36[1]). Moreover, the rest of Psalm 22 has no prophetic connection to Jesus. The bones not being broken also points possibly to three other Hebrew Bible verses, too:

> Exodus 12:46
>
> It is to be eaten in a single house; you are not to bring forth any of the flesh outside of the house, **nor are you to break any bone of it.**

> Psalm 34: 19-21
>
> 19 Many are the afflictions of the righteous,
> But the Lord delivers him out of them all·
> **20 He keeps all his bones,**
> **Not one of them is broken.**
> 21 Evil shall slay the wicked,

> Zechariah 12
>
> 10 "I will pour out on the house of David and on the inhabitants of Jerusalem, the Spirit of grace and of supplication, **so that they will look on Me whom they have pierced**; and they will mourn for Him, as one mourns for an only son, and they will weep bitterly over Him like the bitter weeping over a firstborn. [My emphases.]

Psalm 22 is one of the most popular supposed Hebrew Bible prophecies fulfilled by Jesus. Appearing to have been written sometime in the 6th Century BCE, it apparently predicts a number of events and aspects, as fellow skeptic Bob Seidensticker points out:[2]

> The very first verse of this chapter is, "My God, my God, why have you forsaken me?" which are the last words of Jesus according to Matthew and Mark.

---

[1] Note that there is (as is often the case) debate between Jews and Christians pertaining to this verse, claiming it is a Christian mistranslation (e.g., changing pronouns to fit a Christian purpose).

[2] Seidensticker (2012).

> Verse 7: "All who see me mock me; they hurl insults, shaking their heads. 'He trusts in the Lord,' they say, 'Let the Lord rescue him.'" Sure enough, Mark records the onlookers insulting Jesus and mocking his inability to free himself.
>
> Verse 16: "they have pierced my hands and my feet" sounds like the crucifixion. This form of execution was practiced by many cultures in the Ancient Near East for centuries before the time of Jesus, but it probably didn't go back as far as the writing of this psalm. In that case, this verse looks prophetic.
>
> Verse 18: "They divide my garments among them and cast lots for my clothing," as noted in Mark.

John not only knew this was a prophecy fulfilment, he was very open about it (John 19):

> Pilate then took Jesus and scourged Him. 2 And the soldiers twisted together a crown of thorns and put it on His head, and put a purple robe on Him;...
>
> 23 Then the soldiers, when they had crucified Jesus, took His outer garments and made four parts, a part to every soldier and also the tunic; now the tunic was seamless, woven in one piece. 24 So they said to one another, "Let us not tear it, but cast lots for it, to decide whose it shall be"; this was to fulfill the Scripture: "They divided My outer garments among them, and for My clothing they cast lots." 25 Therefore the soldiers did these things.

This isn't a case of expecting the reader to have a good working knowledge of what would become the Hebrew Bible, it is the case of spelling things out causally: this happened *so that* a prophecy could be fulfilled. This notion of prophecy communicates the importance for God of setting out the universe in such a way that there should be a repetition of events so that people who aren't convinced enough by a man-God dying and rising into heaven as a resurrected being, actually being convinced by a prophecy fulfilment of Jesus' bloody clothes. *Now* he's the real deal.

John doesn't stop there with his theological overlay. He alone recounts the piercing of Jesus' side after they decide not to break his bones. Either the Synoptic authors were not aware of this information, or they deliberately omitted it, or it is an outright fabrication. As John recounts (John 19):

> 31 Then the Jews, because it was the day of preparation, so that the bodies would not remain on the cross on the Sabbath (for that Sabbath was

> a high day), asked Pilate that their legs might be broken, and that they
> might be taken away. 32 So the soldiers came, and broke the legs of the
> first man and of the other who was crucified with Him; 33 but coming to
> Jesus, when they saw that He was already dead, they did not break His
> legs. 34 But one of the soldiers pierced His side with a spear, and immedi-
> ately blood and water came out. 35 **And he who has seen has testified,
> and his testimony is true; and he knows that he is telling the truth, so
> that you also may believe.** 36 For these things came to pass to fulfill the
> Scripture, "NOT A BONE OF HIM SHALL BE BROKEN." 37 And again another Scrip-
> ture says, "THEY SHALL LOOK ON HIM WHOM THEY PIERCED." [My emphasis.]

I have highlighted the agenda-driven claims of John here and I want you, dear reader, to let it sink in. There is a fine line between believing things *so that* a conclusion is true and believing a conclusion *because* the previous factors are true. This is arguably a confluence of propaganda, theology and agenda. It also fits in with the exclusively Johannine theology of Jesus as the paschal lamb.

The breaking of legs (*crurifragium*) is a process used to speed up the death of the crucified. Consequently, it meant the victim would not be able to support their body weight and this would lead to difficulty in breathing. Eventually, chest muscles would become fatigued, leading to asphyxiation and an earlier death than otherwise.

One must wonder why, after knowing that Jesus was dead, the Roman soldiers still pierced his side. If they really wanted to make sure he was dead, they would have simply carried out their orders and broken his legs. It would be a Roman win-win.

John clearly has the Jews wanting to take the bodies down so they are not hanging over the Jewish holy day. The soldiers did not break Jesus' legs because he was presumably already dead. This purported incident allows Jesus to be the paschal lamb based on the Hebrew Bible ruling that the paschal lamb's legs *should not be broken*. As we saw earlier when discussing the day of the crucifixion and the Last Supper, it is only John that has the meal not as the Passover meal because the crucifixion takes its place. Jesus *himself* is the sacrificial lamb dying on the day of preparation when all the lambs are slaughtered for Passover. This information doesn't feature in any other Gospel.

One must assume that, somehow, John knows that no bones were broken from some witness who was able to attest that neither being nailed, hands and feet (wrists and ankle areas?), nor being pierced with a spear, would have broken any bones.

Andy Rau in *Bible Gateway* explains:[1]

---

[1] Rau (2012).

When God gave Moses and Aaron the rules for the Passover, some might have sounded unconventional–for example, the clear prohibition against breaking any bones of the lamb that was sacrificed and eaten by each household. Why did God insist on this?

This command–that the Passover lamb not have its legs broken–carries symbolic weight. When Jesus, whom John the Baptist proclaimed to be "the Lamb of God, who takes away the sin of the world" (John 1:29), was crucified, not one of his bones was broken. John 19:31-34 tells us that when the soldiers came to Jesus to break his legs to hasten his death, they found that he was already dead, so they pierced his side with a spear but did not break his legs. As John testifies, "These things happened so that the scripture would be fulfilled: 'Not one of his bones will be broken'" (John 19:36). The Exodus 12:46 rule is also echoed prophetically in Psalm 34:20: "He protects all his bones, not one of them will be broken." To the last detail of his death, Jesus fulfilled the prophecies concerning the Messiah, verifying that he was, as John the Baptist claimed, the sacrificial Lamb of God.

You simply can't get away from the Gospel of John, with its high Christology, being a much more theological project. But to create this theological treatise, it appears that John has to *generate* the facts (which is polite-speak for making things up); he is not somehow discovering them long after eyewitnesses have died. You either have John making things up to achieve a theological objective concerning his audience, or you have the Synoptics getting things wrong and contradicting John (or omitting very many details for completely unknown reasons leading to accusations of incoherence).

The author of John might be admitting his non-historically veridical objective rather overtly, in writing in John 20:

Why This Gospel Was Written

30 Therefore many other signs Jesus also performed in the presence of the disciples, which are not written in this book; 31 but these have been written so that you may believe that Jesus is the Christ, the Son of God; and that believing you may have life in His name.

That's a very important quote that I think warrants reading again in the present context. The question is, did these events predict the future or did later writers create events that mimicked supposed prophecies (in order to give them validation and purchase amongst their audiences)?

When Prophecies Aren't Prophecies

The problem with prophecy fulfilment, and this is something I discussed in my Nativity book, is that the Gospel authors appear to have trawled through the Hebrew Bible to look for quotes that will support their agenda (that Jesus was the Messiah, and for John more obviously, that Jesus *was* God). However, these cherry-picked verses were not, on most counts, prophetic verses.

The Exodus verses are obviously not prophetic. In reality, these verses were merely instructions on how to prepare lambs for Passover. Some analyses show that John *edits* Exodus, changing the verb tense from the aorist imperative command to the future passive indicative case for his theological ends.[1]

This misappropriation of verses for prophecy is just as much the case for Psalm 34. The idea that this psalm "foreshadows" Jesus' crucifixion is not warranted. As Michael J. Alter observes: [2]

> There is absolutely no indication that Psalm 34 is intended as prophetic.... Furthermore, there is no indication that Psalm 34 applied to Jesus. The theme of Psalm 34 is that the righteous man is saved from the wicked. When the wicked attempt to impose suffering on this righteous man, they could not break any of his bones because God protected him. Not only was this righteous man protected, but also the wicked are slain. In contrast, Jesus was not saved, and the wicked, the Romans, were not slain. Finally, nothing is mentioned about the Messiah being killed. In short, Psalm 34 has nothing to do with Jesus.

There has also been much criticism (particularly from Jewish scholars) concerning the mistranslations that the Gospel authors and biblical compilers have committed to in order to shoehorn in prophecies of Jesus that simply do not do the job desired if understood in proper context and with accurate translations.[3]

Let us now look in more detail at whether each of the supposed prophetic verses were prophecies or prophetic in nature.

Zechariah 12

As far as Zechariah 12 is concerned, it talks about the final onslaught of all nations on Jerusalem, with the "piercing" of Yahweh being mourned as one would mourn the loss of an only son or, indeed, a firstborn son (thus

[1] Waetjen (2005), p. 405-6, cf. Alter (2015), p. 178.
[2] Alter (2015), p.181.
[3] There are many books and articles examining this. One looking just at Isaiah 53 is Roth (n.d.)

highlighting perhaps the cherry-picking of the only son to refer to Jesus). The mourning is then compared to the death of King Josiah, spreading from Jerusalem to the entire land, referencing different clans, and husbands and wives. In the Gospels, we have very few people mourning Jesus' death. Indeed, many Jews (priests, elders, scribes) seem particularly happy about it, mocking him in the process, and then going to Pilate after his death and calling him a "deceiver". There is no mention of Jesus' disciples or other followers mourning him at all, neither in the Gospels, nor in Acts.

Much of Zechariah 12 has the prophet saying God will defend his people, and yet in the forty years after Jesus' death, the Holy Land continued to be occupied and Jerusalem was laid siege and then utterly destroyed (including the holiest of places, the Temple) in 70 CE.

Zechariah 14 later states that the Lord will rescue Israel in that day. This does not happen in any way related to Jesus and his time period. One must also realise that Israel was under Roman occupation and not under attack from "all the nations of the earth".

In fact, if you read through Zechariah 12-14 verse by verse, you will be left with absolutely no doubt that this completely refers to something other than the (life and) death of Jesus. God did not destroy the enemies of Israel after Jesus' death but actually oversaw Israel's occupation, and Jerusalem and its Temple being destroyed with hundreds of thousands of Jews being murdered. Thomas Ice, of (the Christian) Liberty University, declared in his piece writing against *preterism*[1] (and its worth reading his whole analysis on Zechariah and how it *cannot* refer to Jesus):[2]

> Because of the differences between the above contrasted passages, it is impossible to harmonise with events that have already taken place. Impossible as long as two plus two continues to equal four.

There is no way one can relate Zechariah in any way to the destruction of Jerusalem and, without that, you cannot hope to relate it to prophesying Jesus.

But it's not just Jerusalem that it doesn't prophesy. There is a whole raft of claims that make no sense in the context of Jesus (and that are arguably yet to happen). Out of the dozen or so claims, God will remove the land of unclean spirits; will remove from the land two-thirds of the people (who will then die); the living waters will flow out of Jerusalem, half to the eastern sea, half to the western; God will punish all the nations who do not go up to keep the Festival of the Booths; and so on.

---

[1] *Preterism* is the position that Ancient Israel finds its continuation or fulfilment in the Christian church at the destruction of Jerusalem in 70 CE.

[2] Ice (2009).

This is, as ever, the tip of the iceberg. There is a massive amount of lexical and linguistic analysis (including lots of mistranslated pronouns) to show that Zechariah cannot refer to Jesus, the Roman soldiers or anything to do with the Resurrection.[1]

This is a prophecy fail.

Psalms 22 & 69

Psalm 22 can be easily picked to pieces for its supposed prophetic value and I have already discussed some of the issues earlier in this chapter. However, it is also worth mentioning several noteworthy passages:

> 16 For dogs have surrounded me;
>
> A band of evildoers has encompassed me;
>
> They pierced my hands and my feet.

This verse is better translated as (according to an in-depth analysis in *Net Bible*): [2]

> 16 Yes, wild dogs surround me–
>
> a gang of evil men crowd around me;
>
> like a lion they pin my hands and feet.

Indeed, the entry on this single line in the commentary at *Net Bible* shows you what a very intricate process it is correctly translating texts, and this would equally have applied to John, the other Gospel authors and Septuagint (all written in Greek):[3]

> **tc** The Masoretic text reads "like a lion, my hands and my feet." The reading is difficult and the ancient versions vary, so the textual difficulty is probably very early. Without a verb, the syntax appears broken and the role of "hands and feet" unclear. One option is to understand the verb of the previous line to apply again, a poetic technique called ellipsis and double duty. But "my hands and feet" would be an odd object for a verb meaning "they encircled." Otherwise, the broken syntax may represent the emotional outcry of the Psalmist, first mentioning the lion

---

[1] See Alter (2015) and his exhaustive analysis, Chapter 4: Zechariah 12, p. 188-205.

[2] Psalm 22, *Net Bible*, https://netbible.org/bible/Psalms+22

[333] Ibid.

> as part of the third person description, but suddenly shifting to the first person perspective and crying out as the lion attacks, pinning down his hands and feet (a scene depicted in ancient Near Eastern art). But this development seems late textually. All the other witnesses have a verb instead of "like a lion." The LXX says "they dug my hands and feet; the verb ὀρύσσω (orussō) means "to burrow in the ground, to dig." A Qumran witness seems to read similarly, "they dug." Instead of the MT's כארי (k[e]'ariy; like a lion"), the scroll from Nahal Hever has a verb form כארו (ka'aru) ending with vav instead of yod. Supposing that the א ('aleph) is a superfluous spelling variant, the form would be understood as כרו (karu) from the root כרה (karah), meaning "they dug." In that case, the Qumran scroll and the LXX agree because כרה is one of the two verbs translated inn the LXX by ὀρύσσω. But as both these verbs mean "to dig [in the dirt]" this has not helped us understand the context. Assuming that the enemies are still the subject, we might expect "they dug a pit for my hands and feet." In fact the Hebrew words behind "they dug a pit" look similar (כרו בור) so it is not hard to imagine that one of these two would be overlooked by a scribed [sic] and dropped from the text. Some suppose that "to dig [in the ground]" means "to pierce" in reference to hands and feet (possibly from the root כור). Other variants and suggestions include "they bound," or "they picked clean" (from אָרָה, 'arah, "to pluck") my hands and feet. Or "my hands and feet are consumed," or "worn out." The latter two assume a copying error of resh for lamed, making the verb come from כלה. P. Craigie (*Psalms* [WBC], 1:196) opts for this last but also cites Syriac and Akkadian for additional root K-R-H meaning "to be shrunken, shriveled." The Akkadian verb (karu) is said of body parts and can refer to paralysis, which is the kind of metaphor which occurs in battle contexts elsewhere (e.g. Ps 76:5). It would be very natural to read "my hands and my feet" as the subject of the verb because verb-subject is typical word order. There is no decisive answer to the problem and the NET translation includes the lion imagery (cf. v. 13) and supposes a verb that conveys an attack.

I wouldn't normally have included such a large and analytical quote but it does give the reader an idea of the importance of translations and translating correctly. Because, with a more accurate reading, the claims concerning Jesus and the so-called prophecies evaporate into meaninglessness and nonsensical events or an *ex post facto* theological embellishment by the Gospel authors.

Bob Seidensticker looks at Jesus' last words in the context of Gnosticism, an early Christian belief system to which we will later return:[1]

---

[1] Seidensticker (2012).

> Let's reconsider those last words: "My God, why have you forsaken me?" Does forsaking Jesus sound like part of God's plan? This doesn't sound like the cool-headed, in-control Jesus written about in Luke and John.
>
> What it sounds like is Gnosticism (not in the Psalm, but when transplanted into the gospels). The Gnostic Gospel of Philip (third century) explains it this way, "'My God, My God, why, Lord, have you forsaken me?' [Jesus] spoke these words on the cross, for he had left that place." That is, Christ the god entered Jesus the man at baptism (remember the dove?) but then abandoned Jesus at the crucifixion.

Jesus' words can be seen in broadly three different ways:[1]

(1) Jesus repeated the words from Psalm 22 because he had previously read them and for some reason wanted to repeat them near his death.
(2) Jesus repeated the words from Psalm 22 because it was a prophecy and, in this way, he was *bound* to repeat them, asking questions of free will and why this would be desired.
(3) The Gospel writer wrote Jesus as saying these words recorded in the Psalm to suggest a prophecy for theological reasons, but he didn't actually say those things.

The larger problem is that when you look at the whole of Psalm 22, *in its entirety*, it makes no sense as a prophecy of Jesus and his life or death. The Gospel authors (here, John, but even if John's use originally depends on previous Gospel writers) like to quote-mine, to cherry-pick their way through larger chapters or sections in order to find the diamonds that they need, so to set them into the Jesus story. Not only can the rest of the verses in Psalm 22 be seen as nonsensical in relation to Jesus, but also we see no mention of the Resurrection at all! We are receiving prophecy of minor elements of the story, but when it comes to actual resurrection and ascension into heaven, the so-called prophecy is silent.

One response to Seidensticker's article was telling of apologist approaches and reeks of both cognitive dissonance and post hoc rationalisation (looking for reasoning and evidence to fit a belief *already* adhered to):

> [Bob Seidensticker], you have absolutely no idea how prophecy works or is written, you've proven that only prophecy, unlike general doctrine, is scattered throughout the old testament, not highlighted by a chapter at a time, it is mixed in between verses.

[1] Ibid., adapted.

So pointing out that these chapters are not prophetic of Jesus as a whole because they make no sense of Jesus' life is disingenuous since prophecies should only be seen in terms of individual lines written here and there throughout the Hebrew Bible?

On this logic, I could predict my own life by sifting through any old book that predates me and cherry picking a sentence here and a sentence there.

The same commenter writes:

> Isaiah 7:14 Therefore the Lord himself shall give you a sign; Behold, a virgin shall conceive, and bear a son, and shall call his name Immanuel.
>
> Who is this describing...?

For the Christian, there is only one option when they see something that is written before the life of Jesus that has elements of Jesus' life: that these excerpts foreshadowed and predicted Jesus' life. Of course, the skeptic points out the rather obvious alternative reading: that the later writers quote-mined elements of previous holy writing to add these details into Jesus' life. That Jesus was born from a virgin and was named Immanuel by angels does not reflect the predictive nature of the Hebrew Bible, but the quote-mining legendary embellishments of the New Testament. They "named" Jesus Immanuel *from* this excerpt!

Again, it must be asked: what is the most likely explanation of the data? As a Christian, when you read such prophecy *in other religions*, what do you hypothesise? Do you conclude straight away that all instances of prophecy are correct? If you apply skeptical metrics to *another* religion, why do you not apply the same metrics to *yours*?

If you really have to work that hard to make your religion make sense, to harmonise everything, then perhaps your religion isn't all it's cracked up to be. Or, as Seidensticker himself responds in his article to another Christian seeking to harmonise Hebrew Bible prophecy with New Testament Gospel claims:

> The punch line is that I have a far, far higher standard for the ability of an omniscient god to prophesy than you do. That tells me that you're reading into the chapter what you want, not reading out of it what is there.

Many apologists defer to the dual application of prophecy. That is, it can be applied to the original person (say, in Isaiah 53, it is Ahaz) but that it *then* applies to Jesus *as well*. There is no evidence from the writers themselves that this was their intention and only looks to be "a thing" when trying to argue that Hebrew Bible prophecies really do also predict Jesus.

Christian-turned-atheist author John Loftus sums it all up rather well in his chapter "The Resurrection of Jesus Never Took Place" in his anthology "*The Case Against Miracles*:[1]

> But there is literally nothing about Psalms 22 or 69 that have anything to do with the sufferings of a Messiah, much less about Jesus. Contextually these two Psalms are prayers of someone who is suffering and asking for God's help, even though they are misapplied in the Gospel stories of the trial and crucifixion of Jesus (Matt. 27:34, 35, 43, 46). The way they are used looks exactly as if the details about the death of Jesus were created from them. The same thing goes for the suffering servant of Isaiah 53, which describes the sufferings of Israel, god's servant (see Isaiah 49:3 for the context). There's nothing in the Old Testament about a suffering Messiah. It cannot be found. That's why the Jews rightly rejected Jesus as their Messiah.

All of these points, as Loftus concludes, apply to Psalm 69 as much as they do to Psalm 22.

Matthew's Spear Piercing

Here's a problem, no matter which way you look at it. Most Bible translations omit a verse from Matthew (27:49) that seems to be pretty important. The Synoptics don't recount anything to do with a Roman soldier and a spear unless we look at older manuscripts:[2]

> The three synoptic gospels (Matthew, Mark and Luke) do not mention the incident, while John addresses it *after* Jesus "gave up His spirit" (19:30). Where is the controversy?
>
> The contention arises from *a verse that is not even there*! The King James Version leaves out the last part of Matthew 27:49, though it is present in the most ancient manuscripts: "And another took a spear, and thrust it into His side, and out came water and blood." The Moffatt and Fenton translations both include this additional material. What makes it controversial is where these words appear: just *before* Jesus "yielded up His spirit" (verse 50). Which is right?

---

[1] Loftus (2020), p. 500.

[2] "When Was Jesus Stabbed by the Roman Soldier (John 19:34)?", *Church of the Great God,* https://www.cgg.org/index.cfm/library/bqa/id/233/when-was-jesus-stabbed-by-roman-soldier-john-1934.htm (Retrieved 28/11/2020).

However, the source above pleads that the two accounts are harmonisable, that Matthew's spear thrust was before and John's was after Jesus' death, by simply having the translation (concerning tenses) of John as "But one of the soldiers *had pierced* His side with a spear, and immediately blood and water *had come out.*"

Dirk Jongkind at *Evangelical Textual Criticism* gives a fairly honest appraisal of whether the addition in the "earliest and best manuscripts" should be kept or not:[1]

> On external evidence, the addition has definitely a very good shout. Or, to put it in the short-hand principles behind the THGNT [Tyndale House Greek New Testament], "In light of the external evidence, do we have good reason not to print the reading of the 'earliest and best manuscripts'?" And indeed, this is one of those high-profile cases where I think that the transcriptional and internal reasons outweigh the external evidence. We should beware of treating any group of manuscripts as so reliable that we ignore what stares us in the face.

In other words, there are reasons of harmony and coherence that outweigh the external (textual etc.) reasons as to why the addition should be left out. But he continues:

> However, is there any way we can bolster the argument for the inclusion of the addition? Obviously, if original, the removal of the extra words may solve a problem in the sequence of events in comparison to the other gospels: Jesus did not die because of the spear thrust and neither should the text give any suggestion as such. Therefore, the shorter text provides a less difficult reading.

And this quote admits the convenience of ignoring this additional verse. Jongkind continues:

> And then there is Dan Gurtner, in the recent Holmes *Festschrift* (who does an excellent job of discussing the versional evidence). He is also bold enough to put the suggestion forward that it is perhaps John who is editing the original text of Matthew and places it at a different, more appropriate location in his narrative. However, ultimately this possibility (I don't think Dan proposes the originality of the longer text of 27:49) raises so many other problems that the simpler conclusion of influence of parallel accounts is preferable over any complex, redactional

[1] Jongkind (2018).

> theory.... The 'best and earliest manuscripts' do not always present us with the 'best and earliest readings'.

Of course, as an evangelical, he will have a great interest in there not being substantial and lasting issue regarding internal contradictory Gospel claims. The paper by Dan Gurtner, referenced above, is a fair and balanced analysis, including:[1]

> The importance of the variant lies not simply in the connection of a Johannine tradition with the Matthean Passion Narrative, but also in the potentially embarrassing placement of the incident prior to Jesus' death. This placement not only contradicts the Johannine tradition but also the tradition that the crucifixion–not the spear thrust–caused the death of Jesus. In the early fourteenth century a dispute arose as to whether the water and blood issued from Christ before or after his death. Given the importance of these elements as symbols for baptism and the eucharist, it received pointed attention under Pope Clement V at the Council of Vienne. A certain Ubertino da Casala cites a Latin manuscript in support of the Spiritual Franciscans' advocacy of the Matthean, pre-death reading.

Which is to say (and why bother devoting so much time to such a small quote that's most often not there?) that the issue is not solved. Evidence goes both ways and this Matthean verse is redacted in most translations even though it is in the "earliest and best manuscripts". Can we trust the Christian Bible, the translations, the interpretations of people with an agenda, evidenced over time to the highest levels of the Christian churches? Why do the Gospels continually contradict (or "differ from") each other? Is this data better supported by the thesis that the Gospels accurately and truthfully portray supernatural events that they did not witness, or by the thesis that these are ex post facto, agenda-driven accounts written with unknown sources by people who weren't interested in the accurate recounting of historical events?

Blood and Water

Now that I have exorcised some musings and urges for textual criticism, let us return to the blood and water that streamed forth from Jesus' pierced, dead body, continuing in the same vein (pun intended) as the biblical content of the previous section.

---

[1] Gurtner et al (2015), p.135.

The first issue here is how on earth anyone would know about this event or the details? Who would be there to both witness and be able to recognise that both blood and water came out of Jesus' body, especially given the prohibition of close witnesses (certainly at any here meaningful proximity) at crucifixions, and the claim that his followers had scattered? The soldiers were there, as per the text, and so the rules would have been enforced. The only other explanation being that the soldier *was* the source of this information.

Given that there is supposedly one piercing, blood and water would have mingled on exit and in pooling. Really think about the practical considerations here: this really has to be a legendary and theological embellishment.

Why blood and water? Well, several explanations have been given[1] (showing that there is no theological clarity to the event anyway), that it represents...

- The Spirit flowing from Jesus' body.
- A duality: his baptism of water and baptism of blood.
- From Ezekiel 47:1-2, life-giving water flowing from the new Temple.
- The dispensation of the Temple.
- Proof that Jesus died fully human.
- A counter-apologetic to claims that Jesus never really died.
- Proof that he died considering it had been a short crucifixion in John's Gospel.
- Nothing but an actual physiological phenomenon at death: the spear pierced the heart and the lungs causing the pericardial effusion and the pleural effusion to stream out.

The blood and water is definitely something theological. Of this I am certain, though it is rather meaningless if future readers are unable to access the theology that was intended by the writer!

Having said this, remember the *Got Questions* quote concerning Jesus supposedly collapsing and this being "evidenced" in the Gospel narratives? Well, to continue their rather physiological analysis, they conclude:[2]

> Prior to death, the sustained rapid heartbeat caused by hypovolemic shock also causes fluid to gather in the sack around the heart and around the lungs. This gathering of fluid in the membrane around the heart is called pericardial effusion, and the fluid gathering around the

[1] By a number of apologists and exegetes as summarised in Alter (2015), p. 186, adapted and added to.

[2] "Why did blood and water come out of Jesus' side when He was pierced?", (n.d.), *Got Questions*, https://www.gotquestions.org/blood-water-Jesus.html

> lungs is called pleural effusion. This explains why, after Jesus died and a Roman soldier thrust a spear through Jesus' side, piercing both the lungs and the heart, blood and water came from His side just as John recorded in his Gospel (John 19:34).

Although I make a claim that this episode, to me, speaks of a theological overlay, here we have an apologetics website paring it back to a physiological core, that the blood and water can be explained literally and medically. History, not theology.

Take your pick because there is no way John would have any evidence or source for this anyway. It's not history, at any rate.

Hosea

Finally, let us look rather quickly at Hosea 6:2, and another opportunity for the Gospel authors to quote-mine from the Hebrew Bible (as now is):

> He will revive us after two days;
>
> He will raise us up on the third day,
>
> That we may live before Him.

And there you have the tradition of Jesus rising on the third day as we see in the 1 Corinthians 15 creed. A tradition, mind you, that seems rather absent in (the interpolated) Mark, who has Jesus rising on the first day of the week. However, such a reading is not as sound as it may appear, as *Ellicott's Commentary for English Readers* points out:[1]

> **In the third day**–i.e., after a short time. This and the above expression are not identical in the designation of time. Some Christian interpreters (Jerome, Luther, Pusey) consider the passage has sole reference to the resurrection of Christ. But with Calvin, Henderson, Schmoller, &c., we consider this to be contradicted by the form of the expression. To bring in the resurrection of Christ with no authority from the New Testament is far-fetched over-refinement, and breaks the consistency of the passage.

[1] "Hosea 6:2", *Ellicott's Commentary for English Readers* as detailed on *Bible Hub*, https://biblehub.com/commentaries/hosea/6-2.htm (Retrieved 17/12/2020).

Yom Kippur

I will include the idea that the story is a metaphor for Yom Kippur in this section, even though it is not a prophecy: it seems to fit well here.

Yom Kippur is one of the most popular Jewish celebrations throughout the year, known as the Day of Atonement (which should raise eyebrows when considering Jesus died as atonement). The purpose was to undergo individual and collective purification by forgiveness and repentance of sins.

Before the destruction of the Temple in Jerusalem, a sacrificial ceremony involving the high priest took place in the Holy of Holies. This entailed confessing his own sins, the sins of priests, and the sins of all Israel. He was clothed in white linen and entered the Holy of Holies, something only allowed at Yom Kippur. Here, he sprinkled the blood of the sacrifice and offered incense.

The key to the whole ceremony (in terms of our analysis) is then what happened: two goats were selected for two different outcomes. One goat (the "scapegoat"), symbolically carrying the sins of Israel, was driven to its death in the wilderness. The other goat (the immolated goat – the "goat to Yahweh") was consecrated to God. The goats were supposed to be alike, as twins: the commandment required that the two goats be identical in appearance, size, and value. These would appear as twins – the same on the outside – but with different destinies.

There have been different views on which goat is represented by whom in the Resurrection narrative, as discussed by Hans Moscicke in the excellent "Jesus as Goat of the Day of Atonement in Recent Synoptic Gospels Research".[1]

You could present arguments to support Barabbas being set free by Pilate as the scapegoat, but likewise Jesus as the scapegoat, carrying away the sins of Israel. Were Jesus and Barabbas alike, as twin goats? Moscicke details an evaluation that includes:[2]

> Even if Origen's statement (on Matt 27:16-18) that some [manuscripts] of St Matthew in his day read 'Jesus Barabbas' as opposed to 'Jesus called Christ', be not relied on, here yet remains a very singular coincidence of name between the two. Barabbas, son of the Father, stands in a remarkable antithesis to the Son of man, who claimed God as his Father.

Indeed, the analysis shows Matthew's interest in Jewish holy books and customs, such that the narrative follows Yom Kippur as such:

---

[1] Moscicke (2018).

[2] Ibid., p. 68.

> (A) There are two subjects (the two goats and the two prisoners; Mt. 27.17, 21)
>
> (B) One subject is released and the other is put to death (Mt. 27.26)
>
> (C) The two subjects are exact counterparts of each other (Mt. 27.16, 19)
>
> (D) Both subjects are similar in appearance (Mt. 27.16-17) (E) Both rituals include a confession and transference of sin (Mt. 27.24-25)

Although biblical scholar John Dominic Crossan has a slightly different view of the interpretation of Yom Kippur through the Easter story, Moscicke presents Crossan's analysis of the development of the Easter story, and I think it is absolutely spot on:[1]

> Crossan argues (1985: 125-81; 1988: 156-57; 1991: 375-76) that the passion tradition evolved through three primary stages: (P1) the historical passion, (P2) the prophetic passion, and (P3) the narrative passion. During P1, Jesus was crucified, but his earliest followers knew none of the details of his execution. During P2, Jesus' disciples interpreted the meaning of his death in light of the Old Testament, but they did so without reference to the particular details of the passion events. During P3, Jesus' followers organized this complex array of scriptural proof-texts into a coherent and sequential narrative, refining and augmenting the story with verisimilar historical detail.

And this is what we see in the embellishment together with increase in theological complexity of the Gospels. I believe that the narrative was eventually created and/or moulded to fit the theological agendas desired by the different authors.

Helmut Koester built upon Crossan's thesis, pointing out some striking similarities between the Yom Kippur tradition and the Easter narrative, and with reference to the Epistle of Barnabas, written somewhere between 70-130 CE:[2]

> [Koester affirms the] incorporation of the 'royal mocking' motif (pp. 224-25). The Jewish tradition of spitting upon the scapegoat (Barn. 7.8) established a bridge to Isa. 50.6...and the supposed Jewish tradition of piercing (κατακεντέω) the scapegoat (Barn. 7.8) created a link to Zech. 12.10 (pp. 224-25).... Once the scapegoat typology was firmly established, Koester suggests that the passion tradition evolved to integrate

[1] Ibid., p. 61.

[2] Ibid. p. 62-63.

> the theme of royal mockery by means of the following motifs: (A) tying a piece of scarlet wool around the scapegoat's head (Barn. 7.8); (B) placing the scarlet band among thorns (Barn. 7.11); and (C) (possibly) piercing the scapegoat (1990: 224-25; Barn. 7.8). Christian tradents blended these motifs with the theme of royal mocking, and they became: (A′) the purple/scarlet robe placed upon Jesus (Mk 15.17; Mt. 27.28); (B′) the crown woven from thorns (Mk 15.17; Mt. 27.29); and (C′) the reed placed in Jesus' right hand as a mock scepter (Mt. 27.29; cf. Mk 15.19). The Synoptic Gospels finally incorporated this combined tradition.... Lastly, Koester suggests (1990: 225) that Matthew utilized an older christological goat typology independently from Mark. Thus, Mt. 27.28 changes the purple (πορφύρα) garment of Mk 15.17 to a scarlet (κόκκινος) garment to correspond to the scapegoat's scarlet attire, conforming to the tradition preserved in Barn. 7.8. Similarly, Mt. 27.34 and 27.48 preserve the elements of vinegar (ὄξος) and gall (χολή) that were used in the older typology of Jesus as immolated goat retained in Barn. 7.4-5. This passage in Barnabas draws a correspondence between (A) a Jewish custom in which the priests are to eat the intestines of the immolated goat unwashed with vinegar, and (A′) the sacrificial death of Jesus, who was offered gall mixed with vinegar at his crucifixion, and the consumption of his body in the Eucharist. While Mk 15.36 and Lk. 23.36 only transmit the tradition concerning vinegar (ὄξος), Mt. 27.34 includes the tradition involving gall (χολή; cf. Mk 15.23) to conform to an earlier tradition that interpreted Ps. 69.21 (Ps. 68.22 lxx) in light of the immolated goat typology (Koester 1990: 227-30; see Barn. 7.5; Gos. Pet. 5.16).

There is an incredible preponderance of Gospel authors shoehorning in aspects of tradition to the Resurrection narrative in exactly the same way we have seen in the rest of this chapter in terms of prophecy, severely casting doubt on claims of historical accuracy.

We will return to prophecies again when considering Joseph of Arimathea in the next chapter. For now, here endeth the section of the book leading up to the death of Jesus. Next, we will start to examine what happened to Jesus in the days following his death on the cross.

So far, it looks like the whole project for the biblical authors has been to take or develop theology and write a story that best fits and evokes that theology in ways that are most effective for their audiences.

Theology not history.

12 – Joseph of Arimathea – Fact Or Fiction? Fiction…

Joseph of Arimathea was often used by Christian apologist and successful debater William Lane Craig as a pillar of his truth claims for the Resurrection, itself one of the four cornerstones of his apology. It is interesting that Craig appears to no longer reference Joseph of Arimathea in his debates. This decision is quite possibly as a result of the weakness of any positive evidence and the strength of negative evidence for the historicity of this most interesting of biblical characters.

Craig has previously stated:[1] "It is unlikely that the Christian tradition would invent a fictional character and place him on the historical council of the Sanhedrin."

I contest this opinion for the following reasons.

An Embellished Man and a Literary Mechanism

He is one of the most well-known figures in the New Testament. Well known, yet strangely very little is *actually known* about him. In reality, Joseph of Arimathea is an elusive figure. He is purported in all four gospels to have buried Jesus' body in his own[2] empty, rock-hewn tomb. Here are the four accounts:

> Mark 15:
>
> 43 Joseph of Arimathea came, a prominent member of the Council, who
> himself was waiting for the kingdom of God; and he gathered up cour-
> age and went in before Pilate, and asked for the body of Jesus. 44 Pilate
> wondered if He was dead by this time, and summoning the centurion,
> he questioned him as to whether He was already dead. 45 And ascer-
> taining this from the centurion, he granted the body to Joseph. 46
> Joseph bought a linen cloth, took Him down, wrapped Him in the linen
> cloth and laid Him in a tomb which had been hewn out in the rock; and
> he rolled a stone against the entrance of the tomb. 47 Mary Magdalene
> and Mary the mother of Joseph were looking on to see where He was
> laid.

---

[1] Craig (1985), p. 674.

[2] In Mark, notice it is not denoted as how "own" tomb, but just "a" tomb – this becomes an embellishment.

Matthew 27:

57 When it was evening, there came a rich man from Arimathea, named Joseph, who himself had also become a disciple of Jesus. 58 This man went to Pilate and asked for the body of Jesus. Then Pilate ordered it to be given to him. 59 And Joseph took the body and wrapped it in a clean linen cloth, 60 and laid it in his own new tomb, which he had hewn out in the rock; and he rolled a large stone against the entrance of the tomb and went away. 61 And Mary Magdalene was there, and the other Mary, sitting opposite the grave.

Luke 23:

50 And a man named Joseph, who was a member of the Council, a good and righteous man 51 (he had not consented to their plan and action), a man from Arimathea, a city of the Jews, who was waiting for the kingdom of God; 52 this man went to Pilate and asked for the body of Jesus. 53 And he took it down and wrapped it in a linen cloth, and laid Him in a tomb cut into the rock, where no one had ever lain. 54 It was the preparation day, and the Sabbath was about to begin. 55 Now the women who had come with Him out of Galilee followed, and saw the tomb and how His body was laid. 56 Then they returned and prepared spices and perfumes.

John 19:

38 After these things Joseph of Arimathea, being a disciple of Jesus, but a secret one for fear of the Jews, asked Pilate that he might take away the body of Jesus; and Pilate granted permission. So he came and took away His body. 39 Nicodemus, who had first come to Him by night, also came, bringing a mixture of myrrh and aloes, about a hundred pounds weight. 40 So they took the body of Jesus and bound it in linen wrappings with the spices, as is the burial custom of the Jews. 41 Now in the place where He was crucified there was a garden, and in the garden a new tomb in which no one had yet been laid. 42 Therefore because of the Jewish day of preparation, since the tomb was nearby, they laid Jesus there.

Notice how, as I have put these in order of chronological priority, Joseph becomes a little more upright and overt follower of Jesus as the accounts develop. This evolution continues in the non-canonical accounts such as the Gospel of Nicodemus in the Acts of Pilate (in which Joseph is arrested for burying Jesus), until Joseph is embellished to the point of mythical legend where he eventually came to Britain (Glastonbury, of all places) and got thoroughly involved with the Holy Grail and King Arthur! Although later legends do not invalidate earlier historical claims about Joseph, it does mean that you have to draw a somewhat arbitrary line when deciding what is historical and what is not, reflecting that holistic arbitrary line drawn between the "obviously legendary" non-canonical Gospels and the "surely historically accurate" canonical Gospels...

He starts off being merely a pious Sanhedrin member before eventually becoming a secret follower of Jesus. However, there is an oddity in that Mark explicitly states Joseph is a Council member, and Luke is the only other Gospel author to recount this claim: neither Matthew nor John deem this an important fact to include. Or they are correcting Mark's original assertion?

Biblical scholars Marcus Borg and John Dominic Crossan in *The Last Week* state:[1]

> The story of Jesus's burial by Joseph grows in the other gospels. In Mark, Joseph is not described as a follower of Jesus, but at most might be viewed as a sympathizer. Matthew calls him "a disciple of Jesus" (27:57). Luke does not call Joseph a disciple, but adds that he was "a good and righteous man who had not agreed" with the council's condemnation of Jesus (23:50-51). To Mark's account, Matthew adds that it was Joseph's own tomb and new (27:60). Though Luke does not say it was Joseph's tomb, he does say that it was new: no one had ever yet been laid in it (23:53). John also says that the tomb was new, and that Nicodemus (mentioned only in John) assisted Joseph and brought a hundred pounds of myrrh and aloes, an enormous amount of spices (19:38- 42). In John, Jesus is in effect given a royal burial.

When researching and writing my book on the Nativity, it became very apparent that the Gospel writers (well, at least Matthew and Luke) were not averse to using characters as literary vehicles or mechanisms to achieve certain ends. Herod, for Matthew, was a vehicle to get Jesus to Egypt so that he could come out of Egypt and thus fulfil a Hebrew Bible prophecy. In direct contrast, Luke has no such event and has Jesus returning to Nazareth via the Temple of Jerusalem. Herod is essentially utilised as an incarnation of the Pharaoh to allow Jesus to be a newly remastered Moses. In this context, we should be able to see that Joseph of Arimathea is a similar sort of literary mechanism, a means to an end.[2]

---

[1] Borg & Crossan (2008), p. 153.

[2] At this point, it is worth pointing the reader in the direction of the two papers by William John Lyons: "On the Life and Death of Joseph of Arimathea" (Lyons 2004) and "The Hermeneutics

One can easily come away from the Gospels, particularly John, thinking that Joseph was a dedicated follower of Jesus. However, this interpretation would be a charitable reading of Mark, the earliest source, who says he is a "respected council member who was also himself awaiting the kingdom of God". As even Raymond Brown agrees, this probably just means that he was a pious Sanhedrin member who wanted to carry out the Jewish Law in accordance with his Jewish beliefs. This account gets embellished to recounting Joseph as being someone who strongly favours Jesus and who is a secret follower of him.

If Joseph had been merely a pious Sanhedrin member, then would he really have been running around getting Jewish criminals buried on time, or would he have relied on the Roman authorities to do what was expected of them if this was a commonplace occurrence? The Romans would actually have been in a better position to carry out the burial "since they would not have acquired ritual impurity thereby", especially concerning a person who would "only be commonly perceived as crucified scum, the Galilean just as much as the highwaymen".[1]

On the other hand, if Joseph was truly a disciple of Jesus, then it is odd that he does not work in cooperation at all with the disciples or the women who come to the tomb to anoint the body. He has no interactions with anyone at all. He simply disappears. This leads one to favour Mark's account that he was just a pious council member. Raymond Brown concurs:[2]

> No canonical gospel shows cooperation between Joseph and the women followers of Jesus who are portrayed as present at the burial, observing where Jesus was put (Mark 15:47 and par.). Lack of cooperation in burial between the two groups of Jesus's disciples is not readily intelligible, especially when haste was needed. Why did the woman not help Joseph if he was a fellow disciple, instead of planning to come back after the Sabbath when he would not be there?

This quotation is powerful reasoning, in my opinion, and helps to illustrate what appears to be a contradiction between Mark and the other Gospels. One should not take Raymond Brown's conclusions lightly! If Joseph was a secret follower of Jesus, he seems to have absolutely no connection to any other member of the nascent Jesus sect, which rather raises the question as to how he would be such a follower if this were the case.

---

of Fictional Black and Factual Red: The Markan Simon of Cyrene and the Quest for the Historical Jesus" (Lyons 2006).

[1] Kirby in Price & Lowder (2005), p. 244, with reference to the fact that Galilee was looked down upon by people of Jerusalem (as evidenced in John 1 and John 8).

[2] Brown (1994), p. 1218.

There seems to be no sense to make of Joseph of Arimathea, whether he was merely a pious Sanhedrin member with no connection to Jesus or if he was an actual follower as the later Gospels intimate. He was a literary mechanism, as Peter Kirby explains in "Roman Crucifixion and Jewish Burial":[1]

> ... Joseph has all the signs of *deus ex machina* in the Markan plot. Jesus has been abandoned by his disciples, convicted by the Sanhedrin, and executed by Pilate. Yet along comes the noble knight riding in from Arimathea, daring to ask Pilate to be able to meddle in his affairs, disregarding the prohibition on honorable burial for the condemned, and providing proper interment in his own newly rock-hewn tomb before sundown on the sabbath, which just happens to be nearby and which just happens to have never contained anyone yet (lest he defile the grave of his ancestors).

Reversal of Expectation

It is important to note the motif throughout the Gospels of the reversal of expectation. The disciples aren't quite the loyal and brilliant followers of the Messiah people often see them as. They bungle, they doubt and they are consistently acting in ways that are opposite to what we, the reader, would expect.

One of Mark's strengths is his grasp of irony. As atheist author Richard Carrier says, talking of another scholar, Dennis MacDonald's work:[2]

> What I found additionally worthwhile is how MacDonald's theory illuminates the theme of "reversal of expectation" which so thoroughly characterizes the Gospels–not only in the parables of Jesus, where the theme is obvious, but in the very story itself. Though MacDonald himself does not pursue this in any detail, his book helped me to see it even more clearly. James and John, who ask to sit at the right and left of Jesus in his glory, are replaced by the two thieves at Jesus' crucifixion; Simon Peter, Jesus's right-hand man who was told he had to "deny himself and take up his cross and follow" (8:34), is replaced by Simon of Cyrene when it comes time to truly bear the cross; Jesus is anointed for burial before he dies; and when the women go to anoint him after his death, their expectations are reversed in finding his body missing. Later Gospels added even more of these reversals: for instance in Matthew Jesus' father, Joseph, is replaced by Joseph of Arimathea when the duty of burial arose–a duty that should have been fulfilled by the father;

[1] Kirby (2001).
[2] Carrier (2000b).

likewise, contrary to expectation **the Mary who laments his death and visits his tomb is not Mary his mother, but a prostitute; and while the Jews attack** Jesus for healing and doing good on the Sabbath, they in turn hold an illegal meeting, set an illegal guard, and plot evil on the Sabbath, and then break the ninth commandment the next day. This theme occurs far too often to have been in every case historical, and its didactic meaning is made clear in the very parables of reversal told by Jesus himself, as well as, for instance, his teachings about family, or hypocrisy, and so on. These stories were crafted to show that what Jesus preached applied to the real world, real events, "the word made flesh."

Again, this narrative makes Joseph look more like a literary mechanism to act as a reflection of the reader or to emphasise the disciples' lack of foresight and pious sanctity, rather than the actual historical secret Jesus follower who just so happens to have a spare tomb handy before disappearing, never to be heard from again.

A Rich Prophecy Fulfilment

Next, and crucially, the word "prominent" to describe Joseph in Mark is a word that can also mean rich or wealthy, as is used in Matthew. It, in fact, makes more sense to use it thus. This is not, as it seems, a random detail adorning the man. We have already come across the spurious desire for the Gospel authors to seek prophecy fulfilment, and here it raises its head again. Joseph suddenly makes sense as a fulfilment of prophecy mechanism. Isaiah 53, which is a *key* messianic prophecy that Christians like to use to apparently prophetically point to Jesus, says this (53:9):

His grave was assigned with wicked men,

Yet He was with a rich man in His death,

Because He had done no violence,

Nor was there any deceit in His mouth.

This verse is a clear reference to the criminals with whom Jesus was condemned and crucified, and to Joseph. There is no reason why the Gospel author would mention Joseph as a rich man. It seems this is another example of the prophecy fulfilment. Still another verse from Isaiah presumably predicts Jesus' side being pierced (53:5):

But He was pierced through for our transgressions

I have already previously mentioned prophecies concerning piercing sides... This all seems entirely dubious, that there is suddenly this rich man burying Jesus, which so conveniently fits into this contentious messianic prophecy (including the wicked criminals crucified around Jesus, and his side being pierced). If you then argue that God has ensured that this prophecy was fulfilled, then you have to answer why God has ensured this by organising the world in such a way, and *not* ensured that malaria never existed, killing the billions of people that it has. That a prophesied rich man is with Jesus at his death looks to be *a more important design feature* than *not creating malaria* (or Covid-19 or any other disease or pandemic) – a further philosophical point that I have reserved for this section. Simply put, it seems entirely retrojected and casts more doubt upon Joseph's existence, seeing him as another mechanism to achieve certain theological ends. Theology not history!

Where is Arimathea?

Bearing this in mind, the first thing we might want to ask about Joseph of Arimathea is: "Where is Arimathea?" This is a worthy question to which there is no answer. Literally, we don't know. Not only do we not know where it is, but also it is not mentioned as a place in any other contemporaneous source in the world. It is mentioned in the Gospels as a *city*, after all, so one would think...

Richard Carrier, again, has proposed that the key possibly lies in the Greek, discoverable with some lexical analysis. In a personal email to me some years back (as he has also expressed elsewhere), Carrier elucidated what he thinks could be a good explanation.[1] It is not only plausible, but it also coheres with the sort of literary mechanisms used by the Gospel authors. He stated:

> ari- (best) math- (disciple/doctrine) -aia (town/place)
>
> The ari- prefix meaning "best" appears in such words as aristocracy (rule of the best), aripikros (best in bitterness, hence "bitterest"), arideiketos (best in display, hence "glorious"), as explained in standard Greek lexicons (under "ari-"). As stated in the L&S Lexicon [Liddell & Scott], "ari- : insep. prefix, like eri-, strengthening the notion conveyed by its compd.: cogn. with areiôn, aristos, chiefly denoting 'goodness, excellence'." This would have been well-known to anyone educated in Greek of the time, since ancient education emphasized classical and preclassical poetry, including the interpretation of rare words commonly used in such

[1] Private correspondence on 17/01/2011.

literature, where the L&S notes this prefix saw wide use. At least half a dozen examples are listed in the L&S.

The math- root forms the verb mathein (lexically referenced under "mathô"), to teach, and the nouns mathê, lesson or doctrine, and mathêtês, disciple (which can be confirmed in any lexicon).

And the -aia suffix as town or place appears for such regions as Galilaia (Land of the Galiyl) and Judaia (Land of the Jews), and such actual cities as Dikaia (Justice Town) and Drymaia (Thicket Town), the latter examples taken from the Barrington Atlas of the Greek and Roman World[1] (the leading reference for ancient geography).

So a town could in principle be recognizably named mathaia, "teaching town" and hence (by association) "disciple town" (i.e. the town inhabited by people who receive the best teaching), or what we might encounter in English as "Teachton" or "Discipleton."

I have only ever suggested this as a possible mytho-symbolic derivation of the name, not as something anyone has proven (much less myself). I think it probably intentionally evokes the Ramathem repeatedly called Armathaim in 1 Samuel, but it is very suspicious that this spelling isn't preserved, but altered in exactly the way that creates the pun (analyzed above). But suspicion is not a proof.

Since commentators have seen the burial by the outsider Joseph of Arimathea as a contrast to the failure of the disciples and intimates of Jesus, the coincidence that Arimathea can be read as "best disciple town" is staggering. Indeed, it is good evidence that Joseph of Arimathea is a fictional character and that the tomb burial story in the Gospel of Mark is also fictional. With the absence of any evidence anywhere that Arimathea actually exists, and given the clear endorsement of the reversal of expectation motif, we have an outsider, a member of the Jewish Sanhedrin no less (who were responsible for his death) – and *not* his disciples – and this outsider was responsible for giving him a proper burial. It was Joseph, and not any other actual disciple, who ended up being the "best disciple".

The Sanhedrin and Pilate

The next issue is that we know that all, and it states in the Gospels *all* the Sanhedrin (the Jewish council), sentenced Jesus to death. Why on earth would one of the sentencing members then go back to Pilate and ask for his body? We

[1] Talbert (2000).

know in some detail Pilate's (somewhat private) surprise concerning Jesus' early death. It would seem that Joseph could be a first-hand source for the Gospels – however, more on that later. Would Pilate (who has gone through the whole rigmarole of crucifying Jesus, of *not* setting him free in a dubious, unevidenced holy day forgiveness ceremony) be a little hypocritical if he let Jesus' body go and not either rot on the cross, as was the Roman custom, or be buried in the criminals' graveyard as was the Jewish custom (more on *these* later)? The most likely scenario is that Jesus would have been given a dishonourable burial, and that the Sanhedrin would have seen to it that he did receive one, *having just gone to all the effort of getting him crucified.*

So the question remains: why did Joseph of Arimathea go to Pilate to ask for the body? The only possible answer is given by our earliest source, Mark, and only then by *inference*. Mark 15, which had already detailed how Jesus had died at the ninth hour, reads:

> **42** When evening had already come, since it was the preparation day, that
> is, the day before the Sabbath, **43** Joseph of Arimathea came, a prominent
> member of the Council, who was himself also waiting for the kingdom of
> God; and he gathered up courage and went in before Pilate, and asked for
> the body of Jesus. **44** Now Pilate wondered if He was dead by this time, and
> summoning the centurion, he questioned him as to whether He was al-
> ready dead. **45** And after learning this from the centurion, he granted the
> body to Joseph.

As we will learn in the next chapter, it was Jewish law to take a body down from its execution device by sunset if it was dead. There is much evidence from both inside and outside of the Bible to support this custom. The idea that Jesus, very unusually, had died so early (in a matter of hours as opposed to days) is the only possible reason we can infer that Joseph is asking special permission from Pilate; nothing else makes any sense (and I'm not even sure that this cuts the mustard). I can't imagine that Pilate would normally care about such petty things as taking a body down from a cross to fulfil Jewish laws, as it would probably be happening every day or, at least, very often. I would imagine Pilate would have someone else to deal with such small matters and requests. So there must be something out of the ordinary happening – a very early death and an approaching Sabbath.

I still find it hard to believe that this would be of interest to Pilate personally, but at least one can contrive *some sort of sense* from this episode. Here, we have a skeleton of a *possible* narrative based in some kind of historical context, before it is clearly embellished beyond plausibility by later Gospels. Otherwise, Pilate is merely a literary mechanism himself...

Joseph's name, if it were fictional, would have been impossible to verify at any rate, since there were some seventy people in the Sanhedrin, and

Jerusalem was sacked in the meantime (around the time that many think Mark's Gospel was penned), conveniently destroying all such records. This destruction of the Temple records provides an all-too-convenient get-out-of-jail-free card to the Gospel writers. It would arguably have been unlikely that a man from outside of Jerusalem in Arimathea, if it existed at all, would be on the Jerusalem Sanhedrin.

An Empty Tomb

A further point is that it is incredibly unlikely he would have a family tomb that was just at that time empty and ready to use, especially being from another city. Tombs were expensive to build or quarry and were "jealously preserved within families over several generations. The only motivation for a pious Jew to undertake a tomb burial for the man will be a strong belief that the crucified deserves an honourable burial."[1]

Thus, even though it could be that, as a pious Jew, he wanted Jesus to be buried before sunset and Passover (and didn't have time to get him dug into a shallow grave or placed in the criminals' graveyard complex, placing him into a tomb temporarily before moving him elsewhere later, unbeknownst to Jesus' followers), it seems unlikely for someone to actually have and lend an expensive family tomb for the burial. Especially considering Jesus was the highest form of Galilean criminal, a crucified treasonous and blasphemous man. It would also, one might argue, appear to require him to think that his own Sanhedrin had unjustly sentenced Jesus.

It is also unlikely that Joseph would have defiled his own tomb by storing Jesus' body in it, the body of a condemned criminal. This either lends credence to the notion that the tomb wasn't actually owned by Joseph or that he truly was a secret follower. Of course, Mark doesn't claim the tomb was Joseph's or that he was a secret follower – this was a later embellishment.

It seems like, no matter whether you believe Joseph to be a pious Jew or a secret Christian, both hypotheses are less likely than Joseph simply being a fiction. As we shall see, Jesus almost certainly would have been buried in a nearby criminals' graveyard (since what would the point of having nice tombs next to the place of execution, and the criminals' graveyard far away?). Joseph is a mechanism to get Jesus into his own tomb, from whence he can resurrect, and so allow for the empty tomb motif (or vice versa).

[1] Kirby in Price & Lowder (2005), p. 244.

Never to Be Seen or Heard from Again

Finally, it is worth considering that if Joseph was such a prominent member of the Sanhedrin, and *was* an actual follower of Jesus (as per the embellishments), why is he never heard from again? He disappears off the radar immediately after his burial antics. Joseph is *exactly* the sort of person that the Christians would want to head up the early church – rich, powerful, lots of contacts, a secret disciple, a good man, and one who has shown good discipleship. If he *were* all these things, he would have been an exceptionally prominent early Christian. Instead, nothing is heard of him until he pops up in much later, spurious writing with no historical evidence or credence. He is a man who would have been an excellent source for information for the Gospel writers. However, none of the authors list him as a source.

I actually see this as a strong piece of circumstantial evidence to add to the cumulative case that Joseph of Arimathea was a fictional character. However, that is not to say that Jesus' body wasn't stored somewhere temporarily before receiving his "proper" dishonourable burial in an unknown shallow grave or criminals' graveyard complex, or that there was a real human who could have been later legendarily mythologised to become Joseph of Arimathea. More on this topic later.

No matter which Joseph you think is being reported in the Gospels, we have so many problems concerning him that the simplest and most reasonable conclusion is that he is a fictional character utilised as a literary mechanism.

13 – An Honourable Death and Burial? Burial Practices Exhumed.

What happened? Jesus was condemned to death and executed for the highest known crime: blasphemy or high treason. This condemnation for blasphemy was by the Jewish high council (Mark 14:61-64; Matthew 26:65-66; John 19:7). He also had no family in the city willing to provide burial or support for him that we know of. Let us discuss one area of the narratives where we can do a little bit of historical detective work.

Throughout this chapter, I will be presenting historical and exegetical evidence for my claims, and I will also present a few arguments often heard from fellow skeptics with whom I now disagree, having changed my mind on a couple of points (e.g., concerning whether Jesus' dead body would have been left on the cross for days). I will present a range of arguments here, showing where I agree and where I disagree, and in so doing, hopefully illustrating my methodology of following the evidence, even if I have to change my mind.

As previously mentioned, Mark's account alone provides something that *could* allow for historical precedence. The most likely conclusion is that all of the stories are (almost) entirely false; but if one really wanted to extract a narrative with some historical possibility concerning the death and burial, Mark's Gospel can provide the reader a skeleton. Having just said this, Mark falls at the first hurdle.

Jesus Would Have Been Stoned

Before we get onto burials, let us discuss the method of Jesus' execution and death. There is actually good reason to think that Jesus should certainly have been *stoned* for his particular crime and *not* crucified: "Jesus, as a blasphemer, would be ear-marked for stoning and thus for the Graveyard of the Stoned and Burned."[1]

Jewish historian Josephus furnishes us with some details when describing the Mosaic laws concerning execution by stoning, passed down to contemporaneous Jews. This also illuminates the idea of burying the dead afterwards:[2]

[1] Carrier (2002), see especially footnote 17.
[2] JW 4.202, 260.

> Let him who blasphemes God be stoned to death and hung during the day, and let him be buried dishonorably and out of sight...[and]...when he has continued there for one whole day, that all the people may see him, let him be buried in the night. And thus it is that we bury all whom the laws condemn to die, upon any account whatsoever. Let our enemies that fall in battle be also buried; nor let any one dead body lie above the ground, or suffer a punishment beyond what justice requires.

Leviticus has some more evidence for stoning blasphemers:

> The one who blasphemes the name of the Lord shall be taken outside the camp, and let all who heard him lay their hands on his head; then let all the congregation stone him. (Leviticus 24:14)

And this is later confirmed by the New Testament, in Acts 7, where Stephen, who had been performing "great wonders and signs", was stoned for his blasphemy:

> But they cried out with a loud voice, and covered their ears and rushed at him with one impulse.[58] When they had driven him out of the city, they began stoning him; and the witnesses laid aside their robes at the feet of a young man named Saul.[59] They went on stoning Stephen as he called on the Lord and said...

In other words, all the evidence points towards the notion that he simply would not have been crucified. It strongly suggests that this could have been a legendary embellishment that allows all sorts of theology to be introduced. In all likelihood, Jesus would have been stoned to death.

It is also the case that those who were stoned were also usually hung (lashed or nailed up) as further dishonour and deterrence (i.e., stoned and then crucified already dead). This would have been the most likely outcome for Jesus. Even references in Paul (Galatians 3:13 – "Christ redeemed us from the curse of the Law, having become a curse for us – for it is written: 'Cursed is everyone who hangs on a tree [i.e., wood]'"), fits with this narrative. According to Jewish law, and it was Jewish law that was being maintained (as we shall see), it is highly probable indeed that Jesus would have been stoned, with a possibility he could have been strung up after this as a deterrence. None of this is explicitly detailed in the Gospels, though Galatians 3:13 more likely supports a stoning and then being hung, as Mishnah *Sanhedrin* 6.4 details:

> How do they hang the corpse of one who was put to death by stoning? They sink a post into the earth with a piece of wood jutting out, forming

> a T-shaped structure. And the court appointee then places the dead man's two hands one upon the other, ties them, and hangs him by his hands. Rabbi Yosei says: The post is not sunk into the ground; rather, it leans against a wall, and he hangs the corpse on it the way that butchers do with meat. The dead man hangs there for only a very short time, and then they immediately untie him. And if he was left hanging overnight, a prohibition is transgressed, as it is stated: "His body shall not remain all night upon the tree, but you shall bury him that day, for he that is hung is a curse of God"

Jesus hangs on a "tree".

Lastly, if Jesus had been stoned, Pilate almost certainly wouldn't have been involved in the process (there really wasn't recourse for this).

Crossing the 'T's

The first extra-biblical "evidence" we have of Jesus on a "cross" (and even then, no cross is evident, just hands to the side with nails in them) is in 440 CE, *some four hundred years after his death.*[1] Indeed, there is no evidence of anyone being crucified on a cross. Jesus, or whoever was supposed to have carried the cross, simply would not have been able to carry something that big. Such a cross was very likely a T-shaped arrangement, given an abundance of evidence for this, from the language itself and pagan literary comparisons to the Greek letter Tau and visual depictions (e.g., graffiti), and suchlike.[2] It could have been a cheaper (in time and effort) version, an X-shape, as has been found on an early Roman villa mosaic. Even a Pi-shaped scaffold has been known to be used. Or more likely still, the device of execution could have been a simple post (*crux simplex*) for which there is more evidence (some say people were even impaled, though this would probably have been too quick a death for the Romans...).[3]

With crosses (T-shaped devices), victims would usually be lashed to the *crux* (crossbeam) to carry it to the *patibulum*, or post, and then they would be hoisted onto the post where the crossbeam would sit in a notch on top of it (rather like the sail and mast set-ups on ancient vessels). As mentioned, though, in a previous section, there is no evidence *outside of Rome* that prisoners carried the *patibulum* to the site of execution.[4] Is this the Gospel authors taking their knowledge of customs elsewhere and erroneously applying them to Jesus?

---

[1] It appears on a small relief panel on the wooden door of the Church of the Santa Sabina in Rome. See Sheckler & Leith (2010).

[2] See Thoby (1959).

[3] For crucifixion information, see Kennedy (n.d.).

[4] Van Wingerden (2020).

Wood and trees were also scarce in the area, as Romans had to go over ten miles outside of Jerusalem to secure timber for their siege machinery. This meant that devices would have been reused and economically constructed.[1]

Deuteronomy 21:22 says "If a man guilty of a capital offence is put to death and his body hung on a tree...", which again details how people were stoned *and then* hung on a tree or post. Jewish sources agree. Once stoned, the Mishnah tractate Sanhedrin states, a corpse of a blasphemer be further dishonoured: "the corpse was then hung on a pole for display, apparently like a slab of meat, which resembled a crucifixion".[2]

If it was crucifixion, then this was a wholly torturous affair:[3]

> Seneca (d. 65 C.E.) refers to a variety of postures and different kinds of tortures on crosses: some victims are thrust head downward, others have a stake impale their genitals (*obscena*), still others have their arms outstretched on a crossbeam. The Jewish historian Josephus, writing of the Jewish War of the late 60s, is explicit about Jews captured by the Romans who were first flogged, tortured before they died, and then crucified before the city wall. The pity he reports that Titus, father of Josephus's imperial patron Vespasian, felt for them did not keep Titus from letting his troops dispatch as many as five hundred in a day: "The soldiers, out of the rage and hatred they bore the prisoners, nailed those they caught, in different postures, to the crosses for the sport of it, and their number was so great that there was not enough room for the crosses and not enough crosses for the bodies." Josephus calls it "the most wretched of deaths." He tells of the surrender of the fortress Machaerus on the east shore of the Dead Sea when the Romans threatened a Jewish prisoner with crucifixion.
>
> An especially grim description of this punishment, meted out to murderers, highwaymen, and other gross offenders, is the following from a didactic poem: "Punished with limbs outstretched, they see the stake as their fate; they are fasted, nailed to it with sharpest spikes, an ugly meal for birds of prey and grim scraps for dogs."

It seems like Jesus should really have been stoned and then perhaps displayed on a "cross", but the likelihood of Jesus being crucified on a cross as depicted in Christian iconography is very slight indeed.

---

[1] Zias & Sekeles (1985), p. 26.

[2] Carrier (2002).

[3] Sloyan (1995), p. 15-16.

One of the biggest problems with the Gospel narratives is the speed that Jesus died. This was a truly remarkably quick death. Where many crucifixions take three days to kill someone, Jesus dies within the daytime on the first day.

The most likely outcome for Jesus was death by stoning, and then being hung on a "cross". After this (in terms of probability), it is certainly still possible he have had a mere crucifixion, though the likelihood being that it wouldn't have been on an actual cross.

So the next question becomes, where would he have been buried? But before we answer this question, there is the thorny issue of whether or not he was taken off the "cross" early.

Taking the Body down by Sunset

There is a lot debate as to whether Joseph of Arimathea (or any such figure) would have taken Jesus' body down off the cross and this has caused all number of arguments from skeptics and resultant defences from Christians (and even other skeptics). This revolves around whether there is precedence for bodies being taken down before sunset and before a Jewish holy day. Skeptics will naturally see this is an opportunity to poke yet another hole in the biblical accounts. Surely his dead body would have been left on the cross for days! Yet the removal of dead bodies from crosses (or an unknown execution device) before sunset is actually something about which I have changed my mind by following the evidence faithfully.

The skeptic *could* say that the Romans were the ones who ultimately killed Jesus, with an order from Pilate, and so it is very unlikely that the Jews would be able to sanction when a criminal was taken down from their cross. The issue for such a view is that the Romans and the Jews had a treaty that allowed the Jews under their control to continue to adhere to many of their religious observances. Thus, taking a *dead* body down by sunset to avoid a religious curse would be an acceptable custom for the Roman authorities. They would have allowed this to happen.

So it is not a question as to whether the Sanhedrin would go against their intentions and the entire point of punishing Jesus for high treason to allow him to be taken down by sunset, because they would certainly not want to break religious law and invite a curse; all criminals, if dead, we be taken down by sunset as a matter of legal adherence. But what is important here is whether they would subsequently allow him an honourable *burial.*

Skeptics might often argue that, even if Jews wanted to take the body down for reasons of religious observance, Pilate would have been unlikely to acquiesce. The Gospels must be wrong. But we must not be so hasty to confirm our beliefs in this way.

This opinion is often borne out by the use of various sources. Jewish philosopher Philo *seems* to suggest that taking the body down by sunset was something only reserved for holy days (as it would have been for Jesus):[1]

> I know that some of those crucified in the past were taken down when a day-of-rest of such a kind was about to start, and they were returned to their families for the purpose of enjoying burial and the customary rites. For there is need even that the dead enjoy some good upon the birthday of an emperor and, at the same time, that the sacred character of the public holy day be protected.

Moreover, Raymond Brown shows precedence for leaving such perpetrators on the cross:[2]

> But the prefect Flaccus (within a decade of Jesus' death) "gave no orders to take down those who had died on the cross," **even on the eve of a feast.** Indeed, he crucified others, after maltreating them with the lash. [My emphasis.]

However, Flaccus ruled in Egypt and so the Jewish treaty will not have applied, and this is also the context that Philo was writing about, whereby the law wasn't so closely observed for Alexandrian Jews as for those in Judea. This does not concern *Judea*, and Jerusalem as the most holy of Jewish cities. As skeptics, we must be very wary (since we accuse this so often of our interlocutors) of confirmation bias. I originally adhered to the belief that the body would have been left through sunset and so the Gospel accounts are wrong, here, too. But we must be honest with the evidence. And the evidence is that taking a dead body down by sunset is Jewish law and would have been observed, even under Roman rule.

Richard Carrier[3], likewise, *does* think that there exists a very good plausibility of Pilate agreeing to Joseph's (or another pious Jew) request to take down the body (though he is not kinsfolk). A logical rationale is that agreeing to Joseph's request would be in line with Jewish custom and he might not want to annoy some of the local Jews. Mark, after all, doesn't claim it is Joseph's own tomb or that it had never been used before. *These were later embellishments.* Indeed, Mark's Gospel is comparatively thin on details and actually supports, as we shall see, a dishonourable burial narrative.

The Torah Law is unequivocal about this:

---

[1] *In Flaccum*, 83, translation Richard Carrier, Carrier (2002).

[2] Brown (1994), p. 1207-8.

[3] Carrier (2002).

> If a man has committed a sin worthy of death, and he is put to death, and you hang him on a tree, his corpse shall not hang all night on the tree, but you shall surely bury him on the same day, for he who is hanged is the curse of God, so that you do not defile your land which the Lord your God gives you as an inheritance. (Deuteronomy 21:22-23; cf. Joshua 8:29, 10:26-27).

There seems to be little space for doubting the Jewish propensity for burial before sunset,[1] and especially before a holy day. This is also supported by Mishnah tractate *Sanhedrin* (6.4-5). Furthermore, Josephus (in *Antiquities of the Jews* 4.8.24 and 5.1.14) says the following:

> ... and there let him be stoned; and when he has continued there for one whole day, that all the people may see him, let him be buried in the night....
>
> ... He was immediately put to death; and attained no more than to be buried in the night in a disgraceful manner, and such as was suitable to a condemned malefactor.

Again, this clearly indicates that Jesus would have had a dishonourable burial, perhaps being *buried* after sunset, ignominiously in the dark. But, importantly, his dead body would *not* have been left on the cross.

The larger point is that it was the holy duty of the Jews to take down dead bodies from execution posts in order to avoid a curse, as set out in their holy writing: the body must be buried the day it died. We circle back to whether the Romans would allow Jews under their control to observe Jewish law. It seems that, before the Jewish War, this was certainly the case, and with imperial decree. As Josephus has Titus quoting:[2]

> It can therefore be nothing certainly but the kindness of us Romans which hath excited you against us; who, in the first place, have given you this land to possess; and, in the next place, have set over you kings of your own nation; and, in the third place, have preserved the laws of your forefathers to you, and have withal permitted you to live, either by yourselves, or among others, as it should please you...

---

[1] See the "Down by Sunset" section in Carrier (2001).

[2] *The Wars of the Jews*, 6.6.2. https://ccel.org/j/josephus/works/war-6.htm (Retrieved 09/03/2021). See also Phil, *Embassy to Gaius*, 153, 159, 161.

This treaty is well attested to in Josephus' *Jewish Antiquities*. As scholar Evanthia Polyviou explains:[1]

> In book XIV of his *Jewish Antiquities* Flavius Josephus preserves a number of official documents issued by Caesar or voted with his initiative, which are considered to be of great importance for the study of the Jewish political history of this period. Dated between 49 and 44 B.C., they attest the renovation of the Romeo-Jewish "alliance and friendship" and confirm the Jewish right to live according to their ancestral laws and to benefit from all privileges derived from their religious liberty...
>
> The roman recognition of the Jewish right "to live according to their ancestral laws" was part of the religious toleration policy, expressed in the right of free attendance of religious rites, which was conferred on all people residing within the limits of the Roman Empire. In the case of the Jews this right entailed a number of additional privileges concerning respect of the Shabbat and other religious feasts of the Jews, dietary laws, collection of sacred money etc.; privileges which in certain cases involved roman legislation

Christian apologist William Lane Craig, of all people, disagrees with this Jewish legal ruling and Roman allowance of Joseph to bring down the body:[2]

> None of the Gospels suggest that Joseph was acting as a delegate of the Sanhedrin; there was nothing in the law that required that the body to be buried immediately, and the Jews may have been content to leave that to the Romans. That Joseph *dared* to go to Pilate and asked specifically for Jesus's body is difficult to understand if he was simply an emissary of the Sanhedrin, assigned to dispose of the bodies.

Here we return to the idea that Joseph was a secret admirer of Jesus and not a mere pious Sanhedrin member. However, Craig seems to think that the Jews would ordinarily have left the body on the cross, making no mention of exceptions for sunset or holy days, and showing no knowledge of Jewish law. Simply put, the Romans would not have been concerning themselves with the burial of Jews. Craig's reason for arguing this is because it makes Joseph of Arimathea to be this courageous Christ-following Jew that he has become in Christian cultural history, as opposed to the much more probable idea that he was merely a pious Jew doing his religious duty, unconcerned with whom Jesus

[1] Polyviou (2015).
[2] Craig (1989), p. 75-6.

supposedly was. Craig, in arguing for his orthodox Christian view here, is illustrating a dubious methodology whilst contradicting known history.

It is clear that there is plenty of evidence to suggest that the Romans let their Jewish counterparts have a great deal of elbow room when it came to their own customs, religious laws, and observances. I originally didn't personally think that Pilate would have entertained Joseph's request. For Pilate, the Roman authorities and the Sanhedrin to have gone through the whole rigmarole of finding Jesus, hearing and sentencing him, supposedly making a cross for him, which he carries to Golgotha, nailing him up and killing him, only for him to suddenly be taken down and given an honourable burial, for me, went over the mark of plausibility. Peter Kirby agrees with this position:[1]

> Jesus is the least likely of the three for Pilate to release, for not only might it suggest that the crucifixion was unjust, but it also would lend justification to whatever sedition that Pilate suspected and would honor one who had been condemned as a threat to order.

But I am not so sure, now. That's not to say Pilate would have released Jesus' body – I don't think he did, because I don't think Pilate would have had much to do with any of this. According to Paul (Galatians 3:13, 1 Thessalonians 2:14-15) and the Gospels, Jesus was executed by the *Jews*. Since I am using Jewish law and observance to argue how his trial and death would have been carried out, it would be double standards of me to claim that this did not also apply to his body being removed thereafter.

An issue one hears is that it was customary to give bodies to family members, who would bury them in their family tombs (issues with criminality aside), but Jesus' family (depending on what Gospel you read) was notably absent. Because none of Jesus' family was in Jerusalem at the time, here again, we could imagine that Joseph of Arimathea (or some other pious Jew) might have stepped in, to take the body down. Though the Christian would argue that this was precisely because he was allegedly a secret follower of Christ.

Pilate Problems

Joseph supposedly approaches Pilate to have the body taken down. I would see Pilate's involvement in much of the Jesus narrative as unlikely, as mentioned. But even if we grant Pilate a place at the table, so to speak, Michael Alter lists[2] seven problems with Joseph approaching Pilate and the timeframe

[1] Kirby in Price & Lowder (2005), p. 246.

[2] Alter (2015), p. 209-10.

in which he has to do this. It's no easy thing to gain access to Pilate and the time one needs to do this after finding out that Jesus had died.

> Matthew 27:
>
> 57 When it was evening, there came a rich man from Arimathea, named Joseph, who himself had also become a disciple of Jesus. 58 This man went to Pilate and asked for the body of Jesus. Then Pilate ordered it to be given *to* him.
>
> John 19:
>
> 31 Then the Jews, because it was the day of preparation, so that the bodies would not remain on the cross on the Sabbath (for that Sabbath was a high day), asked Pilate that their legs might be broken, and *that* they might be taken away. 32 So the soldiers came, and broke the legs of the first man and of the other who was crucified with Him; 33 but coming to Jesus, when they saw that He was already dead, they did not break His legs. 34 But one of the soldiers pierced His side with a spear, and immediately blood and water came out. 35 And he who has seen has testified, and his testimony is true; and he knows that he is telling the truth, so that you also may believe. 36 For these things came to pass to fulfill the Scripture, "Not a bone of Him shall be broken." 37 And again another Scripture says, "They shall look on Him whom they pierced."
>
> 38 After these things Joseph of Arimathea, being a disciple of Jesus, but a secret one for fear of the Jews, asked Pilate that he might take away the body of Jesus; and Pilate granted permission. So he came and took away His body.

The problem with Matthew's account is that it was evening[1] or certainly late and this probably means that the Sabbath had already started Days start at sunset). The ramifications of John 19:31 with his Jesus as the paschal lamb is that this is avoided. However, the approaching sunset and Sabbath is the whole reason for the body coming down when and how it did. But Matthew's account invalidates this reasoning for the body being taken down.

One further problem is, if Joseph (or whoever may have taken the body down) was observing Jewish custom in taking down Jesus' body, why didn't he take down those around Jesus (i.e., the two thieves)? Perhaps, to help the Christian out, the thieves were still alive, thus meaning they should remain on the cross through sunset. The bigger problem is all of this happening on the eve of a Sabbath or a holy day, and one could not work on these days, including for

[1] See *Young's Analytical Concordance to the Bible* (1979), p. 309, for analysis of the word *opsios* (which "never means an earlier moment than sunset", J. Weiss, *Das Urchristentum*, cited by C.G. Montefiore (1968, 1: p. 392).

burial rites – even moving a body.[1] This almost certainly would have been a case of the thieves being "hurried along" with their deaths and taken down at the same time as Jesus as well. But we never hear about them.

The most sensible option for people wanting the maximum suffering for the worst of crimes, as would be the case for Jesus, would be to have the victim crucified on the Monday in order for the suffering not to require hastening (and note that hastening is itself a mere inference made from both Philo and the Gospel of John).

Even if crucified, the process would still be so routine that Pilate would never even be consulted or involved (to refer back to previous discussions concerning Pilate); the centurion in charge of execution detail would already have a system worked out with the Sanhedrin, and the Sanhedrin would already have staff gravediggers routinely taking care of this.

As mentioned, the only remotely historically plausible account of Joseph requesting the body from Pilate is in the context of the Jewish laws and because it was Sabbath approaching and Jesus had died so early (if, indeed, you believe all of those claims!). But Christians appear to prefer to take the embellished later Gospels as, well, gospel truth. This excerpt is from Jodi Magness's "What did Jesus' Tomb Look Like?" in *The Burial of Jesus* from the Biblical Archaeology Society, and is typical Christian apologetics:[2]

> Jesus was condemned by the Roman authorities for crimes against Rome, not by the Sanhedrin (Jewish council) for violating Jewish law. The Romans used crucifixion to maintain peace and order and punish rebellious provincials for incitement to rebellion and acts of treason. Although victims of crucifixion were sometimes left on their crosses for days, this was not usually the case. According to the Gospel accounts, Pontius Pilate approved Joseph of Arimathea's request to remove Jesus' body from the cross for burial. Presumably Joseph had to make this special request because he wanted to ensure that Jesus received a proper burial before the beginning of the Sabbath.

Not only does this not marry with internal biblical claims (it was the Jews who condemned and killed Jesus), but Joseph is arranging an honourable burial, going against all sense of the narrative and historical precedence, as we shall now see.

---

[1] Talmud: *Sanhedrin* 35a-35b; *Yevamoth* 7a; *Baba Bathra* 100b, *Shabbath* 150-1.

[2] Magness (2007).

Dishonourable Burials

> The impact of crucifixion could go on for days at a time, as the body of one who had crossed the purposes of Rome was left hanging in public view, rotting in the sun, with birds pecking away at it.[1]

What is our background knowledge and what are the prior probabilities when considering such burial claims as those described by biblical archaeologist Byron McCane? Well, we have no known precedent for the highest form of criminal (high treason and blasphemy) being crucified and given anything like honour in their death in Jewish or Roman history. The whole idea of crucifixion is that it is punishment beyond death. This has two ramifications: (1) that the person needs to be punished beyond their death, the dishonour of a protracted death (perhaps involving carrion) and a shallow grave or a criminals' grave complex and (2) the point of crucifixion was as a deterrent – people were kept up on the cross (or similar) in order to serve as a warning to others.

Simply put, crucifixion was intended to torture and humiliate a person as much as possible. In addition, it served to assert the authority of Rome over those looking on or passing by, with an ultimate degradation of the body being left on the cross to be picked at by carrion and wild animals, whilst decomposing to provide sustenance for scavengers (with Jewish bodies being taken down on the day of death sometime by sunset). The historian of religion Martin Hengel states in his book *Crucifixion in the Ancient World and the Folly of the Message of the Cross*:[2]

> Crucifixion was aggravated further by the fact that quite often its victims were never buried. It was a stereotyped picture that the crucified victim served as food for wild beasts and birds of prey. In this way, his humiliation was complete.

We can see some tension between what many scholars (including Christians) state of crucifixion, and the process as understood in *Jewish* contexts (under occupation by the Romans) as we have previously discussed in some detail. Bart Ehrman, in *How Jesus Became God*, details Roman practices at the time, but arguably ignores (or is ignorant of) the point about the Jewish treaty:[3]

> Evidence for this comes from a wide range of sources. An ancient inscription found on the tombstone of a man who was murdered by his slave in the city of Caria tells us that the murderer was "hung . . . alive for the wild beasts and birds of prey." The Roman author Horace says in

[1] McCane (2003), p. 90.
[2] Hengel (1977), p. 87.
[3] Ehrman (2014), p. 157-61.

> one of his letters that a slave was claiming to have done nothing wrong, to which his master replied, "You shall not therefore feed the carrion crows on the cross" (Epistle 1.16.46-48). The Roman satirist Juvenal speaks of "the vulture [that] hurries from the dead cattle and dogs and corpses, to bring some of the carrion to her offspring" (Satires 14.77-78). The most famous interpreter of dreams from the ancient world, a Greek Sigmund Freud named Artemidorus, writes that it is auspicious for a poor man in particular to have a dream about being crucified, since "a crucified man is raised high and his substance is sufficient to keep many birds" (Dream Book 2.53). And there is a bit of gallows humor in the Satyricon of Petronius, a onetime advisor to the emperor Nero, about a crucified victim being left for days on the cross (chaps. 11-12)....
>
> Among the Romans, we learn that after a battle fought by Octavian (the later Caesar Augustus, emperor when Jesus was born), one of his captives begged for a burial, to which Octavian replied, "The birds will soon settle that question" (Suetonius, Augustus 13). And we are told by the Roman historian Tacitus of a man who committed suicide to avoid being executed by the state, since anyone who was legally condemned and executed "forfeited his estate and was debarred from burial" (Annals 6.29h).
>
> Again, it is possible that Jesus was an exception, but our evidence that this might have been the case must be judged to be rather thin. People who were crucified were usually left on their crosses as food for scavengers, and part of the punishment for ignominious crimes was being tossed into a common grave, where very soon one decomposed body could not be distinguished from another. In the traditions about Jesus, of course, his body had to be distinguished from all others; otherwise, it could not be demonstrated to have been raised physically from the dead.

He provides a different rationale as to why the body was taken down early, here. One must again be careful, however, in conflating what Romans did with what Romans did *in Judea*. Or, more accurately, what the Jews in Judea did under Roman occupation. We can't truly know exactly what *did* happen to Jesus' body and so it becomes about probabilities and precedence.

That Jesus should have received a dishonourable burial is corroborated by the Secret Book of James, a non-canonical text, which has Jesus saying:

> Or do you not know that you have not yet been mistreated and have not yet been accused unjustly, nor have you yet been shut up in prison, nor have you yet been condemned lawlessly, nor have you yet been crucified without reason, nor have you yet been **buried in the sand**, as was I myself, by the evil one? [my emphasis]

Some even have this last line written as[1] "nor have you yet been buried *shamefully*, as was I myself, by the evil one?" [Again, my emphasis.] This quote goes to the nub of the matter. The Secret Book of James (Apocryphon of James) describes the secret teachings of Jesus to Peter and James, as they were supposedly given after the Resurrection but before the Ascension. Probably originating in the Jewish Christian community, it appears to show no dependence on the canonical texts, and was probably written in the first half of the 2nd century CE. However, if we are going to cast a lot of suspicion over the sources of the canonical Gospels, we must also treat this source with a skeptical view.

This is an early source that is communicating what at least some early Christians believed. Why would they believe and write this down unless it was some kind of idea that was in some way prevailing? This is another piece of evidence to suggest that Jesus would have received, and that people believed he was given, a shameful burial.

Contemporaneous Jewish historian, Josephus, states:

> He that blasphemeth God, let him be stoned; and let him hang upon a tree all that day, and then let him be buried in **an ignominious and obscure manner**" (*Antiquities of the Jews* 4.8.6) [my emphasis]

By "ignominious and obscure", what Josephus meant was essentially "amongst many others and without a permanent public epitaph". This is pretty straightforward a contradiction of what the later Gospels recount, again pointing to a dishonourable burial (though which you could argue is evidenced in Mark).

There is plenty more biblical and extra-biblical evidence for the dishonourable burial of blasphemous criminals including (from the Hebrew Bible), 1 Kings 13:21-22 and Jeremiah 22:18-19. Also, Jewish historian Josephus recounts a biblical story (from Joshua 7) that ends: "...straightway put to death and at nightfall was given the ignominious...burial proper to the condemned" (*Antiquities of the Jews* 5.1.14 44).

There is a probability that any burial tradition, as it was told and retold amongst early Christians, would have become somewhat embellished, as we can indeed see in many elements of the Gospel stories. Details get added, whether this be names or adjectives or supposed facts. This is what we saw in the previous chapter with Joseph of Arimathea.

Byron R. McCane, in '"Where No One Had Yet Been Laid": The Shame of Jesus' Burial', casts some light over shameful burials.[2]

---

[1] "The Apocryphon of James", translated by Ron Cameron. http://scriptural-truth.com/PDF_Apocrypha/The%20Apocryphon%20of%20James.pdf (Retrieved 28/11/2020).
[2] McCane (1998) p. 431-52.

> Before proceeding any further, there is a point to be noted here about burial practices - not just Jewish burial practices, but burial practices in general. The point is this: they change very slowly. For centuries on end Israelites and Jews had been burying their dead promptly, and burying their dishonored dead in shame, and these customs did not change much over time. Burial practices are in fact among the most traditional and conservative aspects of human cultures, and they are especially so in unsecularized societies. When a society is still embedded in religion - i.e. when religious beliefs still serve as the foundation for social institutions and customs - burial practices function as ritual vehicles for social and cultural cohesion in the face of death. As such, they change very slowly. It is important to note the significance of this fact for the burial of Jesus. Traditions of prompt burial, and of dishonorable burial, would have exerted a powerful influence on the Jewish leaders of first-century Jerusalem. These customs had been handed down for generations and were invested with the aura of sacred authority. The Jewish leaders were devoutly religious. To imagine that they could have disregarded these traditions, out of indifference or inconvenience, is to misunderstand burial customs in a fundamental way. Worse yet, it is to project post-modern secularized ways of thinking back into an era where they do not belong.
>
> The element of shame in Jewish dishonorable burial is most vividly evident in the specific differences between burial in shame and burial with honor. Honorable burial emphasized precisely what shameful burial left out: the family tomb, and mourning.

He actually favours a dishonourable burial (as a Christian), though in a tomb, but this view seems to stretch things to favour some kind of Markan reliability in favour of a shallow grave burial, but one that us hard to accord with history. Raymond Brown adds some detail to this opinion:[1]

> True, we have in the Matthean and Lucan accounts of the burial an early interpretation of Mark; but...there is a very high possibility that these two evangelists have changed and developed the Marcan outlook. Consequently, I shall not use Matthew and Luke as a primary guide to Mark's intention.

This quotation brings up an important point to note here: the Gospel of Mark does not necessarily report an honourable burial. Indeed, it says very little

[1] Brown (1988), p. 233.

and the later Gospels take the opportunity to embellish these scant claims (Mark 16):

> 46 Joseph bought a linen cloth, took Him down, wrapped Him in the linen cloth, and laid Him in a tomb which had been cut out in the rock; and he rolled a stone against the entrance of the tomb.

This could either be a temporary stop-gap for the body or a tomb in a criminals' graveyard complex. I find it more plausible, since the inference is that Joseph did this himself (i.e., that there was no manager or *archon* present), that the tomb was not yet the criminal's complex, though this or a shallow grave would have been the eventual resting place. Let me expand on this piece of historical datum.

Everyone who died on a cross (as discussed) would be removed before sunset and dishonourably buried, as law required, that night in the appropriate criminals' graveyard. This would also be the case for anyone stoned and hung in accordance with Mishnah – probably in the most dishonourable of the two graveyards, owing to the Deuteronomy "curse" rule (21:22-23): those whose corpses were displayed are a curse, and the land is cursed if they are not buried on the same day. As Mishnah *Sanhedrin* 6.5 states:[1]

> Rather, two graveyards were established for the burial of those executed by the court: One for those who were killed by decapitation or strangled, and one for those who were stoned or burned.

Here is what we know to definitely be the case: Jesus, as a criminal, would have been buried in the Sanhedrin's criminal graveyard, almost certainly the Graveyard of the Stoned and Burned.

What we don't know is exactly what this would have looked like, and so we have to do some conjecture based on archaeological finds. The following is inference based on these archaeological finds.

Other towns might have only had a smaller version, but Jerusalem would have needed a very large burial complex. It would have to house at least a hundred persons at a time, given the size of the city and the number of executions. There are two basic options: an earthen burial system or a tomb complex, both of which have been evidenced in Judean archaeology. Plenty of *necropoli* and grave sites exist, so it is a case of piecing together what such a place must have looked like. A single empty tomb is certainly where Jesus was not buried.

Jewish law allows for reburial of criminals after a period of a year for purification (it would also allow rotten flesh to be taken off the bones more

[1] Mishnah Sanhedrin 6.5, https://www.sefaria.org/Mishnah_Sanhedrin.6.5 (Retrieved 10/03/2021).

easily as it was the bones that we reburied, if at all collected). Reburial (even by families of the poor) obviously requires being able to locate the dead after a year, which is highly impractical but not impossible with an earth grave system (most reburials themselves would be in the earth, but only because after that point no one ever needs to dig them up again). The Sanhedrin would be using a location set up centuries ago by an earlier (possibly first) Sanhedrin of the Second Temple, which would have had ample resources to produce any of these, and they would most likely have produced the one that was the most efficient.

As such, I think the forced ranked probabilities for each option would be (1) a stone- or brick-built complex, (2) a natural (underground/hillside/catacomb) cave complex, and (3) a cordoned-off earthen graveyard. Each of these are possible. We could assign a probability, taking into account practicalities of what was needed from such a set up of, say, 60:30:10.

This graveyard, for numerous practical reasons, was therefore most probably a constructed complex of brick or stone, with *loculi* (architectural compartments or niches) where corpses would have been rotated in and out. These *loculi* might more specifically be *arcosolia*, which are arched recesses. An example of this are the Tombs of the Sanhedrin (Tombs of the Judges) built in the first century CE (that later became a pilgrimage site). The largest chamber, just inside the entrance, contains 13 arched *loculi* arranged on two tiers, one atop the other, with *arcosolia* dividing the niches into pairs. Each niche measures 50 centimetres (20 inches) by 60 centimetres (24 inches).[1] There are sixty-three in total with several cubicles for bone collection; ossuaries were also found in vaults within the complex.[2] And, remember, this would have been for respectable burials.

Taking this into account, a criminal complex would have been filled with other criminals' corpses; Jesus' body, shrouded and bloody, would have been deposited in any spare *loculus* (unclaimed bones might even be swept off it to make room, and tossed in a bone heap), and an erasable chalk mark made to identify it. This identification would be a simple name or abbreviation of a name, possibly even just a number (if the gravetender kept a log, though in that case no mark might be made). In this latter case, the *loculus* would have a permanent, chiselled number, and the tender would just update his logbook.

In that place, the body would likely have rotted away, never to be claimed (unless it was, a year or so later as the law allowed, but only by his Galilean family; perhaps Christian cognitive dissonance just omitted that fact from all their sacred stories). If unclaimed, the bones of Jesus would, after a year or so, have been just swept into a random bone heap like all other unclaimed criminals, and the *loculus* reused for some other incoming criminal's corpse. This rotation of corpses, sanctioned by Jewish law to allow for reburial after a year,

---

[1] See Jonathan Price (2010) and James Barclay (1858), p.186-187.

[2] See Har-El (2004), p. 107-108 and "Sanhedriyya – Archaeological Appendix" (2002).

is why there is practical preference to believe it would have been a tomb complex as opposed to mere shallow graves, especially for somewhere so busy as Jerusalem. Such a secondary burial would not be reburial to make space in a tomb (as happened in family tombs when bones could be collected into boxes etc.), but reburial for *honour*: a very different matter.

What we have here is a vision of the sort of criminal grave site that we would absolutely expect given what we already know about burial customs from historical and religious texts, and from archaeology, relevant to the particular time and place. What this *doesn't* look like is the vision produced by Christians reading the Gospels; Gospels that were written outside of the precise time and place of Jesus' execution and burial, and with incorrect knowledge of what was most probable. This vision, that Christians now have – derived from the Gospels and popular culture – is far removed from what (if Jesus both existed and was executed for high treason) would almost certainly have happened.

Christians play fast and loose with probability in order to fulfil theological desires and obligations.

Returning to burial customs, and to confirm that separate graveyards were set apart for criminals (the Jewish requirement not to have family tombs defiled by proximity), we return to the Mishnah *Sanhedrin*:[1]

> ...they did not bury the condemned in the burial grounds of his ancestors, but there were two graveyards made ready for the use of the court, one for those who were beheaded or strangled, and one for those who were stoned or burned.

This is confirmed elsewhere (the Talmud, the Tosefta, and the Midrash Rabbah), and as the Talmud Sanhedrin 47a adds:[2]

> ...and just as a wicked person is not buried beside a righteous one, so is a grossly wicked person not to be buried beside one moderately wicked. Then should there not have been four graveyards. [No, for] it is a tradition that there should be but two.

These sources are at pains to emphasise the biblical basis for these stipulations (e.g., Deuteronomy 21:23; Psalms 26:9). The Midrash Rabbah, a collection of Torah commentaries, says:

> Those slain by a court of law are not buried in their fathers' sepulchres, but in a grave by themselves. (Numbers [XXIII:13 (877)])

---

[1] Ibid.

[2] Carrier (2002).

Richard Carrier confirms these sources:[1]

> The Mishnah itself goes on to explain that only "when the flesh was completely decomposed were the bones gathered and buried in their proper place," i.e. only then could the family rebury the condemned man in their ancestral tomb.... There were no apparent exceptions made for execution by a Gentile government (Talmud, *Sanhedrin* 47b), and there certainly would be none when the Sanhedrin had already condemned the man, since that meant his death was "merited" in the eyes of the Jewish law. Indeed, Talmudic interpretation held that the mere fact of a disgraceful death, and the stain of wickedness it entailed, required burial in a special graveyard, since the corpse could only be placed next to others of like indignity - as noted above, this was the purpose of having two graveyards reserved for different kinds of criminals.

Whether Mark's account relates to this sort of "tomb" is open to debate; what is not, is that the later Gospels most certainly do not. One could possibly, if you really wanted the Gospel to be as accurate as possible, stretch and argument that Mark actually had Jesus dishonourably buried, but that the later Gospels embellished this account (or whitewashed it) to fit their own agendas.

Considering the general belief that you couldn't bury criminals near the righteous, it makes it highly unlikely that anyone owning tombs near Joseph's (or Joseph himself as a pious Jew) would have been happy for Jesus to be buried at the locale. This either makes the claim of Joseph of Arimathea placing him in a tomb very unlikely, or feeds into a greater likelihood of a temporary storage before moving the body on to its proper place (such that leaving the body up was worse than temporarily defiling a tomb). Of course, if you take Mark as already recounting a dishonourable burial, this isn't a problem, but if not, and for the later Gospels, this *is* a problem.

> The bodies of those who are condemned to death should not be refused their **relatives**; and the Divine Augustus, in the Tenth Book of his *Life*, said that this rule had been observed. At present, the bodies of those who have been punished are only buried when this has been requested and permission granted; and sometimes it is not permitted, **especially where persons have been convicted of high treason**. Even the bodies of those who have been sentenced to be burned can be claimed, in order that their bones and ashes, after having been collected, may be buried.[2] [My emphasis.]

---

[1] Ibid.

[2] Ulpian, *Duties of Proconsul*, book 9, Digesta.

Though this is not referring to Judea, I include it to illustrate a pervasive cultural idea: that high treason was an especially heinous crime. We return to the idea that Jesus was particularly toxic, and people went utterly out of their way to get him crucified. The likelihood of going back on the decision to treat him ignominiously, but to give honour in death is preposterous. It makes no sense, from an evaluation of the circumstances and inferring likely behaviour such as an honourable burial. Pilate would sanction the body to be taken down to fulfil Jewish law, but is unlikely to sanction honour to Jesus. The precedent question is more specific – there is no precedence for someone in the same situation as Jesus being given an honourable burial.

On the other hand, in terms of type of burial, there are arguments for a shallow grave as opposed to a tomb complex. Biblical scholar John Dominic Crossan became unpopular for suggesting that Jesus would have been buried in the criminal alternative: a shallow grave, where he would have been likely eaten by wild dogs.[1]

It is also known that, at most, such burials had only an uninscribed stone, pile of loose rocks or whiting (to show uncleanness) to denote the burial.[2] One issue for the shallow grave hypothesis is how pragmatic that is for secondary reburial after time for purification has elapsed and after decomposition.

One of these two options – a criminals' graveyard complex or a shallow grave – is simply what you would expect from anyone in Jesus' position being crucified for the reasons he was. This isn't inflammatory or religiously insensitive; this is history.

Mark's account is important because of its primacy but also because he, and his audience, would understand that Jesus would have normally been buried in a criminals' graveyard with none of his followers being present (Mark says they fled for fear of the law). Consequently, he needs to have the women present *to see where he was buried*. But they would not have had access to this grave unless they were family and only after a year:[3]

> Once the flesh of the deceased had decomposed, they would gather his bones and bury them in their proper place in his ancestral burial plot. And soon after the execution, the relatives of the executed transgressor would come and inquire about the welfare of the judges and about the welfare of the witnesses, as if to say: We hold no grudges against you, as you judged a true judgment. And the relatives of the executed man would not mourn him with the observance of the usual mourning rites,

[1] Crossan (1995), Chapter 6; (1991), p. 392-93; (1985), p. 153-64.
[2] Komarnitsky (2009), p. 29.
[3] Mishnah Sanhedrin 6.6, https://www.sefaria.org/Mishnah_Sanhedrin.6.6 (Retrieved 10/03/2021).

so that his unmourned death would atone for his transgression; but they would grieve over his passing, since grief is felt only in the heart.

The key here is to remember that Jesus, hated by the Jewish council and the Romans for his proclamations, would have been accorded the worst punishment possible. In fact, the lead up to the death in the Gospel accounts themselves strongly supports this conclusion.

Exceptions

We should now ask, as the Christian would, do we have exceptions to the general idea of a prolonged stay on the cross and a criminals' graveyard burial[1] afterwards?

The problem here is that we have Roman practices (and often brutal rulership over their subjects) playing against Jewish desires based on religious law and ritual. Whilst there is evidence that Jews liked to bury their dead before sunset, at the time of Jesus' execution, this was a Roman province. I think I have laid this objection to bed in previous discussions. However, I will present a few sources here that you may be presented by skeptics arguing for a strictly Roman understanding.

We know in Egypt that Jewish philosopher Philo talks about someone being taken off the cross (as quoted earlier) on the Emperor's birthday and given to family members. But we must not get confused here: what Philo is saying here is that the Emperor's birthday can also be seen in terms of a holy day (i.e., that taking a body down always happens for holy days, and sometimes for the Emperor's birthday, too). Obviously, this has nothing to do with Jewish Passover or anything Jewish. We also know that Cicero mentions, in 70 BCE, a governor in Sicily who released bodies to family members for a fee. But, again, this is *not* Judea, and we know that Jesus' family didn't feature in his burial.

The Digesta (a compendium of Roman law, that though written hundreds of years later, is at times referring to previous rulings) suggests that people condemned to death should be given to their kinsfolk. However, this is *explicitly* not for criminals convicted of high treason. Jesus claimed to be king of the Jews and was condemned for such. Most apparent, he *explicitly* does not qualify for exemption: it was for simple crimes and suchlike. Moreover, Jesus had no kinfolk around, and there is no evidence that kinfolk requested his body – it was Joseph of Arimathea. Yet again, however, these sources are often called in to support the skeptic's or the Christian's case for various reasons, but the source

[1] This is the term I will use to cover both options of a criminal's tomb complex and a shallow grave, both of which are possibilities, and either together make a much greater probability than what the later Gospels entail.

is not dealing with Judea, so we must treat it with care. The Digesta is an attempt to universalise Roman law, and ignores the variance we find around certain parts of their empire and at certain times.

My reasons for including this "non-evidence" is in providing something like a cautionary tale for both Christian and skeptic alike.

There is also the case of Jehohanon. We have this one other nugget often thrown in by Christians to show precedence for honourable burials of criminals. There was, found in an ossuary, some ankle bones of a crucified person – therefore (given an ossuary), criminals can be buried in a tomb honourably! Not so fast.

These bones had to be hewn off the legs to get them off the cross. We have no idea how long the person was on the cross, and are pretty sure he was taken first to the shallow grave or criminals' grave. In fact, Carrier discusses this subject, in his essay "Jewish Law, the Burial of Jesus, and the Third Day":[1]

> A cautionary note is needed to prevent confusing temporary storage of a body with secondary burial. It is well known that the Jews practiced secondary burial: a corpse would receive a funeral and burial, then when the flesh rotted away (typically some months to a year later) the bones would be gathered, cleaned, and placed in an ossuary, a small box or chest for holding the bones of the reburied. Hence the Mishnah states "When the flesh has rotted, they collect the bones and bury them in their appropriate place" (Sanhedrin 6.6a; also, Talmud Mo'ed Katan 8a, Tractate Semahot 12.6-9; Tosefta, Sanhedrin, 9.8c, etc.). Numerous ossuaries have been found attesting to the practice, including one case of a clearly crucified man.

The latest analysis of this ossuary (the first was fraught with issues) concluded that he was a criminal crucified on a Pi-like structure upon which he was tied, later dying of asphyxiation. His bones were found in an inscribed ossuary. A nail was found in *one* heel bone:[2]

> The literary sources for the Roman period contain numerous descriptions of crucifixion but few exact details as to how the condemned were affixed to the cross. Unfortunately, the direct physical evidence here is also limited to one right heel calcaneum (heel bone) pierced by an 11.5 cm iron nail with traces of wood at both ends.

[1] Carrier (2002).

[2] Zias & Sekeles (1985), p. 26.

Does this give evidence, then, that a criminal can be buried in a tomb? No, not after crucifixion. It gives evidence of what we already know the Mishnah says: that a family can collect the bones from a registered criminal after a year to properly entomb them after the body has fully decomposed and purged of dishonour. This is not what the later Gospels entail.

In other words, there is this particular occasion of a criminal having his body taken down for proper burial almost certainly after enough time has elapsed for ritual purification and body decomposition. This is why we have the fusing of the nail to the bone in the heel. It was left for a year or so before being moved and placed in an ossuary. In that time of decomposition and rusting, the nail did what nails do. But execution for treason and for immediate honourable burial thereafter, there is simply *no* example of this ever having happened outside of the later, embellished Gospels.

The rites of mourning

There is scholarly agreement that dishonourable burials *disallowed* for public mourning in Jewish jurisprudence and ritual. As Jeremiah 22:18 stipulates: "They shall not lament for him...". The Talmud further verifies this opinion with "For those executed by the court, no rites whatsoever should he observed..." (Semahot 2:6). Mishnah Sanhedrin 6:6 also includes "And they used to not make open lamentation, but they went mourning, for mourning has its place in the heart."

It gets worse because this was a time of religious festival. As another Mishnah passage states (Moed Katan 3:7-9):

> A mourner must not observe mourning on festivals, for it is written: 'And thou shalt rejoice on thy feast'.

Exceptions for next of kin in terms of mourning are invalidated by point of fact that Jesus had no next of kin there in Jerusalem at this time (although John alone includes Jesus' mother at the cross – this is suspicious and arguably a later embellishment).

We are already aware of the "ignominious and obscure manner" of such burials from what I have previously set out. I scarcely think any of Jesus' followers would have been there to mourn – at least not publicly – and would, therefore, likely not know where Jesus was buried. This was a very humiliating time for his followers, and it certainly would have been dangerous for them to be present. The only incentive for there to have been witnesses was really to provide a mechanism for the story of the Resurrection.

And remember, as soon as Jesus was arrested, the disciples scattered like dust in the wind. These were not the sort of people to bravely break the rules at this time. Again, this is evidence from the Gospels themselves.

Therefore, we are beginning to see that the biblical narrative runs against what we know from historical analysis and common sense. If we piece together all of these ideas, like Joseph being fictional (as I set out earlier); the death likely being from stoning; burial in a criminals' graveyard; Pilate and the Sanhedrin being very unlikely to be involved; private discussions being known and written down; and with the yet-to-be discussed accounts of the Resurrection being contradictory; the tomb not being venerated (thus unknown, as discussed later); and so on, then we see the net closing in on the historical credibility of these accounts. Yet we are far from finished in our skeptical analysis.

Such is the colossal job that the Christian apologetic has to do to maintain that Christian beliefs are the most probable hypothesis to explain the data.

Compounding Probabilities

Here is something else methodological to consider concerning the eventual probability of a hypothesis determined by a cascade of dependent factors. I have assigned a number of these events previously discussed a rough percentage chance of happening in the following example. These are somewhat arbitrary and please see them as only proving a mathematical, methodological point rather than being in any way accurate. What we have hopefully learnt is that:

(1) It is unlikely that Jesus would have been crucified (he was more likely stoned to death and hung on a post). (40%)
(2) Had he been crucified, or subsequently hung on a post, there is some possibility he would have been taken down before sunset and the Passover. (60%)
(3) The chances of Joseph of Arimathea being a real person are very small for the reasons noted in the previous chapter. (2%)
(4) The chances he would have had time and access to Pilate, and that Pilate would agree to his request to pull down the body, are slim. (20%)
(5) The probability that criminals' graveyard fit for a criminal who has committed the worst crime, blasphemy, is low. (5%)
(6) It is implausible that Joseph would have had an empty tomb just ready for Jesus.[1] (15%)

[1] This is assuming the narrative of the later Gospels, and not arguing that Mark is, indeed, proposing a dishonourable burial in a criminals' grave.

And I could probably throw in a few more implausibilities on top of those listed above. Let me discuss how compounding percentages works here and why this might be a problem.

For the Resurrection account to be true as stated by the later Gospels, all the above had to take place. But for these particular claims to be true, the previous one in the list must be true. These are *dependent* claims.

How do we work out the overall percentage of all of this happening? It is not a case of looking down the list of percentages and seeing the lowest one and taking that as being the overall chance of this happening, The lowest one is 2% but this does not mean the overall percentage of all of these things happening is 2%. One starts with 40%, takes a 60% chance *of that* 40%, and then a 2% chance of the now-remaining percentage.

Thus, to get to the end of (3), one has to do this calculation (where I am converting percentages to decimals):

0.4 x 0.6 x 0.02 = 0.0048 = 0.48%

So to get to the end of (3), our low probabilities are compounded to leave us with a much lower 0.48%.

If we were to continue this to the end of my arbitrary figures, we would finish with a compounded probability of the story happening of 0.0000072%.

If there are other unlikelihoods, and if my arbitrary percentages are far too generous (they are), then that miniscule chance of this event taking place in the way recounted is even lower.

And then add all of the other problems of the differing, if not conflicting narratives!

That said, some of the other claims are separable from these death claims; as mentioned, the reason I have applied this calculation methodology here is that you can't have (6) without (5) and (4) and (3) before it, whereas you can have the death events and not have the earthquake of Matthew 27, which is independent of these events that are causally connected. This escapes it being a Fallacy of Diminishing Probabilities.

Concluding Remarks

It is worth my while quickly drawing together some conclusions here. For ease of reading, I will bullet point these:

(1) I don't think this likely happened on the Passover week (this is a theological contrivance) or just before Sabbath.
(2) The Christian *could* argue that Mark is recounting a dishonourable burial in a criminals' graveyard and that the later Gospels are correcting the narrative and putting more meat on the bones (yes, pun intended).

(3) I personally don't think Mark *is* recounting this, as, for example, the tomb appears not to be the complex one would expect, and with Joseph doing the "spadework". The later Gospels are still greatly embellishing Mark's lack of details.
(4) Jesus was probably stoned, and then "hung" or displayed, and taken down by sunset when he died.
(5) If he *was* crucified, it almost certainly wasn't on a cross.
(6) Pilate was unlikely involved.
(7) His followers were unlikely there (and not close if they were), and witnesses were only used as mechanisms for an empty tomb narrative and to contrive certain supposed evidence and sayings.
(8) Jesus would not have died so quickly.
(9) Jesus was almost certainly buried dishonourably. There is a possibility his body was stored temporarily and then later moved to a criminal's graveyard.

14 – Matthew's Tomb Guards, Bribes and Not Believing

The earliest accounts of Jesus' burial have him simply "buried" (1 Corinthians 15:4; Romans 6:4) and this could refer to a simple, shallow grave or an ignominious shelf in a Sanhedrin tomb complex littered with the corpses of other criminals. Later empty tomb creations allow for a more ostentatious story of resurrection that befits a God-man. As a later development, we can see a coextensive relationship between the Gospels and growing counter-arguments to them, which Gospel stories get embellished to answer.

This chapter refers to a Resurrection account given by Matthew, an addition found in no other Gospel account: that there were guards stationed at the tomb. Before we look in any detail at this assertion, it is worth noting that the fact that no other Gospel contains this part of the story should give us cause for concern.

According to Matthew, the chief priests were worried that the disciples might steal Jesus' body to fake a resurrection, so they went to Pilate and got permission to post guards at the tomb. When Jesus rose from the dead, the guards reported it to the priests, and the priests bribed them to claim that disciples stole the body while they were asleep. Matthew claims that "to this day" Jews report the body as stolen (as opposed to resurrected).

So what is really going on here? I look to investigate the historicity of this claim and conclude that the guards at the tomb, as according to Matthew, were ahistorical and that this whole section of the narrative serves only the purpose of being a counter-argument to early Jewish naysayers.

Let us look at how contrived the setting of the guard appears to be (Matthew 27):

> 62 Now on the next day, the day after the preparation, the chief priests and the Pharisees gathered together with Pilate, 63 and said, "Sir, we remember that when He was still alive that deceiver said, 'After three days I am to rise again.' 64 Therefore, give orders for the grave to be made secure until the third day, otherwise His disciples may come and steal Him away and say to the people, 'He has risen from the dead,' and the last deception will be worse than the first." 65 Pilate said to them, "You have a guard; go, make it as secure as you know how." 66 And they went and made the grave secure, and along with the guard they set a seal on the stone.

Christian apologists, such as William Lane Craig,[1] have variously attempted to defend the account as being historical. The critical view of this passage, as Craig sees it, is that the guard is a Christian invention aimed at refuting the Jewish allegation that the scheming disciples had stolen the body.

The first problem here that defenders need to deal with is the idea that, at the time of making these veiled claims, nobody believed Jesus, not even his disciples. And it is not even a case of *believed* – they simply didn't *understand* what he was talking about. And suddenly, after his death, you have a collection of worried Pharisees who seem to know *exactly* what could be in store (see John 2:18-22 and Matthew 27:39-40) and arouse themselves to action.

The second problem here is that the Pharisees are demanding a guard after an entire night has already passed, giving ample opportunity for the body to have been stolen already. In an article on *Alethian Worldview*, "Gospel Disproof #38: The guards at the tomb", we read a good skeptical counter:[2]

> They're too late! Jesus' body has already been unguarded all night. Considering that one of the things Jesus was executed for was his relaxed attitude towards Sabbath prohibitions, there has been ample opportunity for some small group of unnamed disciples to get to the unguarded tomb, remove the body, and get away before the Sanhedrin even asked for a guard. Even if they had posted a belated guard, once the body was gone then their excuse would be "disciples took it before we got there," not "disciples took it while we were sleeping on the job." Matthew screwed up again.
>
> It's just not a plausible story. We know it's intended to deny that disciples took the body, because that's what Matthew tells us it "proves." And as a form of denial, it's psychologically effective for believers.
>
> As reliable history, though, it really sucks.

Let us see how Matthew 28 continues:

> **28** Now after the Sabbath, as it began to dawn toward the first day of
> the week, Mary Magdalene and the other Mary came to look at the
> grave. **2** And behold, a severe earthquake had occurred, for an angel of
> the Lord descended from heaven and came and rolled away the stone
> and sat upon it. **3** And his appearance was like lightning, and his cloth-
> ing as white as snow. **4** The guards shook for fear of him and became
> like dead men. **5** The angel said to the women, "Do not be afraid; for I

[1] Craig (1984).

[2] "Gospel Disproof #38: The guards at the tomb", *Alethian Worldview*, https://freethoughtblogs.com/alethianworldview/2012/02/27/gospel-disproof-38-the-guards-at-the-tomb/ (Retrieved 12/12/2020).

> know that you are looking for Jesus who has been crucified. [6] He is not here, for He has risen, just as He said. Come, see the place where He was lying. [7] Go quickly and tell His disciples that He has risen from the dead; and behold, He is going ahead of you into Galilee, there you will see Him; behold, I have told you."
>
> [8] And they left the tomb quickly with fear and great joy and ran to report it to His disciples. [9] And behold, Jesus met them and greeted them. And they came up and took hold of His feet and worshiped Him. [10] Then Jesus *said to them, "Do not be afraid; go and take word to My brethren to leave for Galilee, and there they will see Me."
>
> [11] Now while they were on their way, some of the guard came into the city and reported to the chief priests all that had happened. [12] And when they had assembled with the elders and consulted together, they gave a large sum of money to the soldiers, [13] and said, "You are to say, 'His disciples came by night and stole Him away while we were asleep.' [14] And if this should come to the governor's ears, we will win him over and keep you out of trouble." [15] And they took the money and did as they had been instructed; and this story was widely spread among the Jews, and is to this day.

The next thing to notice is how different this account is from the other Gospels. The guards simply did not feature in the other Gospels. At all. Not one single reference. One must assume that since there were incredibly few witnesses of this event (and this, too, depends on what Gospel you read, from Mary to Salome to Peter); it means that the Gospel writers could only have had no more than four witnesses to use as original sources. Even then, writing at the time they did, and even if they did have access to the original first-hand witnesses, there would most likely have only been one alive and findable to interview if we could even stretch plausibility that far. Since the Gospels were written in different places and in foreign languages, it raises the question as to whether the writers had *any* access to such witnesses. Thus, it is a tough call as to whether we can trust accounts such as the Gospels with unknown sources and accounts that differ so much on such basic details. To make matters worse, the Gospel of Mark has the Marys and Salome going to the tomb to anoint the body. If they knew guards would be there, then they would simply not do this (that and the fact that he had already been anointed in Bethany – double incoherence).

The problem for Matthew is that the only witnesses to this purported event are the guards themselves, which makes one wonder where the testimony for this story really originated. One further issue here is of conversations. Again, we have the problem of how personal conversations are recorded and known.

These are private conversations amongst Jews and one wonders how Christians would find out about them. Moreover, as the *Alethian Worldview* article reads:

> The problem Matthew is facing is that by putting the guards around the tomb, he's creating a narrative in which the guards are the only actual eyewitnesses to the resurrection itself. He can't write a Gospel in which the only eyewitnesses are giving plausible testimony about the disciples stealing the body. So he gives them a stupid testimony instead, sacrificing realism for agenda.

Craig claims because Matthew is less embellished than the Gospel of Peter, the non-canonical Gospel that *does* include the story,[1] that, therefore, it demonstrates its historical validity.

Craig claims:

> By contrast in Matthew's story the guard is something of an afterthought; the fact that they were not thought of and posted until the next day could reflect the fact that only Friday night did the Jews learn that Joseph had, contrary to expectation, placed the body in a tomb, rather than allowing it to be discarded in a common grave. This could have motivated their unusual visit to Pilate the next day.

Of course, the "coulds" here speak volumes. There is nothing to suggest that this addition is anything less than a mechanism similar to the apologetics of Peter, just slightly less fanciful.

Craig continues:

> But perhaps the strongest consideration in favor of the historicity of the guard is the history of polemic presupposed in this story. The Jewish slander that the disciples stole the body was probably the reaction to the Christian proclamation that Jesus was risen. This Jewish allegation is also mentioned in *Justin Dialogue with Trypho* 108. To counter this charge the Christians would need only point out that the guard at the tomb would have prevented such a theft and that they were immobilized with fear when the angel appeared.

Well, so far so good. This is entirely what the mechanism seems to set out to do, and indeed what it achieves (if believed).

---

[1] See Raymond Brown's translation here: http://www.earlychristianwritings.com/text/gospelpeter-brown.html (Retrieved 09/03/2021).

In my opinion, the account goes like this – with this dialogue developing over some time within early Christian and Jewish polemics:

Christian: Jesus resurrected from his tomb.

Jew: No he didn't. Anyway, how do you know his body didn't get stolen – this is a more probable explanation.

C: ... Um, aah, because there were guards outside the tomb on the insistence of the Pharisees.

J: Okay, but what if the guards were asleep.

C: The guards were not asleep.

J: How do you know?

C: Because we know that they saw it.

J: But why didn't they tell anyone? Why is this not known everywhere since this is the Resurrection of the Messiah?

C: Because the guards told their superiors and were bribed to keep silent and then disappeared.

J: That's...suspiciously convenient.

We can see the way that this narrative clearly (to me) developed. What is plainly in the critical evaluator's favour is the notion that the guards, having seen one of the most incredible sights – God resurrecting like lightning in the middle of an earthquake – decide that this is not life-changing enough and simply go back to their superiors and say...

"You know what, that man only went and resurrected!"

"Did he really! Well, I'll be! Here are some shekels for you. Don't say anything about witnessing the *real and actual* God resurrecting in human form to the heavens. Run along, like a good chap."

"Right you are sir. Nothing to see here."

It's just ridiculous that, if the guards *actually* witnessed this supposed event, and the Pharisees heard their account, they would continue to be loyal-to-the-nonbelieving-Sanhedrin guards and nonbelieving Pharisees and even attempt to cover it up! If you saw God in such a way as this, you would say, "Wow, that's God. I now believe!" It's just utterly nonsensical. As one commentator adds:[1]

> These soldiers allegedly have front-row seats to the most important and impressive miracle of all time.

[1] "Bible: Outrageous Resurrection Account -- Gospel of Matthew", *Conversational Atheist*, (2011).

> They don't, however, start worshiping the obvious God-man whose death and resurrection bring about earthquakes, darkness in the middle of days and angels descending from heaven.
>
> Instead, they return to the priests that sent them to guard this "impostor's" tomb and tell them everything that happened.
>
> These priests are now in quite a situation. They had to deal with all the stresses of organizing the Passover, and then they had to deal with this rabble-rousing Jesus character. And, as soon as they get Jesus sentenced to death, the trouble really begins.
>
> There was an earthquake, the temple curtain being ripped from the ceiling to the floor, darkness that covered all the land, and now another earthquake.
>
> On top of that there are all these reports of all kinds of dead saints that are walking around today, and to top it all off, the guards that the priests THEMSELVES had posted to guard the tomb came running back, terrified, telling them, "Hey! That guy that you sent to death for falsely proclaiming to be sent by God... Turns out, He is God! We were there, guarding the place... earthquake happens, angel comes blazing in from the sky rolls away the stone, Jesus came back to life just like he said would happen!"
>
> At this point, if you don't know how the story goes in Matthew, you might guess that the soldiers and priests became Christians and followed Jesus for the rest of their days.
>
> You'd be wrong.

I can't stress this enough, but that account above is incredibly important to showing how patently ridiculous is the whole Easter story and how it is devoid of any historical veracity. It makes no historical sense and it makes no common sense. These characters, absolutely guaranteed, would not have reacted in such a manner.

Christian apologist William Lane Craig, though, seems to ignore this common-sense reality. His first real defence is as follows:

> In the first place it is unlikely that the Christians would invent a fiction like the guard, which everyone, especially their Jewish opponents, would realize never existed. Lies are the most feeble sort of apologetic there could be. Since the Jewish/Christian controversy no doubt originated in Jerusalem, then it is hard to understand how Christians could have tried to refute their opponents' charge with a falsification which would have been plainly untrue, since there were no guards about who claimed to have been stationed at the tomb.

Of course, this prompts one to say that most of the Gospels look like a lie of sorts, and this further claim is no different. There are flat-out contradictions and there is ripping of the Temple curtains, there are resurrected saints parading around inner Jerusalem. None of this material is attested to elsewhere and so it seems like the material looks rather like lies to me. Also, as discussed earlier, in writing after the destruction of the Temple, the Temple records would have been destroyed. There would be no verification available to such questioners. It is the perfect time, indeed, to lie! Moreover, the city was kept a perpetual ruin by a Roman garrison until Hadrian rebuilt it half a century later, and even then as a pagan city from which Jews remained at times banned; Craig seems to imagine Matthew being published, inexplicably in the wrong language, in a thriving Jerusalem, not one whose population had decades ago been killed off or sold abroad into slavery and banned from even reinhabiting the place. Simply appealing to it being a feeble form of apologetic does not get the Gospel off the hook.

As implied, if this claim originated in the writing of Matthew, then this occurred some fifty to sixty years after the death of Jesus. Verification would be utterly impossible. This is a poor defence from Craig, who goes on to say:

> But secondly, it is even more improbable that confronted with this palpable lie, the Jews would, instead of exposing and denouncing it as such, proceed to create another lie, even stupider, that the guard had fallen asleep while the disciples broke into the tomb and absconded with the body. If the existence of the guard were false, then the Jewish polemic would never have taken the course that it did. Rather the controversy would have stopped right there with the renunciation that any such guard had ever been set by the Jews. It would never have come to the point that the Christians had to invent a third lie, that the Jews had bribed the fictional guard.

However, as I set out above, this would not necessarily be a lie, but a hypothesis. This defence is simply misplaced. The Jews could not verify whether a guard was posted or not, and so the dialogue would simply have progressed as I listed earlier in the chapter. Both sides make claims that were simply not falsifiable. The renunciation, as Craig claims, would be nothing more than an unverifiable assertion by the Jews that would allow the Christians to make their own unverifiable assertions. It's just another big Easter mess.

Craig concedes that his evidence is in the balance – not particularly strong either way – whilst saying that even if it were a lie, it doesn't affect the truth of the core Resurrection claim (covering both bases). How convenient:

> So although there are reasons to doubt the existence of the guard at the tomb, there are also weighty considerations in its favor. It seems best to leave it an open question. Ironically, the value of Matthew's story for the evidence for the resurrection has nothing to do with the guard at all or with his intention of refuting the allegation that the disciples had stolen the body.
>
> The conspiracy theory has been universally rejected on moral and psychological grounds, so that the guard story as such is really quite superfluous. Guard or no guard, no critic today believes that the disciples could have robbed the tomb and faked the resurrection. Rather the real value of Matthew's story is the incidental – and for that reason all the more reliable – information that Jewish polemic never denied that the tomb was empty, but instead tried to explain it away. Thus the early opponents of the Christians themselves bear witness to the fact of the empty tomb.

Trying to devalue the thesis that it is an ahistorical addition by trying to smear it as a mere conspiracy theory is a fairly poor show. "Universal rejection" is shorthand, it seems, for William Lane Craig and other theists interested in (and often doctrinally contracted to) maintaining the truth of the Gospel accounts. Afterwards, he proclaims, "no critic today believes that the disciples could have robbed the tomb and faked the resurrection", amounts to nothing more than an Argument from Incredulity, asserting what nonbelievers supposedly believe, rhetorically daring the reader to disagree. Yet such a hypothesis is one amongst many far more plausible explanations than simply accepting that the "Godmanspirit" died for our sins and was resurrected, all whilst the world continues to sin in exactly the same way.

This kind of mere assertion is similar to the "75% of New Testament scholars" claim we saw earlier and is nothing if not a little lazy. Nonetheless, it will undoubtedly work well on the non-discerning Christian reader keen on confirming their worldview.

Another problem is that the guards would clearly have been Roman since they were issued by Pilate. If this was not the case, the Sanhedrin would simply have got their own men and not bothered Pilate. Furthermore, in the exact passage about the bribe, the members of the guard are referred to as *stratiotai*, a Greek word that unambiguously meant "infantry soldiers".[1] Accepting bribes is punishable by death, so what would cause them to be so rash? Why would they then have confessed to this bribe, presumably, to the Gospel writers or someone

[1] See Liddell & Scott, *A Greek-English Lexicon*, Στρατιώται, https://tinyurl.com/2kxx9jez (Retrieved 09/03/2021).

else to pass it on to the writers, since that might as well be signing their own death warrant!

In conclusion, the guards weren't there! In itself, not earth-shattering. But what this episode does is open the floodgates further still to continue to raise questions as to what other Gospel claims and what other aspects of the Resurrection claims are false. How can we differentiate that which is false from that which is true, if indeed *any* of the account is based on historical fact?

Raymond Brown, the Catholic scholar who I have already referenced several times, has this to say on the matter:[1]

> Yet there is a major argument against the historicity that is impressive indeed. Not only do the other Gospels not mention the guard at this sepulchre, but the presence of the guard there would make what they narrate about the tomb almost unintelligible. The three other canonical Gospels have women come to the tomb on Easter, and the only obstacle to the entrance that is mentioned is the stone. Certainly the evangelists would have had to explain how the woman hoped to get into the tomb if there were a guard placed there precisely to prevent entry.... There are other internal implausibilities in Matt's account.... The lack of harmony with the other Gospels touches on the heart of the story, i.e., the very existence of the guard.... More accurate is the observation that as with other Matthean material (e.g., Herod's slaughtering the children at Bethlehem and the flight to Egypt - a story with functional parallels to the present story), there is neither internal nor external evidence to cause us to affirm historicity.
>
> That, of course, does not mean the story is without value. I have suggested that the polemic and apologetic functions were probably secondary, and that the more fundamental thrust was an apocalyptic eschatology or dramatization of the power of God to make the cause of the Son successful against all human opposition, no matter how powerful.

I couldn't have put it better myself. Or, the account didn't actually occur. If you don't believe me, then perhaps one of the foremost Christian biblical exegetes will pass the muster.

---

[1] Brown (1994), p. 1311-12.

15 – A Tomb; an Empty Tomb

The empty tomb thesis is the claim that Jesus' tomb, where Joseph of Arimathea supposedly buried him, was eventually found empty. This is often seen by Christian apologists as a central component of the Resurrection story – as historical evidence to back up the claim. Concerning this supernatural event, I must stress here that the Resurrection in question is a resurrection of the flesh because this view is somewhat contested, as we will see in a later chapter. To whet your appetite, here are Bart Ehrman's words from his section called "The Need for an Empty Tomb" in a chapter on the Resurrection in *How Jesus Became God*:[1]

> I want to stress that adjective [*physically*]. Without an empty tomb, there would be no ground for saying that Jesus was *physically* raised.... [S]ome early Christians believed that Jesus was raised in spirit, but that his body decomposed. Eventually, this view came to be prominent among different groups of Christian Gnostics. We can see evidence of its presence even in the communities of the authors who produced our canonical Gospels. The later the Gospel, the more the attempt to "prove" that Jesus was raised bodily, not simply spiritually.[2]

So the empty tomb is not only essential for the Resurrection narrative but a particular type of resurrection – a "physical" (bodily) one – to fit the agendas of the later Gospel writers.

William Lane Craig is a famous exponent of the idea that the empty tomb is fundamental to historically validating the Easter Story. The support he gives for the empty tomb is as follows:[3]

> (1) Paul's account suggests the historical authenticity of the empty tomb, (2) the existence of the empty tomb text in the pre-Markan passion narrative supports its historical authenticity, (3) the usage of 'on the first day of the week' rather than 'on the third day' indicates the primitiveness of the oral history, (4) the account is theologically

[1] Ehrman (2014), p. 168.
[2] It is well worth noting here that Ehrman might slightly misunderstand matters with his use of the word "physically". There were no versions of the Resurrection that didn't feature "physical bodies"; the dispute even among Christians was only over *which* body one rose in, so a tomb with a body still in it did not mean resurrection without a body, but resurrection in a different body; the contrary was never the case. More on this in a later chapter devoted to the topic.
[3] More recently rewritten into an updated version of his argument, "The Historicity of the Empty Tomb of Jesus" – Craig (n.d.b).

unembellished and non-apologetic, (5) the finding of the tomb by women is very likely, (6) the inspection of the empty tomb by the apostles is historically likely, (7) it would have not been possible for the apostles to declare the resurrection in Jerusalem had the tomb not been empty, (8) the Jewish polemic presumes the empty tomb.

He originally included a few more claims on his list, such as the lack of veneration of the tomb, as further evidence, but these seem to be missing from his later writings. I deal with a lack of veneration and conclude antithetically to him in a later chapter. The superb book, *The Empty Tomb: Jesus Beyond the Grave* (edited by Robert M. Price and Jeffery Jay Lowder) is an exhaustive refutation of these points above. You can see the trouble I will have in summing up a huge book into a short chapter.

Although I will mention naturalistic hypotheses later in this book, it is worth briefly mentioning one of my favoured theories: the relocation hypothesis.[1] This theory is based on the notion that Jesus was crucified, died on the cross and was hastily buried in a tomb for a short while due to the approaching holy festivities. Shortly afterwards and unbeknownst to his followers, Jesus was then reburied in a dishonourable manner. This would mean that those followers who thought that Jesus was still there in the original tomb would have had no idea that the body had been relocated and would have returned to the tomb to find it empty. This hypothesis seems a far more plausible explanation than a resurrecting man-God. I say this now because it gives you some idea of what could have happened in the context of discussing the empty tomb as reported in the Gospels.

The Tomb Itself

Before I go on, I would like to quickly discuss the tomb itself. Or, more pertinently, the stone that supposedly enclosed it. I have already discussed the unlikeliness of a Sanhedrin member having an empty tomb conveniently available for Jesus (and not the other criminals) to be buried in.[2] However, a further problem involves the shape of the stone door.

The stone that blocked the entrance is described as a "very large" stone with the woman visiting the tomb asking "Who will roll away the stone for us?" (Mark 16:3)

The issue here is that archaeological evidence suggests that Jesus would almost certainly have had a square-shaped ("cork-shaped", counter-intuitively, despite what we imagine by corks) stone door. For instance, Megan Sauter

[1] As set out by Jeffery Jay Lowder in Price & Lowder (2005), p. 266-301.

[2] This still allows for Mark's account, lacking in the embellishment of the later Gospels.

states in her article "How Was Jesus' Tomb Sealed?" for *Biblical Archaeology Society*:[1]

> In fact, of the more than 900 Second Temple-period burial caves around Jerusalem examined by archaeologist Amos Kloner, only four have been discovered with disk-shaped blocking stones. These four elegant Jerusalem tombs belonged to the wealthiest–even royal–families, such as the tomb of Queen Helena of Adiabene.
>
> Was the tomb of Jesus among the "top four" Jerusalem tombs from the Second Temple period?
>
> Since disk-shaped blocking stones were so rare and since Jesus' tomb was built for an ordinary person–because it was actually the borrowed, but unused, tomb of Joseph of Arimathea (Matthew 27:60)–it seems highly unlikely that it would have been outfitted with a disk-shaped blocking stone.

Matthew, Mark and Luke have the stone as being "rolled away", with John having it "taken away". However, even the archaeologist mentioned above, Amos Kloner, himself argues that the Gospels are still referring to a square stone, which would make more sense for the angels to be able to sit on. This prompts apologists to look more closely at the word for "to roll". The problem, perhaps, is either a potential contradiction of known archaeology or something that can be solved with a little bit of lexical give and take.

One critical position to take that has some sound reasoning behind it is the fact that when the Gospels were written, after 70 CE, round stones were much more likely at tombs. As a result, tombstones at the door literally would have been rolled away. Therefore, if you were writing at that time and locale, and using words historically au fait with your tomb door construction knowledge, you would assume a round stone covering the entrance. In reality, however, the tomb would be covered with a square-shaped stone that would be pretty difficult to shift, especially if you were a couple of women coming to anoint the body without any prior organisation (no sexism intended).[2] More on that subject later.

---

[1] Sauter (2019).

[2] Though the Gospels even have the women themselves admit they would not be able to do it themselves, which the authors certainly thought to be accurate (e.g., Mark 16:3).

The Silence of Paul

Of course, I have dealt with this idea in the earlier chapter on the subject and I do not want to belabour the point.

The simple fact of the matter is that there is no mention of the empty tomb in Paul's epistle to the Corinthians, as the earliest source; there is just a burial. No tomb, no Joseph of Arimathea, and no discovery of an *empty tomb*. It is an interesting observation that Paul only provides two types of evidence for the Resurrection at all, namely scripture and personal epiphanies, neither of which count for much at all.

Bart Ehrman has this to say on the topic:[1]

> The discovery of the empty tomb presupposes that there was a tomb in the first place, and that it was known, and of course that it was discovered. But if serious doubt is cast on whether there ever was a tomb, then the accounts of its discovery are similarly thrown into doubt. Christian apologists often argue that the discovery of the empty tomb is one of the most secure historical data from the history of the early Christian movement. I used to think so myself. But it simply isn't true. Given our suspicions about the burial tradition, there are plenty of reasons to doubt the discovery of an empty tomb....
>
> But all of this is beside the point, which is that we don't know whether the tomb was discovered empty because we don't know whether there even was a tomb.
>
> In this connection I should stress that the discovery of the empty tomb appears to be a late tradition. It occurs in Mark for the first time, some thirty-five or forty years after Jesus died. Our earliest witness, Paul, does not say anything about it.

This quotation goes right to the heart of the matter; the tomb appears to be a critical claim in the Easter story. Indeed, whenever we think about the narrative, we think cross and tomb. For Paul to be so silent on these matters is to raise serious concerns.

For Paul, as we learnt at the beginning of this book, the Resurrection was everything. You would certainly expect, if someone was proposing a hugely crucial element to their belief, that they would provide evidence of that core event, or at least reference some aspect of that event. But there is *nothing*! I remind you of absence of evidence *being* evidence of absence if the absence is of something you would otherwise very much expect.

---

[1] Ehrman (2014), p. 164-65.

Mark: simple and early

Mark 16 recounts events as follows:

> When the Sabbath was over, Mary Magdalene, and Mary the mother of James, and Salome, bought spices, so that they might come and anoint Him. 2 Very early on the first day of the week, they came to the tomb when the sun had risen. 3 They were saying to one another, "Who will roll away the stone for us from the entrance of the tomb?" 4 Looking up, they saw that the stone had been rolled away, although it was extremely large. 5 Entering the tomb, they saw a young man sitting at the right, wearing a white robe; and they were amazed. 6 And he said to them, "Do not be amazed; you are looking for Jesus the Nazarene, who has been crucified. He has risen; He is not here; behold, here is the place where they laid Him. 7 But go, tell His disciples and Peter, 'He is going ahead of you to Galilee; there you will see Him, just as He told you.'" 8 They went out and fled from the tomb, for trembling and astonishment had gripped them; and they said nothing to anyone, for they were afraid.

Remember that this is where Mark's Gospel originally finished, with the rest of the narrative being an interpolation (see as follows).

> 9 Now after He had risen early on the first day of the week, He first appeared to Mary Magdalene, from whom He had cast out seven demons. 10 She went and reported to those who had been with Him, while they were mourning and weeping. 11 When they heard that He was alive and had been seen by her, they refused to believe it.

Apologists such as William Lane Craig argue that the Markan tradition of the empty tomb is early and simple, and this points to it being likely true. Where he says the others "are coloured by theological and other developments", he says of the Markan account that it "is a simple, straightforward report of what happened."[1] What is interesting about this quote is that it rather implies that the later Gospels of Luke, Matthew and John are legendary embellishments. Therefore, we have claims that are not true if Mark's straightforwardness is a sign of truth! Quite some tacit admission!

There are two issues with this approach:

---

[1] As cited in Lowder, from Price & Lowder (2005) p. 280-82, citing William Lane Craig, *Did Jesus Rise*, p. 151.

a) This still doesn't mean that Mark is true or even likely true.
b) We return to the matter of arbitrary lines of embellishment and legendary character talked about earlier that lies behind the choice of the four canonical Gospels.

This second point is important. Just because Mark may be the least embellished and outlandish of the Gospels, including the non-canonical Gospels, that reality doesn't mean that it isn't outlandish in itself. "The least racist person is still racist", as the saying goes (I am analogising a point, not poisoning the Christian Bible with racism). Not only does Mark's Gospel still entail all the theological issues with its narrative, but also it still contains an incredibly improbable and miraculous claim. As Jeffery Lowder observes:[1]

> And most of the "theological and other developments" in the latter documents are found precisely within the sections that the Markan account of the resurrection lacks. Most of the motifs listed by Craig as legendary - including a description of the resurrection itself, reflection on Jesus's triumph over sin and death, quotation of fulfilled prophecy, or a description of the risen Jesus - are found within the empty tomb stories of the Gospel of Peter and the Ascension of Isaiah. In other words, while the resurrection stories in both the Gospel of Peter and the Ascension of Isaiah are "theologically adorned," the empty tomb stories of both accounts do not appear to be significantly more theologically adorned than that of the Gospel of Mark.

Mark doesn't explain who the "young man" is (to be discussed later) and so the assumption is, particularly from Christians, that this man was an angel. The probability of this claim being true will depend upon whether you believe in angels or not, and we have discussed ideas of presuppositions and background knowledge earlier. But, even so, if you did believe in angels, then any given claim is still incredibly improbable in terms of being true, given the vast number of claims that have existed over time. So again, if you do believe in angels, you still need a very high level of evidence to support any such claim. Do these verses in Mark qualify as exceptionally high levels of evidence? Do we accept these claims on the historical grounds of a mere Gospel assertion? However, it gets worse because, as we will see in the next chapter, some evidence that suggests that this "young man" isn't actually an angel but a recurring figure throughout the Gospel (and its longer version, the Secret Gospel of Mark).

---

[1] Lowder, in Price & Lowder (2005), p. 280-81.

Even Catholic historian E.L. Bode, a man whom William Lane Craig relies heavily upon, concludes:[1]

> Rather, our position is that the angel appearance does not belong to the historical nucleus of the tomb tradition. This omission does not call into question the existence of angelic beings. The stance is taken for two reasons: (1). The kerygmatic and redactional nature of the angel's message and (2) the omission gives a better insight into the tomb tradition and its development.

There is no doubt that angels are typical mechanisms that act as divine messengers from God and prove very useful tools for biblical authors to employ and Mark is no exception.

Simply put, "simpler" does not necessarily mean true.

One final point to add to this is brought up by Richard Carrier. This could be utilised in my chapter on the guards at the tomb but I will employ it here:[2]

> Matthew's stated excuse for introducing guards into the story of the empty tomb narrative...reveals a rhetoric that apparently only appeared after the publication of Mark's account of an empty tomb. For Mark shows no awareness of the problem. It clearly hadn't occurred to Mark when composing the empty tomb story that it would invite accusations the Christians stole the body (much less that any such accusations were already flying). Which should be evidence enough that Matthew invented that story, as otherwise surely that retort would have been a constant drum beat for decades already, powerfully motivating Mark to answer or resolve it (if his sources already hadn't, and they most likely would have). There can therefore have been no such accusation of theft by the time Mark wrote.

This Gospel reality is an argument against the empty tomb story itself: if no "you just stole the body" polemic had arisen in forty years of evangelism (i.e., by the time Mark wrote his Gospel), that strongly suggests there had been no "empty tomb" claim circulating for Jews to react against; therefore, Mark clearly is the first to invent it, provoking the "you just stole it" response *afterward*, which Matthew is *then* forced to respond to. This supports Ehrman's claim that we heard earlier concerning the silence of Paul: "Our earliest witness, Paul, does not say anything about it."[3]

---

[1] Bode (1970), p. 166.
[2] Carrier (2012), p. 128.
[3] Ehrman (2014), p. 165.

Verifiability

William Lane Craig, in his many reasons as to why the empty tomb is a historical narrative, argues that the investigation of the empty tomb by Peter and John is evidence of the claim being historical. He states, as evidence:[1]

> *6. The investigation of the empty tomb by the disciples is historically probable.* Behind the fourth gospel stands the Beloved Disciple, whose reminiscences fill out the traditions employed. The visit of the disciples to the empty tomb is therefore attested not only in tradition but by this disciple. His testimony has therefore the same first hand character as Paul's and ought to be accepted as equally reliable. The historicity of the disciples' visit is also made likely by the plausibility of the denial of Peter tradition, for if he was in Jerusalem, then having heard the women's report he would quite likely check it out. The inherent implausibility of and absence of any evidence for the disciples' flight to Galilee render it highly likely that they were in Jerusalem, which fact makes the visit to the tomb also likely.

Of course, if the account is made up, then this is a rather moot point. In other words, if the women didn't discover the empty tomb, then there would be no story for John and Peter to verify or their verification is itself false. The idea that two disciples went to check the women's claim of the empty tomb is equally as fictional as the empty tomb claim itself (being in the very same sources). It is just self-referential. William Lane Craig seems to think that the empty tomb is evidenced by a supposedly historical attestation to verification by Peter and John through tradition (Luke 24, esp. 24:12; John 20:3) and Peter's denial (Mark 14:66-72); this denial would supposedly make Peter want to check out the women's story. Craig believes that John's testimony "has therefore the same first-hand character as Paul's and ought to be accorded equal weight".[2]

The problem here, in presupposing the truth of the empty tomb, is one of having the cart before the horse; undoubtedly, such post hoc rationalisations look to shore up the apologists' case.

John 20, in contradiction of Mark *having the women tell no one,* reads:

> Now on the first day of the week Mary Magdalene came early to the tomb, while it was still dark, and saw the stone already taken away from the tomb. 2 So she ran and came to Simon Peter and to the other disciple whom Jesus loved, and said to them, "They have taken away the Lord out of the tomb, and we do not know where they have laid

[1] Craig (n.d.b.).

[2] Craig (1989), p. 368.

> Him." [3] So Peter and the other disciple went forth, and they were going to the tomb.

Luke 24 states (of "the women who had come with Him out of Galilee"), *again in contradiction of the earlier* (as Craig says, straightforward and trustworthy) *Mark*:

> [8] And they remembered His words, [9] and returned from the tomb and reported all these things to the eleven and to all the rest. [10] Now they were Mary Magdalene and Joanna and Mary the mother of James; also the other women with them were telling these things to the apostles. [11] But these words appeared to them as nonsense, and they would not believe them. [12] But Peter got up and ran to the tomb; stooping and looking in, he saw the linen wrappings only; and he went away to his home, marveling at what had happened....
>
> "... [24] Some of those who were with us went to the tomb and found it just exactly as the women also had said; but Him they did not see."

It is worth noting that there is much discussion (isn't there always!) that verse 12 is an interpolation since it is missing from certain manuscripts. If the original Gospel were without this verse, then Luke would contain no disciple verification (it doesn't even mention the disciple John, as the Gospel of John does with "the other disciple"). Thus, the latest and arguably most different Gospel might be the only one to have apparent disciple verification. This isn't particularly a great piece of evidence for Craig to cite for the claim of the empty tomb being historical!

And Mark and Matthew, two of the earliest Gospels, do not mention such disciple verification of the empty tomb at all. Why would this be?

Craig maintains[1] that this lack of verification was because women weren't considered legal eyewitnesses.[2] But he can't have his cake and eat it too (though that is, indeed, what cakes are for). Either the women were not legal eyewitnesses, and so we have the disciples visiting the tomb *in all accounts*, or the legal witness issue is not relevant as this is not a legal case, and the women should suffice *in all accounts*. Craig is trying to cover both bases.

If the women were supposed to be silent, as we learn from Mark, then how long was this silence? We can make sense of a medium- to long-term silence as things often tend to get out anyway, and they would need to for there to be a story at all. But, if Luke and John are to be trusted, this silence would

---

[1] Craig (1995), p. 151.

[2] Worth noting that Richard Carrier shows this not to be the case in Chapter 11, Carrier (2009), p. 297-321.

have to be only momentary. Importantly, it wouldn't be a silence at all. This incident is an open contradiction of Mark, as already stated, because the implication is that they told the disciples *straight away* for them to run to the tomb to witness what they did!

Either the women's silence is pure fiction, or the verification is pure fiction. But Craig has told us that the simpler, more straightforward character of the Gospel of Mark is evidence of its truth.

So either Craig is wrong, or he is wrong. Or he is wrong twice.

Either way, this apologetic doesn't even provide evidence for the historicity of the empty tomb. At any rate, as discussed at the beginning of this section, nearly all of the claims recorded in the narratives are most probably legendary embellishment or made up "information".

Finally with regard to verifiability, Homuyan Sidky has this to say about whether Caiaphas and the Jewish community would demand an exhumation of a body:[1]

> ...the assertion about the public display of a corpse is based on four presuppositions: (1) that the Jews and the general public knew precisely where the grave was located; (2) that the Galilean missionaries who came back to Jerusalem were outstandingly successful; (3) that Caiaphas and his colleagues had an urgent need to refute the proclamations of the Jesus cultists about their risen rabbi; (4) that the biblical narratives about Jesus's burials are accurate. There are no grounds for accepting any of these suppositions.

One can add some further arguments here: (5) Jewish law held that identification of bodies after just *three days* was illegal and *never* admissible in court, specifically due to expected decay; (6) Exhuming a dead body for any purpose was punishable by death in both Roman and Jewish law. Therefore, this whole narrative was neither verifiable nor falsifiable, even if one had wanted to check the claims being made.

Jerusalem

Another one of Craig's arguments for the historicity of the empty tomb is where the events took place, namely Jerusalem. The argument goes something like this: Because the purported events took place in Jerusalem, the Jewish authorities would easily have been able to locate the tomb and draw people's attention to the body. This approach is connected to the argument I presented

[1] Sidky (2019), p. 472.

in the chapter concerning Matthew's guards at the tomb. Personally, I think this argument is exceptionally weak.

Although I haven't talked in any depth about alternative theories, if something like the relocation hypothesis (and certainly if Jesus had been buried in a shallow grave or given another sort of dishonourable burial) is at all plausible, then no one would have known where his body was located. And since this is what the evidence points towards anyway, the greater point here is somewhat debateable.

The decomposition of the body in such an environment would have invalidated any realistic identification process. Remember, this is first-century Jerusalem and not modern-day TV shows involving post-mortem identification. John 11 includes the verse concerning Lazarus:

> 39 Jesus said, "Remove the stone." Martha, the sister of the deceased, said to Him, "Lord, by this time there will be a stench, for he has been dead four days."

That's four days and we know from Acts 2 that the disciples didn't start spreading the news of these events until Pentecost, fifty days later. Several days at local temperatures would have made a face unrecognisable, let alone seven weeks.[1]

Jewish midrash here doesn't particularly come to the help of Craig, either:[2]

> Bar Kappara taught: until three days [after death] the soul keeps on returning to the grave, thinking that it will go back [into the body]; but when it sees that the facial features have become disfigured, it departs and abandons [the body].

This is not just a case of the body not being identifiable due to decomposition but a case of not being identifiable under Jewish law. And even if the Jewish authorities paraded this body around town, a rotting corpse removed from a grave or tomb weeks after burial, what will this have achieved? Early Christians would be able to deny that this was Jesus, *even if it was his body*. Neither the Jews nor the Christians would have been able to identify the body and the whole parade would have looked rather grotesque and arguably petty.

It seems that Craig's evidence doesn't really get off the ground. But it doesn't get any better for him...

---

[1] Lowder in Price & Lowder (2005), p. 289, with evidence from retired pathologist John Nernoff III.

[2] Midrash Rabbah Genesis C:7 (994). Further talk of identification being only within three days can be seen explicitly in Mishnah *Yemahot* 16:3a-e, as well as in a host of other Midrash.

The idea that Christianity would already have been, in the week after Jesus' supposed resurrection, a significant enough movement for the Jewish authorities to be spending time and effort in providing counter-arguments for their claims is a little far-fetched. Two thousand years later, Christianity is one of the world's largest belief systems with billions of adherents and attracts far more attention than it would have done in the nascent days after Jesus' execution. Do not judge events of virtually two thousand years ago in the context of today.

Moreover, its early days saw the movement attracting people from the lower echelons of society, passing under the radar of the authorities and working secretively. As Jeffery Lowder observes:[1]

> Robert L. Wilken, a Christian historian, points out that "for almost a century Christianity went unnoticed by most men and women in the Roman Empire.... [Non-Christians saw] the Christian community as a tiny, peculiar, antisocial, a religious sect, drawing its adherents from the lower strata of society."[2] First-century Romans had about as much interest in refuting Christian claims as twentieth century skeptics had in refuting the misguided claims of the Heaven's Gate cult: they simply didn't care to refute it. As for the Jews, Jewish sources do not even mention the resurrection, much less attempt to refute it.[3] As Martin writes, "this hardly suggests that Jewish leaders were actively engaged in attempting to refute the resurrection story, but failing in their efforts."[4]

What is desperately missing here is any kind of actual evidence to support Craig's claim. At best, this is speculative and circumstantial support of Jesus' purported resurrection.

I have discussed other elements of the empty tomb thesis that required their own chapters elsewhere: Matthew's guards at the tomb, and the fact that the tomb was not venerated. Both of these chapters, together with the aforementioned arguments, should lead the open-minded and reasonable reader to conclude that there was no empty tomb – it was a later embellishment. There are just too many problems with the Christian's thesis, all of which are solved

---

[1] Lowder in Price & Lowder (2005), p. 288.

[2] Wilken (1984), p. xiv.

[3] Lowder footnotes: "The text of Josephus' *Antiquities of the Jews* (18.3.3 & 63-64) might seem to contain an authentic reference to Jesus' resurrection, but there are clear signs of Christian tampering with the text. Moreover, even the New Testament does not claim that the Jews ever bothered to check the tomb.

[4] Martin (1991), p. 91. And we can see from the later *Dialogue with Trypho* that they even dispute his existence.

by the more probable claim that it was a later legendary embellishment. This is where notions of coherence also aid probabilities.

Motivated Reasoning

To wrap this chapter up, let us look briefly at motivated reasoning: why we believe what we do and who has the most to lose by not doing so (or believing it to be false).

What is *motivated reasoning* (an idea that I mentioned at the beginning of the book)?

Similar to the cognitive bias of confirmation bias, motivated reasoning can be defined as the tendency to find arguments in favour of conclusions we want to believe to be stronger than arguments for conclusions we do not want to believe. The reward or consequence for believing or not believing something is what drives our evaluation of the evidence and reasons for that belief. The desired outcome filters our processes of evaluation.

Again, who has the most to lose from the empty tomb arguments that the skeptics provide finding their mark? As such, will the theist apportion more value to certain arguments, such as Craig does with his Jerusalem argument, than a more objective third party? Almost certainly; it's human nature. Will the Christian apportion less value to skeptical arguments? Almost certainly; it's human nature.

If the arguments that I am presenting here are sound, and they work, what happens? For the skeptic, it is another reason out of the many not to believe (in the empty tomb and then) in the Resurrection. And as we discussed at the start of the book, with no Resurrection, you have no death of Christ and rising of Christ, and, without these two, you have no atonement. Without atonement, Jesus is pointless. Furthermore, there is no theological or narratival point to the existence of Jesus. And even so proclaims Paul, in 1 Corinthians 15: 1-20!

The Christian has an awful lot more to lose from the skeptical arguments against the empty tomb being on point. They are motivated to believe in the empty tomb – there is a lot on the line.

Skeptics, on the other hand, can have their arguments miss the bullseye and still happily get on with not believing the Resurrection or in God. The empty tomb is *not* foundational to an atheist but it is *somewhat* foundational to the Christian. If the empty tomb isn't, then the Resurrection as a whole most certainly *is* theologically foundational. If the empty tomb arguments that I present here fail to persuade the objective third party, then all the skeptic is left with is that the tomb might well have either been empty (and something else explains the other data, naturalistically), or there was no tomb, or it was *never really empty*.

The evidence and arguments to any of these conclusions are not weak, and apologists struggle even to deflect them. The Gospels, therefore, can in no way even be good evidence for Christian beliefs, far less extraordinary evidence. As I've shown, this evidence is all – at best – highly suspect. Which also means that, if the historical validity of the empty tomb is seriously challenged, then the historical validity of *all* of the Gospel claims are likewise thrown into doubt. How can we be certain if those claims over there have veracity if these similar ones here are false?

There are many ways for the skeptic or atheist to get to their conclusion. We could use philosophical arguments against God, other biblical arguments and so on. In direct contrast, for the Christian worldview to be correct, all of the foundation and philosophical, theological, and biblical masonry need to be present and in place.

Belief in the burial and the disappearance of the corpse of Jesus is not terminal for the atheist or skeptic in the manner it is for the Christian.

This is why apologists such as William Lane Craig argue so vehemently for the empty tomb – they have everything to lose.

Does this point about motivated reasoning prove anything by itself? No, it has no bearing, ceteris paribus, on truth values or truth claims. But it should give you context and give you an understanding of why a Christian might weight a particular reason with a completely different evaluation than a skeptic.

Many Christians are fairly desperate for the empty tomb to be true because it is *absolutely necessary* that the Resurrection is true, for which the empty tomb arguably provides a pivotal foundation.

16 – The Women at the Tomb: Who Were They?

I have briefly discussed that the women who discovered the empty tomb did not work in co-operation with Joseph of Arimathea. This leads to either the conclusion that Joseph of Arimathea did not exist or that he was, as Mark implies, merely a pious Sanhedrist and not the secret Jesus disciple that the embellished later Gospels claimed. Although I have also mentioned the women in the previous empty tomb chapter, it is worth lingering on the topic.

Let us look a little more closely at those who supposedly discovered the empty tomb.

Spices and Embalming

The women who turned up at the empty tomb appeared to be trying to anoint Jesus' body for embalming purposes, as according to the most embellished Gospel, John. This is a rather bizarre procedure by point of fact that "the embalming of a body was apparently not in accordance with contemporary custom since there is not a single example available".[1] Let us remember that no other Gospel recounts this. Mark's original claim was that the women went to "anoint" the body, which does not mean "embalm".

Bodies were usually washed and anointed before they were placed in the tomb: there is no such thing as a second anointing. What the Gospels (other than Mark[2]) are suggesting is arguably contrary to Jewish custom.[3] Christian apologists like to claim that they were just carrying out procedures that are described in the Mishnah. However, they fail to note that this action is usually done prior to burial (though tombs are arguably a different matter).

As *Talmud, Shabbat* 23.5 elucidates:[4]

> One may perform all of the needs of the dead on Shabbat. One may smear oil on the body and rinse it with water, and all of this is permitted provided that one does not move any of its limbs, which would constitute a violation of the laws of set-aside objects. When necessary, one may also remove a pillow from beneath it and thereby place it on cold sand in order to delay its decomposition. Similarly, one may tie the jaw

---

[1] Hendrickx (1984), p. 44.

[2] Though it is interesting to note that they waited until after the Sabbath, though the law allows this to be done on the Sabbath. Was this a mistake?

[3] Kirby in Price & Lowder (2005), p. 243; von Campenhausen (1968), p.58.

[4] https://www.sefaria.org/Mishnah_Shabbat.23.5 (Retrieved 09/03/2021).

of a corpse that is in the process of opening. One may not move it directly so that it will rise back to its original position, but so that it will not continue to open.

Matthew and John, who are thought to be more knowledgeable of Jewish customs, do not include the desire to anoint. This makes it look like (and not for the first time) they are correcting the erroneous Mark, who gets some claims of Jewish custom wrong in his Gospel.

It is also worth noting that the women would be unable to buy the spices in and around the Sabbath and Passover holy time. The purchase supposedly takes place after the Sabbath has passed, when one assumes that it was then dark. The women would have to travel by night to find a merchant who had reopened after the Sabbath so that they could buy their spices. However, we know that in this time, after dark, people would be sleeping.[1] That said, we could also assume that not everybody was asleep for twelve hours, and there were certainly Passover meals taking place!

Of course, this assumes that the whole event took place just before the Sabbath – a claim that is thoroughly problematic at best. Indeed, as previously discussed, it almost certainly didn't happen at this time.

Luke has a different chronology with the spices. Consequently, Christian apologists like William Lane Craig[2] get themselves into something of a twist trying to create apologetics that make sense of this chronology. I won't go into details here for the sake of parsimony. However, it is worth checking out Michael J. Alter for a discussion of this topic and the deconstruction of what Craig claims.[3]

Essentially, there was no time to purchase the spices since any stall or shop would have been closed, as this was a holy festival and the night time. Therefore, the whole process of anointing the body is itself problematic.

Again, we get the sense that every single detail of the Gospels is contestable and problematic.

Visiting the Tomb

As with the problem of acquiring the spices, people these days tend to forget the importance of sunrise and sunset for dictating the activities of humans who were somewhat constrained by natural light. One might generally

[1] Jeremias (1966), p. 44-46.
[2] Craig (1989), p. 201.
[3] Alter (2015), p. 302-4.

infer that, soon after sunset, people went to sleep. On the other hand, at sunrise, people woke up to go to work.[1]

Mark declared that the women arrived at the tomb at the rising of the sun and to do this, they would have to have been travelling when it was dark, very early in the morning. Matthew mentions that it was beginning to dawn, when the women came to see the tomb. John said it was still dark, whereas Luke declared it was very early in the morning. John is vaguer and this is potentially because, as a non-Jewish writer (contested by some conservative Christians who see him as a disciple), he is using the sources of the other Gospels to piece together his own narrative without sometimes fully understanding Jewish custom. There is some confusion when reading the accounts because Jewish days begin at sunset, which in Jerusalem in April would be the evening at around 6 pm. Consequently, we could have the woman leaving in Matthew in the darkness of the evening to visit the tomb.

Quite a lot of ink has been spilled trying to tie up both when the women left their residence and when they arrived at the tomb because there are some apparent contradictions amongst the Gospels in the chronology of both of these events.[2] It is always revealing when Christian apologists disagree with each other over such harmonisations[3] (I am inclined to sit back and let them battle it out). Whilst these particular contradictions might not be the most critical, they are still contradictions. Alter says of the difference between Mark and John:[4]

> There are definite and incontrovertible contradictions between the Gospel narratives. Either it is dark or not dark when the women *arrive* at the tomb.

The question is, do they represent reliable or non-reliable sources?

Finding the Tomb Empty

Each Gospel recounts differently the discovery of the empty tomb (remember the rather weak four newspaper accounts analogy). Here, I list them with the total number of people claimed to have been there (as well as the time the discovery took place):

---

[1] There is some generalisation here since there is plenty of archaeological evidence of torches and torch use; it wasn't as if, when darkness came, everyone dutifully went to bed…

[2] See extended discussion in Alter (2015), p. 305-17.

[3] Ibid, p. 312-14.

[4] Ibid, p. 314.

Mark (16:1): When the Sabbath was over, **Mary Magdalene, and Mary the mother of James, and Salome**, bought spices, so that they might come and anoint Him. (3)

Matthew (28:1): Now after the Sabbath, as it began to dawn toward the first day of the week, **Mary Magdalene and the other Mary** came to look at the grave. (2)

Luke (23:49, 55): And all His acquaintances and the women who accompanied Him from Galilee were standing at a distance, seeing these things.... **Now the women who had come with Him out of Galilee followed**, and saw the tomb and how His body was laid. (Unspecified, at the very least 4)

John (20:1): Now on the first day of the week **Mary Magdalene** came early to the tomb, while it was still dark, and saw the stone already taken away from the tomb. So she ran and came to... (1)

Theists like to dismiss the contradictions here as being harmonisable or not at all important. Personally, I don't see them as harmonisable. John is very clear in stating one woman and you would have to really want to achieve an agenda to translate that as "at least one woman, Mary...".

Mark continues (16:3-4) with the women asking:

> "Who will roll away the stone for us from the entrance of the tomb?" Looking up, they saw that the stone had been rolled away, although it was extremely large.

This account is highly suspect since they travel to a tomb with a huge stone blocking their way, without working out *how to get into* said tomb. But they needn't worry because there is literally a *deus ex machina* to save them having a totally wasted journey. Peter Kirby notes:[1]

> It would seem more likely that they would have inquired at the house of Joseph for permission or assistance, or at least that they would have brought someone who would be able to help, rather than acting like the fools that Mark depicts. This tends to lower the likelihood of the story.

As I mentioned with the discussion on the shape of the stone covering the tomb, if it was indeed square-shaped, these two women would not have had any chance of shifting it. Conversely, if the tomb entrance stone was circular, they might well have struggled, but possibly could have done it if there had been three or four of them...

---

[1] Peter Kirby's chapter "The Case Against the Empty Tomb" in Price & Lowder (2005), p. 242.

Also recall the brief mention of the relocation hypothesis that I mentioned in the last chapter. Whoever returned to the tomb to find it empty might well be returning not to Jesus' final resting place, but to where he was only temporarily stored.

Women as Witnesses

Apologists (such as N.T. Wright[1]) often claim that the fact that lowly women are the first people to discover the tomb points towards it more likely being true: why would the Gospel writers make up what might be more embarrassing first witnesses (particularly in terms of *legal* witnesses)? However, remember the mechanism of reversal of expectation that Mark liked to employ. And, after all, the women weren't being used as *legal* witnesses (and they *could* actually be used as legal witnesses if there were no men available). We also know that historians such as Josephus and Pliny the Younger used women witnesses. Besides, we also have John referencing women witnesses in John 4:39.

Therefore, I don't think this claim, the idea that women witnesses being used gives the Gospels a much greater ring of truth, has any merit. Ehrman certainly disagrees with the apologetic defence:[2]

> I used to hold this view as well, and I see its force. But now that I've gone more deeply into the matter, I see its real flaw. It suffers, in short, from a poverty of imagination. It does not take much mental effort to imagine who would come up with a story in which the female followers of Jesus, rather than the male followers, discovered the tomb.

There seems to be very little surprise that women were first witnesses perhaps because women were incredibly important in the early church. For example, we have New Testament mention of "Chloe's" people and Lydia. Additionally, the work of James Crossley, in *Why Christianity Happened*, seeks to emphasise the importance of *households* in the conversion to and growth of Christianity.[3] Women seemed to be accepted as important in the development of the early church and not some sort of gender-based embarrassment.

There is every reason to think that, since the male disciples had all run away for some time (the Gospels dispute as to how long, and where they went), women were quite possibly the *only* sources for the early Pauline and Gospel narratives. Ehrman continues:[4]

---

[1] Wright (2003), p. 607-8.
[2] Ehrman (2014), p. 166.
[3] Crossley (2006).
[4] Ehrman (2014), p. 166-67.

> The first thing to point out is that we are not talking about a Jewish court of law in which witnesses are being called to testify. We're talking about oral traditions about the man Jesus. But who would invent women as witnesses to the empty tomb? Well, for openers, mainly women would. We have good reasons for thinking that women were particularly well represented in early Christian communities. We know from the letters of Paul - from passages such as Romans 16 - that women played crucial leadership roles in the churches: ministering as deacons, leading the services in their homes, engaging in missionary activities. Paul speaks of one woman in the Roman Church as "foremost among the apostles" (Junia in Rom.16:7). Women are also reputed to have figured prominently in Jesus's ministry, throughout the Gospels. This may well have been the case, historically. But in any event, there is nothing implausible in thinking that women who found their new-found Christian communities personally liberating told stories about Jesus in light of their own situations, so that women were portrayed as playing a greater part in the life and death of Jesus than they actually did, historically. It does not take a great deal of imagination to think that female storytellers indicated that women were the first to believe in the resurrection, after finding Jesus's tomb empty.

Women would be far more likely to prepare bodies for burial, and so it would be of no surprise that they would discover the empty tomb (if there was one). This is hardly evidence of historical accuracy: value based on the notion that the Gospel writers would not *choose* women to be the first witnesses. If there were an empty tomb, it would be rather bizarre that men would go there at all. And if you are making up a story, in which all the relevant men had properly run away, you really only have women left to do the discovering:[1]

> In addition, our earliest sources are quite clear that the male disciples fled the scene and were not present for Jesus's crucifixion. As I stated earlier, this may well be a historical fact - that the disciples feared for their own lives and went into hiding or fled town in order to avoid arrest. Where would they go? Presumably back home, to Galilee - which was more than one hundred miles away and would have taken at least a week on foot for them to reach. If the men had scattered, or returned home, who was left in the tradition to go to the tomb? It would have been the women who had come with the apostolic band to Jerusalem, but who presumably did not need to fear arrest.

[1] Ibid., p. 167.

Remember that Mark originally ended his Gospel with the women running away and telling "no one". This looks to like Mark could well be explaining why an empty tomb claim had not developed already. Mark's empty tomb is possibly the earliest source and he is explaining it with the fact that the witnesses told no one. Of course, the fact that Mark knew of these events means that he wants us to assume that they did eventually let their story out. Paul, the earliest writer about Jesus, mentions nothing about the women witnesses.

Let us now consider the interactions that the women had with the angels that they had purportedly seen, in differing quantities.

The "Angels"

As I might have already hinted (since you would never guess that there would be a divergence between the Gospel accounts), there is, in fact, a divergence between the Gospel accounts on the subject of angels.

Let me be clear, no one, in any explicit manner, is said to have *witnessed* Jesus' Resurrection. At most, you could infer that one or two angels (if you agree they were angels) might have seen it happen. And Paul, the earliest source, does not even mention these events.

In the Gospels, at the tomb, we have the following claims:

Mark: Mary, Mary and Salome "[e]ntering the tomb, they saw a young man sitting at the right, wearing a white robe; and they were amazed".

Matthew: Mary, Mary and some guards were there, as an earthquake hit and "an angel of the Lord descended from heaven and came and rolled the stone away and sat upon it. And his appearance was like lightning, and his clothing as white as snow."

Luke: "[T]he women who had come with Him out of Galilee" entered the empty tomb, with the stone rolled away, and "they did not find the body of the Lord Jesus. While they were perplexed about this, behold, two men suddenly stood near them in dazzling clothing..."

John: Mary Magdalene alone came to the tomb when it was dark, saw the stone rolled away, found it empty, got some disciples, who saw it empty and, walking away, "saw two angels in white sitting, one at the head and one at the feet, where the body of Jesus had been lying."

Here, we see, *if* (more on this in a few pages) we can assume all of these men are angels,[1] angels appear in every account, but the accounts differ as to whether there were one or two angels. Rather than say, "This is a discrepancy but it is not the end of the world; it could be due to a variety of sources,"

---

[1] Because if some really were just men, then there are some accounts that show there were *no* angels – see in a few pages the discussion of this regarding Mark.

Christians most often prefer to offer such terrible arguments that it poisons the rest of their case. The ubiquitous one here is "Well, two is at least one."

In other words, if I am in a court of law, and I was asked, "How many men ran into the bank with guns?", I could answer "One man ran into the bank with a gun" and this could mean anywhere from one man to an almost infinite number!

CARM (the Christian Apologetics and Research Ministry) states this interpretation explicitly:[1] "If there were two angels in the tomb, then there was at least one." Similarly, *Bible Answer* gives us the same get-out-of-jail-free card:[2]

> Just because two authors choose to mention only one of the angels doesn't mean there is a contradiction in scripture. If Matthew or Mark had said there was only one angel, then that would have contradicted the other two writers. These first two Gospels never say there was **only** one angel, they just simply chose to write about one of the two.

Imagine going through life thinking like this: That every time you gave a numerical answer, you could actually be referring to any number above the actual quantity referenced. This was truly one of the first, simple contradiction arguments I got into when I first started arguing about Christianity and the Bible. It was precisely this type of rationalisation that opened my eyes to what I saw as people being dishonest with *themselves*. If you are the sort of person who can convince yourself with this type of argument, then we probably shouldn't be talking. You are probably convincing yourself of an awful lot of other nonsense that you really shouldn't believe (Young Earth Creationism is a prime example).

Or, cognitive dissonance[3] isn't just an issue for Jesus' early disciples; it remains equally problematic for his modern-day followers.

What is worth dwelling on is the young man in Mark wearing a linen cloth. Was this young man really an angel? Mark 14 places this bizarre interlude in the garden of Gethsemane during the arrest of Jesus.

> **51** A young man was following Him, wearing nothing but a linen sheet over his naked body; and they seized him. **52** But he pulled free of the linen sheet and escaped naked.

This event is not reported anywhere else. And yet the same language is used to describe the young man (νεανίσκος, *neaniskos*) in the tomb, in a white

---

[1] Slick (n.d.).

[2] "How many angels were at the tomb of Jesus?", *The Bible Answer*, https://thebibleanswer.org/how-many-angels-tomb-jesus/ (Retrieved 10/12/2020).

[3] We will come back to this term later to more formally investigate it.

robe. It is a bizarre, nonsensical addition to the narrative in Mark 14 and makes little sense without further delving into. So let us delve further into this episode.

Secret Mark (or the Secret Gospel of Mark) is a longer Markan text alluded to (and left to the church in Alexandria) in a now-lost letter, the Mar Saba letter from Clement of Alexandria[1]. We now only have photographic evidence of this letter. Some scholars suggest that this young man is the same young man that Jesus raises from the dead in Secret Mark.

Marvin Meyer, the late Director of the Coptic Magical Texts Project of the Institute for Antiquity and Christianity, sees the young man as a symbol of discipleship who follows Jesus throughout the Gospel story. This interpretation makes a good deal of sense, as we shall now understand through the following analysis.[2]

We first see this young man in Mark 10:17-22 in the story of the rich man whom Jesus loves, a man "who is a candidate for discipleship".[3] We then see him in the first Secret Mark passage (after Mark 10:34) as someone whom Jesus raises from the dead and subsequently teaches him the mystery of the kingdom of God, with the young man coming to love Jesus. The third instance is found in the second Secret Mark passage (at Mark 10:46) in which Jesus rejects Salome, the sister of the young man, and his mother. Next, we see him in the story of the escaping naked young man in Gethsemane (Mark 14:51–52). Lastly, he is found in the story of the young man in a white robe inside the empty tomb, when he informs Salome and the other women that Jesus has risen (Mark 16:1–8). Seen chopped up with missing parts, in the canonical Gospel of Mark, this narrative is somewhat lacking in this coherence. However, as a repeated figure in the Secret Gospel of Mark, he is much more coherent.

And, not an angel.

This, then, becomes an outright contradiction because the motif and narrative make a lot more sense when read in such a way. You will understand the motif elaborated upon in what Marvin Meyer also says of him:[4]

> This is a youth, the sort of character we have seen who crops up in ancient literature in stories of fear and flight as well as scenes of initiation and discipleship. The youth, presented with familiar literary images, may function as everyman, everywoman, everydisciple, in a manner that recalls aspects of the presentation of the beloved disciple in the Gospel of John. Mark's youth, termed a *neaniskos*, is a rich inquirer who hesitates but eventually turns to Jesus as a disciple that loves Jesus and is loved by him. He is brought from death to life by Jesus. Still, his

[1] It must be noted that there is considerable discussion as to whether or not the letter is a forgery/hoax. The debate still rages.

[2] Meyer (2003), Meyer (2013), p. 152-56, and Fowler (1998).

[3] Meyer (2013), p.153.

[4] Meyer (2013), p. 155-56.

> uncertainties follow the uncertainties of the other disciples, and as they flee from the crucifixion, so he also flees. But at the end of the Gospel, it is the youth, and only the youth, who is in the tomb, identifying with Jesus in life and in death.

This, in my opinion, shows a more coherent analysis of this young man in several different ways: lexically, literarily and theologically.

Again, we have an example of another contradiction and yet more legendary, theological embellishment.

What can we learn from this chapter? As with all other elements of the Resurrection narrative, every claim appears to be flawed: Whether it be (1) time of day, (2) what Jesus said, (3) who was present, (4) what the details of the crucifixion were, whether (5) he should have been killed and (6) buried differently, (7) who was at the empty tomb, (8) whether there even was a tomb, and (9) what happened thereafter. We are met with issue after problem after discrepancy after outright contradiction.

Do these myriad problems better support a legendary embellishment of a story created through a process of building fiction from various unknown sources. Or is there a more probable thesis that the Christian account is a historically accurate representation of the most incredible set of events in human history and that these sources rise up to the evidentiary challenge that such a claim demands?

By now, you can probably guess my answer.

17 – Flesh and Blood or Spirit: Old Body Restored or New Spiritual Body?

Many skeptics prefer to concern themselves with arguments about history, archaeology, science and cold hard facts. As a consequence, when analysing claims such as the birth narratives or the Resurrection of Jesus, skeptics might shy away from engaging with more theological and abstract arguments. However, theological arguments are often useful tools for the skeptic that can arguably supersede the whole enterprise of scrutinising more tangible claims. For example, if we can theologically confirm (and I think we can) that Jesus' atonement is completely nonsensical, then we can pretty much write off the Resurrection claims as read in the Bible.

Before I discuss additional theological topics, it is worth pointing out that only 43% of the cells on and within the human body are...human (sources vary wildly on this estimate). Most of the cells on and within a human body are bacteria, fungi and archaea. Therefore, in order for Jesus to experience a "proper" bodily resurrection, there needs to be a resurrection of literally millions upon millions of non-human organisms. You cannot eat (break bread, eat fish, drink) without the proper function of this microbiome. The resurrection of one human is the resurrection of millions more entities. (If what "resurrection" means is being restored to one's previous life.)

Of course, Christians will always assert unfalsifiable claims, such that God changes the rules for resurrected bodies. It is a case of moving the pea in the conman's shell game at a flea market. Whenever something is challenged, use a sleight of hand to change the rules and cheat reality. Be warned!

While we are talking about very flesh-and-bloody ideas that the Gospels claim of Jesus, there is something of a spiritual bent to their claims as well: as well as eating fish, Jesus could pass through walls (John 20:19, 26), or appear out of thin air (Luke 24:36), and also disappear at will (Luke 24:31, 51). Consequently, we are starting to understand that if Jesus did experience a bodily resurrection, his body wasn't the body it was beforehand, becoming apparently imbued with even more special abilities.

Further, a theological consideration that is crucial to the empty tomb narrative is the argument over whether Jesus resurrected in a new spiritual body or whether the Resurrection meant the rising from death of the same flesh and blood body that had died.

As is often the case, whole books could be written on this topic and there is much more research that can be done. I would advise the reader to pore over Richard Carrier's chapter, "The Spiritual Body of Christ and the Legend of the Empty Tomb", and Robert M. Price's chapter, "By This Time He Stinketh: The

Attempts of William Lane Craig to Exhume Jesus" (amongst other sources for a superb discussion of this topic); both appear in *The Empty Tomb: Jesus Beyond the Grave*. Moreover, Robert Greg Cavin's opening chapter, "Is There Sufficient Historical Evidence to Establish the Resurrection of Jesus?" is also pertinent. In the chapter, he brilliantly takes seriously what Paul says the Resurrection body was like, and shows that the Gospels come nowhere near evincing *that* view. Apologists like to try and hide this fact; they want Jesus to be flesh and blood and "also" somehow supernatural as well, a soft contradiction in their worldview (and a hard contradiction to what Paul, and hence their own Bible, actually says).

The issue is this: Christian apologists like William Lane Craig argue that the empty tomb is a vital historical basis and evidence for the Resurrection of Jesus, and thus for the whole of the Christian worldview and belief system. You can see why he puts so much effort into it, given that Craig sees the centrality of the Resurrection. But, if the skeptic can show that Paul, the earliest source for these events, did not believe in a resurrection of the flesh – that it was spiritual, supernatural, instead – then there was no recourse to there being an empty tomb since the body buried there stayed put. Jesus effectively switched houses (2 Corinthians 5:1-5), rising in an entirely new body (1 Corinthians 15:35-55), leaving the old one behind, like a discarded shell. And if there was no empty tomb, then this casts serious doubt on the Easter Story, especially since Christians like Craig see the empty tomb as being fundamental evidence for the Resurrection.

So, although it might seem that Paul argues for the Resurrection still, this reality is perhaps a *spiritual* resurrection. This scenario would mean that the empty tomb claim is a later embellishment to the story. Furthermore, this would then mean that the claims of resurrection are nothing but (Pauline) assertion without any real evidence to support them. It is not until the Gospels come along at a later date and look to (progressively) embellish/invent the story that there is a fundamental change to the understanding of what resurrection was (for Paul or those who adhered to his position). The "reanimation and glorification of the body" could be more aligned with their thinking.[1]

On the other hand, the later Gospel writers could well be in the train of thought of Jesus as an apocalyptic Jew, with him being the first of the general resurrection of *corpses* of the dead.

Let us rewind: does Paul really make a claim for a spiritual resurrection that would invalidate an empty tomb?

[1] Ehrman (2014), p. 186.

Biblical Quotes

Paul says nothing of the resurrected body being of flesh or being the same body that died (1 Corinthians 15):

> [3] For I delivered to you as of first importance what I also received, that Christ died for our sins according to the Scriptures, [4] and that He was buried, and that He was raised on the third day according to the Scriptures, [5] and that He appeared to Cephas, then to the twelve.

There is nothing about a tomb, nothing about the Marys and the women who discovered it: nothing but an empty silence. Robert M. Price states of this fact, and Craig's approach to the vagueness:[1]

> The whole trend of his argument seems to me to belie the points he is ostensibly trying to make, namely that any differences between the two traditions do not imply that 1 Corinthians allows only sightings, subjective visions, while the gospels depict more fulsome encounters replete with dialogue, gestures, touching, and eating. Nothing in 1 Corinthians 15 rules out such scenes, he says. But surely the very urgency of the matter shows that Craig would feel himself at a great loss if he had to cut loose all those juicy gospel resurrection stories to be left with the skimpy list of terse notes in 1 Corinthians 15. By itself, 1 Corinthians 15 just wouldn't mean much. He wants the appearances of 1 Corinthians 15:3-11 to be read as if they had in parentheses after them "See Luke 24; Matthew 28; John 21."

It is clear that the Gospels (Mark excepted due to issues of later interpolation and the original finishing with the silence of the women) are explicit. For example, Luke 24:39 reads:

> [39] See My hands and My feet, that it is I Myself; touch Me and see, for a spirit does not have flesh and bones as you see that I have."

Paul, in 1 Corinthians 15, states in apparent contradiction of this sort of resurrection:

> [45]The last Adam became a life-giving spirit.... [50] Now I say this, brethren, that flesh and blood cannot inherit the kingdom of God; nor does the perishable inherit the imperishable. [51] Behold, I tell you a mystery; we will not

[1] Price in Price & Lowder (2005), p. 426-27.

> all sleep, but we will all be changed, [52] in a moment, in the twinkling of an eye, at the last trumpet; for the trumpet will sound, and the dead will be raised imperishable, and we will be changed.

Flesh and blood cannot inherit the kingdom of God. And the perishable cannot inherit the imperishable. These words are strong prima facie evidence that Paul makes great distinctions between spiritual and physical bodies. Paul's epistle, 1 Corinthians 2, also contains some abstract thought concerning spiritual manifestation:

> [14] But a natural man does not accept the things of the Spirit of God, for they are foolishness to him; and he cannot understand them, because they are spiritually appraised. [15] But he who is spiritual appraises all things, yet he himself is appraised by no one.

Moreover, 2 Corinthians 5:1 states of the resurrection:

> ...if the earthly tent which is our house is torn down, we have a building from God, a house not made with hands, eternal in the heavens

Craig's main defence of the "flesh and blood" quote from the earlier Pauline writing is to say it is a synecdoche. A synecdoche is a figure of speech where the parts represent the whole. So that Craig interprets "flesh and blood" as "mortality", but this is stretching matters to the point of bastardising language.

As Robert Price points out, if we were to say "all hands on deck", we would expect these parts of the whole to represent the whole, so *everybody* should be on deck to help as represented by *all hands*. What we don't mean is "everybody on deck, but you can leave your hands behind". Though they are part of the whole, the whole requires those parts for any sense to be made. Flesh and blood may represent mortality, but mortality is dependent on both flesh and blood; they are integral to the turn of phrase. You cannot have mortality that is not of flesh and blood, nor flesh and blood that is not mortal, or if you did, you are clearly using the wrong figurative language! Price concludes:[1]

> It is simply absurd for Craig to suggest that one might say "flesh and blood shall not inherit the kingdom of God," meanwhile supposing that someone who had in fact inherited that kingdom did so while wearing a body of flesh!

---

[1] Price in Price & Lowder (2005), p. 429.

Thus, Craig's defence is exceptionally weak!

The Gospel writers see a clear evolution in the development of a flesh-and-blood resurrection, where, in Mark, it is Jesus' body that is raised because the tomb is empty. Later, Matthew adds that Jesus appears to his followers, and some of them touch him. (Matthew 28:9). Luke builds on these claims with increased clarity because Jesus appears to his disciples and tells them explicitly that he has flesh and bones, unlike "a spirit", telling them to experience this themselves by handling him (Luke 24:39-40). Luke has Jesus eating food in front of them to convince them of this (Luke 24:41-43). In John, the last of the Gospels, Jesus cooks and eats with the disciples (John 21:9-14, though there is no explicit claim he eats) and when Thomas doubts him, he invites his disciple to place their finger in his wounds to verify that it is indeed his dead body that has been physically raised from the dead (John 20:24-29).

Arguments for a Spiritual Resurrection

Richard Carrier's 126-page chapter "The Spiritual Body of Christ and the Legend of the Empty Tomb" (Price & Lowder 2005) is effectively a book-length thesis to argue for Paul claiming that the Resurrection was spiritual, leaving one body to enter another (not made of flesh or blood). He then points out that this is evidence that the empty tomb narrative was a later legendary embellishment. It will be hard to do his case justice in my short chapter.

Much of the conversation and thesis derives from the argument that Paul had with the Corinthians in his epistles. The problem here is that we do not know exactly what the Corinthians stated. They were certainly disagreeing with some aspect of the Resurrection that itself points towards Paul having a two-body approach to Jesus' resurrection.

Below, I will list Carrier's arguments as succinctly as possible for reasons of parsimony:

- The two-body doctrine is very clearly demonstrated by Philo, Josephus, the Jewish apocrypha, certain Pharisees and even supported by biblical sources (see Ecclesiastes 12:7).[1]
- The discussion Paul has with the Corinthians underwrites how neither of them had an understanding or access to the Resurrection narrative accounts we see in the Gospels. The Corinthians are not doubting the Resurrection per se (as Paul makes clear what would happen in a full lack of Resurrection belief) but some *aspect* thereof, the details of which are unclear. It seems that the Corinthians may have believed that Jesus was always a spiritual body. Paul counters with a two-body thesis (more on this in a later bullet point).

---

[1] Carrier in Price & Lowder (2005), p. 110-13.

- When Paul comes up against some detail in opposition to the Resurrection (1 Corinthians 15), he doesn't employ common Rabbinic defences of resurrection:[1]

> We can also conclude that, whatever doctrine Paul was espousing, scripture provided scant assistance in proving it. If, for example, he meant that our bodies would be reformed from the dirt into which they had dissolved, he would surely have cited passages supporting such a view (like Daniel 12:2, Isaiah 26:19, and Ezekiel 37:5-10), and used the familiar Pharisaic analogies (like clayworking or glassmaking). But he didn't.

- The crux of the Corinthians passage is that Paul is arguing back against the Corinthians about *how* the body was raised.[2] I think Carrier correct because it is clear that this is the case from 1 Corinthians itself, where he explicitly denies continuity and claims the bodies are different types of body. The idea is that the Corinthians would understand that Christ's body was still in situ, so how could he, and by extension they, resurrect to the heavens? This argument makes sense of Paul's explanation – why would this talk (exchange of letters) even exist or be relevant if everyone understood a bodily resurrection with an empty tomb?

> **35** But someone will say, "How are the dead raised? And with what kind of
> body do they come?" **36** You fool! That which you sow does not come to
> life unless it dies; **37** and that which you sow, you do not sow the body
> which is to be, but a bare grain, perhaps of wheat or of something
> else. **38** But God gives it a body just as He wished, and to each of the seeds
> a body of its own. **39** All flesh is not the same flesh, but there is one flesh of
> men, and another flesh of beasts, and another flesh of birds, and another
> of fish. **40** There are also heavenly bodies and earthly bodies, but the glory
> of the heavenly is one, and the glory of the earthly is another. **41** There is
> one glory of the sun, and another glory of the moon, and another glory of
> the stars; for star differs from star in glory.
>
> **42** So also is the resurrection of the dead. It is sown a perishable body, it is
> raised an imperishable body; **43** it is sown in dishonor, it is raised in glory;
> it is sown in weakness, it is raised in power; **44** it is sown a natural body, it
> is raised a spiritual body. If there is a natural body, there is also a spiritual body.

[1] Carrier in Price & Lowder (2005), p. 117.

[2] Ibid.

Concerning the Corinthians with whom Paul is arguing, why would they have any doubt at all about the form in which Jesus resurrected? According to the Gospels, Jesus rose and appeared, ate and drank with plenty of witnesses, and left his tomb empty. Unless, of course, this legend *hadn't yet developed* (as we see it in the later Gospels). Personally, the whole basis of the conversation with the Corinthians is a strong argument for this thesis.

- On this same point, if Paul had knowledge of all of these events, why did he not bring them into play (apart from in very generic "appeared to" terms, but not being handled, not eating fish etc.)? Paul makes no reference to any "eyewitness" to Jesus' Resurrection, beyond what he calls an inner revelation.
- In Philippians 3, we have further confirmation of Paul's belief in transforming old bodies into new ones (where the lexical analysis of the word "transform" means to change location[1]):

> **20** For our citizenship is in heaven, from which also we eagerly wait for a Savior, the Lord Jesus Christ; **21** who will transform the body of our humble state into conformity with the body of His glory.

- Since early church fathers, post-Gospels, toed the Gospel line (such as Justin with "the resurrection is a resurrection of the flesh, which died."[2]), why didn't Paul say anything like this at all? Athenagoras and Tertullian concerned themselves with trying to prove that God could keep track of all the parts of a decomposing body in order to reassemble it for resurrection. Yet Paul clearly has a totally different understanding of how a resurrection would take place, without even hinting at any kind of reassembly.
- Similarly, Christians more than a century later...

> ...would readily appeal to things Jesus said to prove their point about the nature of the resurrection, but Paul, only a decade or two away, can't summon a single word from Jesus in his own defence? Nor, apparently, could his Corinthian opponents. Even more bizarre, how can it be that, more than a century later, Christians would have all kinds of eyewitness testimony to cite in proof of their position, and had no problem citing both Old Testament and New Testament resurrection examples, yet Paul, only a decade or two away, fails to summon a single example? No witnesses are cited - not even his own eyewitness encounter with Jesus!

---

[1] Carrier in Price & Lowder (2005), p. 119.

[2] Justin Martyr, *On the Resurrection* 2, 4. See also Tertullian, *On the Resurrection of the Flesh* 57-59

No analogous resurrections are used as an illustration, or a point of contrast. No physical evidence is mentioned. So it begs all credulity to maintain that Paul believed in the resurrection of the flesh.[1]

- The early church fathers argued at great length that "the flesh is not dishonourable, not disgusting, not unworthy of restoration, but that it is fundamentally good, that it would be evil for God to destroy what he thought good to create in the first place."[2] Paul, again, says absolutely nothing remotely connected to this claim (other than to actually argue against it, e.g. in Romans 7:18).
- These early Christian thinkers are at pains to denigrate those who attack the flesh (meaning there were those who believed that flesh was not something worthy of resurrection) as they really believe in resurrection referring to the dying body being restored rather than, as Paul argues, a new body being occupied.
- Returning to the Corinthians: since Paul had to write a second letter to them, we know that ideas of resurrection were not simple and straightforward (see 2 Corinthians 5 for further distinction).
- You can imagine their worry in seeing dead bodies of family members and descendants still being on Earth and thus apparently contradicting the claims of resurrection, or at least leading to very particular lines of questioning. However, under a two-body hypothesis, we can make sense of this.
- The fact that Paul appears to be missing all these lines of reasoning that supported continuity of the bodily resurrection, *later Christians had to invent a third letter to the Corinthians* and ascribe it to Paul.[3] It had *the sole intention* of correcting supposed misconceptions with Paul's theology. Of course, what we are arguing here is that Paul was very clear with his theology. It's only that it didn't agree with later legendary embellishments of the Gospels (or they with it). This here is a hugely important and persuasive piece of the puzzle.
- Carrier, in an article called "Spiritual Body FAQ", writes, to answer the question:[4]

Q: Your theory is that some of the Corinthians were bothered by the fact that the body of Jesus remained in the grave, even though he was resurrected as a spiritual being, because they apparently thought Jesus

[1] Carrier in Price & Lowder (2005), p. 124
[2] Ibid.
[3] 3 Corinthians 5:24-35. This is a non-canonical text written by "pseudo-Paul" in the third century CE.
[4] Carrier (2014).

was, unlike us, already a spiritual being, and therefore if we died we could not be resurrected as he was. But wouldn't Paul have already taught the Corinthians these things when he originally converted them?

A: Had that been so, then Paul would not be teaching them these details again in 1 Corinthians and yet again in 2 Corinthians. Obviously, they did not understand something very fundamental about "how they would be raised" and "with what body they would come," so much so that some of the Corinthians were concluding that the dead would not be raised at all--which they could not possibly have concluded if Paul had "already taught them" all about how they would be raised. Therefore, these letters entail there was a large gap in their education (at least that faction's education--and they may have been evangelized after Paul, while those converted and taught by Paul were having a hard time explaining Paul's views to them). But that Paul himself would leave them in the dark should come as no surprise, since Paul's "introductory course" in Christianity (represented by his letter to the Romans) is a lengthy discourse packed with details about what they were expected to believe, yet it never discusses anything about the mechanics of resurrection--in fact, its discussion of resurrection is so scanty and ambiguous that it practically ensures confusion (hence see my discussion on pp. 149-50). [Page references to Carrier's chapter in Price & Lowder (2005).]

I think I have identified what must have been missing from their education--and to date, I have not seen any plausible alternative that is actually consistent with the text and the facts (e.g. pp. 120-26, 139-41). They had to have been worried about Jesus being so different from themselves that they would not be raised from the dead, and the only such worry that makes sense of the actual text we have is a worry attached to the corpse of Jesus, as I explain in the book. There is only one alternative that makes sense of the same evidence: if everyone in this dispute (Paul and all the Corinthians) believed Jesus was incarnated and raised only in the heavens, and thus he was never on earth in the first place (see my review of *The Jesus Puzzle*), then their worry would make even more sense, because then Jesus would be a purely cosmic being, very much unlike us, so his resurrection would have been a cosmic act, not the raising of a buried corpse. However, if we conclude this, then it still follows that there was no empty tomb nor any corpse on earth.

- Paul's word to describe the new bodily form is *pneumatikos* and is contrasted with "flesh and blood" of the *psychikos* body. Carrier carries out a detailed lexical analysis[1] of Paul's language throughout his body of

[1] Carrier in Price & Lowder (2005), p. 126-39.

writing (no pun intended) to leave the reader in no doubt as to what Paul was referring to: that the *pneumatic* body of the Resurrection of Jesus was a different body to the *psychic* one that was crucified. And rather than saying that one *becomes* another, or transforms into the other, he "emphasises their separateness".[1]

- The separate bodies may look the same (have the same image) but they are different. Let me remind you of 1 Corinthians 15 again:

> **45** So also it is written, "The first MAN, Adam, BECAME A LIVING SOUL." The last Adam became a life-giving spirit. **46** However, the spiritual is not first, but the natural; then the spiritual. **47** The first man is from the earth, earthy; the second man is from heaven. **48** As is the earthy, so also are those who are earthy; and as is the heavenly, so also are those who are heavenly. **49** Just as we have borne the image of the earthy, we will also bear the image of the heavenly.

- Paul, throughout his writing, seems to be very clear in saying that we live and die as Adam, made of dirt and sharing in his nature and fate. However, in resurrection, we are made of a different material, a heavenly spirit, and the nature and fate that we have is shared with Jesus. The flesh and blood and bones of our bodily existence are perishable and cannot enter heaven and so have no place in any resurrection.
- Luke 24:39 ("See My hands and My feet, that it is I Myself; touch Me and see, for a spirit does not have flesh and bones as you see that I have.") *flatly and explicitly* contradicts Paul's claims that our raised bodies are glorious, indestructible[2] and not made of flesh and, as mentioned, cannot eat food, as 1 Corinthians 6 states:

> **13** Food is for the stomach and the stomach is for food, but God will do away with both of them. Yet the body is not for immorality, but for the Lord, and the Lord is for the body.

- Carrier's lexical analysis of 2 Corinthians is also a detailed confirmation of the idea that Paul was always talking about a two-body resurrection.[3]
- The further epistles of Paul support a two-body hypothesis for the resurrection of Jesus.[4]
- Carrier lists numerous problems and nonsensical issues with the one-body hypothesis, *all* of which are solved by the two-body hypothesis.

---

[1] Ibid., p. 132.
[2] 1 Corinthians 15:50, for example.
[3] Carrier in Price & Lowder (2005), p. 139-47.
[4] Ibid., p. 147-50.

- Paul's own personal experiences of witnessing Jesus can both be understood in terms of a second body, but can also, with a further lexical analysis, be understood in terms of a religious *experience* (as opposed to a concrete visual experience of seeing a Jesus figure). Paul's 2 Corinthians 12 is evidence of a lack of clarity concerning his own experience and recount, and provides reference to a generalised, mysterious experience:

> Boasting is necessary, though it is not profitable; but I will go on to visions
> and revelations of the Lord. [2] I know a man in Christ who fourteen years
> ago—whether in the body I do not know, or out of the body I do not
> know, God knows—such a man was caught up to the third heaven. [3] And
> I know how such a man—whether in the body or apart from the body I do
> not know, God knows— [4] was caught up into Paradise and heard inexpressible words, which a man is not permitted to speak.

My concluding remarks would be that, and I have merely skimmed the surface in a way that does little justice to the scope and power of the argument, Paul is clearly referring to a two-body resurrection. This is wholly important because it shows:

(1) A disconnect and contradiction between the earliest source, Paul, and the later Gospels.
(2) That Paul did not have access to those same Gospel traditions and narratives.
(3) That the Gospels *do* look like legendary embellishments.
(4) That the empty tomb is a later embellishment.
(5) That the empty tomb is in direct contradiction to the claims of Paul's "exchange" of bodies.

And so on. This then means, as mentioned at the start of this chapter, that the level of evidence for the Easter story is especially poor, since:

a) Paul, as the earliest and most reliable source, is merely asserting the "fact" of the Resurrection without recourse to evidence such as witnesses and events (for example, the empty tomb).
b) Using the empty tomb as a primary source of "historical" evidence for the Resurrection of Jesus is unsound, based on the beliefs and claims of the earliest (most reliable) source – Paul.

So, whilst such an approach in terms of in-depth lexical analysis and theological exegesis might be somewhat drier and less exciting than other more prima facie obvious contradictions, there is a lot of mileage to be gained from looking at Paul's very clear disagreements with the Gospels that came after him.

But there is yet more support for this thesis that I think needs to be brought to bear here, if you for some reason find Carrier's thesis, as communicated here, unsatisfactory. It is now time to turn to the Gnostics, an interesting group of early Christians.

The Gnostics and Early Support for this Theory

Whilst mainstream Christians will have an agenda-driven rationale for dismissing a spiritual resurrection (because it does away with the whole empty tomb narrative and bodily resurrection as a later embellishment qua counter-argument), this is a thoroughly reasonable theological summary of Paul's position. We know this because factions of one of the early Christians, the Gnostics, *did* believe this.

Before I go on, let me throw in some caveats. There has been a recent movement within New Testament studies to reverse prevailing thought that the Gnostics were a distinct category of Christians: it is a loose title at best.[1] It's not that the ideas didn't exist, but that communities of people coalesced around them into a distinct group. There were many diverse sects, and so my points can be seen in light of differing beliefs amongst different sects, vying for primacy (even if not accurately labelled as "Gnostic" vs "Orthodox"). Different groups had different sets of beliefs with huge overlaps – but there was no one "Gnostic" sect.

I will now use the term "Gnostic" as a refined term with caveats to refer to "many beliefs or sects other than the ones represented by the New Testament Gospels".

For Gnostics, the physical world was evil and fallen and they escaped this conceptual scenario by having secret *gnosis* ("knowledge") in order to return to their spiritual home – and Jesus was the fount of this knowledge, and this knowledge has a different content to that understood by the Gospel writers and their sects.

For many Gnostics, the prevalent belief was that Jesus was two entities: the *divine spiritual Jesus* who inhabited the *human body of a man*. The physical body, as part of the fallen, physical world, was far more inferior than Jesus' spiritual being. In this context, the spirit escaped the physical body at crucifixion rather like many modern people would understand ghosts, not to attempt to belittle the theory as many would reject ghosts as merely cultural folklore. However, it is a useful analogy. As long as we understand that these sects

---

[1] See Taussig (2015).

understood this phantasmal body to be physically superior to the body of flesh, and not actually a formless ghost.

One of the famous textual discoveries took place in 1945 near Nag Hammadi, Egypt (often being called "The Gnostic Gospels"). The *Coptic Apocalypse of Peter* is of great interest in this context because it lays out exactly what we have been discussing in terms of what, it seems, Paul *actually* believed. Here, Peter is having a vision in the temple, of something that isn't happening and didn't happen, which the real Jesus sitting next to him is explaining (like an some dream-reality mentor); it is therefore more like the strange symbolic content we find in the Book of Revelation. There are actually three Jesuses in the scene: the real one speaking, who is sitting next to Peter, in the temple, and the two others that Peter sees in a vision (who are not real persons, any more than the blanket that descends from heaven in Peter's vision in Acts is a real blanket). In this vision, one of those "symbolic vision Jesuses" is depicted (in the future) crucified in a body of flesh and the other is depicted as nearby watching but as somehow also being the physical Jesus that was taken at his arrest and thus not actually "incorporeal". This is a symbolic vision, so none of what Peter is seeing is meant literally:

> He whom they crucified us the firstborn, and the home of demons, and the clay vessel in which they dwell, belonging to Elohim, and belonging to the cross that is under the law. But he who stands near him is the living Savior, the primal part in him whom they seized. And he has been released. He stands joyfully looking at those who persecuted him.... Therefore he laughs at their lack of perception.... Indeed, therefore, the suffering one must remain, since the body is the substitute. But that which was released was my incorporeal body. (Apocryphon of Peter 82)[1]

The theology here and elsewhere shows that a spiritual resurrection was a belief held by early Christians. The flesh and blood body belongs to the God of this world (Elohim, the Hebrew term for God we so often see in the Hebrew Bible) as opposed to the true God. The bodily Jesus laughs at the idea that Jesus can be killed, as the enemies think, when the heavenly spirit actually escapes.[2]

We know that these views were definitely held in the mid-second century period and possibly earlier, as evidenced above (for example).[3] But if we look at Paul's letters to the Corinthians, the very strong inference would be that these sorts of views were around earlier than 35 CE: Carrier's thesis proposes very

[1] Translated by James Brashler Robinson (1996).

[2] Ehrman (2014), p. 180.

[3] Further evidence is Ignatius, who argues against Christians who appear to deny Jesus rose in the flesh, as seen in his letters to the Trallians and the Smyrnaeans.

robustly what Paul's view is and how it is a response to other such similar or non-Gospel views.

The Gospels were a real counter-argument against this notion of spiritual resurrection. For instance, as we shall see in the next chapter, Luke really over-emphasised the bodily nature of Jesus, having the disciples not believe their eyes until Jesus eats broiled fish in front of them. This is a bizarre event that makes a whole lot more sense when understood in the spiritual versus fleshly resurrection theological argument. John also does this with his Doubting Thomas "episode" (John 20:24-29). Indeed, one can argue that John ever more does this, as he even more than Luke includes the target of "non-flesh resurrectionists" and indeed all adherents to Paul's theology, and with his reference to wounds. Paul, on the other hand, clearly imagined a resurrection body would not and could not have such wounds, being untaintable and perfect. Understanding the *context* allows one to better understand the *content*.

Thus some people, like Bart Ehrman, see Paul believing that the body of Jesus "transforms" into the spiritual body. This differs from the usual understanding in the Gospels in that respect, and differs again from the Gnostics such that we have three distinct positions in the debate. On the other hand, Carrier goes to great lengths to lexically analyse the word "transform" to lead one to conclude that Paul, too, was in the Gnostic camp when considering the nature of the Resurrection being spiritual, and that the Resurrection was a spiritual one, leaving flesh and blood behind and rising in an entirely new, glorious body.

What we learn from this variety of views is that the empty tomb narrative is on very shaky *historical* grounds not least because it is on very shaky *theological* grounds. It is much better understood as ad hoc "evidence" inserted to supposedly prove a point to those who were both arguing against a resurrection of the flesh (Gnostics or similar) and those who were arguing against a resurrection at all (Jews and gentiles).

18 – Post-Resurrection Appearances: Elvis Is in Town

> The story of Jesus Christ appearing after he was dead is the story of an apparition, such as timid imaginations can always create in vision, and credulity believe. Stories of this kind had been told of the assassination of Julius Caesar, not many years before; and they generally have their origin in violent deaths, or in the execution of innocent persons.
>
> –Thomas Paine, *The Age of Reason* (1795)

> If this Jesus were trying to convince anyone of his powers, then surely he ought to have appeared first to the Jews who mistreated him–and to his accusers–indeed to everyone, everywhere. [...] When he was punished, everyone saw; yet risen from the tomb, almost no one.
>
> –Celsus, *On the True Doctrine* (circa 185 CE)

For Christians, and previously people like myself, to compare sightings of Jesus to sightings of Elvis is something of an insult. I thought long and hard about whether I should flippantly include Elvis in the chapter title because there is a chance it devalues the subject, particularly in terms of trying to convince a committed Christian. When we talk about people sighting Elvis, we dismiss it out of hand as being ridiculous: just the sort of thing that huge, cultish fans *wanted* to happen.

And then I realised that this is *precisely* the point.

Elvis fans came to love him so much (and some as a *result* of his death) that their minds and the wonderful world of psychology brought about all sorts of purported phenomena and still do. As atheist philosopher Keith Parsons says, "The postmortem 'sightings' of Jesus are no more remarkable than the similar reports about Elvis Presley and Jimmy Hoffa."[1]

So who experienced appearances of Jesus? Paul himself famously did:

> The essential thing to note about Paul's understanding of the appearances to him is that it was identical with every other appearance on his

[1] Keith Parsons's chapter "Peter Kreeft and Ronald Tacelli on the Hallucination Theory", in Price & Lowder (2005), p. 437. I would heartily recommend reading this chapter for an insight into the argument from Christians looking to defend from accusations of hallucination, and a skeptic's sound rebuttal. Furthermore, Homuyan Sidky shuts down Kreeft and Tacelli's case, and other Christian thinkers such as Edwin Yamauchi, in Sidky (2019), p. 499-504.

> list. That is, it was not a physical, historical encounter but a revelatory manifestation of the living Christ from heaven.

The words of Bishop John Shelby Spong[1] prime you beautifully for the rest of this chapter. We will get onto his experience later. Paul lists the people to whom Jesus posthumously appeared:

- Cephas
- The Twelve
- More than five hundred at one time (most of them still alive)
- James
- All the apostles
- Paul himself

The first thing to note is that Paul's list, as a claim, is mere, uncorroborated assertion (and we could just leave it at that). Where did Paul get his information? Is it reliable? Were there motivated reasons on the part of the source *and* Paul? Are the claims now and were the claims then verifiable? Atheist author and former minister John Loftus agrees with such problems:[2]

> So let's sum up so far. If this list of eyewitnesses is supposed to be considered evidence Jesus had been raised from the grave it just does not work, especially in those cases where he doesn't give us names. When it comes to the people Paul named, it seems highly improbable the Corinthians had personally met any of them. So why would the Corinthians believe Paul? Why should we do so today? I would have wanted to talk with a few or all of these so-called witnesses so that I could ask them some questions. I might even have wanted to withhold judgment because I had not personally seen the risen Jesus myself. Such a stance would be no more unreasonable than it would be to doubt Balaam's tale until he made his ass talk in front of us. When it comes to such a claim as this, we should all be doubting Thomases who would also doubt the story of doubting Thomas (John 20:24–29).

But there is something that the skeptic needs to take notice of here: the early Christians really did seem to believe Jesus appeared to people, either themselves or to others whom they believed.

Did Paul, in his 1 Corinthians passage, actually mean visions as opposed to actual physical appearances? Keith Parsons expresses the following view:[3]

---

[1] Spong (1995), p. 50, cf. Loftus (2020) p. 503.

[2] Loftus (2020), p. 508.

[3] Keith Parsons in Price & Lowder (2005), p. 434.

> Recently, NT scholar Gerd Lüdemann offered extensive and cogent reasons for thinking that the postmortem "appearances" were in fact visionary. For instance, the earliest kerygmatic proclamations, such as Paul's famous testimony in 1 Corinthians 15, made no distinction between "seeing" the risen Jesus with the physical eye or with the inner mental or spiritual "eye." The Greek word used to characterize these appearances is *ophthe*, the aorist passive form of the verb *horao*, which in this context means "appeared" in a sense that is neutral with respect to literal, visual appearance or appearance to the eye of the mind of spirit. Paul uses this same verb in Colossians 2:18 to denigrate false visions. Apparently for Paul the important distinction was not between literal seeing and visionary seeing, both of which could be veridical. The important distinction was between true and false visions.

As a reaction to early Jewish and gentile accusations of ghost story peddling, the theory goes, the Gospel writers then embellished these Pauline claims with more physical appearance stories.

The initial thing to say is that one must not presume that the Pauline accounts are accurate in the first place because (other than his own experience) he was not a primary witness and had his own agenda and ex post facto belief structure. In other words, the skeptic has every right to argue that Paul's claims are legendary or mistaken and the reported events did not take place. But if the skeptic concedes that at least some of the alleged appearances were "real", then the most we can say is that Paul was really referring to some sort of *experience* of Jesus as opposed to actual physical and bodily resurrected appearances of Jesus, *especially given the conclusions of the previous chapter.*

Secondly, in other religions and secular scenarios, there are also countless numbers of post-death appearances. In other such religious and secular contexts (ghosts, unexplained phenomena etc.), Christians don't (generally, especially concerning other religions) believe these myriad claims, often putting them down to hallucinations. This is simply a case of double standards. Skeptics just add another religion (Christianity, in this case) onto the rest of the list of post-death appearances.

The counter-argument to (Paul's claims of) hallucinations for the initial appearances is that hallucinations are private and these appearances listed are often to groups.

Mass hallucinations are well attested: there have been many throughout history and the world, including those in the context of Christianity such as the Virgin Mary at Fatima.[1] It is important to point out that neither the Gospels nor

[1] Though the hallucination/illusion was of a dancing sun, there was a mass sensory hallucination of Mary.

Acts specifically mention the appearance to more than five hundred people. Why would this be? Again, I would refer you back to the idea that, in such a context, this silence *is* evidence of absence. Indeed, the earliest Gospel, Mark (in its original form), mentions no appearances at all.

Some writers claim that the appearance to more than five hundred refers to the events at Pentecost.[1] Of course, this was not a physical appearance of Jesus at any rate, so this doesn't really help the rationale.

Remember, these claims are in a letter sent to Corinth in Greece. How many people would have had the time, resources and wherewithal to travel to Palestine (Roman Judea) to verify these claims? Paul blithely stated that many were still alive, and some were dead, but gave no details or names, and I can hardly imagine new converts to the faith getting up and going to Palestine to fact-check Paul's epistle claims.

The differences between Paul and the Gospels are marked, as Keith Parsons states:[2]

> Again, for Paul and the earliest Christians, it was not important to distinguish between a visionary and a physical encounter with the risen Christ. Only later, in response to anti-Christian polemics, did it become important to emphasize that the appearances were physical and not visionary. Clearly, the appearance stories grew in the telling, and the telling may well have obscured their original nature.

I will return to the subject of visions later in this chapter. Let us first look briefly at the appearance claims before we start looking at what could explain those visions.

The Gospel Claims of Appearances: The First, and an Evolution

Of course, as we have discussed, Paul utterly fails to mention the empty tomb and, as such, he disagrees with the Gospel writers as to whom Jesus first appeared. Mark, in his original ending, has Mary Magdalene, Mary the mother of James, and Salome visiting the tomb and seeing a man in a white robe (an angel?) inside who tells them Jesus has risen. The resurrection appearances thereafter are an interpolated ending (and most often written in brackets in Bibles for this accepted reason). According to tradition and some lines of evidence, Mark's main source is Peter. However, he does not mention Peter as

---

[1] An event recounted in Acts where disciples gathered and there was a "mighty rushing wind" (a common symbol for the Holy Spirit),i and "tongues as of fire" appear. They were "filled with the Holy Spirit, and began to speak in other tongues as the Spirit gave them utterance".

[2] Parsons in Price & Lowder (2004), p.444.

being appeared to first. This is a problem considering two other Gospels arguably do.

The first appearances are thoroughly contradictory:

Paul: Cephas (Peter?)
Mark: Mary Magdalene
Matthew: Mary Magdalene and the other Mary
Luke: Simon[1]
John: Mary Magdalene

The chronology, if one is to believe both Paul and the Gospels, is thoroughly problematic for Peter, notwithstanding the outright contradictions.

Paul's claims are utterly lacking in detail and Matthew and Luke very much look to be counter-arguments to early Jews and gentiles. We start to see a coherent narrative develop:

(1) Early Christians (e.g., Paul) claim that Jesus died and appeared to those among them.
(2) Early non-Christians make counter-arguments such as a body being in a tomb and that these appearance claims are fairly worthless or low-grade.
(3) Christians retort that, no, these were real, *bodily* resurrections.
(4) Non-Christians refute this claim with various arguments.
(5) Christians claim that no, there was an empty tomb to verify this bodily resurrection and there were witnesses to this empty tomb.

And so on. You can even agree that there was an empty tomb because Jesus might have been taken out of a temporary tomb to be buried anonymously. This would have led these Christians to genuinely believe in an empty tomb and would have perhaps even inspired visions.

But we will discuss this topic later in depth.

For now, let us consider the later, seemingly embellished appearance accounts of Matthew and Luke.

Matthew has two resurrection appearances that he recounts. Firstly, he has Jesus appearing to Mary Magdalene and "the other Mary" at the tomb and then later to all of the disciples on a mountain in Galilee.

---

[1] Or actually, not Simon – and there's some serious weirdness here…
The appearance to the two on the road to Emmaus (24:13-35) is the first appearance of the risen Jesus in Luke; Peter only finds the discarded linen cloths (24:12). Despite this, when the two finally *do* catch up with the disciples, they oddly exclaim "The Lord has appeared to Simon!" (24:34) – even though he hasn't yet! – and only *then* does Jesus actually appear to Simon/Peter (and the rest of them at the same time; 24:36).

Luke (24), on the other hand, is in explicit contradiction of Matthew, stating that Mary Magdalene did not see Jesus but an angelic vision:

> **23** "...and did not find His body, they came, saying that they had also seen a vision of angels who said that He was alive. **24** Some of those who were with us went to the tomb and found it just exactly as the women also had said; but Him they did not see."

The women had visions of angels, and did not see Jesus, after which people returned to the tomb and likewise did not see Jesus.

Luke is also at odds with Matthew in terms of location. For him, events do not take place in Galilee but in Jerusalem. Luke also includes the famous "Road to Emmaus" story in which Jesus appears to Cleopas and an unnamed disciple, an appearance to Peter and to the eleven disciples (with others) at a meeting. On a mountain outside Jerusalem, Luke has Jesus ascending into heaven in front of the disciples.

Acts adds Paul's experience on the Road to Damascus, an alleged appearance to the martyr Stephen, and Peter hears Jesus' voice.

John has Mary Magdalene not at first recognising Jesus at the tomb and then understanding him as being the resurrected Jesus. He then has Jesus appearing to the disciples (with the Doubting Thomas). A later addition (interpolation) to John (21) has Jesus appearing in Galilee to Peter and six of the disciples (importantly, not all of them).

Again, the main point to note is the lack of coherence or corroboration across all of the Gospels.

There is potentially an evolution of ideas and theology here. As mentioned in an earlier chapter, there is an argument as to whether Paul meant a spiritual resurrection. As stated earlier in this chapter, we can see the appearances become more physical, perhaps as the audience and writers move towards a setting more heavily influenced by Greco-Roman thinking and context.

The question is whether these later, embellished stories of physical resurrection and experiences are, indeed, embellished. And if they are real and veridical, why did Paul not indicate this?

One issue concerning the appearance narratives (and Gospels/Epistles in general) is the notion that apologists claim that Simon, Peter, Simon Peter and Cephas are all the same person. We can probably accept, on the explicit claims, that Simon, Peter and Simon Peter are the same, but the claim that Peter is Cephas is more problematic. Peter is mentioned twice by Paul, Cephas eight times, and he uses Peter and Cephas both in one sentence. He doesn't say Peter is Cephas at all and it is perhaps a stretch to assume they are the same person.

As briefly discussed before, Mark's source is, according to many apologists, Peter (originally according to Papias, who heard this from John the Presbyter). But if Peter was his source, how come Mark does not have any claim as to Peter being appeared to, let alone appeared to first? This could be prima facie evidence that Peter is *not* actually Simon or Cephas.

Paul's claim of Jesus appearing to Cephas first is perhaps at odds with his claims in Galatians 2 that Peter was arguably a false apostle. This is part of the apparent rift between the Paul faction and the James and Peter faction of the early Christian sect.

The point being that we just have a mass of confusion as to who was the first to "witness" Jesus.

Matthew doesn't even mention the name of Peter in any of his references to appearances, and Luke's actual mention is about as insightful as Paul's (Luke 24):

> **33** And they got up that very hour and returned to Jerusalem, and found gathered together the eleven and those who were with them, **34** saying, **"The Lord has really risen and has appeared to Simon."** [My emphasis]

If this material is evidence of an appearance, then this is literally the poorest form of evidence in the poorest quality of sources (the Gospels, as discussed previously in this book many times). Luke is usually a richer storyteller with far more detail, so this pithy statement perhaps speaks volumes. Indeed, this may simply be a reflection of Paul's very short 1 Corinthians 15:4-5 claim, as Richard I. Pervo states:[11]

> Luke 24 follows the order of 1 Corinthians 15:4-5, with the same words, mentioning an appearance to "Simon" followed by an appearance to the entire group. "The Lord has been raised and appeared to Simon".... The combination of "raise" and "appear" in the passive voice may seem unremarkable, but it is found only in these two places. Wolfgang Schenk has developed a detailed argument based upon the similarities among Luke 24, 1 Corinthians 15, and Galatians 1. Although the relation may seem tenuous at first sight, the question deserves serious attention. Luke 24:34 may well be a reflection of 1 Corinthians 15:4-5.

Both Luke and Paul have single sentence "accounts" for Jesus' appearance to Peter and they are worth not a lot to the evidential case for the Resurrection.

---

[11] Pervo (2006), p.70.

With regard to Mary, there is more detail, fleshed out as the Gospels progress in writing chronology (no surprise there) with John's account being the richest. Mary mistakes Jesus for a gardener and then has a conversation with him. On the other hand, Matthew has a short episode of two Marys worshipping at Jesus' feet after meeting him upon returning from the tomb for him. Here, Jesus commanded them to tell the disciples to meet him in Galilee, something that does not happen in John.

What do we make of these divergent accounts that do not take place in Luke (with Mark 16:9-10, an interpolation, reporting only a couple of sentences lacking any real detail)? Again, this is very low-level evidence amounting to nothing more than progressively embellished, and contradictory, assertions.

As an independent third party, I am not convinced by the evidential force of the case for the Resurrection continually being presented by the Gospels and Paul (or by people using these sources) considering the exceptionally high bar that they are required to meet and surpass in order for the Christian hypothesis to be seen as the most probable one to explain the data.

Eleven or Twelve in Jerusalem or Galilee…

Things are no clearer with the appearance to the Twelve. Or Eleven.

Paul and Mark claim that Jesus next appeared to the disciples – Paul says twelve; Luke has Jesus appear to "the Eleven" in Jerusalem. You might assume that this missing disciple was Judas, but John (20:24), in his account, claims it was Thomas. If Judas is already dead, as according to Matthew, this is a problem. To confirm how much of a problem this is, later copyists *changed* Paul's Greek use of "twelve" with a Latin "eleven" for the Vulgate Bible (the Latin translation for the Greek Bible). There is contradiction here, no doubt. And things aren't made easier by claiming there are twelve when one is dead and as yet unreplaced.

Luke and John have this appearance to the disciples sometime late on Easter Sunday in Jerusalem. In contrast, Mark and Matthew have it what must be some days later (at least three days of travel) in Galilee.

Apologists generally claim this is a second appearance, but this assertion is fraught with problem. Obviously, and given Matthew's dependence on Mark, why would Mark and Matthew omit any mention of earlier appearances in Jerusalem? Why would Luke, in his Gospel and Acts, completely exclude any appearances in Galilee by having the disciples remain in Jerusalem until after Jesus ascends to heaven? Only John thinks to harmonise these by imagining an appearance in Jerusalem and *then* a later one in Galilee.

Concerning the place, Matthew is simply in open contradiction as he not only says the meeting is in Galilee, but also, like Mark, has the risen Jesus in

Matthew 28:10 commanding the women to tell the disciples *to go to Galilee* where he will meet them.

The appearances were crucial, politically speaking. It seems important that the disciples were appeared to for early church authority, as philosopher Donald Viney states (referring to the work of biblical scholar Elaine Pagels):[1]

> If Pagels is correct, then not only do we know that the Gospel writers increasingly emphasized the bodily reality of the risen Christ, we have some understanding of why they did. The motives had more to do with building church structure than with historical accuracy.

There are many attempted Christian rationalisations to this (for the Christian, apparent) contradiction, ranging from "the Twelve" being a colloquialism to designate "the apostles", to being a rough rounding, and all such similar reasoning. Of course, since the Church itself deemed it important enough to *change the wording*, it seems like these weren't decent enough reasons for those actually changing the wording. (Twelve is an important number in the context of the Hebrew Bible and this would account for why there were originally twelve chosen disciples.)

As ever, it often seems like attempted harmonisations are so many and so disparate that they are mutually exclusive and show an approach of throwing as many things at the wall as possible to see what, if anything, sticks. Again, it's *possibiliter ergo probabiliter*, or "it's *an* answer, so therefore it's really reasonable and thus *the* (most probable) answer".

The Details of the Appearances to the Disciples

This is where, for the sake of time and space, I am not going to delve much further into the finer details, contradictions and speculations of the meeting(s) with the disciples. There are contradictory (or "differing") messages, responses from both Jesus and the disciples, issues concerning the disciples' lack of belief, doubting Thomas only being in John (with Jesus showing his hands, feet and side in John but not his side in Luke) and so on. I implore the reader to read and research further into these matters.[2]

The one thing I will say is that Jesus most probably did not appear to the disciples all at once, as according to Paul's account:[3]

[1] Viney (1989), p.134 [cf Alter (2015), p. 566].
[2] See Alter (2015) and his detailed analysis, p. 569-665.
[3] Carrier (2018).

> First, this is the only appearance on Paul's whole list that is "all at once" (*ephapax*). That means none of the other appearances he lists were "all at once." So when he says Jesus appeared "to the twelve" in verse 5, he means individually, on separate occasions; not to all twelve "at once." Otherwise, he'd have said so. As he does here, for the five hundred. Likewise, to "all the apostles" in verse 7 means individual apostles had individual experiences over time. Not a mass appearance all at once. Indeed, Paul can be read as including himself in that number, simply specifying that he was the last one. Because he does not say "then" Jesus appeared to him, but "then" Jesus appeared to all the apostles "and last of all me too," meaning, he was the last of the apostles he just mentioned.

The Road to Emmaus

There is still much debate as to where Emmaus is located, the famous Lukan destination of the two travellers to whom Jesus appears. Robert Price offers up an interesting theory on why Luke, proficient with Greek and Greek texts, might have chosen the name Emmaus:[1]

> My guess is that Luke intends a punning reference to the name from the Odyssey, that of Emmaeus, the faithful servant to whom Telemachus and Odysseus reveal their secret identities, as Jesus does to the Emmaus disciples.

Knowing Luke, as an author, this is a good theory. Luke's audience was educated Greeks, and he wrote in a polished Greek literary style. The traditional leading geographical contender for Christians for Emmaus is, unfortunately for them, 160 *stadia* (a Greek unit of distance) from Jerusalem as opposed to the 60 that Luke claims.

The story goes as follows, in the interpolated Mark 16:

> **12** After that, He appeared in a different form to two of them while they were walking along on their way to the country. **13** They went away and reported it to the others, but they did not believe them either.

And then in Luke 24 – I will lay it all out here as it is worth reading in context of our discussion and to see how unlikely it is and that, at best, it is an

[1] Price (2003), p. 339.

"unevidenced" assertion that most probably acts as theology rather than history:

> 13 And behold, two of them were going that very day to a village named
> Emmaus, which was about seven miles from Jerusalem. 14 And they were
> talking with each other about all these things which had taken
> place. 15 While they were talking and discussing, Jesus Himself approached
> and began traveling with them. 16 But their eyes were prevented from rec-
> ognizing Him. 17 And He said to them, "What are these words that you are
> exchanging with one another as you are walking?" And they stood still,
> looking sad. 18 One of them, named Cleopas, answered and said to Him,
> "Are You the only one visiting Jerusalem and unaware of the things which
> have happened here in these days?" 19 And He said to them, "What
> things?" And they said to Him, "The things about Jesus the Nazarene, who
> was a prophet mighty in deed and word in the sight of God and all the
> people, 20 and how the chief priests and our rulers delivered Him to the
> sentence of death, and crucified Him. 21 But we were hoping that it was He
> who was going to redeem Israel. Indeed, besides all this, it is the third day
> since these things happened. 22 But also some women among us amazed
> us. When they were at the tomb early in the morning, 23 and did not find
> His body, they came, saying that they had also seen a vision of angels who
> said that He was alive. 24 Some of those who were with us went to the
> tomb and found it just exactly as the women also had said; but Him they
> did not see." 25 And He said to them, "O foolish men and slow of heart to
> believe in all that the prophets have spoken! 26 Was it not necessary for
> the Christ to suffer these things and to enter into His glory?" 27 Then be-
> ginning with Moses and with all the prophets, He explained to them the
> things concerning Himself in all the Scriptures.
>
> 28 And they approached the village where they were going, and He acted
> as though He were going farther. 29 But they urged Him, saying, "Stay with
> us, for it is getting toward evening, and the day is now nearly over." So He
> went in to stay with them. 30 When He had reclined at the table with them,
> He took the bread and blessed it, and breaking it, He began giving it to
> them. 31 Then their eyes were opened and they recognized Him; and He
> vanished from their sight. 32 They said to one another, "Were not our
> hearts burning within us while He was speaking to us on the road, while
> He was explaining the Scriptures to us?" 33 And they got up that very hour
> and returned to Jerusalem, and found gathered together the eleven
> and those who were with them, 34 saying, "The Lord has really risen
> and has appeared to Simon." 35 They began to relate their experiences on
> the road and how He was recognized by them in the breaking of the
> bread.

The most obvious issue with Cleopas and the other disciple being appeared to is that they did not recognise Jesus. Jesus had been beaten, scourged (it is worth noting that Luke misses out this detail in his account), forced to wear a crown of thorns and did not have his clothes, and was only initially wrapped in linen. How was he not recognised in this state? His body must somehow have transformed back to what it was before he was crucified and his clothes magically rematerialised. This is bizarre! But, with the supernatural, you can make anything up and claim it is true.

It is even more bizarre since we know Jesus later showed his nail wounds in his hands and feet to the eleven (twelve) disciples in Jerusalem! The only explanation, given that he would have had three-day-old wounds on his body is that, oddly for this appearance, he did not have those particular wounds. Indeed, the only way they recognised him, even after saying all he did, was the way he broke bread with them shortly before he simply "vanished". The wounds must have healed just enough, but not fully for the later appearance. There seems to be an arbitrary nature to the details of Jesus' appearance and wounds throughout the Gospels.

Perhaps, as is hinted by Luke, the travellers' eyes were supernaturally veiled. How would they *know* that their eyes had been supernaturally shut? What is the divine purpose for doing this to these people (other than to give it literary value when later converted to text in Luke)?

Far more likely, as ever, is that this pericope is theological and not historical. We might ask how two people could walk all that way conversing with Jesus in broad daylight and then sit and eat with him and not recognise him. We would be more reasonable to answer that this was not something that happened but was as story of theological value. And that theology is about the Eucharist, the meal shared in Christian ritual, as well as the idea: "I was blind but now I see".

Not recognising Jesus is a common motif in these appearance accounts: it happens to John's Mary Magdalene (who thinks he is a gardener) and to John's fishing disciples who do not recognise Jesus when speaking to him until the "beloved disciple" does.

In terms of theology, it also looks to be a retelling of a story motif that happened in the Hebrew Bible with some frequency, such as in Genesis 18 and 19, Joshua 5:13-15 and particularly Judges 13. Indeed, as atheist Neil Godfrey opines, such analysis could give us a clue as to the chosen place name:[1]

> When Jacob was travelling the sun set (early Jewish legends explained the pointed reference in Genesis 28:11 by saying God had caused it to set prematurely to force Jacob to stop there) and he had a dream that he was in the presence of God. God spoke to him there. And the name

[1] Godfrey (2007).

> of the place was originally known as Luz – in the Septuagint it is Oulammaus. In the Codex Bezae this is the name used for Emmaus in Luke 24. In an early reading of Luke (perhaps the earliest) the Emmaus road revelation happened at the same place that Jacob dreamed he was visited by God.

This is a very interesting observation, indeed. He also goes on to show the number of times Luke borrows language and ideas from the Hebrew Bible, as well as the story form being a very common fictional motif:

> A most common motif was the resolution of the narrative through a gradual series of recognition scenes at the end. Throughout so many plots of novels character's identities had become confused, changed, or lost.

It is worth reading Godfrey's article for a host of enlightening and incisive observations concerning the Road to Emmaus story.

These observations certainly point to a literary creation of Luke to fulfil a theological and/or literary agenda, as opposed to a real and veridical appearance account.

The 500 and the One

This claim, due to the number, sounds impressive. No, that does not do it justice. This would have been one of the most momentous events in the whole of human history (for Christians claim it *was* history) – the resurrection of God who had died when in human form, and then an appearance to more than five hundred witnesses all at once. But we hear nothing. From anyone. Anywhere. However, we do have one source: a single sentence in an agenda-driven evangelical convert's letter. This claim does not even feature in the Gospels.

We have absolutely no details about this claim: Who were the people Jesus appeared to? Can we check the claim with them? When did it happen? Was it a bodily appearance of Jesus, or just a sensation? Did Jesus interact with the alleged witnesses? If so, what language did he use? Where did this appearance occur? Was he amongst the crowd? So on and so forth – there is no information at all that helps the reader to assess Paul's claim.

However, be aware that over five hundred people have claimed an alien abduction and various UFO shenanigans (even if not all at once, though over three hundred Melbourne students and staff had a UFO experience in 1966[1]). You could argue, adopting the logic of a Christian apologist, that the best explanation of *all* of the data is, indeed, an alien in a spacecraft, from another galaxy, with probes, wanting to travel across space and time to find out what the inside of... and so on. But we know better. Or, at least, we *should* know better. Nevertheless, these stories and beliefs prevail amongst certain people. We will also later deal with, for example, mass hallucinations and miracles taking place in Smyrna, in the context of Sabbatai Zevi.

As you gather, the initial problem with the claim of the appearance to more than five hundred people is believing the Gospels (are accurate sources of data). No actual evidence of this event happening is given: it is a mere Pauline assertion attributed to a creed. Even Luke's claim that his information was passed down by eyewitnesses is merely an assertion. Yet again, the absence of evidence *is* evidence of absence because we would *absolutely* expect someone in that group of five hundred-plus people to have recorded the event somehow. We would *expect* multiple attestations. Yet we do not get them. This should invoke terminal doubts. Richard Carrier is dismissive of Paul's claims:[2]

> So all we have left to count on is Paul, whose letters constitute the only text we have from anyone claiming to be an eyewitness to a risen Jesus, and someone who tells us he knew and met some of the eyewitnesses before him (though he didn't meet them until years after he himself saw Jesus and was already evangelizing across the Middle East). But here's the huge disconnect. Nothing in Paul, connects with anything in the Gospels. That's right. Not a single detail in the Gospels, matches anything in Paul. Paul never mentions anyone hanging out with the undead Jesus eating and drinking and fondling him for weeks on end. And Paul's only reported sequence of events, corresponds to no Gospel we know.
>
> Paul tells us Jesus was seen, and preached his gospel of resurrection and salvation, *in revelations* (Romans 16:25-26; Galatians 1:11-16; 1 Corinthians 9:1). Not by showing up at the apostles' door and asking for a hot breakfast. In fact, what Paul does tell us, rules that out. The most detailed account Paul ever gives is in 1 Corinthians 15:5-9...

Homuyan Sidky refers to the writing of theologian Ernest Barnes to dismiss this claim:[3]

---

[1] And then there was the Phoenix Lights phenomenon in 1997 being the largest mass UFO experience in history.

[2] Carrier (2018).

[3] Sidky (2019), p. 485.

> The theologian Ernest Barnes (1948: 173) dismissed the reference to the appearance of the 500 as non-historical and a later redaction. Otherwise, he adds, this incredible bit of evidence would have been the centerpiece of Christian apologetics. However, there are no mentions of this event in any other source. From this, he concluded that this story was invented after Paul's time. Barnes is generous by attributing this tale to the work of some later religious enthusiast rather than deception on the part of Paul, who is given deference because he is an important Christian saint.

There is only one event that the appearance to the five hundred-plus witnesses remotely refers to if it does at all, and that is the Pentecost event of Acts 2:1-4. This ecstatic experience of a violent wind coming from heaven, what seemed like tongues of fire coming and resting on each of the people there and filling them with the Holy Spirit. That event happened fifty days after Jesus died, hence the name Pentecost.

Acts states there were one hundred and twenty apostles present (conveniently ten times twelve, a rather biblical number). There is good evidence to support the idea that Paul is actually referring to Pentecost in his appearance to five hundred-plus claim:[1]

> Could this be because Paul's letters did not then say "above five hundred brethren" when the author of Acts consulted them? It's distinctly possible. There are three pieces of evidence for that conclusion: (1) that no Gospel ever mentions an appearance "to over 500," not even Luke-Acts (yet how could they have failed to have built that out, if they had such a precious verse in Paul to work from?); (2) that "over five hundred" looks suspiciously similar in Greek to "over the Pentecost"; and (3) Paul actually links the resurrection of Jesus to the Pentecost, and indeed in the very same chapter of First Corinthians that he mentions an appearance to hundreds of brethren.

Indeed, if you read the whole of Carrier's piece, and understand the lexical analysis of the Greek, it is almost certainly a copyist error that gets made that later writers had to fudge to fix (See Appendix 2).

In order to evaluate the appearance of the "five hundred", then, we need to consider the author of Acts, and his reliability concerning the Pentecost account. The author, we know, has a habit of spinning and exaggerating events. We can't tell whether "speaking in tongues" was a magical ability to actually speak in foreign languages to others or the glossolalia we see and dismiss in

---

[1] Ibid.

today's Pentecostal churches. It might be worth considering our skepticism of the "mass hallucination" events (or mass hysteria events) of those same modern Pentecostal churches, with pastors laying on hands to congregants and all sorts of bizarre reactions that we see and, quite frankly, dismiss. If something *is* happening there, then it is a psychological phenomenon resulting from manipulation. The events recorded in Acts could have been something similar to what we see in such churches every Sunday.

Moreover, Paul himself refers to such Pentecostal activities. Hence, we know the early followers were exhibiting such religious and psychological fervour: see 1 Corinthians 14:1-33; 12:1-11; 1 Thessalonians 5:19. As Carrier continues:[1]

> The most famous example being the Fatima Sun Miracle, which we know (because we had the ability to carefully record the events and interrogate those present at them) was really just an ecstasy-inspired hallucination of some unusual light phenomena associated with the sun, really only experienced internally. Just an altered state of consciousness; a perceptual confabulation of the human brain. This isn't the only example in history. Other kinds of mass hallucination of light occurred at Our Lady of Assiut and Our Lady of Zeitoun. Many a mass UFO report appears to relate to misperception of an amorphous light phenomenon. Similar experiences have been studied in Buddhists.
>
> The significant fact for us is that everyone who experienced the "vision" at Fatima came away claiming they had "seen" a miracle of (and thus proof of the existence of) the Virgin Mary; to their minds, a celestial woman named Mary could at some point have been said to have "appeared" to them "by means of" her miracle. Only upon careful interrogation would you even know that what they *meant* was just an ambiguous dance of light (much as Acts claims is the way Jesus "appeared" to Paul). And yet *unlike* the Fatima incident, for the event Paul refers to we don't get to access what anyone *actually* was saying or claiming.

There is good reason to believe that Paul, then, is referring to very personal or "amorphous" (in relation to the Pentecost appearance) appearances that are visions – hallucinations – and not real events that relate to external objects in reality. Let us consider these phenomena in a little more depth.

When considering Paul's own experience, this is almost certainly, by his own admission, a generalised religious experience of Jesus as opposed to an actual vision of a figure of Jesus (long-ascended into heaven, given this was some years later). In Galatians 1, we learn that God saw fit "to reveal His Son in

[1] Ibid.

me" and that Paul did *not* receive the Gospel from man but "received it through a revelation of Jesus Christ". Indeed, these "visions and revelations of the Lord" are communicated in such a fashion by Paul (2 Corinthians 12) that it has led some to believe he was schizophrenic, which is a condition highly associated with hallucinations. Many exegetes believe that the man he is talking of/to in this passage is himself.

Acts (a source of questionable reliability here) describes a flash of light, a loud noise, a loss of sight and the inability to eat or drink for three days. Some critics have opined that this phenomenon could easily be described by a lightning strike. The odds, as a modern US citizen, of being struck by lightning in one's lifetime are as low as 1 in 3,000.

One must also be careful not to confuse Paul's own writing with the overtly and legendarily embellished accounts of the events from the later Acts, and so working out what *really* happened to Paul at the very best takes a lot of investigation and inference, and guesswork at what is true and what is not; at very worst, it's impossible.

Paul, like so many other people in so many different religions in so many different eras, had religious experiences that he interpreted as revelations.

Simply put, this is nothing unusual and should not, in any way, convince the reader to equate them to real and actual visions of an external, mind-independent Jesus. Not unless we really *wanted* to believe that, absent the required level of quality evidence to do so.

And, yet again, we have incredible claims; actually, very poorly detailed claims. Bluntly stated, we do not have the level of evidence that we should require to establish such claims as being true.

Visions of Jesus

When I previously read about *visions* (as something seen, whether or not it is really *there*) as applied to Jesus, well over a decade ago when first looking in-depth at the Resurrection story, my initial reaction was to be quite scornful of ideas of them. Really? *Visions* explain much of Resurrection and appearance claims? But as time has passed, and I've understood more about cults, about "UFO abductions", about skepticism (thank you Carl Sagan), about religious experiences from people and cultures of many religions in the world (mutually exclusively), and so on, and even though I have not had a visionary experience myself, I understand far better the power of such explanations and the wonders of the human brain and mind.

I say I have not had a visionary experience, but I have had many wondrous experiences. Actually, and rather *less* wondrously, I have suffered several times from sleep paralysis, both occasions of which were incredibly disturbing and possibly do count as (sleep) visions. Once, a horde of "demons" moved through my backpacker's dormitory in New Zealand to leave from the window next to me. I was utterly unable to move. So, perhaps I have had visions or hallucinations, and pretty scary ones at that.

One far more pleasant experience that I had – which had the motifs of mountains and clouds and strange lights – happened to me in the mountains of Slovakia some years back. I was hiking over a beautiful peak near to a friend's place in the Tatras Mountains, and we were just nearing the summit (not a huge affair) when we started being surrounded by low cloud, the sort that feels like a cross between fog and mist. I guess that's cloud for you.

The whole experience was surreal and I was left thinking that, had I been religious, I almost certainly would have interpreted it as being a religious experience; I really would have, I am sure. The clouds descended all around us and it was eerily quiet and serene in a way I can't describe, and then the sun tried to break through. Except, we were surrounded by low mountain cloud; the end result was that we couldn't see the sun at all but were surrounded by the most *incredible* bright sun-cloud-mist-light, with an obvious source in the direction of the sun. The effect was visually and experientially incredible. I won't do it the injustice of trying to describe it any more but suffice to say that it was an astonishing (and utterly naturalistic) experience and phenomenon that will stay with me forever. We eventually reached the peak and the cloud dissipated, as the day drew on, for us to be left with stunning views and disappointed that no god-like figure had descended from the heavens to accompany us. Or, perhaps, taken off from us to join the heavens. We were all present and accounted for...

That was not a vision but, given a different context for me, or happening to someone else, could that have been a "vision", a religious experience? Or, given a different person, could they have run with those experiences and developed those phenomena and their experiences *into* a vision retrospectively (within the context of their worldview and desires)? Who knows?

What we *do* know is:

(1) People really do have visions and hallucinations.
(2) People really do lie about having visions and hallucinations.
(3) People really do mistake experiences as visions and hallucinations.
(4) People really do misrepresent memories and re-present them as misformed versions of what they originally experienced.

This state of affairs is all very uncontroversial. Until you apply these ideas to Christian sources and relate them to Christians. Then, all of a sudden, such a naturalistic explanation is ridiculous (according to Christians). How could billions of people come to believe in such a worldview, based on such hallucinations? Well, there is Islam and the visions of the angel Gabriel that Muhammed had upon which the entire religion is based. So, there is that. Then there are Joseph Smith's visions that gave rise to Mormonism. So, there is that as well. And Zoroaster's vivid revelatory visions in which he was instructed by Ahura Mazda, the 'Wise Lord'. So, there is that, too. Then there is *makyo,* or hallucination, in Buddhism, *siddhi* in Hinduism...and...and...

Visions are surprisingly common in the inception of different religions throughout time and geography. If, as a Christian, you are to dismiss hallucinations as applied to Christian claims as somehow not worthy, or too "out there" as an explanatory tool, then you are in serious trouble, because the same logic and arguments could be used to defend almost every other (foundation of) religion in the world. And the Christian will be using the hallucination argument to dismiss these.

Christian, Beware the double standard.

I cannot belabour this point enough. To dismiss visionary hallucinations out of hand is to take away your major rebuttal of all the other claims of visions and appearances in every other religion, religions that you do not adhere to given your use of the sorts of hallucination argument you do not allow to be applied to your own religion.

As Homuyan Sidky, Professor of Anthropology, states in *Religion, Supernaturalism and the Paranormal: An Anthropological Critique*:

> Many supernatural and paranormal experiences, past and present, are hallucinations misinterpreted and ascribed celestial meaning by the percipients. As Beyerstein (2007: 320) sums this up, the sense of presence, out-of-body experiences (OBEs), and visions of ghosts and other supernatural beings have for millennia[1] produced new religions. While these have been accepted as proof of afterlife, higher planes of existence, and cosmic consciousness, he adds, they have prosaic explanations....
>
> Although commonalities exist across different societies, the metaphysical attitudes of time and place influence the contents of hallucinations. Religious phenomena, we might recall, are part and parcel of cultural traditions. They cannot be otherwise. Moreover, the culturally determined content of hallucinations can change over time. For example, Aleman and Larøi (2009: 30) point out that unlike the present-day pattern in Europe, during the Middle Ages hallucinations were universally religious in nature, involving messages from God, saints, and interactions with angels or demons. Moreover, the recorded cases from the Middle Ages were almost entirely visual hallucinations (Kroll and Bachrach 1982). Such occurrences are rare at present.
>
> There are also cross-cultural variations in the predominance of particular kinds of hallucinations. For example, visual hallucinations associated with schizophrenia predominate in Africa and the Middle East, while

[1] Sidky (2019), p. 298-99.

> these hallucinatory phenomena are the least frequently reported symptoms among European and American patients (Aleman and Larøi 2009: 30; Bentall 2000: 96–97). One would not expect such variations if these experiences were actually tapping into some singular universal cosmic source or ultimate reality beyond the material universe, rather than being the effects of the human brain and nervous system with input from culture. The significant cultural component of such experiences is a rationality defeater for such claims.

Visual hallucinations, common in the Middle East at that time, would have been overwhelmingly religious in character (whereas today we have visions of UFOs and all sorts).

As Sidky goes on to discuss, temporal lobe epilepsy is commonly associated with such hallucinations and this has led people to theorise that Paul suffered from such. One might counter that the duration of the phenomena doesn't fit too well with an epilepsy explanation, but this is taking Paul's claims concerning the duration as accurate.

He continues:[1]

> One conclusion someone could reach regarding the phenomenological similarities between religious experiences and a psychotic worldview is that religions "are a form of madness and the religious merely insane." Alternatively, we could take the cultural relativist perspective that clinically diagnosed psychotics in this culture are merely prophets and visionaries falsely labeled as mad by those who lack their "sensitivities and insights" (Clarke 2010: 75). Most researchers do not make such determinations. The type of hallucinatory phenomena associated with psychosis is now known to also occur among a significant proportion of the nonclinical population (David 2004: 111; Johns and van Os 2001). These include individuals ranging from the psychologically well-adjusted to those who display some symptoms of psychopathology but do not fit the category of clinically psychotic (Aleman and Larøi 2009: 83; Peters 2010: 127).

So that when many Christians claim (without any evidence, mind) that the Christian followers such as Paul were not prone to such clinical problems, the evidence suggests prevalence in the nonclinical population as well.

Why all of this preamble?

We need to take hallucinations seriously. Not as seriously as people did before our modern times because they ended up believing them as real, but we need to take them seriously as naturalistic manifestations of biology, of mind

[1] Ibid, p. 291.

and brain, of experience. We need to apply our doubts and skeptical analysis *fairly* across all claims, not leaving our favoured worldview inoculated to the high levels of skeptical analysis we apply to competing worldviews.[1]

These visions are important because they are the foundations of the Christian faith. On this point, Christians and nonbelievers might have some agreement: at least some of the disciples had visionary experiences of some kind. One must be careful of language here because, for the Christian who believes in veridical visions, these are not "visions", these are people empirically seeing things. But let us park that issue for now and stick with the term "vision" to include both and differentiate it from "hallucination".

I believe the empty tomb was a later legendary addition to give force to the claims that originally arose from the disciples' visions. The question, therefore, is whether these visions were real or not, and by "real", I mean actually reflecting a physical appearance ("seeing"). At least some of these people had some sort of vision, but was their vision in reality just a hallucination?

Paul, as our earliest source, said he had a vision and this had nothing to do with the empty tomb (which he does not mention at all, and arguably knew nothing about as it had not yet been legendarily invented). It seems important to point out that Paul tells us his knowledge comes from his study of scripture and revelation from God – but never tells us anything remotely like Luke's Road to Emmaus story – not even when justifying his apostleship (see Galatians 1).

Luke even tells us that the empty tomb was not what convinced the disciples: (Luke 24:11) "But these words appeared to them as nonsense, and they would not believe them." They did not believe the empty tomb on its own but they *did* believe their appearance visions. It is the following formula that gives the disciples strength of conviction, apparently: vision of a risen Jesus + empty tomb = confirmed belief in Jesus' resurrection.

James Crossley, New Testament scholar, observes of this:[2]

> But some things are not so different. Jesus may well have been accompanied by a blinding light in Paul's vision according to Acts rather than someone being of light or the source of light, but the presence of bright light also echoes revelatory experiences from different cultures. Michael Goulder points to Susan Atkins (involved with the serial killer Charles Manson) who was converted in prison by a blinding white vision where the human form at the centre of the vision was recognized as Jesus and he spoke to her." ...but given it is our most detailed account...it is telling that it lacks any evidence in favour of Jesus as a real live flesh and blood figure who can be touched and who might want a shared meal, and it would hardly be out of place in a discussion of cross-cultural

[1] See John Loftus's superb book *The Outsider Test for Faith* (Loftus 2013).
[2] Crossley (2005), p. 175.

visionary experiences. Again, this is not, of course, to deny that what was seen was not thought of as real. But it does not follow from this that there had to be an empty tomb.

In terms of the visions of Jesus' followers, Christians will say that they are veridical in that they referred to an external reality. Visions that do not refer[1] to something physical (or perhaps even nonphysical but somehow mind-independent of the agent) are events I will term as *hallucinations*. Hallucinations come in many different guises: visual hallucinations, olfactory hallucinations, gustatory hallucinations, auditory hallucinations, tactile hallucinations. As one typical paper concerning hallucinations includes:[2]

> There is a growing recognition that hallucinatory experiences attend a wide variety of psychiatric diagnoses and can be part of everyday experience for people who do not meet criteria for mental illness. For the experiencer, hallucinations can have important personal meanings...

Here, we are dealing with the question as to whether it is more probable that the visions that the disciples had related to an external object (or misrepresented it), or more probable that they were hallucinations.

In terms of some of the claims such as the Road to Emmaus and Doubting Thomas, we need ask a slightly different question: is it more probable that the visions reported were historically accurate (were these real events at all?), or more probable that the sources shouldn't be trusted and they are in some way legendary embellishments?

Visionary behaviour was nothing if not ordinary in the context of the Christian Bible and its authors. As Richard Carrier points out in his chapter "Why the Resurrection Is Unbelievable":[3]

> In fact, Paul reveals the earliest Christians were hallucinating on a regular basis, entering ecstatic trances, prophesying, relaying the communications of spirits, and speaking in tongues–so much, in fact, that outsiders thought they were lunatics (e.g., 1 Corinthians 14). The whole book of Revelation, for example, is a veritable acid trip, and yet it got into the Bible as an authoritative document. That's how respectable even the craziest of hallucinations were. Not only were they constantly channeling spirits and speaking in tongues and having visions of angels and strange objects in the sky, they were also putting on faith-healing acts and exorcising demons by laying on hands and shouting words of

[1] Or perhaps end up representing them in mis-formed ways.
[2] Waters & Fernyhough (2017).
[3] Carrier (2010), p. 300.

> power. In other words, the first Christians behaved a lot more like crazy cultists than you'd ever be comfortable with. These aren't the sort of people whose testimony you would ever trust if you met them today. And if you wouldn't trust what they said now, you shouldn't trust anything they said then.

Considering all these appearance occurrences, then, we have four options: (1) an accurate report of a vision of a real, external object; (2) an inaccurate (legend/lie or mistaken) report of a real, external object; (3) an accurate report of a hallucination; (4) and/or an inaccurate report of a hallucination.

Just as a reminder, the first option is, by any measure and no matter who you are, the least probable event given what we know about the world, and notwithstanding any particular evidence. So, these Gospel accounts need to constitute exceptional evidence in order to overcome that low prior probability.

Let me emphasise something really important here: Paul's list of appearances is almost certainly referring to visionary qua hallucinatory experiences:[1]

> Second, Paul cannot mean Jesus hung around with his followers for days or weeks. Paul's use of "all at once" for only one single event, and his entire sequence (Cephas, and *then* each of the Twelve, and *then* the brethren, and *then* James, and *then* each of the Apostles, and *then* Paul), entails these were isolated, momentary visions. They came, and went. Paul therefore cannot mean a lingering Jesus who stuck around and dined with them for days on end. That simply isn't what he is describing here. At all. And yet this fact strongly supports explanations from the cognitive science of religious experience: these were visions; not a reanimated body. A reanimated body would stick around.

This explanation definitely points towards Paul giving an account of momentary hallucinations, which sits in direct opposition to what we read in the Gospels. But, by now, we are getting used to a great divergence that takes place between Paul and the Gospel narratives.

Bishop N.T. Wright, though, claims, in *The Resurrection of the Son of God* that visions are insufficient to account for the Resurrection narrative, that if visions were somewhat "normal" then they would not do the job effectively. People "knew the difference between visions and things that happen in the 'real'

---

[1] Carrier (2018).

world".[1] Of course, if visions are *interpreted* as an actual bodily appearance, as James Crossley counters to Wright,[2] then this point is moot.

But, as we see with Mark's earliest account, it is not so easy to assume an empty tomb, as Crossley replies:[3]

> As it tums out this [1 Cor. 15.4] in fact provides evidence in favour of there being no genuine eyewitness knowledge of the empty tomb, particularly when compared with the Markan resurrection narrative. Mark 16.8 famously says that the women at the tomb told no one out of fear. Is it not possible that this indicates that the empty tomb story, known only to 'unreliable' witnesses if we take our earliest narrative source, was not in fact properly established and had no genuine eyewitness support?... Now compare the evidence from Paul. Paul may indeed assume that there was an empty tomb in 1 Cor. 15.4 but this is a general handed-on tradition for which he gives no eyewitness support. It is therefore hugely significant that when Paul does give eyewitness support for appearances of Jesus in the immediately following 1 Cor. 15.5-8, which includes his own, they are, as noted above, presumably similar to the one Paul experienced on the road to Damascus, that is, no indication of eating, drinking or touching. This provides important support for my argument that a vision could be interpreted in a bodily sense with the assumption of an empty tomb, yet at the same time the empty tomb itself being historically inaccurate.

Crossley bemoans that Wright "has underestimated creative storytelling in early Judaism"[4] to the point that claims made of people in similar religious contexts can "hardly be said to give genuine historical insight as to what really happened".[5] Stories that the Hebrew Bible claims of featured figures are rightly not to be treated by historians as historically accurate accounts of what actually happened thousands of years ago.

Homuyan Sidky, the anthropologist who I earlier quoted, has worked with many people who have had religious visions. Excuse the long quote, but so much of what he says is worth contemplating:[6]

> Such visionary or ecstatic events, involving communication and interaction with the sacred or paranormal realm, was almost a daily part of my fieldwork with shamans, mediums, mother-goddesses, god-men, and

---

[1] Wright (2003), p. 690.
[2] Crossley (2005), p. 177.
[3] Ibid., p. 177-78.
[4] Ibid., 178.
[5] Ibid., p. 179.
[6] Sidky (2019), p. 266-67.

oracles. Their behaviors and claims are highly reminiscent of the prophets of old. In many instances, I was able to observe such specialists before, during, and after their encounters with supernatural beings and paranormal realities....

The major problem with revelatory experiences, or revelations, as I found out early in my field research, is that they are private. By this, I mean that during such encounters with the extraordinary only a particular individual is the recipient of the paranormal communiqué. While it was possible for me to observe the behaviors and listen to pronouncements of such miracle workers, I had no access to the subjective perceptions and sensations of what the percipients claimed had transpired between them and the supernatural and the paranormal realms. Long ago, the ever-insightful Thomas Paine (1880 [1794]: 3) noted the problem with such God-to-human communications in the context of his critique of Christianity:

admitting, for the sake of a case, that something has been revealed to a certain person, and not revealed to any other person, it is a revelation to that person only. When he tells it to a second person, a second to a third, a third to a fourth, and so on, it ceases to be a revelation to all those other persons. It is a revelation to the first person only, and hearsay to every other, and consequently they are not obliged to believe it.

What this means is that religious adherents must take their visionary's word – that is, the words of another human being–that the revelation was genuine and was related to them accurately. Thus, the God-to-human communicative exchange is, in reality, a human-to-human message transmission. Believers, however, ascribe mystical and cosmic significance to such revelatory messages of their messiahs, prophets, and vatics, forgetting that ultimately the source of these magical memoranda is other human beings.

There is no doubt that in some cases the percipients are genuinely convinced of the veridicality of their extra-worldly encounters. It must be stressed, however, that this only means that a person comes to sincerely believe that he or she sees or senses the presence of something extraordinary, not that such an extraordinary something necessarily exists outside their minds. In other words, contrary to the assertion by the sociologist Rodney Stark (1999), the ubiquity of purported experiences of God, or whatever label one wishes to use, and how powerfully the percipient believes that the experience is genuine do not justify that such a supernatural being exists as an objective, mind-independent entity. The reason for this is that large numbers of people have experienced seeing and are true believers in comparably unwarranted things, such as UFOs (over 1 million cases since 1947), alien abductions, angels, ghosts,

> vampires, night demons, cryptids, and fairies, but this does not mean that such things exist anywhere, in any form, at any time (cf., Sagan 2006: 162).

For such visions to be interpreted as activity involving a mind-independent figure or veracity, for them to be veridical, we would need further evidence. Evidence that we do not have. Again, if we believe Paul on his word, we would need to believe every other claimant of a religious experience, no matter his or her religious heritage or claim.

These claims are for the religious claimant, for all intents and purposes, claims of miracle, and the prior probability of miracles being true is, well, rather low. And what do we know about claims with low priors? Yes, they need an awful lot of very good evidence in order to warrant assigning truth to them.

Muhammad

The foundation of the Muslim religion is that the prophet Muhammad had a series of visions, including hearing voices, of the Archangel Gabriel. Sometimes, these occurrences were through meditation. Miraculously, he later ascended into the skies himself. These events, according to Muslims and Islamic scholars, have tremendous provenance and provide evidentiary basis for belief in the religion. And yet Christians and other non-Muslims do not believe them.

One of the following possibilities reflects reality:

(1) The Archangel Gabriel really did appear to Muhammad for some divine reason.
(2) Muhammad really had hallucinations that he interpreted as revelations from God.
(3) Muhammad did not have hallucinations and made the whole lot up.
(4) The story (including Muhammad) has no basis in reality to begin with.[1]

For the Christian, (2) and/or (3) are true. In other words, as mentioned previously, they are happy to place either outright deception or falsely attributed hallucinations as visions at the foundation of a massive world religion.

This is a plausible scenario.

For Islam.

---

[1] And, yes, some people surmise that Muhammad never ever existed, rather like Jesus Mythicism. See Carrier (2015).

But not for Christianity?

What, then, Happened?

> Who beheld this? A half-frantic woman, as you state, and some other one, perhaps, of those who were engaged in the same system of delusion, who had either dreamed so, owing to a peculiar state of mind, or under the influence of a wandering imagination had formed to himself an appearance according to his own wishes, which has been the case with numberless individuals; or, which is most probable, one who desired to impress others with this portent, and by such a falsehood to furnish an occasion to impostors like himself.[1]

That Christianity arose from hallucinations (or claimed hallucinations), as we can see from this Celsus quote, was an accepted explanation for and counter-argument to Christianity in the times of the early Christian church.

The first thing to recognise is the quality of the evidence. Paul aside (and he gives us only a little to work with – "a kerygmatic assertion wholly lacking in detail"[2]), the people who experienced the visions did not write anything down that we know of. The sources for the Gospel accounts are unknown. We know very little indeed about the provenance and accuracy of the appearance claims. And, as we have discussed, we should have serious doubts when assessing the probability of these claims as being true. The appearance claims look like outright inventions or embellishments.

My thesis would be that, probably, at least one of Peter, Paul and Mary Magdalene (where mention of Peter and Mary are so common, and Paul seems sincere in his early claims) had visions of Jesus that were hallucinations. As time went on and the movement gathered momentum and popularity, and as others believed the three aforementioned people, these accounts were embellished and there were legendary additions of other appearance stories, some overtly theological in nature. These accounts were written into the Gospels and became part of the canonical "history" of the figure of Jesus. The embellished stories stretched into accounts of a bodily raised, physical Jesus, as counter-arguments to doubters or people with a different theological understanding.

Though many people would have believed these three purported witnesses, others would have doubted, and this is what we see reflected in the Gospel accounts where there is a good deal of doubt surrounding the

---

[1] Ante-Nicene Fathers translation, *New Advent*, https://www.newadvent.org/fathers/04162.htm (Retrieved 09/03/2021).

[2] Keith Parsons in Price & Lowder (2005), p. 444. "Kerygma" refers to the preaching or proclamation of the Gospel.

appearance accounts from disciples themselves. It is this doubt that leads to the up-levelling of claims, so that they become more and more obviously incredible and, in some ways, more detailed.

Do I have justification for believing this thesis as more probable than the thesis of the Christian? Absolutely!

Scientific investigations have been carried out (with differing levels of methodology over time), looking into the phenomena of hallucinations. The most commonly cited study found that some 13.3% of people have claimed to have had at least one vivid hallucination. Moreover, 39% of college students studied said they had had auditory hallucinations.[1] In addition, around 1% of people have visual hallucinations of a dead person with whom they also have a conversation.[2] That is one in one hundred not only visually hallucinating but auditorily hallucinating, too.

For cultures that are more superstitious, and for this, we can probably count all historical cultures, these incidences are higher. In one informal study of Hawaiian natives, a not insignificant 40% of people were found to have had auditory or visual encounters with dead people.[3]

What is important is that, where, say, schizophrenia affects some 1% of the population, these results show that hallucinations happen more frequently. Or, to put it another way, hallucinations happen to "ordinary" people (without wanting to be pejorative, I prefer the term "neurotypical", but you often hear "nonpsychotic" as well) not uncommonly. What we also know is that the hallucinations are often of dead people or involving religious content, which makes sense given that two of the most common forms of vision "involve the comforting presence of a deceased loved one or of a respected religious figure":[4]

> How does one explain these large numbers? Bentall argues that the ability to distinguish between self-generated events (that is, imaginary sensations, originating in the mind) and externally generated ones (that is, those induced by causes exterior to the mind) is a real skill that humans acquire, and like all skills, it "is likely to fail under certain circumstances."[5] This skill is called *source monitoring* - since it is the skill of monitoring where the source of a sensation comes from, either inside or outside the mind. Bentall argues that source monitoring judgments are affected by the culture in which a person grows up. If a person's culture subscribes to the existence of ghosts or the reality of dead people appearing, the chance that one "sees" what will be assumed to be a ghost or a dead person is obviously heightened. Moreover, and this is

---

[1] Bentall in Cardeña et al (2000), p. 86.
[2] Slade & Bentall (1988), p. 70-72.
[3] Ibid, p. 77-78.
[4] Ehrman (2014), p. 194.
[5] Bentall in Cardeña et al (2000), p. 102.

> a key point, stress and emotional arousal can have serious effects on a person's source monitoring skills. Someone who is under considerable stress or experiencing deep grief, trauma, or personal anguish, is more likely to experience a failure of source monitoring.

We also know from research that people who have hallucinations (whether UFO abductions or ones related to bereavement) *really do believe* their experiences to be veridical. They *really are* being visited by a dead person, so they think. They aren't hallucinations to *them*, they are lived experiences of seeing something tangible.

Furthermore, when there is a sensation of guilt, people are more likely to experience such visions. Ehrman explains:[1]

> Such visions are more commonly experienced when a person has a sense of guilt over some aspect of his or her relationship with the one who has died (recall: the disciples had all betrayed, denied, or fled from Jesus during his hour of need). Often they are accompanied by anger at the circumstances or the people who caused the loved one's death (another obvious parallel to the disciples and Jesus). Strikingly, after the loved ones have died, the survivors idealise them, smoothing over the difficult aspects of their personalities, or remembering only their good sides. And not infrequently, those suffering bereavement seek to form community with others who remember the loved ones and tell stories about them. All of these features relate closely with what we have in the case of Jesus, the beloved teacher and master who met an untimely death.

What this information tells us is that, from a modern standpoint, at least some of Jesus' followers will have had hallucinations in their lives. However, it is more powerful than that. Given the cultural context, and the context of a beloved religious leader and friend dying (horrifically), and given their feelings of guilt and anger, this probability then rises considerably and can be well applied to the disciples in the period following Jesus' death.

We have a scenario where, in first-century Roman-occupied Judea, Jesus followers were *likely* to have had hallucinations. This isn't just some crackpot theory trying to justify something highly improbable. There would have bee'n a high probability that at least some of Jesus' disciples would have had some form of hallucination. The feeling, in bereavement, that the person is still with you there in the room – the seeing, the hearing, and so on – this is in no way unusual and certainly to be expected, especially in that culture and context.

---

[1] Ehrman (2014), p. 195.

There is also substantial evidence that people in such scenarios of bereavement who have vivid visions of such loved ones in dreams believe that these were not dreams, but were genuine communications from the dead.[1]

As Homuyan Sidky states:[2]

> These were the characteristics of the group that entered Jerusalem with high expectations. Hope turned into a calamity for the disciples with the violent death of their leader. Fearing for their own lives, the disciples renounced their faith in Jesus whose mortifying death exposed him in their minds at that time as a false messiah, scattered, and fled back to their homes in Galilee. In shock and deep despair over their shattered hopes and expectations, and mourning for their master, they were left pondering how to make sense of the tragedy and horror that befell them. These are all universal human responses to events of this kind. Bereavement associated with the murder of a loved one, as this was, is often associated with very intense emotional reactions of anger, bewilderment, traumatic stress, denial, and guilt.
>
> Moreover, the disciples had to come to terms with the absence of the deceased's body. This is a particularly important point. The corpse represents tangible evidence that death has taken place. Viewing it dispels all doubts as to its appearance, serves as a final confirmation of the death, and provides the bereaved an opportunity to express regrets, take away a keepsake, such as a lock of hair, or leave one behind, and to say farewell (Klein and Alexander 2003: 266-67). Observing the body provides closure. The disciples were denied all of this because Jesus's body was disposed of by others in some unknown location. These factors thus precluded appropriate burial rites honoring the dead and comforting the mourners, which are two crucial commandments in Jewish tradition regarding death (Levine 2006: 98). For the cultists, there was no sense of closure that happens upon seeing the mortal remains of a loved one and knowing their proper ultimate disposition. These conditions would have been especially emotionally painful and disturbing. Such factors alone, as the cognitive scientist Ilkka Pyysiäinen (2007: 59) points out, could have resulted in the disciples' memories of their teacher to become deindividuated, leading to sightings of the apparition of the risen Lord.
>
> In the weeks after the crucifixion, the cultists struggled with sadness, confusion, hopelessness, doubts, self-reproachment, denial, and survivor guilt for abandoning Jesus to a lonely death at the hands of his

[1] See the huge collection of anecdata collected by Bill and Judy Guggenheim at http://www.billguggenheim.com/a-summary.html.

[2] Sidky (2019), p. 503-5.

> enemies. Survivor guilt commonly occurs in circumstances that involve wars, accidents, major tragedies, and especially when a loved one dies violently, but others are spared (Shuchter 1986-35). It is also very likely that the disciples felt an overwhelming need for forgiveness because of their betrayal and desertion (Allison 2005: 370; Lüdemann 1994: 95-100).
>
> At this stage, two concurrent processes came into play: (1) grief hallucinations; (2) the psychological process involved in coming to terms with the disconfirmation of deeply held beliefs.

"Grief hallucinations" and, as we shall discuss later, cognitive dissonance make for a powerful recipe for visionary experiences. The closer one is to the death, the more prevalent and intense the hallucinations. Sidky details the voluminous research into grief hallucinations, and it makes for fascinating reading. I would advise further researching this phenomenon for a greater grasp on the subject and how it is both common and powerful. Indeed, this phenomenon helps explains the scenario that the disciples found themselves in, and the likelihood of having hallucinations qua visions.

By convincing others of their visions, they end up convincing and confirming their own beliefs. This is why catastrophic failures of a cult leader turn into more intense belief and evangelisation of their success: believers will try harder to convince others that their "excuse" (their "apologetic" explaining away that failure into a success) is true. Moreover, this will lead them to exaggerate, lie to themselves, or even alter their memory of things to effect that persuasion. And the intensity of their belief causes that persuasion to be successful: they gain fellow believers, and that success reinforces their own belief in the lies, exaggerations, or altered memories they developed to effect that persuasion.

The historical and psychological context created a perfect storm of conditions for Jesus' followers to have had hallucinatory experiences. This is what we should *expect* of Jewish apocalypticists living in such a time and having gone through such experiences.

Apologists may retort, "Then why did it only happen this one time? Other messianic claimants who died didn't inspire these things!" To this, I would reply: (1) we actually don't know that – in many cases, we have insufficient information (i.e., we don't have the writings of survivors of those movements so as to declare what did or did not happen to them afterward); (2) not all leaders will have been so charismatically effective, and we will only see phenomena like this arise from those few who were successful; and (3) even insofar as the confluence of all the conditions necessary to inspire something this extensive may be rare, we should thus texpect to see it rarely. Which means that the rarity of Christianity conforms to that natural statistical expectation; it is not evidence against it.

Bart Ehrman, in his *How Jesus Became*, showed how reasonable naturalistic explanations of the appearance stories were developed, and psychologists agree. In "Hallucinations of Loss, Visions of Grief" at *PsychCentral*, Ronald Pies M.D. writes:

> Recently, the theologian [sic] Bart Ehrman presented a very controversial argument[1], in his book *How Jesus Became God*. I have not read the book, but in an interview published in the Boston Globe (April 20, 2014), Ehrman argued that the belief in Jesus's resurrection may have been founded on visual hallucinations among Jesus's bereaved and grief-stricken disciples. Ehrman speculated that, "...the disciples had some kind of visionary experiences...and that these...led them to conclude that Jesus was still alive."
>
> Now, I am in no position to support or refute Prof. Ehrman's provocative hypothesis, but there is no question that after the death of a loved one (bereavement), visual hallucinations of the deceased are quite common. Sometimes, post-bereavement hallucinations may be part of a disordered grieving process, known variously as "pathological grief" or "complicated grief" – a condition my colleagues have been investigating for many years, and which had been proposed as a new diagnostic category in psychiatry's diagnostic manual, the DSM-5. (Ultimately, a version of this syndrome was placed among disorders requiring "further study.")
>
> Though visual hallucinations usually are reported by a single individual, there are reports of "mass hallucinations" following some traumatic events; in such contexts, clinicians often speak of "traumatic grief." A report from Singapore General Hospital noted that, following the massive tsunami tragedy in Thailand (2004), there were many accounts of "ghost sightings" among survivors and rescuers who had lost loved ones. Some would-be rescuers were so frightened by these perceptions that they ceased their efforts. There may well be a cultural or religious contribution to the Thai experience since many Thais believe that spirits can be put to rest only by relatives at the scene of the disaster.
>
> But "visionary experiences" also may be seen in normal or uncomplicated grief, following the death of a loved one, and appear to be common in many different cultures. In one Swedish study, researcher Agneta Grimby looked at the incidence of hallucinations in elderly widows and widowers, within the first year after the spouse's death. She

[1] Pies is playing it conservatively given many of his audience will undoubtedly be Christian.

> found that half of the subjects sometimes "felt the presence" of the deceased – an experience often termed an "illusion." About one-third reported actually seeing, hearing and talking to the deceased....
>
> Whatever the neurobiology of bereavement-related visual hallucinations, it seems plausible that these experiences often serve some kind of psychological function or need. Psychiatrist Dr. Jerome Schneck has theorized that bereavement-related hallucinations represent "... a compensatory effort to cope with the drastic sense of loss." Similarly, neurologist Oliver Sacks has commented that "... hallucinations can have a positive and comforting role... seeing the face or hearing the voice of one's deceased spouse, siblings, parents or child... may play an important part in the mourning process."
>
> On the one hand, there may be sound psychological reasons why Jewish tradition advises that mirrors be covered during the mourning period for a lost loved one. For some bereaved persons, visualizing the deceased while expecting to see one's own reflection might be very distressing – even terrifying. On the other hand, such "visions of grief" may help some bereaved loved ones cope with an otherwise unbearable loss.

The case in Thailand referenced here is something to which I will shortly return.

Of course, Jesus (and the Virgin Mary, and any number of other religious figures throughout the world) still appears in visions to people. To this day, many Christians believe such visions are veridical; however, many believe they are not. The whole arena is something of a mess. I could recount to you the number of times that the Virgin Mary has appeared (really appeared!) to individuals and groups and masses over time and geography. I could relay the time four Coptic bishops authenticated the Virgin Mary appearing on the roof of an Egyptian church (in Zeitoun in the 1960s). They really saw her. Or so they think.

Or, I could recount the many times religious believers (fervent, dedicated believers) have experienced visions and completely believed them to be veridical and even had these experiences authenticated by religious leaders or elders. In *other* religions. And yet, as mentioned, to the Christian, these were nonveridical.

Reminder: beware the double standard!

For the skeptic, there is no double standard. For the skeptic, there is consistency and coherence (within worldviews and the context of natural laws). For the skeptic, *all* of these various visions are either hallucinations (common) or made up (very common). We simply apply this rationale across the board and do not cherry-pick.

One further point that remains to be emphasised is that it doesn't require a vision to be veridical for someone or a group of people who had it to have a significant effect (moral, religious, comforting, social etc.) going forward. It requires a vision merely to be *believed* (to be veridical). Hence, as mentioned, we can see visions in Islam, Mormonism and a good deal of other religious movements in this context.

Supposed Messiah Sabbatai Zevi is a fascinating individual. In the 1600s, he was a Jewish Rabbi and Messiah-figure, who converted to Islam. His action caused great cognitive dissonance amongst his followers. For example, one group (the Dönmeh – his wife and three hundred followers) immediately outwardly converted to Islam so to follow their leader, but kept their Jewish faith and Kabbalistic beliefs secret – this is how they harmonised that dissonance. What also happened, concerning his early rise to prominence, speaks of the sort of fervour with which we are dealing (actually, far more so):[1]

> ...but the excitement surrounding him quickly burst forth in the most sensational manner. Outbreaks of prophesying, visions of the prophet Elijah, reports of miracles, and massive penitential movements erupted in both cities....
>
> Letters written by both Jews and Christians in Aleppo and Izmir had been reaching Europe for months. The earliest ones were reports of the reappearance of the Lost Ten Tribes of Israel from their long exile beyond the mythical Sambatyon River. **A clearer picture emerged as Sabbatai's name and alleged miracles were transmitted, enhanced by copyists, and passed along to others. Nathan's missives were likewise distributed and studied.** [My emphasis.]

Nathan of Gaza had seen Sabbatai Zevi in a vision and believed he was the Messiah. Nathan, Zevi, Messiah, visions, miracles, letters. If you can't dismiss the claims of Nathan – that he wrote himself in 1673 of a vision[2] – due to the risk of double standards, then that should lead you down a Jewish rather than a Christian path. These accounts are written with more detail than Paul's letters. Therefore, if you dismiss the claims of Zevi, you should also be dismissing Paul's claims. Let that sink in!

And, talking of mass hallucinations, and in the Sabbatai Zevi context, hundreds of people supposedly saw the long-dead prophet Elijah walk the streets of Smyrna.[3] Quite how they recognised him in the pre-photographic era is beyond me, but these sorts of claims are not unique to Christianity.

---

[1] Karp & Sutcliffe (2017), p. 498.

[2] Scholem (1973), p. 417, cf Komarnitsky (2009), p. 203-5

[3] Scholem (1973), p. 417, cf Komarnitsky (2009), p. 81-82.

I have emphasised that last section of the quote above because it should certainly ring some bells. Of course, Christians don't like such powerful and accurate comparisons because it highlights potential double standards; supposedly, the fervour and activity of early Christianity point towards historical reliability of *their* claims.

If we were to believe the claim that Jesus appeared to five hundred-plus people (or even one hundred and twenty or just a large group), rather than it being a legendary embellishment, is there evidence that such a thing can happen, naturalistically? Mass hallucinations are referred to as mass hysteria events and are not uncommon. I won't take up space listing the incredibly interesting mass hysteria events recorded over time. A simple web search should help you, including referring to the Wikipedia list that splits the accounts into time categories due to there being so many. However, I will relay reports of a number of mass hallucination events after the terrible 2004 tsunami that took place in Thailand (from the report "Thai tsunami trauma sparks foreign ghost sightings"[1]):

> A second surge of tsunami terror is hitting southern Thailand, but this time it is a wave of foreign ghosts terrifying locals in what health experts described as an outpouring of delayed mass trauma.
>
> Tales of ghost sightings in the six worst hit southern provinces have become endemic, with many locals saying they are too terrified to venture near the beach or into the ocean....
>
> The majority of Thais are deeply superstitious, believing ghosts reside in most large trees and keeping a spirit house in every home where daily offerings of food and drink are given to calm nearby paranormal entities.
>
> Mental health experts warn tsunami survivors have picked up on this cultural factor as a way of expressing mass trauma after living through the deadly waves and witnessing horrific scenes in their aftermath.
>
> "This is a type of mass hallucination that is a cue to the trauma being suffered by people who are missing so many dead people, and seeing so many dead people, and only talking about dead people," Thai psychologist and media commentator Wallop Piyamanotham said....
>
> Mr Wallop said widespread trauma began to set in about four days after the waves hit.

---

[1] From the ABC News/AFP article, "Thai tsunami trauma sparks foreign ghost sightings", https://www.abc.net.au/news/2005-01-14/thai-tsunami-trauma-sparks-foreign-ghost-sightings/618946 (Retrieved 12/12/2020).

> "This is when people start seeing these farangs (foreigners) walking on the sand or in the ocean," he said, adding the sightings started about the same time as people "began calling for help, crying, some scared".
>
> Many people said they could not escape the smell of death or the sights they had seen while assisting in the crisis, he said.
>
> Mr Wallop said the reason almost all ghost sightings appear to involve foreign tourists stems from a belief that spirits can only be put to rest by relatives at the scene, such as was done to many Thai victims.
>
> "Thai people believe that when people die, a relative has to cremate them or bless them. If this is not done or the body is not found, people believe the person will appear over and over again to show where they are," he said.

Neurologist Oliver Sacks observes,[1] "a deeply superstitious and delusional atmosphere can...foster hallucinations arising from extreme emotional states and these can affect entire communities."

Even if we do grant historical accuracy for the vision claims in the New Testament, we are still well within our epistemic warrant to claim that they are naturalistic in provenance. More than that, though, given the preponderance of data, we are obliged to give a naturalistic explanation a much higher probability of explaining the data.

Later, I will expand upon several naturalistic explanations for the data, notably something already mentioned: cognitive dissonance. Additionally, I will show how this will have played into the psychological disposition of the rather crestfallen disciples.

Finally, Visions as Giving Religious Authority

Lastly, let's explore the idea that supposed visions gave the experiencer religious authority in the nascent Christian community. We all know that organisational and social psychology is hugely important in maintaining structure and hierarchy in communities and community organisations. This would have been incredibly important in the birth of the Christian religion.

In 1 Corinthians 9:1, Paul pertinently asks: "Am I not free? Am I not an apostle? Have I not seen Jesus our Lord? Are you not my work in the Lord?" Kris Komarnitsky, in *Doubting Jesus' Resurrection: What Happened in the Black Box?*, succinctly spells out this phenomenon:[2]

---

[1] Sacks (2012), p. 244.

[2] Komarnitsky (2009), p. 93.

> In the weeks and months after Jesus's crucifixion, what the emerging Christian community must have needed badly were people who had the ability to lead, that is, the ability to teach, preach, and defended their new beliefs. It is therefore plausible that the traditions of the appearance to the Twelve and to all of the apostles was born out of a desire to designate who had the authority to lead, not out of a desire to accurately record appearances. This would be consistent with the hierarchical structure in the two appearance traditions above - Peter apparently being the leader of the group, known as "the Twelve", James apparently being the leader of the group, known as "all the apostles". We know too that an appearance of Jesus was *required* in order to confer authority to someone in the early church. For Paul says [so]...(1 Cor 9:1). If authority designation was the primary motivation for these appearance traditions, it is probable that some of these people, possibly even James, did not experience an individual appearance by Jesus, but were nevertheless still very suitable for and designated as leaders

Prominent members of Jesus' disciples would have had a vested interest in having had an appearance experience. This need for sectarian authority then gives motive for making up claims of visions and experiences.

Do we have any good parallels, any precedence for this kind of embellishment happening? Certainly!

What is particularly germane to this sense of falsely creating divine experiences in order to create and maintain religious organisational authority is set out in the 1838 case of Martin Harris. I cannot stress enough the importance of this case in showing precedence for lying in contexts utterly analogous to that of the early Christian church. John Loftus explains:[1]

> A parallel case might be the golden plates Joseph Smith claimed the angel Moroni led him to discover, which he "translated," producing the Book of Mormon. Smith carefully chose eleven men beside himself who became "eyewitnesses" to these plates, and their "testimonies" are found in the front of modern editions of the Book of Mormon. Their testimony is that they "beheld and saw the plates and the engravings thereon" and that they "know of a surety that the said Smith has got the plates of which we have spoken." Let's say this is all we know. Is it enough to believe? Wouldn't we want to know more about who these men were and why they claimed what they did, rather than simply trust their testimony? We would simply want to investigate it for ourselves. We would want to know what they knew and how they knew it, if they

[1] Loftus (2020), p. 508-9.

> knew anything at all. Surely it would be important to know, if we could, that all the witnesses were family, close friends, or financial backers of Joseph Smith, which was the case. It would also be important to know, if we could, that they didn't actually physically see these plates but rather saw them in visions, since they were visionaries, some of whom recanted because of this, which is also the case.

These are all valid and necessary questions. But the actual case of Harris is powerful in raising more parallel issues. Martin Harris, along with two others (Oliver Cowdery and David Whitmer), constituted what became known as the "Three Witnesses". These three men were supposedly shown the golden tablets that formed the revelatory experience that founded Joseph Smith's Mormon religion. David Whitmer, one of the other two witnesses, stated:[1]

> It was in the latter part of June, 1829... Joseph, Oliver Cowdery and myself were together, and the angel showed them [the plates] to us.... [We were] sitting on a log when we were overshadowed by a light more glorious than that of the sun. In the midst of this light, but a few feet from us, appeared a table upon which were many golden plates, also the sword of Laban and the directors. I saw them as plain as I see you now, and distinctly heard the voice of the Lord declaring that the records of the plates of the Book of Mormon were translated by the gift and power of God.

Let's see these revelatory experiences as on a par with the appearances of Jesus for the early Christians. Each witness signed a joint statement and it has been included in every copy of the Book of Mormon printed. It reads in part:

> And we declare with words of soberness, that an angel of God came down from heaven, and he brought and laid before our eyes, that we beheld and saw the plates, and the engravings thereon; and we know that it is by the grace of God the Father, and our Lord Jesus Christ, that we beheld and bear record that these things are true.

The problem is that Harris, in 1838, *recanted the experience*, claiming that it was only a mental vision, and this reality was the same for the signatories. The Three Witnesses had never seen or handled the golden plates, and this, in turn, caused five very influential members (of which three were apostles) to leave the church.

---

[1] David Whitmer, interview with the Kansas City Journal, June 1, 1881, in Cook (1991), p. 63.

Sometimes you hear the term "liars for Jesus". Well, here we have a case of lying for Smith and the Mormon Church.

And yet the Mormon (LDS) Church is presently about the only church *not* losing followers and has actually enjoyed rapid growth. In fact, early Mormonism outgrew early Christianity and the parallels between the two sects are astounding. They are analysed in a fascinating piece by John W. Welch called, "Early Mormonism and Early Christianity: Some Providential Similarities".[1] He creates an exhaustive side-by-side table of the similarities. The major difference, of course, being that one of the main original disciples admitted to lying in the Church of Jesus Christ of Latter-day Saints. However, no such admission is recorded within Christianity (that we now know of!). But the chance of it being the case in Christianity is orders of magnitude more likely than a Godmanspirit dying and resurrecting to atone for the sins of humanity that he had designed and created in order to sit on his own right hand in heaven[2] for eternity just after appearing to a small number of his disciples who were in the process of establishing a religious movement that would have handily profited from early members being miraculously appeared to by this actual god.

Which hypothesis has greater probability?

In addition, one must ask whether appearing to only a handful of followers in a very short time span and in a very particular geography is the best way of revealing oneself to humanity as a whole from the beginning of time to the end. Savour this point. Does this parochial account lend itself more probably to the skeptic's thesis or to the Christian's? Is this apparent biblical scenario the absolute best that God could do to lead humanity to a relationship with him, to reveal himself to all of humanity?

I will leave you with the words of eminent Catholic exegete and scholar, Raymond Brown:[3]

> Truth, conveyed by drama can at times be more effectively impressed on people's minds than truth conveyed by history.

Theology not history! But what is theology without history? Nothing but a castle in the air.

---

[1] Welch (2005).

[2] Again, I am not ridiculing the spatial implications from reading this at face value, but of the philosophical issue of God somehow giving a position of favouritism to himself.

[3] Brown (1994), p. 1312.

19 – The Veneration of the Tomb that Never Happened. Well, the Wrong Tomb and Much Later.

I will add a few caveats to the beginning of this chapter in light of a change in my own views concerning veneration of the tomb. My change was a consequence of talking to others and being presented new arguments and data. This is the art of skepticism.

The force of this argument isn't nearly as strong as I thought it once was, though it still has validity in a cumulative case. Later in the chapter, I will lay out the counter arguments in presenting the argument against the historicity of the empty tomb narrative based on the idea that no tomb was venerated.

The main area of contention to bear in mind whilst reading this chapter is the fact that, in 70 CE, Jerusalem was razed after its siege. This has significance for the ability to "do history" about this time and context. Furthermore, there were theological and religious ramifications that were at play, helping the divergence of Christianity and Judaism (including Christians thinking the destruction of the Temple was God's punishment for the Jewish rejection of Christ). I admit that such destruction could have caused the loss of the actual location, or knowledge of the location, of Jesus' burial place.

At various times over the next one hundred years or so, Jews had difficulty entering or living in Jerusalem (at points having to pay the Jewish Tax) as the Romans wanted to stamp out the Jewish Revolt and make Jerusalem pagan. It is perhaps less sure as to whether Christians were differentiated enough from Jews during these times as to be treated differently (i.e., as Jews or not).

That said, if you believe that the site still would have been venerated (I do, on balance, but I don't have the full strength of conviction I once did), then the following case acts as part of the cumulative case against the existence of the empty tomb.

In the context of the earlier tomb chapter, it is suspect that the place of the greatest spiritual and religious significance in the whole world seems not to have been venerated (at least not until the 4th century CE onwards). Let that point sink in with all we know about the behaviour of religious people. What best explains this data? Again, we get back to a Bayesian analysis.

It then prompts these questions:

(1) Was Jesus actually buried in a tomb?
(2) Was the position of the tomb unknown?

And these sorts of questions lead onto others, such as:

(3) Did the Jesus' death actually happen as reported?
(4) Did the physical resurrection take place?

As such, let us look at the veneration of the tomb, or lack thereof.

Before we do this examination, it is worth noting that we still do not know where Jesus' empty tomb *really* is or was located. Constantine claimed to have found it in a religio-political and ideological stunt (more precisely, his mother on his behest), and built a church around it now called the Church of the Holy Sepulchre. The Emperor, with the help of his mother Helena, went about destroying pagan temples and supplanting them with Christian ones. The story of how they came to knock down a Hellenistic temple from Hadrian's time, and then came to realise long after it was levelled, that there was supposedly the tomb of Jesus beneath (partly known because they found three crosses in the tomb itself, one of which cured someone, with nails and an inscription written by Pilate himself!) is an interesting read. At best, it is part-fantasy, part-cynical political and religious power dynamics.

There are actually three proposed sites for Jesus' tomb: Talpiot Tomb, the Garden Tomb and the Church of the Holy Sepulchre (the latter being the preferred option for most Christians). These are not the site of Jesus' empty tomb, assuming that he had one anyway; all of them have archaeological and historical issues associated with the theses that claim their heritage. I am not going to devote any time here to a historical or archaeological analysis of their provenance.

So let us return to ideas of veneration and the fact that, whether the three hundred year-later findings were genuine or not. In the intervening period, there is absolutely no evidence that anyone venerated Jesus' tomb.

By veneration, I mean the worship or religious and spiritual respect given to (dead) people or places deemed as important to the religion or cult. In Catholic traditions, veneration of Saints has been a long-held behaviour. Places like Lourdes garner particular reactions from Christians, and stories involving the spiritual powers and importance of such places abound. What we need to do is look at Judaism, since this is the bedrock upon which Christianity was built and the context within which early Christianity and the Jesus story were set.

If such traditions did not pre-exist Christianity, then it was the Christians who brought veneration into the spiritual spotlight. However, there are certainly records of Jewish veneration of tombs such as Joseph's tomb dating back to around the 5th century CE and Rachel's tomb to the 4th century CE.

Raymond Brown, Catholic exegete, notes:[1]

---

[1] Brown, ibid., p. 1280.

> There was in this period an increasing Jewish veneration of the tombs of the martyrs and prophets.

To which William Lane Craig, as a Christian apologist, adds:[1]

> During Jesus' time there was an extraordinary interest in the graves of Jewish martyrs and holy men, and these were scrupulously cared for and honored. This suggests that the grave of Jesus would also have been noted. The disciples had no inkling of any resurrection prior to the general resurrection at the end of the world, and they would therefore not have allowed the burial site of the Teacher to go unnoted. This interest also makes plausible the women's lingering to watch the burial and their subsequent intention to anoint Jesus' body with spices and perfumes (Luke 23:55, 56).

As Jesus himself says, in castigating the Pharisees (Matthew 23:29):

> "Woe to you, scribes and Pharisees, hypocrites! For you build the tombs of the prophets and adorn the monuments of the righteous." ["[A]dorn the monuments" can also be translated as "decorate the graves".]

You don't get a much better source than Jesus in the Gospels, right? At least this source should appeal to the Christian reader or interlocutor. This verse clearly shows that tomb veneration was something that happened contemporaneously.

Nicholas de Lange, a professor of Hebrew and Jewish studies at Cambridge University, agrees:[2]

> Of the many Jewish shrines of the Middle East, some of which are undoubtedly of very great antiquity, the most famous were traditionally the supposed tombs of the prophet Ezekiel at el-Kifl and of Ezra the Scribe at Kurna, both in Babylonia (modern Iraq).

In *An Introduction to Judaism,* De Lange also mentions such "practices as veneration of tombs of patriarchs and saints, often associated with pilgrimage".[3]

---

[1] Craig "Did Jesus Rise from the Dead?" in Wilkins & Moreland (1995) p. 148-49.
[2] "The Pilgrim's Way", *The UNESCO Courier,* May 1995. https://unesdoc.unesco.org/ark:/48223/pf0000100245 (Retrieved 09/03/2021).
[3] De Lange (2000), p. 69.

Furthermore, Jews have always seemed to venerate ancient scrolls of the Torah, and buildings such as the Temple. Indeed, in '"The Odour of Sanctity," and the Hebrew Origins of Christian Relic Veneration', Lionel Rothkrug (a professor who had worked on pilgrimages) saw the later relic veneration rampant in Christianity as rooted in a Jewish context.[1] Indeed, in the Book of Tobit, there is precedence for leaving bread and wine at tombs of the just. Rothkrug observes:[2]

> God's special esteem for the dead helps Tobit to justify ritual offerings made at the graves of the pious. But not all the dead are worthy of God's favour. Tobit admonishes his son to make offerings "on the tomb of the just, and give not to sinners." For Tobit, just as for Philo, the wicked remain in oblivion. Moreover, to offer bread and wine at the tomb of the just was to participate in a communal meal with those dead who enjoyed God's special recognition.

Jesus and his tomb would certainly fit into this mould.

So I think we can successfully conclude that Jews did venerate sites and even artefacts. Would it then seem likely that early Jewish Christians would give the tomb of Jesus such veneration? Absolutely! Remember, this tomb is probably the greatest site of spiritual interest in the world, bar none. This site is where God, incarnate as man and dying nearby, was given life again to rise into heaven magnificently in order to pay for our sins and give us hope. It also acts as the birthplace, if you like, for the entire Christian religion. It would be wildly implausible to think that the site would not be venerated and given special accord.

Let us ask whether the site would be known and remembered. According to Matthew, Luke and John, the tomb was that of Joseph of Arimathea, a member of the Sanhedrin. Even if one didn't know exactly where this tomb was located, one could surely find out. His description within the New Testament hints at him being of some notoriety, though this assumes the historical reliability of the documents in the first place... Moreover, there are a number of people who visited the tomb who clearly *had* to have been, in some way, the sources to the resurrection accounts. Whether it was Mary, the other Mary, Salome, or Simon Peter, we have a number of candidates who qualify for having such geographical knowledge. It would be strange if they could recount all the details of the resurrection to their fellow apostles and disciples, and yet somehow couldn't remember where it took place. This is almost a moot point since

---

[1] Rothkrug (1981).

[2] Ibid., p. 118.

in describing the visitors to the tomb; it is clearly implicit that they knew where it was located!

So if they knew where it was, and if they were culturally and spiritually likely to venerate the spot, why didn't they? Let us look briefly at the reasons why they would not want to do so, as offered by apologists.

One posited reason that the early Christian followers would not venerate the site is out of fear for their safety. The Sanhedrin had already, perhaps it could be claimed, placed a guard there (in worrying about such a site), assuming that Matthew is historically accurate – an assumption I contest. In other words, they had sentenced this man(-God) to death and venerating such a tomb might get one into trouble. Yet we know that early Christians show later disregard for their own safety, dying, apparently, with relative ease for their beliefs (as Acts verifies). Veneration, of course, would not have to be public, either. A secret pilgrimage of one or two local Christians would be well understood. And yet, even given secrecy, we have nothing about such early followers venerating the tomb, or certainly no growth to the idea beyond the critical mass required to maintain secrecy. Not a single word about the tomb after the resurrection had taken place. As the Christian movement grew and gained credence, *nothing* ensued concerning the location of Jesus' death and burial.

Other reasons have been suggested, but they get the Christian into trouble. For example, Byron McCane states:[1]

> The shame of Jesus' burial is not only consistent with the best evidence, but can also help to account for an historical fact which has long been puzzling to historians of early Christianity: why did the primitive church not venerate the tomb of Jesus? Joachim Jeremias, for one, thought it inconceivable (undenkbar) that the primitive community would have let the grave of Jesus sink into oblivion.

The shame of a dishonourable burial, as McCane espouses, not only contradicts the later Gospel accounts (I think he is right, here, as we saw in the burial chapter), but also would not stop the followers from venerating the tomb unless it was completely unknown. Thus, to use the shameful burial hypothesis to explain a lack of veneration is to show all the resurrection accounts that related the empty tomb of Jesus as false. It certainly fits a good critical analysis from nontheists, but hardly does the theist any favours.

Given Jesus being buried in a shallow grave or a whole building filled with continuously rotating criminal corpses, you aren't realistically going to get veneration.

Christian theologian James Dunn offers:[2]

---

[1] McCane (1998).
[2] Dunn (1985), p. 67-68.

> Christians today of course regard the site of Jesus' tomb with similar veneration, and that practice goes back at least to the fourth century. But for the period covered by the New Testament and other earliest Christian writings there is no evidence whatsoever for Christians regarding the place where Jesus had been buried as having any special significance. No practice of tomb veneration, or even of meeting for worship at Jesus' tomb is attested for the first Christians. Had such been the practice of the first Christians, with all the significance which the very practice itself presupposes, it is hard to believe that our records of Jerusalem Christianity and of Christian visits thereto would not have mentioned or alluded to it in some way or at some point.

Thank you James Dunn! (Though the point about records is mitigated somewhat by the destruction of Jerusalem.) The problem for Dunn is that he goes on to reason that this lack of veneration in the early church was because there were no bones in the tomb, which is simply nonsense. As if this lack of bones would stop a site being venerated, especially since they would understand the idea of bodily resurrection (at least as far as the Gospels were concerned)!

Bearing in mind the earlier brief discussion of the destruction of Jerusalem, where does this analysis leave us? Well, one of these further conclusions must follow:

(1) Early Christians wouldn't have venerated due to "Gnostic" beliefs of Christ's body being of "inferior" substance. (Though later Gospel Christians thought otherwise, as we see by the Gospels themselves, and we know there was a diversity of thought, anyway.)

(2) The strongest counter-argument: that the time period between the death of Jesus and the destruction of Jerusalem could have been too brief a period for veneration. Within forty years, the war reduced Jerusalem to a ruin and at times Jews were banned from, after which the site was razed for new construction of a pagan city by Hadrian. (Though whether *Christians* were included with this anti-Jewish approach is difficult to decipher.)

(3) Connected to (2) – it *was* venerated, but all evidence of veneration was lost in the destruction of Jerusalem.

(4) The later Gospel writers made up claims of an empty tomb. Hence, the place was never really empty (and the resurrection accounts should be wholly doubted as accurate). Later Christians either did not think that these claims were "doing history", or could not find such fictitious places.

(5) There really was no veneration as Jesus was actually buried in an unknown criminals' graveyard as was customary for a dishonourable burial. An argument for the empty tomb itself.
(6) Jesus did not exist. Similar to (4), but the whole gamut of Gospel claims is false.
(7) Posited by Byron McCane is the theory that earliest Christians were obsessed with apocalyptic eschatology and that the end times would happen imminently. In reality, they were more interested in the here and now over venerating anything that likely wouldn't be there much longer in any meaningful way.

These conclusions are all problematic for the Christian apart from (2), (3) and (7) (I think that (1) is answerable by the diversity of thought point).

As far as (7) is concerned, charismatic Christians who believe this is Jesus' burial site still flock to Jerusalem to venerate the supposed tomb. Moreover, Christians who presently believe we are living in the End Times still venerate the tomb site. This leaves the points concerning the destruction of Jerusalem.

That said, I find it odd that, only suddenly after 400 CE, did Christians become obsessed with venerating all sites to do with Jesus, and yet before this there was nothing. Absolutely nothing.

To quickly conclude: the lack of veneration leads me to believe with marginally greater epistemic warrant (ceteris paribus) that the empty tomb was a later legendary Gospel embellishment. However, I also concede that the destruction of Jerusalem can also provide a somewhat satisfactory explanation as to why there was no known veneration of the site until centuries later.

I will leave you with Peter Kirby's opinion as he offers his hypothesis and why the lack of veneration is an important consideration:[1]

> The hypothesis I support in the essay is that Jesus wasn't given burial in a tomb. What might that look like on such a hypothesis? I answer just so as to give a concrete picture of the general suggestion. Jesus could have been hung for crucifixion for several days outside of Jerusalem for the impact, as was often the case for a crucifixion. The small group of close followers, who were not residents of Jerusalem, may have fled the city to go home in fear for their own safety. Jesus may then have been given an inexpensive, unmarked burial somewhere with nobody around to observe it that would care to communicate it to the post-crucifixion movement. This is an illustration of one possibility under the general alternative hypothesis of there being no tomb burial in the first place.

[1] His comment below "Why Wasn't There any Veneration of Jesus' Empty Tomb?" [regarding his own essay (Kirby 2001)] on John Loftus's *Debunking Christianity,* Loftus 2007),

20 – Naturalistic Theories. What Do *I* Think Happened?

I Don't Really Need to Believe Any Particular Theory

The first thing to say here is to echo an earlier quote from Bart Ehrman. He thinks that almost any explanation for the data that I can think of is more probable than the Christian hypothesis. As he says:[1]

> I don't subscribe to any of these alternative views because I don't think we know what happened to the body of Jesus. But simply looking at the matter from a historical point of view, any of these views is more plausible than the claim that God raised Jesus physically from the dead. A resurrection would be a miracle and as such would defy all "probability." Otherwise, it wouldn't be a miracle. To say that an event that defies probability is more probable than something that is simply improbable is to fly in the face of anything that involves probability.

I could end this chapter there because, quite frankly, that quote does the job. But let me expand on it with that in mind. Let us briefly look at some of the main theories before I offer you what I think clearly best explains the data of the Gospels and resulting Christian religion. Some of these seem prima facie very implausible indeed, but the question is "Is this implausible naturalistic explanation still far more probable than the Christian thesis?"

Previously, in this text, I have quoted variously from James Crossley, and I would like to draw on a conclusion he offered in countering the work of N.T. Wright, and Wright's own staunch beliefs in the historicity of the Resurrection accounts:[2]

> 'I regard this conclusion as coming in the same sort of category, of historical probability so high as to be virtually certain, as the death of Augustus in AD 14 or the fall of Jerusalem in AD 70.'[3] This eyebrow-raising claim concerning the empty tomb must be completely rejected. Yes, historically something happened shortly after Jesus' death, but the evidence hardly demands anything as spectacularly dramatic as a bodily resurrection in the sense that it would be an unparalleled event in

---

[1] Ehrman (2014), p. 165.
[2] Crossley (2005), p. 185-86.
[3] Wright (2003), p. 710.

> human history and would leave an empty tomb. The list of eyewitnesses in 1 Cor. 15.5-8 gives no evidence pointing in the direction of the bodily resurrection as an historical event, except in the sense of a visionary experience. The earliest empty tomb story we have (Mk 16.1-8) suspiciously makes it clear that the only witnesses to the empty tomb told no one (16.8). All the other Gospel narratives make good sense in the context of creative storytelling, including the grounding of present beliefs in the life, death and resurrection of Jesus. I would suggest that these conclusions are much more historically probable than there being a bodily resurrection and empty tomb in the sense Wright claims.

For the following alternative that I give, you can see at the least the initial ones as cascading on from each other. There is certainly an interconnectedness to these ideas that feeds from one section to the next (or vice versa). I hope to have built the case here that the Gospels are far from reliable, and largely outright fiction, and there are many reasons for this reality, from the psychological to the technical, the cultural to the historical. The naturalistic theories simply have greater probability and/or precedence to support their greater plausibility.

Fiction

It is probably wise to start with an approach about which I have been consistently talking: the notion that the accounts are in some way made up, that they are fictionalised. There is a range of options here from being completely made up to partially made up by certain Gospel writers for differing reasons. This is not mutually exclusive to any of the other theories, either, and you will hopefully conclude, after getting this far, that there has been at least some degree (I would argue an awful lot) of legendary (fictional) embellishment.

For example, it is incredibly likely that the account of a Jewish blasphemy trial might be fiction, meant to cover up what really happened: Jesus was executed by the Romans for sedition, without any involvement of the Sanhedrin. That was a common fate in Judea, so there is nothing inherently unlikely about it. It only looks unlikely if you "believe" the Gospels' tales of a Sanhedrin blasphemy trial in the first place.

Some even argue the Gospels are *entirely* fiction.

Obviously incorporated into this category, then, is the idea that Jesus didn't exist at all and that the Gospels are mythology created from nothing (from scratch). I mentioned earlier that I am not a mythicist though I differ only marginally since I think there is merely some kernel of history. For example, I can see Jesus as being an itinerant preacher, but the historical reality is almost wholly removed from the claims within the Christian Bible to the point of said

Bible practically being myth. I am, however, fairly ambivalent and am happy to be swayed either way.

That said, Jesus mythicism is a divisive position between non-Christians and Christians (obviously!), and also between atheists. For example, some atheists argue very vehemently for it and others against, as can be seen in arguments between, say, Richard Carrier (a strong proponent of mythicism) and Bart Ehrman (now a non-Christian, but someone who thinks there is at least some historical kernel to Jesus).

Jesus mythicism explains early Christianity in terms of early Christians having visions (hallucinations, real or pretended), and a movement and writing building from there to a religious belief system built on illusory history. Remember, there are many religions throughout history that are essentially mythological, and Jesus mythicism is not invoking something a priori unrealistic. We have pantheons of gods that, in modern times, are seen as myth but were once not. And it could be said that even many modern religions are lacking in the kernels of historical truth their adherents claim as true.

But, to reiterate, this is not what I personally adhere to. For me, even if there is some historical core about Jesus in the Gospels, it is so surrounded by fictional additions and embellishments that we can't trust them to tell us much reliable truth about the historical Jesus.

Wishful Thinking and Motivated Reasoning

This expands upon the concept of fiction as a whole; connected to the previous section is the idea that people, such as Paul and the Gospel authors, really wanted certain things to be the case, and through this desire we get fictionalisation. This explanation is more of the reason *why* fictionalisation might have taken place. Paul, in being an important early source (but also never having met Jesus though supposedly having visions of a person he had never met), had an interesting conversion to Christianity after persecuting Christians. An awful lot of psychology would have been at play here in his development of the early church.

Wars and fights don't generally end suddenly for political reasons. It would amount to an admission that it wasn't right in the first place. In the context of Jesus' resurrection, Paul wanted to have something to say as he began to stop persecuting Christians. He had the motivation to invent or modify a story as to what happened: he had visions (even if they existed) that were arguably fictionalised in some way, as he would have no way of knowing that it was Jesus, not knowing what Jesus' face looked like. We can see Paul claiming many things, and that he clearly did not do any fact checking. This was combined with the above effects to result in exaggerated claims made later by others.

The whole Christ narrative justified or balanced Paul's previous anti-Christian actions in some way. He needed this narrative to make sense of what he had done and what he had stopped doing. Yes, Christian followers already existed, but he could add visions and hallucinations to the canon of Christian beliefs to somehow justify some facet of his behaviour.

Cognitive Dissonance

Expanding upon motivated reasoning is a term already used plentifully in this book that explains the power and extent that wishful thinking can go. Cognitive dissonance is a psychological phenomenon that arises when we hold a core belief (a very strongly-held belief) and we are then introduced to rational evidence that is contrary to that core belief. It is what our brain does to harmonise the dissonance, the disharmony, that the brain experiences. The brain does not enjoy that disharmony because it is incoherent. If the rational evidence (perhaps "reality") is at odds with a core belief, then the brain can do a range of things to reduce the feeling (cognitive dissonance reduction):

(1) Refuse to accept the disconfirming evidence – it is simply wrong or doesn't exist. Confirmation bias can be used to give more weight to criticisms of the disconfirming evidence than is warranted.
(2) Adapt the evidence: Harmonise the two (belief and evidence) by manipulating or explaining the evidence so it coheres with the belief, often in ways that involve a lot of mental contortion (think how Creationists "explain" away fossil evidence by claiming that the Devil planted it to fool humanity).
(3) Adapt the belief: Create a third way that fuses both the disconfirming evidence with the core belief, perhaps creating a new belief from the evidence.

Leon Festinger first developed the theory after infiltrating a UFO cult. The members of the cult believed, after receiving mental messages through their leader from spacemen, that there would be an end times rapture of sorts. The cult very publicly announced there would be a cataclysm on December 21st 1954, but that they themselves would be removed to safety at midnight on the eve of the date, having to wait in certain parked cars for this rapturous transportation to happen. There were three social psychologists that infiltrated this cult and observed the whole process from build-up to non-rapture.

When the "religious" event of sorts did not happen, one would have expected a rational response to be that, well, this was a lot of bunkum. Two of the eleven members did indeed do this and left the group. Nine did not. Instead, they rationalised what had (not) happened, from wrong dates to postponement to symbolism (of parked cars to bodies) and so on. When one of the psychologists feigned frustration during this process of developing explanations, a committed cult member (a medical doctor) came outside to him to say this:[1]

> I've had to go a long way. I've given up just about everything. I've cut every tie. I've burned every bridge. I've turned my back on the world. I can't afford to doubt. I have to believe. And there isn't any other truth.... I won't doubt even if we have to make an announcement to the press tomorrow and admit we were wrong. You're having your period of doubt now, but hang on boy, hang on. This is a tough time but we know that the boys upstairs are taking care of us.... These are tough times and the way is not easy. We all have to take a beating. I've taken a terrific one, but I have no doubt.

According to Kris Komarnitsky, in *The Fourth R* magazine of the Westar Institute:[2]

> In the end, the group settled on a rationalization provided by the group's leader, which was based on a timely message she received from the spacemen. She said that the steadfast belief and waiting by their small group had brought so much "good and light" into the world, that God called off the pickup and the cataclysm. This rationalization was received with jubilation. According to Festinger, "The group was able to accept and believe this explanation because they could support one another and convince each other that this was, in fact, a valid explanation."
>
> Although the mental health of all the cult members was not open for examination, there was an opportunity for professional psychiatrists to evaluate one of the hardcore cult members, the physician quoted above. The only reason this psychiatric examination was conducted was because relatives questioned his sanity and sought to gain custody of his children. This doctor, a believer in the cult all the way through the disconfirmation and beyond, was cleared by two court-appointed psychiatrists. They concluded that although the physician had some unusual ideas, he was "entirely normal."

There are many examples of cognitive dissonance within religious movements such as with the Millerite movement in the 1800s, when Jesus was predicted to have a second coming several times. But the several non-events

---

[1] Sidky (2002), p .412.
[2] Komarnitsky (2014).

didn't deter belief, with the rationalisation eventually being that it *had* happened, just in heaven.

Likewise, the previously mentioned Jewish messianic figure of Sabbatai Zevi became an apostate by converting to Islam, much to the chagrin of his many, many followers:[1]

> In order to survive, the movement had to develop an ideology that would enable its followers to live amid the tensions between inner and outer realities.... The peculiar Sabbatian doctrines developed and crystalized with extraordinary rapidity in the years following the apostasy. Two factors were responsible for this, as for many similar developments in the history of religions: on the one hand, a deeply rooted faith, nourished by a profound and immediate experience...and, on the other hand, the ideological need to explain and rationalize the painful contradiction between historical reality and faith. The interaction of these two factors gave birth to Sabbatian theology, whose doctrine of the messiah was defined by the prophet Nathan in the years after the apostasy....
>
> When discussing the Sabbatian paradox by means of which cruel disappointment was turned into a positive affirmation of faith, the analogy with early Christianity almost obtrudes itself.

With even more of a parallel to the Jesus story, the 1990s saw the further development of the Lubavitch Hasidic Jewish movement (which started in the 1700s) and the prominence of their leader Rebbe Menachem Mendel Schneerson. The "Rebbe" never claimed to be the Messiah, but many of his fervent followers genuinely thought him to be. In March, 1992, the Rebbe had a stroke that paralysed his right side. How did his followers deal with this reality? Luckily, a psychiatrist and social anthropologist was living with the community at the time, doing other work – Dr. Simon Dein – who observed:[2]

> Despite his profound incapacity, messianic fervor in the Lubavitch community intensified, culminating in plans to crown him as Mosiach [the Messiah]. Lubavitchers referred to Isaiah 53, "a man of sorrows, and familiar with suffering", and argued that his illness was a prerequisite to the messianic arrival.... that the Rebbe himself had chosen to become ill and had taken on the suffering of the Jewish people.

---

[1] Scholem (1973), p.792-95, cf Komarnitsky (2014).
[2] Dein (2010), p. 542.

Bear in mind that his followers were not Christians, so they did not believe in the prophecies fulfilling the claimed history of Jesus, yet they followed the same formula.

A few years later, Rebbe had another stroke, inducing a coma. Dein observed:[1]

> [Rebbe Schneerson's] faithful followers saw this [the second stroke] as a prelude to his messianic revelation and the arrival of the redemption. As he lay dying in intensive care, several hundred followers assembled outside Beth Israel Medical Centre singing and dancing–anticipating the imminent arrival of the redemption.... Supporters and believers signed petitions to God, demanding that he allow their Rebbe to reveal himself as the long-awaited Messiah and rise from his sickbed to lead all humanity to their redemption.

Three months later, he died. However, still the cognitive dissonance reduction prevailed, as Dein records: "Many Lubavitchers expressed the idea that he would be resurrected."[2] At his funeral, followers danced and sang and waited for his resurrection, expecting him to rise from the dead. Indeed, the belief swept through the community.

I would advise reading Dein's accounts and Komarnitsky's summary of the events and the incredible cognitive harmonisations that the community went through over time. And there is some safety in numbers, as what people can rationalise when comforted by others around them in their own rationalisation can be quite staggering. Dein explained:[3]

> [The] Lubavitch are not a group of fanatics.... They are sane people trying to reason their way through facts and in the pursuit of understanding.... Like many groups whose messianic expectations fail to materialize, resort is made to eschatological hermeneutics to explain and reinforce the messianic ideology.... The Rebbe's illness and subsequent death posed cognitive challenges for his followers. They made two predictions that were empirically disconfirmed: that he would recover from his illness and that he would usher in the Redemption. In accordance with cognitive dissonance theory...they appealed to a number of post hoc rationalizations to allay the dissonance.

---

[1] Dein (2001), p.58, Dein (2010), p. 543.

[2] Dein (2001), p. 397.

[3] Dein (2001, 2010, 2011), cf Komarnitsky (2014).

The Chabad-Lubavitcvh movement, now 250 years old, is still with us and the events concerning Schneerson are still prominent in their belief system with many followers continuing to maintain that he was the Messiah.

Let me bring anthropologist Homuyan Sidky back into play in drawing parallels to Christianity here:[1]

> The crucifixion was an unthinkable catastrophe for the cultists who had staked their hopes and desires, indeed their entire lives, on Jesus's triumph as the Messiah. Horrified, dumbfounded, and fearing for their own lives, the disciples deserted their master, scattered, and fled (Mark 14:50) from Jerusalem back to Galilee (Funk 1998: 466-67). According to theologian Herman Hendrickx (1978: 15), "The men left for Galilee after the tragedy of the day of Preparation, and there is no indication that they left with any knowledge of an empty tomb." To the Jews, as the classical scholar Reginald Macan (1877: 81) put it, "the death of Jesus on the cross was [...] the divine judgment upon him as an imposter [and] blasphemer." All this amounts to a sad tale of false prophecies, failed disciples, betrayal, abandonment, and disgrace. These were terrible things, the correction of which would require that the authors of the Gospels who wrote a couple of generations after the events engage in reverse-engineering or retrocorrecting of the narrative.

The parallels to Christianity and to Jesus are obvious. The disciples believed that Jesus was the Messiah (there are actually very good criticisms of this idea such that the disciples neither really believed he was the Messiah or God, but we will leave that for now) and that he would be the Saviour of Israel. However, this supposed miracle-worker ended up being crucified and dying. Not only did they feel somewhat responsible for the death, but also they reacted in a cowardly way and would have felt strong guilt, and also couldn't understand how the Saviour could be killed. Therefore, their brains produced mechanisms that allowed both the core belief and the disconfirming evidence to hold (since they couldn't deny outright that Jesus had been crucified). We will return to this idea of cognitive dissonance in the section where I offer my own theory of what happened. Suffice to say that cognitive dissonance is prevalent with all humans at different points in our lives, and it explains how we react to any number of scenarios on a monthly basis. However, when it comes to significant, life-changing scenarios, it really comes into its own.

In short, cognitive dissonance is a crucial component of the Resurrection narratives. I will end this section with the words from biblical scholar Robert

---

[1] Sidky (2019), p. 432.

M. Price, who puts cognitive dissonance neatly into the context of the Resurrection story:[1]

> When a group has staked everything on a religious belief, and 'burned their bridges behind them,' only to find this belief disconfirmed by events, they may find disillusionment too painful to endure. They soon end up with some explanatory rationalization, the plausibility of which will be reinforced by the mutual encouragement of fellow believers in the group. In order to increase further the plausibility of their threatened belief, they may engage in a massive new effort at proselytizing. The more people who can be convinced, the truer it will seem. In the final analysis, then, a radical disconfirmation of belief may be just what a religious movement needs to get off the ground.

Littlewood's Law

Perfectly natural improbable events or conjunctions are ready fuel to be noticed and seized upon to justify solutions to cognitive dissonance, and in this way, this section builds upon the last. The Archbishop of Canterbury William Temple once observed, "When I pray, coincidences happen, when I don't, they don't." Such "miraculous" experiences only demonstrate a selection bias that counts the hits and ignores the misses.

John Littlewood, a mathematician, developed Littlewood's Law, which can be stated as follows:[2]

> Littlewood defines a miracle as an exceptional event of special significance occurring at a frequency of one in a million. He assumes that during the hours in which a human is awake and alert, a human will see or hear one "event" per second, which may be either exceptional or unexceptional. Additionally, Littlewood supposes that a human is alert for about eight hours per day.
>
> As a result, a human will in 35 days have experienced under these suppositions about one million events. Accepting this definition of a miracle, one can expect to observe one miraculous event for every 35 days' time, on average – and therefore, according to this reasoning, seemingly miraculous events are actually commonplace.

[1] Price (1993), Section II, Chapter 6.
[2] "Littlewood's Law", *Wikipedia*, https://en.wikipedia.org/wiki/Littlewood's_law (Retrieved 15/06/2020).

In general terms, we can all expect things that are seemingly incredibly improbable to happen with alarming regularity, especially over time and populations. Many of these things will appear to be inexplicable. The Resurrection, together with some of these other ideas previously talked about in this chapter, could be an invocation of this law.

Regarding Temple's claim above, it's not that such coincidences don't happen when he doesn't pray, but rather, he only *notices* them when he *has* prayed. And that is Littlewood's point, that we mistakenly give credence to improbable events as miracles only when they are meaningful and thus noticed by us. But, really, they are no more miraculous than millions of other events we ignore or fail to notice.

Hallucinations

Though individually rare, hallucinations are culturally and historically significant. In a sense, these are an example of the very thing Littlewood was talking about: singularly improbable but collectively common events one can seize on or even drive oneself to in resolving cognitive dissonance and wishful thinking.

All sorts of things have been hallucinated throughout the history of the world. If we committed them all to books and religions and saw them all as objective, mind-independent facts, we would have the most wonderful, disturbing, amazing, dark, essentially mythological culture and history imaginable.

But we don't! Why? Because hallucinations aren't reality and we have broadly learnt to accept this point in the modern era. I will elucidate more on the part hallucinations may have played in these accounts in proceeding sections.

Hearsay and Unreliable Witnesses

All the preceding phenomena can then be built on over time with further, and quite commonplace (indeed universal) mechanisms of fiction-production. As has previously been mentioned, eyewitnesses are notoriously unreliable. The Yerkes-Dodson Law[1] looks at how performance is impaired by pressure. These early disciples were highly aroused by grief, guilt, sadness, anxiety, anger,

[1] "This law states that a relationship between arousal and behavioral task performance exists, such that there is an optimal level of arousal for an optimal performance. Over- or under-arousal reduces task performance." Cohen (2011).

embarrassment, resentment and so on, and these characteristics can impair both eyewitness testimony and judgement of eyewitness testimony by others.

The skeptic will add into this mix that many of these people were perhaps hallucinating, which they themselves would have been unreliable at communicating accurately. Furthermore, there would have been an unreliable communication process from the subject, to someone else, to a community, to an eventual author or scribe, and to future generations, accumulating exaggeration and error over time. Given these issues, we have some serious problems regarding the asserted accuracy of these claims and sources.

How much would be rumour, or hearsay, so that original kernels grow into embellished accounts? Without either knowing the witnesses (now or then) or being able to verify their claims, we are left with too many unknowns. But what we do know is that witnesses are unreliable, even more so when in the contexts of the early Christian disciples, and even more when further generations of storytelling and story making intervene before anything gets written down (and we only get to hear what got written down).

Scribal Alteration

Even after we have all the preceding issues, and even after inaccurate and unreliable things (or not) are written down, we have the compounded issue of scribal alteration. Sticking with our methodological approaches, the fiction can be explained not only in terms of embellishment from the original authors – a mythologisation of some sort of events, but also in terms of corrupted details. This "fiction" might be copyists' error, or copyists' cynical theological agenda driving changes and so on.

The problem the Christian faces is that the earliest extant biblical tracts and fragments are copies of the long-lost original autographs. Dating of these manuscripts is accurate to a range of perhaps 50-100 years with radiocarbon dating, and again mainly 50-100 years with palaeography. The earliest fragment is a section of the Gospel of John that possibly dates, at the *very best* for the Christian, to the first half of the second century CE (some Christians will try to argue it is from about 90 CE, but it is not).[1] The first complete book does not

[1] The early date has been challenged over time, as David Fitzgerald sets out in a note in *Jesus: Mything in Action, Vol I* (Fitzgerald 2017), p. 215: "Noted paleographers Pasquale Orsini and Willy Clarysse have recently chastised biblical scholars for embracing insupportably early dates for their manuscripts, including P52. They remind us there are no first century New Testament papyri, and the few that can be assigned to the second century (P52 and two other tiny fragments, P90 and P104), are probably all from the later half of the 2nd century – or even the early third century; almost a century later than apologists wish." The whole note contains further arguments to support this: the topic is well worth researching more deeply.

appear until around 200 CE, with the first New Testament in around 300-400 CE.

This gives a lot of time for Chinese Whispers (the Telephone Game) to take place, for copyists to make errors or theological additions and editions. And, indeed, we have caught dozens of examples of this happening, and know that there must have been many more instances than we have been able to catch.[1] For example, there are five different endings of the Gospel of Mark fabricated in New Testaments by the 4th century CE![2]

Again, deciphering fact from fiction is difficult.

Remember that this sort of error is again different from the problem that already exists: Matthew is just a creative rewrite of Mark, and Luke a creative rewrite of them, and John a creative rewrite of all of them, exhibiting this very change and evolution over time, before we even get to the additional problem of *the manuscripts* of these texts.

A Religious Ghost Story

This title may sound dismissive but there is quite a bit to say on whether the Resurrection fits in the cultural context in which it is set as a ghost story. We already know that the New Testament authors believed in ghost stories (Matthew 14:25–26; Luke 24:37). In *Apparitions of Jesus: The Resurrection as Ghost Story*, Robert Conner states:[3]

> When it came time to tell the central story of Christianity, to explain how and why a man came back from the grave, the New Testament writers used the only resources available to them: the language and frames of reference current in their culture – the culture of Judaism and the Old Testament, and the wider Greco-Roman culture in which Judaism was embedded. So it's hardly surprising that we've encountered visions in the New Testament similar to stories of visions from Greco-Roman sources, or that terms from the nearly ubiquitous mystery cults find their way into the letters of Paul and his imitators. That common elements of ghost lore should also appear in stories of Jesus, returned from the grave to make a brief appearance to his disciples, is less surprising still.

He continues later:[4]

---

[1] See Stewart (2011) and Ehrman (2011).
[2] See Chapters 16 and 16, Carrier (2014c).
[3] Conner (2018), p. 153, cf Loftus (2020), p. 504.
[4] Ibid.

> Every essential feature of the resurrection stories - sudden appearance and disappearance, the fear and confusion of witnesses, the empty tomb and tokens found within it, speaking, eating, and drinking as proof of life, tangible presence, the brevity of the appearances, the display of pre-mortem wounds, encouraging and admonishing – is also found in contemporary Greco-Roman ghost stories.

Whilst this account may not in totum explain all aspects of the narrative and subsequent belief system (as an influence on the writers) there is something to be said for it. The biblical writers, who were not (let us remember) objective historians in the sense we would have today, by any means, would have had an awful lot of contextual baggage. For example, cultural influences would have heavily influenced their writing. So the fiction could be expanded this way as well.

The Wrong Tomb

Subsequent fictions might also have been built on top of a kernel of real, and perfectly natural, but misunderstood events. We now have a number of naturalistic alternatives to the events of the Christian narrative.

Most obviously, it appears to me, is the idea that the wrong tomb was visited. The tomb visited by Jesus' early followers was indeed empty because Jesus happened to be in another tomb. They made some kind of mistake. As a result, panicked witnesses run back to announce that the body is missing and, lo and behold, such grief-stricken sect-members, who believe Jesus is the Messiah, think that he has risen from death in line with Jewish understanding of the general resurrection. The empty tomb story is born.

After that, wishful thinking and cognitive dissonance would prevent early Christian believers ever swaying from this belief no matter what corrective evidence might even have been produced thereafter, just as we saw commonly happens in religious movements.

The Body was Moved

One way they could fix on the wrong tomb is if the body was moved. This is another plausible theory. Jesus' followers return to the correct tomb, where Jesus *was* buried, but it's no longer the *right* one. Unfortunately, the body was only stored there temporarily by a (perhaps anonymous) pious Jew. He was observing Jewish ritual and took the body down from the cross before the holy day began at sunset. However, as soon as possible, the body was subsequently moved from that tomb (an honourable, generous burial place) to the proper burial place for criminals. It might have been that the tomb used only temporarily was closer to the site of execution and there were no grave diggers available to bury Jesus at dusk, or not enough time to complete the task before the onset of the Sabbath. Perhaps, even, the person who gave up the tomb had a change of heart, but we don't even need to suppose that. So the pious Jew used his or another tomb temporarily before Jesus was then afforded a burial more appropriate for a treasonous criminal. Perhaps the followers saw the tomb he was taken to or were not told the body would be taken away.

This theory is plausible and could include Joseph of Arimathea if you believe the claims of his existence. Perhaps he wanted the body out of his tomb after the Sabbath. Maybe he died soon after or moved back to his hometown. Maybe he remained as a pious Jew, lost now in history.

Later, the followers returned to the tomb to find the body missing, and they know it *was definitely* in that tomb. They flee and the story of a risen Jesus is born, becoming embellished thereafter.

The Body Was Stolen

A variation of the previous hypothesis is that some unknown Jews stole the body and spread rumours that Jesus' disciples had taken the body themselves.[1] Or, it could have been that the Christian disciples did actually steal the body as pious fraud and started the sect with creating the story that Jesus rose from the dead.[2] After all, John 20:13 has Mary saying: "...they have taken away my Lord, and I do not know where they put Him." This is a *very* pertinent quote.

Another version of this theme is that third parties stole Jesus' body. Body snatching was a well-known problem in this time and place[3] and this is a plausible suggestion.

Perhaps the women who claimed to see men or angels at the tomb really did see men – body-snatchers.

Significantly, too, Matthew's guards at the tomb are prima facie evidence of this being a plausible hypothesis. Rather than Matthew countering a Jewish hypothetical, this could be cognitive dissonance at work in explaining the data of an *actual* (perhaps unbeknownst to them) stolen body! Matthew claims the accusation of theft was bogus and invents a story to discredit it, but it could very easily be that this accusation existed *because it was true*, and Matthew is trying to cover that fact up. In other words, Matthew's apologetic is itself evidence the

---

[1] Allison (2005), p. 200-13.

[2] For the plausibility of this, see Carrier's chapter "The Plausibility of Theft" in Price & Lowder (2005), p. 369-92.

[3] De Zulueta (1932), and Ibid.

body was in fact stolen, and the stuff about bribing the guards to lie is itself the lie. Again, cognitive dissonance has a lot to answer for.

Swoon Theory

This theory comes from the verb "swoon" meaning to fall unconscious. There are a number of swoon theories that basically claim that Jesus did not die on the cross but merely fell unconscious. These were popularised from the 1700s onwards and a good deal of ink has been spilled over the theory. Whether Jesus was resuscitated by Joseph of Arimathea, or simply came to himself in a tomb he was taken to, there is a range of possibilities. You even have extensions of Jesus travelling to India to continue his ministry.

It probably depends on whether or not you also believe Jesus was pierced by a spear, or indeed whether you believe any other of the ancillary Gospel claims. The point is that someone surviving crucifixion is highly unlikely, but possible. Historian Josephus does recount someone surviving crucifixion (well, three, but two eventually dying despite a physician's help) though it is difficult to say whether this account was comparable to Jesus' crucifixion:[1]

> And when I was sent by Titus Caesar with Cerealio, and a thousand horsemen, to a certain village called Thecoa, in order to know whether it were a place fit for a camp, as I came back, I saw many captives crucified, and remembered three of them as my former acquaintance. I was very sorry at this in my mind, and went with tears in my eyes to Titus, and told him of them; so he immediately commanded them to be taken down, and to have the greatest care taken of them, in order to their recovery; yet two of them died under the physician's hands, while the third recovered.

Interestingly, Muslims (given that they see Jesus as a prophet, and not in divine God-incarnated terms) sometimes advocate for swoon theories, probably because of the Quranic verse:[2]

> And their saying, 'We did kill the Messiah, Jesus, son of Mary, the Messenger of Allah;' whereas they slew him not, nor crucified him, but he was made to appear to them like one crucified; and those who differ therein are certainly in a state of doubt about it; they have no definite knowledge thereof, but only follow a conjecture; and they did not convert this conjecture into a certainty;

[1] Flavius Josephus, *Life of Flavius Josephus*, 414-21

[2] The Quran - Chapter: 4: An-Nisa, 4:158.

Other evidence that could be brought in to support this theory is that Jesus did not stay long on the cross and there is no evidence of his body. Indeed, there are no eyewitnesses outside of the claims (gradually embellished) of the actions taken by Joseph of Arimathea.

Either way, again we ask whether any swoon theory is still more probable than the Christian thesis?[1]

Twins and Moved Bodies

Jesus happened to have an identical twin. The first twin, leader of a sect, was crucified, and the identical twin had the dead twin's body removed. This living twin could have taken on the role of the dead Jesus, "appearing" to the followers. Or, the roles were reversed and the second twin sacrificed himself to be arrested, seeing the writing on the wall for his sect leader brother, who later "appeared" as himself to his followers.

You could also have a slight variation of this theory but with the added mistake of getting the wrong tomb, so the dead twin is still in situ, and the live twin takes on the role of Jesus to give the impression that he has risen from the dead, without having to remove the body.

Sounds unlikely with not much positive evidence going for it, but isn't it still more plausible than the Christian thesis? We know of plenty of examples of identical twin frauds taking place, such as the Italian judge and lawyer who substituted in her twin sister to take on the role of judge in order to receive legal fees whilst she worked elsewhere.[2] These sorts of stories are not unheard of.

The Stecher Theory

As mapped out by Carl Stecher, the late skeptic previously referenced, and as John and Luke themselves depict, not an identical twin but a completely different person just posed as Jesus, and though they admit he didn't look like Jesus, they were nevertheless convinced it was him; cognitive dissonance was working its will again. This doesn't even require someone to have posed as Jesus; disciples clearly could just convince themselves in the right state of mind that any stranger was Jesus in disguise, as that is what Luke and John both

---

[1] One of the best cases for swoon theory is from Robert M. Price, in his chapter "Explaining the Resurrection without Recourse to Miracle" in Loftus (2011), p. 219-32 & p. 398-402.

[2] "Twins who swapped roles charged with fraud", Reuters Staff (2008), *Reuters*, https://www.reuters.com/article/us-italy-twins-idUSTRE48P66N20080926 (Retrieved 11/03/2021).

appear to suggest was originally the case. This also fits Matthew's statement that some disciples doubted it was Jesus (28:17); this can also be evidence that the man mistaken as (or presenting himself as) the risen Jesus really wasn't. Then, fiction and embellishment ensues (as previously set out) from there to build the story out into something more than really happened.

Primary and Composite Naturalistic Explanations

Building on the last point, and hopefully obvious from what I have said, though some of these theories can be seen on their own, in reality, many of these final theories will have elements of most of the above. Indeed, the most plausible theories, as I see them, *will* have elements of *most* of the above, being composite explanations.

My Preferred Explanation

For what it is worth, I will now set out what I think is the most plausible explanation of the Resurrection story. In my opinion, this will serve as the best explanation of what we read in Paul, the Gospels, and what we can infer from what we think the events were in the early Christian church.

I am going to assume here that the disciples believed Jesus to be the Messiah. I don't believe his original disciples had any notion that he was God as understood by the Holy Trinity. This idea came later and was retrospectively inserted into the narrative, mainly by John (I don't think the Synoptics had any such sophisticated theology). As the Messiah, Jesus would have been believed to be the leader and Saviour of Israel (in terms of ridding the land of Roman occupation) in his life in a way that he clearly wasn't. Luke (24:21) admits as much: "But we were hoping that it was He who was going to redeem Israel." This isn't really a contentious issue.

However, his death was massively unexpected. If it hadn't been, if the disciples had understood all the supposed prophecies that were retrojected into the Jesus narrative, they would not have reacted in the way they did. Additionally, the women would not have gone to anoint a dead body since they would have expected some divine thing to happen or have happened. But, to them, Jesus was not actually God. Moreover, with the later Christian theological understanding, the disciples would not have been so unprepared, so downhearted.

Jesus was captured by the Jewish authorities and was sentenced to death for treason (partially explaining the Gospel animus towards the Jews). My opinion is that this much is probably true, and probably with little Roman interaction (though, on the other side of the coin, you could also argue that Jesus was arrested by the Roman authorities for sedition – either is plausible). An itinerant preacher, purported to do miracles (all of this common to the time) was heralded as the Messiah by his followers and was executed.

Whether he was crucified or stoned is open to debate. Jesus could have been stoned, as is very likely; but whether stoned or crucified, he would still have been buried in a criminal's grave, and probably would have been hung up in some way for display, too. Out of this event, through cognitive dissonance and perhaps even visions, a resurrection narrative was created.

But what explains the Resurrection narrative as far as the empty tomb is concerned?

Given this hypothesis, then, there are two plausible explanations that I remain torn between, as I will explain. Either:

(1) Jesus was stoned and/or crucified and was buried in a graveyard reserved for criminals, in this case fit for a treasonous criminal. He may have been taken down from the cross early as it was a holy day and his followers did not know precisely where he was buried. There was no empty tomb narrative.

(2) Jesus was crucified and, due to it being a holy day, was taken down by a pious Jew (not Joseph of Arimathea as he was almost certainly a legendary embellishment but perhaps someone who presented as the kernel to this myth). His body was temporarily stored in a tomb of which the followers knew the location. The body was then removed from the tomb to be buried more appropriately in a criminals' graveyard.

The first option gives us an explanation that requires the empty tomb narrative be created later, out of this non-tomb account, with claimed hallucinations (whether real or not, but not referring to an objective, mind-independent figure of Jesus roaming around) feeding into the construction of that narrative. In reality, it is little different from proposing that he was stoned and buried in a shallow grave, though it explains better the existence of the crucifixion motif.

The second option, though historically less plausible to a degree (as discussed in the preceding chapters), does a slightly better job of explaining the eventual empty tomb narrative and Resurrection claims. This account would then receive an awful lot of embellishment encouraged (or even inspired) by hallucinations.

But, and this is a big but... Though the second option better explains the eventual empty tomb narrative, it does not cohere with Paul's silence. Paul seems utterly unaware of an empty tomb narrative and he is our earliest source. That Mark has no knowledge of a theft polemic is evidence the empty tomb story was not circulating for decades; which is evidence he is the first to invent it.

Therefore, I am marginally convinced that the empty tomb narrative was a later embellishment.

If I was a betting man and had to wager on one explanation only, I would say that Jesus was in some way "crucified", *after* being stoned, and buried in a specific grave location that his followers could not identify.

The Christian thesis would be my last bet, the least likely to be true.

Or, (1) above is slightly more likely than (2), which is itself more likely than the other alternatives I have provided, all of which are far more likely than a reanimated corpse of the Christian narrative. This is not only a prior probability established without needing to look at the evidence, but it is massively supported precisely *by* looking at the evidence, as this book has shown.

Homuyan Sidky summarises:[1]

> Many scholars who are not votaries have now concluded that the story of the burial in a tomb is a later invention by the evangelists who wrote the gospels. They transform Jesus's ignominious death, betrayal, and abandonment by the disciples, who scattered and hid not knowing or caring about their master's body or the location of his grave, and the dishonorable disposal of his remains at the hands of the Jews who had crucified him. Crossan's reflections on this are, "I find [here] a trajectory of hope but not history. Behind that hope lies, at worse, the horror of a body left on the cross as carrion, or, at best a body consigned like others to 'a lime pit.'" In the place of this horrible reality, the gospels supply a royal entombment of Jesus by a faithful but hitherto unknown devotee. Along the same lines, Spong (1994: 240-41) says that the phrase "they all forsook him and fled" means that Jesus died alone, executed as a criminal, and his remains were probably unceremoniously buried in a common unmarked grave in an unknown location. The story of Joseph of Arimathea, Spong (1995: 225) concurs, was invented to mask over the pain of the disciples that they had no clue about the disposition of their teacher's body. Lüdemann (1995: 23- 24) grants a bit more stating that it was probably the Jews who buried Jesus. A man named Joseph of Arimathea may have been in charge of the burial detail, but it is unlikely that he was a disciple or a friend of the deceased (cf., Brown 1994: 1240). He adds that neither the disciples nor Jesus's next of kin bothered about his body and did not know its final disposition.
>
> To recap, as Crossan (1995: 186-87) suggests, either the Roman soldiers placed the body in a shallow grave under a layer of lime and dirt, or it was left on the cross to decompose. In his words, this means "lime, at best, and the dogs again, at worst." Crossan (1995: 187) concludes

[1] Sidky (2019), p. 450-51.

> that the burial stories are not historical memories but "are hope and hyperbole expended into apologetics and polemics."

After his burial, as mentioned, and after scattering to the winds, cognitive dissonance reduction takes over: these disciples would have felt somewhat responsible and thus guilty, but also angry, upset, disappointed, confused, anxious, and so on. As we know with cognitive dissonance and the difficulty humans have with cutting our losses (we throw good money after bad), the disciples wouldn't have split the faith. They wouldn't have given up their core beliefs. As mentioned, there are numerous precedents and examples of such behaviour, *especially* in religious contexts.

Jesus must still be the Messiah.

How can Jesus be a Messiah who dies?

This is where Jesus' followers would have scoured the Hebrew Bible for justification, for scriptural rationale, for comfort. Dying and sacrifice are in no short supply in the Torah. Just as prevalent is the Jewish holy day of Yom Kippur – the Day of Atonement – the holiest day of the year where sacrifice is integral, and such theology would have formed a bedrock for how the disciples came to understand the disappointing string of events. According to Numbers 29:8-11, "one must sacrifice a young bull, a ram and seven lambs who are a year old. As well, for a sin offering, one must sacrifice a male goat." Jesus is now *that offering*. Jesus becomes some kind of sacrificial lamb.

This hypothesis fully explains Jesus dying and how his disciples would have felt and acted.

Religious hallucinations and experiences would most certainly have been had by at least some of his followers, and others may have claimed these for reasons concerning social and structural authority and hierarchy. Religious fervour can account for many things as we see in virtually every religion in the world. And, remember, the Christian denies the veracity of all other religions, and so any arguments used to explain away religious origins, experiences, miracles and so on for those religions can be applied equally to Christianity. Although Christians may think otherwise, I see no real purchase to the idea of Christian exceptionalism in this context.

Paul became convinced by the people he was sent to persecute and convert, converting himself (perhaps "transforming" is a better word). We know how evangelical people can when they convert away from incredibly strong belief in a given religion. The number of "militant atheists" who were originally evangelical Christians is no surprise – the anger at perceiving a wasted life, of being hoodwinked, of falling for perceived falsehoods, means that they can embrace atheism with all the religious fervour they exhibited with Christianity. Paul's move from being a Jew persecuting Christians to being a believer in Jesus himself would have brought with it an awful lot of psychological baggage in a similar manner. Additionally, there are good reasons to suggest that he may have already had psychological issues at any rate.

This perfect storm of events would have meant that Paul was a prime candidate for hallucinating or having religious experiences in a manner no different to so many other religious converts or "gurus" or "holy men" from other religions. Of course, Christians equally discount these explanations as I and other skeptics discount the Christian claims concerning Paul. He starts to build, or helps to build, the edifice of the early church, to foster a new and evangelical movement. Over time, received accounts of these early followers are embellished and adorned with theological accoutrements such that the end result has only the tiniest of commonality with the original events.

In this way, an itinerant preacher with passionate followers disappointingly dies, but his followers pick up the pieces and go with it. They take their cognitive dissonance reduction and they raise it with a mythological enhancement and a theological overlay. Given time, experiences and visions, we get the New Testament.

And that chain of events, dear reader, is not so improbable. That explanation is not implausible, for it is not too dissimilar to how a good many other religions or religious movements have begun.

In sum, this is a damn sight more plausible than the Christian thesis and, as an added bonus, it doesn't break the known laws of nature.

21 – Concluding Remarks

> When it comes to the resurrection, Paul, our only witness, doesn't give us any details; and we can't prove the Gospels actually come from any witnesses. We therefore can establish nothing as true. And in the end, in context, there is nothing all that remarkable about Christianity's origin or success. Dreams or visions are all we have first-hand accounts of as having happened. Mass ecstasies tell us nothing. And the history of Christianity itself is far too mundane to require actual resurrection as the initial inspiration.[1]

Richard Carrier's conclusion in *Resurrection: Faith or Fact?* pulls on a previous conclusion in his chapter "Christianity's Success Was Not Incredible", in John Loftus's *The End of Christianity*:[2]

> If Jesus was a god and really wanted to save the world, [one would expect] he would have appeared and delivered the Gospel personally to the whole world. He would not appear only to one small group of believers and one lone outsider, in one tiny place, just one at a time, two thousand years ago, and then give up. But if Christianity originated as a natural movement inspired by ordinary hallucinations (real or pretended), then we would expect it to arise in only one small group, in one small place and time, and especially where, as in antiquity, regular hallucinators were often respected as holy and their hallucinations believed to be divine communications. And that's exactly when and where it began. The ordinary explanation thus predicts all we see, whereas the extraordinary explanation predicts things we don't see at all.

Excuse the long quote (you should be used to them by now!), but this opinion is absolutely spot on. This is, in effect, the very conclusion of this work in your hands or on your screen. What better explains the data – the orthodox claims of Christianity or a naturalistic explanation such as those given here?

Before finally critiquing Christian Craig Blomberg's case against fellow skeptic Carl Stecher in the book, Carrier states of the above quote:

> This statement holds as well for every other scenario and combination of scenarios Carl proposes. There really isn't any way to get around this,

[1] Carrier in *Resurrection: Faith or Fact?*, Stecher & Blomberg (2019), p.217-18.
[2] Loftus (2011), p. 70-71.

> And Craig [Blomberg] has provided none. All he has are rationalizations and speculations. But what we need is *evidence*.

I couldn't have put it better myself. So I didn't.

The point is that it is clear, to someone like me and hopefully to you by now, that the evidence available to support a traditional Christian thesis of Christ resurrecting, from the data we have (Paul, the Gospels, etc.), makes the Christian hypothesis far less probable than any combination of the naturalistic explanations that I have given here, or, indeed, many I haven't. It is not that I am presupposing naturalism and the idea that divine resurrections are a priori impossible; rather, it is that the evidence is not good enough to support the Christian thesis.

Not by a long shot!

As such, the Christian is not epistemically warranted in believing the Gospel accounts as being historically true and accurate. Certain stories become culturally embedded before they can be vetted by skeptical cognitive mechanisms, and this is one of them.

Where does this then leave the Christian?

Well, as stated at the beginning of this book, such a conclusion leaves them, essentially, as no longer a Christian.

Or, at least, it *should*. However, they have *faith*. And what is faith? It is belief absent of evidence. And for that ailment, I have no cure.

APPENDIX 1

Here is a list of contradictions, differences and speculations found in Paul's writings, the Gospels concerning the Resurrection accounts, and Acts, taken from Michael J. Alter's tour de force, *The Resurrection: A Critical inquiry*. This is a comprehensive list well worth perusing and further checking out. It was simply not possible for me to include all of these issues and problems to consider for a summary of this size. There are 120 "Differences and Contradictions" and 217 "Speculations". I have listed a few of them here, to whet your appetite, and the rest can be found at Pearce (2021).

DIFFERENCES and CONTRADICTIONS
#1: The Year Jesus Was Crucified
#2: The Controversy Regarding the Garments
#3: Nisan 14 or Nisan 15
#4: The Last Supper as a Passover Meal
#5: The Wrong Name in Mark 14:12
#6: The Day of the Week Jesus Was Crucified
#7: John Contradicts Mark
#8: Differing Accounts
#9: John 20:17 Contradicts Luke 23:43
#10: Significant Omissions of Luke's Narrative in Three Gospels
#11: The Viability of the Dialogue
#12: When Jesus Spoke His Last Words
#13: Source and Lack of Verification
...

SPECULATIONS
#1: Was the Crucifixion Really in the Fall and Not in the Spring?
#2: Anomaly 1—Unexplained Rupture of the Storyline
#3: Anomaly 2—the Consequences of Following Judas
#4: Jesus as the Paschal Lamb
#5: John's Theological Agenda of the Lamb of God
#6: Questions Raised about the Lamb of God
#7: John Writing to Appeal to the Gentiles
#8: The Use of Artos (Bread)
#9: Symbolism of the Bread and Wine and the Lack of a Lamb
#10: Jesus Left the Last Supper
...

APPENDIX 2

This excerpt is taken from Carrier (2018), and is a useful reference to show some evidence for copyist error in getting from "Pentecost" to "500":

> Shortly after listing the appearance sequence, Paul writes "Christ has indeed been raised from the dead, **the firstfruits** of those who have fallen asleep" (1 Corinthians 15:20). The firstfruits is a reference to the Pentecost ritual of offering the "first fruits" of the harvest to God (per Exodus, Numbers, and Deuteronomy). It seems a remarkable coincidence that Paul said the risen Jesus was akin to the Pentecost offering in the same place he mentions an appearance to over a hundred "all at once," and Acts narrates an appearance to over a hundred on Pentecost "when they were all together in one place" (Acts 2:1). Might Paul's letter have originally read *epi* ***pentêkostês*** *adelphois* rather than *epanô* ***pentakosiois*** *adelphois*? That would have meant Paul said Jesus appeared "during the Pentecost to the brethren." In other words, he didn't say how many brethren were there, only that "the brethren" all experienced a vision, at the Pentecost. This would explain where the author of Acts 2 got the idea for a mass vision of the brethren on Pentecost.
>
> If someone screwed up on copying Paul's original text–say, slipping from *epi* into *epô*, or *pentekostês* to *pentekostois*, or any of a number of common errors we find throughout ancient manuscripts–a later corrector would have had to make sense of the resulting mishmash and come up with a fix. They could easily assume *epô* must have meant *epanô*, and therefore *pentêkostês* must have been a mistake for *pentakosiois*; or that *epi pentêkostois* must have been a mistake for *epanô pentakosiois*. We have examples throughout ancient manuscripts of these very kinds of corrections and emendations. And we know the early copyists of the New Testament were unprofessional amateurs prone to all kinds of mistakes [see Three Things to Know about New Testament Manuscripts at richardcarrier.info/archives/11209]. Such an emendation is even more likely if the corrector faced with the garbled text was a Gentile not fully immersed in the Jewish ritual calendar, and thus "Pentecost" wouldn't have been the first thing occurring to him as what Paul could have meant.
>
> The spelling is even weirdly close. Acts says the event happened *tês pentêkostês*, the day "of the Pentecost"; 1 Corinthians now says the event involved *pentakosiois*, over "five hundred" brothers. Acts says the event occurred *epi to auto*, "in the same place"; 1 Corinthians, that the

event was *epano*, to "more than" a certain number. Acts says the event happened when *pantes homou*, "all were together"; 1 Corinthians, that the event happened *ephapax*, "all at once." The similarities seem too numerous to be a coincidence. Has Luke remodeled Paul? Or did Paul originally describe a Pentecostal appearance and not an appearance to "more than five hundred"?

BIBLIOGRAPHY

Albright, William and Mann, C.S. (1971), *The Anchor Bible. Matthew*, New York: Doubleday.

Aleman, André, & Larøi, Frank (2009), *Hallucinations: The Science of Idiosyncratic Perception*, Washington, DC: American Psychological Association.

Allison, Dale (2005), *Resurrecting Jesus: The Earliest Christian Tradition and Its Interpreters*. New York: T&T Clark.

Alter, Robert and Kermode, Frank (1990), *The Literary Guide to the Bible*, Harvard: Harvard University Press.

Alter, Michael J. (2015), *The Resurrection: A Critical Inquiry*, Bloomington, IN: Xlibris.

Anderson, Hugh (1965), The Easter Witness of the Evangelists", *The New Testament in Historical and Contemporary Perspective. Essays in Memory of G.H.C. MacGregor*, edited by Hugh Anderson and William Barclay, 33-55, Oxford: Basil Blackwell.

Barclay, James Turner (1858), *The City of the Great King*, Arno Press.

Barclay, William (1961), *Crucified and Crowned*, London: SCM Press.

Barens, E.W (1947), *The Rise of Christianity*, London: Longmans, Green.

Barker, Dan (2008), *Godless: How an Evangelical Preacher Became One of America's Leading Atheist*, New York: Ulysses Press.

Barnes, Ernest William (1948), *The Rise of Christianity*, London: Longmans, Green.

Beyerstein, Barry (2007), "The Neurology of the Weird: Brain States and Anomalous Experience." In *Tall Tales about the Mind and Brain: Separating Fact from Fiction*, edited by Sergio Sala, 314–35. Oxford: Oxford University Press.

Beal, Tarcisio (2009), *Foundations of Christianity: The Historical Jesus and His World*, Bloomington, IN: AuthorHouse.

Bentall, Richard P. (2000), "Hallucinatory Experiences", in Cardeña, Etzel et al (2000), *Varieties of Anomalous Experience: Examining the Scientific Evidence*, Washington: American Psychological Association.

Bode, Edward Lynn (1970), *The First Easter Morning*, Rome: Biblical Institute Press.

Brown, Raymond (1977), *The Birth of the Messiah*, London: Geoffrey Chapman.

Brown, Raymond (1988), "The Burial of Jesus," *Catholic Biblical Quarterly*, Vol. 50.1 (Jan 1988): 233-34.

Brown, Raymond (1994), *The Death of the Messiah: From Gethsemane to the Grave: A Commentary on the Passion Narratives in the Four Gospels*, 2 volumes, London: Geoffrey Chapman.

Brown, Raymond (1997), *Introduction to the New Testament*. New York: Anchor Bible.

Burkett, Delbert (2002), *An Introduction To The New Testament And The Origins Of Christianity*, Cambridge: Cambridge University Press.

Callahan, Tim (2002), *The Secret Origins of the Bible*, Altadena: Millennium Press.

Campbell, Patrick (1965), *The Mythical Jesus,* Waverley.

Carrier, Richard (2000), "Luke and Josephus", http://www.infidels.org/library/modern/richard_carrier/lukeandjosephus.html (Retrieved 17/10/2020).

Carrier, Richard (2000b), Review of *The Homeric Epics and the Gospel of Mark*", *The Secular Web*, https://infidels.org/library/modern/richard_carrier/homerandmark.html (Retrieved 23/08/2020).

Carrier, Richard (2002), "Jewish Law, the Burial of Jesus, and the Third Day", *The Secular Web,* https://infidels.org/kiosk/article/jewish-law-the-burial-of-jesus-and-the-third-day-125.html (Retrieved 20/09/2020).

Carrier, Richard (2006, 6th Ed.), "Why I Don't Buy the Resurrection Story" http://www.infidels.org/library/modern/richard_carrier/resurrection/2.html (Retrieved 20/10/2020).

Carrier, Richard (2006b), "Carrier's Opening Statement: Naturalism Is True, Theism is Not", *The Secular Web,* https://infidels.org/library/modern/richard_carrier/carrier-wanchick/carrier1.html (Retrieved 20/12/2020).

Carrier, Richard (2009), *Not the Impossible Faith*, lulu.com.

Carrier, Richard (2010), "Why the Resurrection Is Unbelievable" in *The Christian Delusion* (Ed. By Loftus, John W.), Amherst: Prometheus.

Carrier, Richard (2011), "Christianity's Success Was Not Incredible", in *The End of Christianity*, (Ed. By Loftus, John W.), Amherst: Prometheus.

Carrier, Richard (2012), "Crucifixion Quake! An Unusual Movie about an Unusual Passion", *Richard Carrier Blogs,* https://www.richardcarrier.info/archives/17618 (Retrieved 29/01/2021).

Carrier, Richard (2012b), *Proving History: Bayes's Theorem and the Quest for the Historical Jesus*, Amherst: Prometheus Books.

Carrier, Richard (2013), "Innumeracy: A Fault to Fix", *Richard Carrier Blogs,* https://www.richardcarrier.info/archives/4857 (Retrieved 20/08/2020).

Carrier, Richard (2014), "Spiritual Body FAQ, *Richard Carrier Blogs,* https://www.richardcarrier.info/SpiritualFAQ.html (Retrieved 15/09/2020).

Carrier, Richard (2014b), *On the Historicity of Jesus: Why We Might Have Reason for Doubt*, Sheffield: Sheffield Phoenix Press.

Carrier, Richard (2014c), *Hitler Homer Bible Christ: The Historical Papers of Richard Carrier 1995-2013,* Richmond, CA: Philosophy Press.

Carrier, Richard (2015), "Did Muhammad Exist? (Why That Question Is Hard to Answer)", *Richard Carrier Blogs*, https://www.richard-carrier.info/archives/8574 (Retrieved 09/03/2021).

Carrier, Richard (2017), "Why Do We Still Believe in Q?", *Richard Carrier Blogs*, https://www.richardcarrier.info/archives/12352 (Retrieved 20/08/2020).

Carrier, Richard (2017b), "What Is Bayes' Theorem & How Do You Use It?", *Richard Carrier Blogs*, https://www.richardcarrier.info/archives/12742 (Retrieved 05/03/2021).

Carrier, Richard (2018), "Then He Appeared to Over Five Hundred Brethren at Once!", *Richard Carrier Blogs*, https://www.richardcarrier.info/archives/14255 (Retrieved 10/11/2020).

Celsus (1830), "The Arguments of Celsus against the Christians." In *Arguments of Celsus, Porphyry, and the Emperor Julian against the Christians*, Translated by Thomas Taylor, London: Rodd. https://www.gutenberg.org/files/37696/37696-h/37696-h.htm (Retrieved 17/07/2018).

Celsus, (1987), *On the True Doctrine: A Discourse against the Christians*, Translated by R. Joseph Hoffmann, New York: Oxford University Press.

Clarke, Isabel (2010), "Psychosis and Spirituality: The Discontinuity Model." In *Psychosis and Spirituality: Consolidating the New Paradigm*, edited by Isabel Clarke, p. 101–14. Oxford: Wiley-Blackwell.

Cline, E.H. (2009), *Biblical Archaeology: A Very Short Introduction (Very Short Introductions)*, OUP USA.

Cohen, R.A. (2011), "Yerkes–Dodson Law", In Kreutzer J.S., DeLuca J., Caplan B. (eds) *Encyclopedia of Clinical Neuropsychology*, New York: Springer.

Cohen, S.J.D. (1979), *Josephus in Galilee and Rome, his Vita and Development as a Historian*, Leiden: E.J. Brill.

Cohn, Haim (2000), *The Trial and Death of Jesus*, Old Saybrook, CT: Konecky & Konecky.

Conybeare, Fred Cornwallis (2nd Ed 1910; reprint 2010), *Myths, Magic and Morals*, Whitefish, MT: Kessinger Publishings.

Cook, John D. (2011), "Absence of evidence", *John D. Cook Consulting*, https://www.johndcook.com/blog/2011/02/22/absence-of-evidence/ (Retrieved 15/08/2020).

Cook, Lyndon (1991), ed., *David Whitmer Interviews: A Restoration Witness*, Orem, Utah: Grandin Book.

Cox, Harvey (2006), *When Jesus Came to Harvard: Making Moral Choices Today*, New York: Mariner Books.

Craig, William Lane (n.d.a), "The Resurrection of Jesus", *Reasonable Faith*, https://www.reasonablefaith.org/writings/popular-writings/jesus-of-nazareth/the-resurrection-of-jesus/ (Retrieved 14/09/2020).

Craig, William Lane (n.d.b), "The Historicity of the Empty Tomb of Jesus", *Reasonable Faith*, https://www.reasonablefaith.org/writings/scholarly-writings/historical-jesus/the-historicity-of-the-empty-tomb-of-jesus/ (Retrieved 201511/2020).

Craig, William Lane (1984), "The Guard at the Tomb", *New Testament Studies* 30, p. 273-81 http://www.leaderu.com/offices/billcraig/docs/guard.html (Retrieved 20/09/2020).

Craig, William Lane (1985), William Lane Craig, *The Historical Argument for the Resurrection of Jesus during the Deist Controversy*, Lewiston, N.Y.: E. Mellen Press.

Craig, William Lane Craig (1985b), "Contemporary Scholarship and the Historical Evidence for the Resurrection of Jesus Christ", *Truth* 1 (1985), p. 89-95.

Craig, William Lane (1989), *Assessing the New Testament Evidence for the Historicity of the Resurrection of Jesus*, Lewiston: Edwin Mellen.

Craig, William Lane (1995), "Did Jesus Rise from the Dead?" in eds. Wilkins, Michael J & Moreland, J.P (1995), *Jesus under Fire: Modern Scholarship Reinvents the Historical Jesus*, Grand Rapids: Zondervan, p. 147-82.

Craig, William Lane (2008), *Reasonable Faith: Christian Truth and Apologetics*, Wheaton, IL: Crossway/Good News Publishers.

Craveri, Marcello (1967), *The Life of Jesus*, London: Secker & Warburg (RandomHouse).

Crossan, John Dominic (1985), *Four Other Gospels*, Minneapolis: Winston

Crossan, John Dominic (1988), *The Cross that Spoke: The Origins of the Passion Narrative*, San Francisco: Harper & Row.

Crossan, John Dominic (1991), *The Historical Jesus: The Life of a Mediterranean Jewish Peasant*, San Francisco/Edinburgh: HarperSan Francisco/T. & T. Clark.

Crossan, John Dominic (1995), *Who Killed Jesus? Exposing the Roots of Anti-Semitism in the Gospel Story of the Death of Jesus*, New York: HarperOne.

Crossley, James G. (2006), *Why Christianity Happened*, Louisville, Kentucky: Westminster John Knox PressDeVries, Dawn (1996), *Jesus Christ in the Preaching of Calvin and Schleiermacher*, Louisville, Kentucky: Westminster John Knox Press.

Crossley, James G. (2005), "Against the Historical Plausibility of the Empty Tomb Story and the Bodily Resurrection of Jesus: A Response to N.T. Wright", *Journal for the Study of the Historical Jesus*, Volume 3: Issue 2.

David, Anthony (2004), "The Cognitive Neuropsychiatry of Auditory Verbal Hallucinations: An Overview." Cognitive Neuropsychiatry 9, nos. 1/2: 107–23.

Davies, Martin F., Griffin, Murray & Vice, Sue (2001), "Affective reactions to auditory hallucinations in psychotic, evangelical and control groups", *British Journal of Clinical Psychology*, 40, p. 361-70.

Davies, William David and Allison, Dale C., (2nd ed 2000), *A critical and exegetical commentary on the Gospel according to Saint Matthew: in three volumes. Introduction and commentary on Matthew 1-VII, Volume 1*, London: T & T Clark.

Davis, Mike (2008), *The Atheist's Guide to the New Testament*, Denver: Outskirts Press.

Davis, Stephen T. (1993), *Risen Indeed*, Grand Rapids: William B. Eerdmans

Dawes, Gregory W. (2001), *The Historical Jesus Question: The Challenge for History to Religious Authority*, Louisville, Kentucky: Westminster John Knox Press.

Dein, Simon (2001), "What Really Happens When Prophecy Fails: The Case of Lubavitch", *Sociology of Religion,* OUP, Vol. 62, No. 3 (Autumn, 2001), p. 383-401.

Dein, Simon (2010), "A messiah from the dead: cultural performance in Lubavitcher messianism", *Social Compass*, Volume: 57, Issue: 4, Pages: 537-554.

Dein, Simon (2011), *Lubavitcher Messianism: What Really Happens When Prophecy Fails?,* London: Continuum.

De Lange, Nicholas (2000), *An Introduction to Judaism*, Cambridge: Cambridge University Press.

Dunn, James (1985), *The Evidence for Jesus: The Impact of Scholarship on our Understanding of How Christianity Began*, London: SCM.

Ehrman, Bart (2011), *The Orthodox Corruption of Scripture: The Effect of Early Christological Controversies on the Text of the New Testament*, Oxford: Oxford University Press.

Elder, John (1960), *Prophets, Idols, and Diggers: Scientific Proof of Bible History*, New York: Bobbs Merrill Co.

Esler, Philip F. (1989), *Community and Gospel in Luke-Acts: The Social and olitical Motivations of Lucan Theology*, Cambridge: Cambridge University Press.

Eusebius of Caesarea, Tr. W.J. Ferrar (1920), *Demonstratio Evangelica*, http://www.tertullian.org/fathers/eusebius_de_00_epreface.htm (Retrieved 28/11/2020).

Evans, Craig A. (2003), *The Bible Knowledge Background Commentary: Matthew-Luke*, Colorado: Victor (Cook Communications Ministries).

Finegan, Jack (1998; rev. Ed), *Handbook of Biblical Chronology*, Peabody, MA: Hendrickson Publishers.

Fitzgerald, David (2010), *Nailed: Ten Christian Myths That Show Jesus Never Existed at All*, Lulu.com.

Fitzgerald, David (2010), *Jesus: Mything in Action, Vol I*, independently published.

Fowler, Miles (Spring 1998), "Identification of the Bethany Youth in the Secret Gospel of Mark with Other Figures Found in Mark and John", *Journal of Higher Criticism*, 5:1, p. 3–22.

France, R.T. (1994), "Matthew", *New Bible Commentary: 21st Century Edition*, edited by D.A. Carson , R.T. France, J.A. Motyer and G.J. Wenham, 904-45, Downers Grove: InterVarsity.

France, R.T. (2007), *The Gospel of Matthew (New International Commentary on the New Testament)*, Grand Rapids, MI: Wm. B. Eerdmans Publishing Co.

Funk, Robert (1998), *The Acts of Jesus: What Did Jesus Really Do?*, New York: HarperCollins.

Galli, Mark (2011), "The Problem with Christus Victor", *Christianity Today*, https://www.christianitytoday.com/ct/2011/aprilweb-only/christusvicarious.html (Retrieved 10/12/2020).

Garland, David E. (2001), *Reading Matthew: A Literary and Theological Commentary*, Macon, Georgia: Smyth & Helwys Publishing Inc.

Geddert, Timothy J. (1989), *Watchwords: Mark 13 in Markan Eschatology* Sheffield: JOST.

Gers-Uphaus, Christian (2020), The Figure of Pontius Pilate in Josephus Compared with Philo and the Gospel of John", *Religions,* 2020, 11, 65.

Godfrey, Neil (2007), "The origin and meaning of the Emmaus Road narrative in Luke", *Vridar*, https://vridar.org/2007/11/17/the-logic-and-meaning-of-the-emmaus-road-narrative-in-luke/ (Retrieved 10/18/2020).

Grant, Robert M. (1963), *A Historical Introduction to the New Testament*, New York: Harper and Row.

Green, Joel B. (1997), *The Gospel of Luke*, Grand Rapids: Wm. B. Eerdmans Publishing.

Grim, Brian J. & Grim, Melissa E. (2016), "The Socio-economic Contribution of Religion to American Society: An Empirical Analysis, *Interdisciplinary Journal of Research on Religion*, Volume 12, Article 3.

Guignebert, Charles (1935), *Jesus*, London: Kegan Paul.

Gurtner, Daniel M. (2015), "Water and Blood and Matthew 27:49: A Johannine Reading in the Matthean Passion Narrative?", Chapter 6 (p.134-150) in *Studies on the Text of the New Testament and Early Christianity*, ed. D. Gurtner, J. Hernández Jr. and P. Foster, Leiden: Brill.

Habermas, Gary (n.d.), "Minimal Facts on the Resurrection that Even Skeptics Accept", *Southern Evangelical Seminary & Bible College*, https://ses.edu/minimal-facts-on-the-resurrection-that-even-skeptics-accept/ (Retrieved 15/11/2020).

Habermas, Gary (2004), *The Case for the Resurrection of Jesus*, Grand Rapids, MI: Kregel Publications.

Habermas, Gary (2009), 'Why The "Minimal Facts" Model is Unpersuasive'. *Evaluating Christianity*, https://evaluatingchristianity.wordpress.com/2009/03/05/why-the-minimal-facts-model-is-unpersuasive/ (Retrieved 18/09/2020).

Har-El, Menashe (2004), "Golden Jerusalem", Jerusalem: Gefen Publishing House.

Hebblethwaite, Brian (2001), *Ethics and Religion in a Pluralistic Age*, London: T&T Clark International.

Hendrickx, Herman (1984), *The Resurrection Narratives of the Synoptic Gospels*, London: G Chapman.

Hengel, Martin (1977), *Crucifixion in the Ancient World and the Folly of the Message of the Cross*. Philadelphia, PA: Fortress.

Hinnells, John R. (2010), *The Routledge Companion to the Study of Religion*, Oxon: Routledge.

Hume, David (1902), "Of Miracles", in L.A. Selby-Bigge, ed., *An Enquiry Concerning Human Understanding*, 2nd edn., p. 108-131, Oxford: Clarendon Press.

Ice, Thomas (2009), "Preterism and Zechariah 12-14", Scholar Crossing, Pre-Trib Research Center, Liberty University, https://digitalcommons.liberty.edu/cgi/viewcontent.cgi?article=1067&context=pretrib_arch (Retrieved 26/08/2020).

Jackson, Samuel Macauley Ed. (1953), *The New Schaff-Herzog Encyclopedia of Religious Knowledge, Vol. VI: Innocents – Liudger*, Grand Rapids, Michigan: Baker Book House.

Jeremias, Joachim (1966), *The Eucharistic Words of Jesus*, Philadelphia: Fortress Press.

Johns, Louise, & Os, Jim (2001) "The Continuity of Psychotic Experiences in the General Population." *Clinical Psychology Review* 21: 1125–41.

Jongkind, Dirk (2018), "Matthew 27:49 Was Jesus Pierced before His Death?", *Evangelical Textual Criticism*, http://evangelicaltextualcriticism.blogspot.com/2018/02/matthew-2749-was-jesus-pierced-before.html (Retrieved 14/08/2020).

Josephus, *Jewish War*, translation referenced at http://perseus.uchicago.edu/perseus-cgi/citequery3.pl?dbname=GreekTexts&query=Joseph.%20BJ&getid=1 using the Perseus Digital Library at Tufts (Retrieved 06/09/2020).

Karp, Jonathan & Sutcliffe, Adam (2017), The Cambridge History of Judaism: Volume 7, The Early Modern World, 1500–1815, Cambridge, Cambridge University Press.

Käsemann, Ernst (1954), "The Problem of the Historical Jesus", in *Essays on New Testament Themes*, translated by W. J. Montague (1982), Philadelphia: Fortress, 1982.

Kennedy, Titus (n.d.), "Roman Crucifixion and the Execution of Jesus", *Drive Thru History Adventures*, https://drivethruhistoryadventures.com/roman-crucifixion-execution-jesus/ (Retrieved 08/03/2021).

Kirby, Peter (2001), "The Historicity of the Empty Tomb Evaluated", *The Secular Web*, https://infidels.org/library/modern/peter_kirby/tomb/ (Retrieved 11/03/2021).

Klein, Susan, & Alexander, David (2003), "Good Grief: A Medical Challenge." *Trauma* 5, no. 4: 261–71.

Komarnitsky, Kris, (2009), *Doubting Jesus' Resurrection: What Happened in the Black Box?*, Draper, UT: Stone Arrow Books.

Komarnitsky, Kris, (2014), "Cognitive Dissonance and the Resurrection of Jesus", *The Fourth R* magazine, Volume 27, Issue 5, September/October 2014, from the *Westar* Institute, https://www.westarinstitute.org/resources/the-fourth-r/cognitive-dissonance-resurrection-jesus/ (Retrieved 25/08/2020).

Köster, Helmut (1990; 2nd ed. 2004), *Ancient Christian Gospels: their History and Development*, Harrisburg, PA: Trinity Press International.

Kraus, S. (1904), "Jesus of Nazareth", *The Jewish Encyclopaedia*, New York: John Shelby Spong, *Resurrection: Myth or Reality* (HarperOne, 1995),Funk & Wagnalls.

Kremer, Jakob (1977), *Die Osterevangelien–Geschichten um Geschichte*, Stuttgart: Katholisches Bibelwerk.

Lachs, Samuel Tobias (1987), *A Rabbinic Commentary on the New Testament: The Gospels of Matthew, Mark and Luke*, Ktav Publishing House.

Lampe, G.W.H. (1966), "Easter: A Statement" in *The Resurrection*, ed. Purcell, William (1966), Philadelphia: Westminster. https://www.religion-online.org/book-chapter/chapter-4-easter-a-statement-by-g-w-h-lampe/ (Retrieved 03/03/2021)

Levine, Ellen (2006), "Jewish Views and Custom on Death." In *Death and Bereavement across Cultures*, edited by Colin Parkes, Pittu Laungani, and Bill Young, 98–130, New York: Routledge.

Licona, Michael R. (2010), *The Resurrection of Jesus: A New Historiographical Approach*, Downers Grove: IVP Academic.

Liddell, H.G., & Scott, R. (1996), 9th Ed., *A Greek-English Lexicon*, Oxford: Clarendon Press.

Loftus, John W. (2007), "Why Wasn't There any Veneration of Jesus' Empty Tomb?", *Debunking Christianity* https://www.debunking-christianity.com/2007/02/why-wasnt-there-any-veneration-of-jesus.html (Retrieved 16/02/2021).

Loftus, John W. (2010), *The Christian Delusion*, Amherst: Prometheus Books.

Loftus, John W. (2011), *The End of Christianity*, Amherst: Prometheus Books.

Loftus, John W. (2013), *The Outsider Test for Faith*, Amherst: Prometheus Books.

Loftus, John W. (2019), *The Case Against Miracles*, Hypatia Press.

Lowder, Jeffrey Jay (2012), "The Evidential Argument from the History of Science (AHS)", *The Secular Outpost*, https://www.patheos.com/blogs/secularoutpost/2012/06/16/the-evidential-argument-from-the-history-of-science-ahs/#ixzz3PwEz8UxQ (Retrieved 25/11/2020).

Luc, Ulrich (2005), *Matthew*, 21-28, Translated by Rosemary Selle, Philadelphia: Augsburg Fortress.

Lüdemann, Gerd (1994), *The Resurrection of Jesus: History, Experience, Theology*, Minneapolis, MN: Fortress Press.

Lüdemann, Gerd (1995), *What Really Happened to Jesus: A Historical Approach to the Resurrection*, Louisville, KY: Westminster John Knox Press.

Lyons, William John (2004), "On the Life and Death of Joseph of Arimathea", *Journal for the Study of the Historical Jesus,* 2, January 2004, p. 29-53.

Lyons, William John (2006), "The Hermeneutics of Fictional Black and Factual Red: The Markan Simon of Cyrene and the Quest for the Historical Jesus", *Journal for the Study of the Historical Jesus*, 4, June 2006, p. 139-54.

McGrath, James F. (2008), *The Burial of Jesus: History and Faith*, Charleston, SC: BookSurge Publishing.

MacGregor, Kirk R., "Is the New Testament Historically Accurate?" (No longer available online at the time of publishing).

McCane, Byron (1998), '"WHERE NO ONE HAD YET BEEN LAID": The Shame of Jesus' Burial', in Chilton, B.D. & Evans, C.A. (eds.), *Authenticating the Activities of Jesus, (New Testament Tools & Studies)*, 28.2, Leiden: E.J. Bril, http://enoch2112.tripod.com/ByronBurial.htm (Retrieved 10/10/2020).

McCane, Byron (2003), *Rolled Back the Stone: Death and Burial in the World of Jesus*, Harrisburg: Trinity Press.

McLeod, S. A. (2014), "Loftus and Palmer", *Simply Psychology*, https://www.simplypsychology.org/loftus-palmer.html (Retrieved 22/11/2020).

McRay, John (1991), *Archaeology and the New Testament*, MI: Baker Book House.

Macan, Reginald (1877), *The Resurrection of Christ: An Essay in Three Chapters*, London: William & Norgate.

Maccoby, Hyam (1987), *The Mythmaker: Paul and the Invention of Christianity*, New York: Harper Collins.

Magness, Jodi (2007), "What Did Jesus' Tomb Look Like?" in *The Burial of Jesus*, Washington: Biblical Archaeology Society

Martin, Michael (1991), *The Case Against Christianity*, Philadelphia: Temple University Press.

Mason, Steve (1992), "Josephus and Luke-Acts," *Josephus and the New Testament*, Peabody, Massachusetts: Hendrickson Publishers.

Meyer, Marvin W. (2003), *Secret Gospels: Essays on Thomas and the Secret Gospel of Mark*, Harrisburg, PA.: Trinity Press International.

Meyer, Marvin W. (2013), "The Young Streaker in Secret and Canonical Mark", in Burke, Tony (ed.), *Ancient Gospel or Modern Forgery? The Secret Gospel of Mark in Debate. Proceedings from the 2011 York University Christian Apocrypha Symposium*, Eugene, OR.: Cascade Books, p. 145-56.

Malina, Bruce & Neyrey, Jerome (1996), *Portraits of Paul: An Archaeology of Ancient Personality*, Louisville, KY: Westminster John Know Press.

Montefiore, C.G. (1968), *The Synoptic Gospels In Two Volumes*, New York: KTAV.

Morrison, Stephen D. (n.d.), "7 Theories of the Atonement Summarized", *Stephen D. Morrison*, https://www.sdmorrison.org/7-theories-of-the-atonement-summarized/ (Retrieved 14/12/2020).

Moscicke, Hans (2018), "Jesus as Goat of the Day of Atonement in Recent Synoptic Gospels Research", *Currents in Biblical Research*, 2018, Vol. 17(1) 59–85.

Oakes, John (2006), "How can you explain the apparent contradiction between John 19:17 and Matthew 27:32? (who carried the cross?)", *Evidence for Christianity*, https://evidenceforchristianity.org/how-can-you-explain-the-apparent-contradition-between-john-1917-and-matthew-2732-who-carried-the-crossr/ (Retrieved 29/05/2020).

Orsini, Pasquale & Clarysse, Willy (2012), "Early New Testament Manuscripts and Their Dates; A Critique of Theological Palaeography", *Ephemerides Theologicae Lovanienses*, 88/4, p. 443–474.

Packer, J. I. (1993) [1973], *Knowing God*, 20th anniversary ed., InterVarsity Press, p. 185.

Paine, Thomas (1880), *The Age of Reason: An Investigation of True and Fabulous Theology*. London: Freethought Publishing Company (Part I [1794], Part II [1795], Part III [1807]). https://openlibrary.org/works/OL60357W/The_Age_of_Reason (Retrieved 12/01/2018).

Pearce, Jonathan MS (2012), *The Nativity: A Critical Examination*, Fareham: Onus Books.

Pearce, Jonathan MS (2016), "Again, Why Do Normal People Believe Ridiculous Things?", *A Tippling Philosopher*, https://www.patheos.com/blogs/tippling/2016/02/07/again-why-do-normal-people-believe-ridiculous-things/ (Retrieved 12/01/2020).

Pearce, Jonathan MS (2020a), "Josephus on Jesus", *A Tippling Philosopher*, https://www.patheos.com/blogs/tippling/2020/10/02/josephus-on-jesus/ (Retrieved 12/11/2020).

Pearce, Jonathan MS (2020b), "More on Josephus", *A Tippling Philosopher*, https://www.patheos.com/blogs/tippling/2020/10/04/more-on-josephus-on-jesus/ (Retrieved 14/11/2020).

Pearce, Jonathan MS (2021), "Differences, Contradictions and Speculations of the Resurrection Listed", *A Tippling Philosopher*, https://www.patheos.com/blogs/tippling/2021/03/11/differences-contradictions-and-speculations-of-the-resurrection-listed/ (Retrieved 11/03/2021).

Pervo, Richard I. (2006), *Dating Acts: Between the Evangelists and the Apologists*, California: Polebridge Press.

Pervo, Richard I. (2008), *The Mystery of Acts: Unraveling Its Story*, California: Polebridge Press.

Peters, Emmanuelle (2010), "Are Delusions on a Continuum? The Case of Religious and Delusional Beliefs." In *Psychosis and Spirituality: Consolidating the New Paradigm*, edited by Isabel Clarke, 127–38. Oxford: Wiley-Blackwell.

Polyvious, Evanthia (2015), "Caesar's Jewish Policy according to Flavius Josephus", Anistoriton Journal, vol. 14 (2014-2015), Essays, http://www.anistor.gr/english/enback/2014_1e_Anistoriton.pdf (Retrieved 11/03/2021).

Price, Jonathan J. (2010), 'Sanhedriya – "Tomb of the Judges" or "Tomb of the Sanhedrin"', and "Inscribed ossuary lid with Hebrew/Aramaic inscription, 1 c. BCE-1 c. CE", in *Corpus Inscriptionum Iudaeae/Palaestinae*, Volume 1: Jerusalem, Part 1, 1-704, Ed. Cotton et al, Berlin: De Gruyter.

Price, Robert M. (1993), *Beyond Born Again: Towards Evangelical Maturity*, https://infidels.org/library/modern/robert_price/beyond_born_again (Retrieved 19/02/2021).

Price, Robert M. (2003), *Incredible Shrinking Son of Man: How Reliable Is the Gospel Tradition?*, Armherst, NY: Prometheus Books.

Price, Robert M. (2004), "New Testament Narrative as Old Testament Midrash", http://www.robertmprice.mindvendor.com/art_midrash1.htm (Retrieved 17/02/2021).

Price, Robert M. & Lowder, Jeffery Jay (2005), *The Empty Tomb: Jesus Beyond the Grave*, Amherst: Prometheus.

Purcell, William (1996), *The Resurrection*, Philadelphia: Westminster Press.

Pyysiäinen, Ilkka (2007), "The Mystery of the Stolen Body: Exploring Christian Origins." In *Explaining Christian Origins and Early Judaism: Contributions from Cognitive and Social Science*, edited by Luomanen, Petri, Pyysiäinen, Ilkka and Uro, Risto, p. 57–72. Atlanta, GA: SBL Press.

Ranke-Heinemann, Uta (1995), *Putting Away Childish Things*, San Francisco: HarperSanFrancisco.

Rau, Andy (2012), in "Questions About Easter: What Is Significant About the Lamb's Bones Not Being Broken?", *Bible Gateway*, https://www.biblegateway.com/blog/2012/02/questions-about-easter-what-is-significant-about-the-lamb%e2%80%99s-bones-not-being-broken/ (Retrieved 12/10/2020).

Robinson, James M. (1996), ed., *The Nag Hammadi Library in English*, 4th Ed., Leiden: E.J. Brill.

Ross Jnr., Bobby (2011), Interpretation Sparks a Grave Theology Debate by Bobby Ross Jnr., *Christianity Today*, http://www.christianitytoday.com/ct/2011/november/interpretation-sparks-theology-debate.html (retrieved 12/12/2011).

Roth, Marshall (n.d.), "Isaiah 53: The Suffering Servant", *Aish.com*, https://www.aish.com/sp/ph/Isaiah_53_The_Suffering_Servant.html (Retrieveed 18/03/2021).

Rothkrug, Lionel (1981), '"The Odour of Sanctity," and the Hebrew Origins of Christian Relic Veneration', *Historical Reflections/Réflexions Historiques,* Vol. 8, No. 2 (Summer 1981), p. 95-142, Berghahn Books.

Sacks, Oliver (2012), *Hallucinations*, New York: Vintage Books

Sagan, Carl (2006), *The Varieties of Scientific Experience: A Personal View of the Search for God.* New York: Penguin Books.

Sanders, E.P. & Davies, Margaret (1989), *Studying the Synoptic Gospels*, Norcross, GA: Trinity Press International.

Sauter, Megan (2019), "How Was Jesus' Tomb Sealed?", *Biblical Archaeological Society*, https://www.biblicalarchaeology.org/daily/archaeology-today/biblical-archaeology-topics/how-was-jesus-tomb-sealed/ (Retrieved 12/06/2020).

Schnakenburg, Rudolf (1982) , *The Gospel According to John*, New York: Crossroads.

Scholem, Gershom (1973), *Sabbatai Sevi, The Mystical Messiah*, Princeton, NJ: Princeton University Press.

Shuchter, Stephen (1986), *Dimensions of Grief: Adjusting to the Death of a Spouse*, San Francisco, CA: Jossey-Bass.

Seidensticker, Bob (2012), "Failed Prophecy: Psalm 22", *Cross Examined,* https://www.patheos.com/blogs/crossexamined/2012/09/failed-prophecy-psalm-22/ (Retrieved 22/09/2020).

Seidensticker, Bob (2013), "Contradictions in the Resurrection Account", *Cross Examined*, https://www.patheos.com/blogs/crossexamined/2013/03/contradictions-in-the-resurrection-account-3/ (Retrieved 12/12/2020).

Sheckler, Allyson E. & Leith, Mary J.W. (2010), "The Crucifixion Conundrum and the Santa Sabina Doors", *The Harvard Theological Review,* Vol. 103, No. 1 (Jan., 2010), p. 67-88.

Sidky, Homuyan (2019), *Religion, Supernaturalism, the Paranormal and Pseudoscience: An Anthropological Critique*, London: Anthem Press

Slade, Peter & Bentall, Richard (1988), *Sensory Deception: A Scientific Analysis of Hallucination*, Baltimore: Johns Hopkins University Press.

Slick (n.d.), "How many men or angels appeared at the tomb?", *Christian Apologetics & Research Ministry,* https://carm.org/how-many-men-or-angels-appeared-tomb (Retrieved 20/09/2020).

Sloyan, Gerard Stephen (1995), *The Crucifixion of Jesus: History, Myth, Faith,* Minneapolis: Fortress Press.

Smith, Jay; Chowdhry, Alex; Jepson, Toby; & Schaeffer, James (n.d.) "101 'Cleared-Up' Contradictions In The Bible", https://gluefox.com/min/contrad.htm (Retrieved 16/11/2020).

Spong, John Shelby (1995), *Resurrection: Myth or Reality,* San Francisco: HarperOne.

Spong, John (1995), *Resurrection: Myth or Reality: A Bishop's Search for the Origins of Christianity*, San Francisco, CA: HarperCollins.
Spong, John Shelby (1997), *Liberating the Gospels: Reading the Bible with Jewish Eyes*, San Francisco: HarperSanFrancisco.
Stark, Thom (2011), *The Human Face of God: What Scripture Reveals When It Gets God Wrong (And Why Inerrancy Tries To Hide It)*, Eugene, OR: Wipf & Stock Publishers.
Stecher, Carl & Blomberg (2019), *Resurrection: Faith or Fact?*, Durham, NC: Pitchstone Publishing.
Stein, Robert H. (1993), *Luke: The New American Commentary*, B & H Publishing Group.
Stewart, Don (n.d.), "How Important Is the Resurrection to Christianity?", *Blue Letter Bible*, https://www.blueletterbible.org/faq/don_stewart/don_stewart_811.cfm (Retrieved 20/05/2020).
Stewart, Robert (2011), *The Reliability of the New Testament: Bart Ehrman and Daniel Wallace in Dialogue*, Minneapolis: Fortress Press.
Strauss, D.F. (4th Ed 1860) translated by Evans, Marian, *The Life of Jesus*, New York: Calvin Blanchard.
Strobel, Lee (1998), *The Case for Christ: A Journalist's Personal Investigation of the Evidence for Jesus*, Grand Rapids, MI: Zondervan
Strobele, Lee (2018), *The Case for Easter*, Grand Rapids, MI: Zondervan.
Tabor, James (2012), *Paul and Jesus: How the Apostle Transformed Christianity*, New York: Simon & Schuster
Talbert, Richard J.A. (2000), *Barrington Atlas of the Greek and Roman World*, New Jersey: Princeton University Press.
Taussig, Hal (2015), "Fall 2014 Christianity Seminar Report on Gnosticism", 28-2, March-April 2015, *The Fourth R*, Westar Institute, https://www.westarinstitute.org/projects/christianity-seminar/fall-2014-meeting-report/ (Retrieved 09/03/2021).
Theissen, G., Merz, A (1998 trans. Bowden, J.), *The Historical Jesus : A Comprehensive Guide*, Fortress Press.
Thoby, Paul (1959), *LE CRUCIFIX Des Origines Au Concile De Trente. Etude Iconographique*, Nantes: Bellanger.
Tinsley, E.J. (1965), *The Gospel According to Luke*, Cambridge: Cambridge University Press.
Tomasino, Anthony J. (2003), *Judaism Before Jesus: The Events & Ideas That Shaped the New Testament World*, Westmont, Illinois: IVP Academic.
Tuggy, D. (2003), "The Unfinished Business of Trinitarian Theorizing", *Religious Studies*, 391, p. 65–83.
Tuggy, D. (2016), "Trinity", *The Stanford Encyclopedia of Philosophy*, https://plato.stanford.edu/entries/trinity/ (Retrieved 09/11/2020).
Van Wingerden, Ruben (2020), "Carrying a *patibulum*: A Reassessment of Non-Christian Latin Sources", *New Testament Studies*, Volume 66, Issue 3, 05 June 2020.

Viney, Donald Wayne (1989), "Grave Doubts About The Resurrection", *Encounter* 50 (2), p. 125-40.

Von Campenhausen, Hans (1968), *Tradition and Life in the Church: Essays and Lectures in Church History*, (trans. A.V. Littledale) Philadelphia: Fortress Press.

Waetjen, Herman C. (2005), *The Gospel of the Beloved Disciple*, London: T&T Clark.

Warner Wallace, J. (2015), "How Many Angels Were Present at Jesus' Tomb?", *Cold-Case Christianity*, https://coldcasechristianity.com/writings/how-many-angels-were-present-at-jesus-tomb/ (Retrieved 23/10/2020).

Waters, Flavie & Fernyhough, Charles (2017), "Hallucinations: A Systematic Review of Points of Similarity and Difference Across Diagnostic Classes", *Schizophrenia Bulletin*, Volume 43, Issue 1, 1 January 2017, p. 32–43.

Wedderburn, Alexander J.M. (2004), *A History of the First Christians*, London: Continuum Publishing Group.

Welch, John W. (2005), "Early Mormonism and Early Christianity: Some Providential Similarities," in *Window of Faith: Latter-day Saint Perspectives on World History*, ed. Roy A. Prete, Provo, UT: Religious Studies Center, Brigham Young University, 2005, p. 17–38.

Whitlark, Jason A. & Parsons, Mikael C. (2006), "The 'Seven' Last Words: A Numerical Motivation for the Insertion of Luke 23.34a", *New Testament Studies*, Volume 52, Issue 2, April 2006, p. 188-204.

Wilkins, Michael J. and Moreland, J.P (1995), *Jesus Under Fire: Modern Scholarship Reinvents the Historical Jesus,* Grand Rapids: Zondervan.

Wright, N.T. (1999), *The Challenge of Jesus: Rediscovering Who Jesus Was and Is*, Downers Grove: InterVarsity Press.

Wright, N.T (2003), *The Resurrection of the Son of God*, Minneapolis: Fortress Press.

Yadin, Yigael (1985), *The Temple Scroll: The Hidden Law of the Dead Sea Sect,* New York: Random House.

Zauzmer, Julie, "Study: Religion contributes more to the U.S. economy than Facebook, Google and Apple combined" *The Washington Post,* https://www.washingtonpost.com/news/acts-of-faith/wp/2016/09/14/study-religion-contributes-more-to-the-u-s-economy-than-facebook-google-and-apple-combined/ (Retrieved 17/09/2020).

Zias, J & Sekeles, E (1985), "The Crucified Man from Giv'at ha-Mitvar: A Reappraisal", Israel Exploration Journal, 35, p.22-27.

Zindler, Frank (1998), "Did Jesus Exist?", *American Atheist Magazine*, Summer 1998.

Zulueta, F. de. (1932), "Violation of Sepulture in Palestine at the Beginning of the Christian Era" *Journal of Roman Studies* 22: 184–97.

Articles/websites with no author/date attribution:

"Bible: Outrageous Resurrection Account -- Gospel of Matthew", (2011), *Conversational Atheist*, Website no longer online, archived at https://web.archive.org/web/20180606184046/http://conversational-atheist.com/christianity/matthew-resurrection-account/ (Retrieved 09/03/2021).

"Doctrine of Atonement", *Catholic Encyclopedia*, https://www.newadvent.org/cathen/02055a.htm (Retrieved 10/11/2020).

"Gospel Disproof #38: The guards at the tomb", *Alethian Worldview,* https://freethoughtblogs.com/alethianworldview/2012/02/27/gospel-disproof-38-the-guards-at-the-tomb/ (Retrieved 12/12/2020).

"Hosea 6:2", *Ellicott's Commentary for English Readers* as detailed on *Bible Hub*, https://biblehub.com/commentaries/hosea/6-2.htm (Retrieved 17/12/2020).

"How many angels were at the tomb of Jesus?", *The Bible Answer*, https://thebibleanswer.org/how-many-angels-tomb-jesus/ (Retrieved 10/12/2020).

"Littlewood's Law", *Wikipedia*, https://en.wikipedia.org/wiki/Littlewood's_law (Retrieved 15/06/2020).

"Miracle" on the reference website *Sensagent*, http://dictionary.sensagent.com/miracle/en-en/ (retrieved 18/11/2020).

"Sanhedriyya - Archeological Appendix", Jerusalem Municipality, Spring 2002, http://www.antiquities.org.il/images/archinfo//001-030/018.pdf (Retrieved 12/03/2021).

Studies in the Bible and Early Christianity 16 (1989), *Assessing the New Testament Evidence for the Historicity of the Resurrection of Jesus*, Lewiston: Edwin Mellen.

"Thai tsunami trauma sparks foreign ghost sightings", ABC News/AFP, https://www.abc.net.au/news/2005-01-14/thai-tsunami-trauma-sparks-foreign-ghost-sightings/618946 (Retrieved 12/12/2020).

"Twins who swapped roles charged with fraud", Reuters Staff (2008), *Reuters*, https://www.reuters.com/article/us-italy-twins-idUSTRE48P66N20080926 (Retrieved 11/03/2021).

"What is propitiation?", *Got Questions,* https://www.gotquestions.org/propitiation.html (Retrieved 11/11/2020)

"When Was Jesus Stabbed by the Roman Soldier (John 19:34)?", *Church of the Great God,* https://www.cgg.org/index.cfm/library/bqa/id/233/when-was-jesus-stabbed-by-roman-soldier-john-1934.htm (Retrieved 27/08/2020).

"Why did blood and water come out of Jesus' side when He was pierced?", (n.d.), *Got Questions*, https://www.gotquestions.org/blood-water-Jesus.html (Retrieved 22/10/2020).

'Why The "Minimal Facts" Model is Unpersuasive', *Evaluating Christianity*, https://evaluatingchristianity.wordpress.com/2009/03/05/why-the-minimal-facts-model-is-unpersuasive/ (Retrieved 08/03/2021).

CPSIA information can be obtained
at www.ICGtesting.com
Printed in the USA
BVHW070407160921
616806BV00004B/281

9 780993 510281